CW00797206

35—

Urban Nature Conserva

Urban Nature Conservation

Landscape Management in the Urban Countryside

Tony Kendle

Department of Horticulture and Landscape,
The University of Reading

and

Stephen Forbes

Kings Park and Botanic Gardens,
West Perth

E & FN SPON
An Imprint of Thomson Professional

London · Weinheim · New York · Tokyo · Melbourne · Madras

Published by E & FN Spon, an imprint of
Thomson Professional, 2–6 Boundary Row, London SE1 8HN, UK

Chapman & Hall, 2–6 Boundary Row, London SE1 8HN, UK
Chapman & Hall GmbH, Pappelallee 3, 69469 Weinheim, Germany
Chapman & Hall USA, 115 Fifth Avenue, New York, NY 10003, USA
Chapman & Hall Japan, ITP-Japan, Kyowa Building, 3F, 2-2-1 Hirakawacho, Chiyoda-ku,
Tokyo 102, Japan
Chapman & Hall Australia, 102 Dodds Street, South Melbourne, Victoria 3205, Australia
Chapman & Hall India, R. Seshadri, 32 Second Main Road, CIT East, Madras 600 035, India

First edition 1997

© 1997   Tony Kendle and Stephen Forbes

Designed and Typeset in Times by John Saunders Design & Production
Printed in Great Britain by The Alden Press, Osney Mead, Oxford

ISBN   0 419 19300 6

Apart from any fair dealing for the purposes of research or private study, or criticism or review, as permitted under the UK Copyright Designs and Patents Act 1988, this publication may not be reproduced, stored, or transmitted, in any form or by any means, without the prior permission in writing of the publishers, or in the case of reproduction only in accordance with the terms of the licences issued by the Copyright Licensing Agency in the UK, or in accordance with the terms of licences issued by the appropriate Reproduction Rights Organization outside the UK. Enquiries concerning reproduction outside the terms stated here should be sent to the publishers at the London address printed on this page.
   The publisher makes no representation express or implied, with regard to the accuracy of the information contained in this book and cannot accept any legal responsibility or liability for any errors or omissions that may be made.

♾ Printed on acid-free text paper, manufactured in accordance with ANSI/NISO Z39.48 1992 (Permanence of Paper).

Contents

    A.D. KENDLE, R. CANDY AND S. FORBES

    Choosing the appropriate management method and pattern   282
    The economics of urban vegetation management   286
        Revenue opportunities from urban landscapes   294
        Critical inputs and risk assessment   295
    Safety in the urban countryside   297
        Poisonous plants   300
    The use of agrochemicals   301
        Can 'safe' pesticides be identified?   301
        Prioritizing weed problems   304
    Community participation in urban land management   306
        The principles of community involvement   309
        User participation in the environment   311
        Enabling – the new professional services   312
        The local authority as facilitator   313
        Ensuring effective participation   313
        Finding a suitable 'entry point' to participation   315
        The threshold of participation   315
        Working in groups   316
    Conclusions   316

9   Nature for people   319
    C.L.E. RHODE AND A.D. KENDLE

    Psychological value of nature for people in urban areas   319
        Psychological well-being and landscapes   321
    Creating ecological landscapes that are valued   322
        Unexpected or subversive nature   323
        Mysterious and complex nature   323
        Unrestrained nature   324
    People who do not value wildness and people who only value
        wildness   325
        The values of formal landscapes   328
    Conflicts between the objectives of amenity and conservation   330
    Education for urban conservation   332

    Bibliography   336
    Index   345

Acknowledgements

We would like to acknowledge the help of everyone who aided the development of this book both through their written work and through personal communications. Particular thanks go to Terry Wells, Gerd Londo, George Barker, Brita von Schoenaich, Mike Oxford, John Box, Peter Buckley, Junko Oikawa, Richard Scott, Oliver Gilbert, John Handley, Allan Ruff, Richard Bisgrove, Peter Gilbertson, James Hitchmough, David Goode, Bill Jordan, Judy Wong, Susan Humphries and Roland Gustavvson. Jane Stoneham played a key role in support and the development of the text, and especially the sections on human use.

Thanks also go to Danny Cooper, Ralph Candy and Christa Rohde for their vital contributions to chapters 3, 8 and 9.

The most important people in the inspiration and understanding of many of the issues here were Peter Thoday and Tony Bradshaw for whom no amount of thanks is adequate.

Illustration Acknowledgements

The authors and publishers would like to thank the following individuals and organizations for permission to reproduce material. We have made every effort to contact and acknowledge copyright holders, but if any errors have been made we would be happy to correct them at a later printing.

Individuals and organizations

Belhaven Press 23 24
Bristol Naturalists Society 2
Cambridge University Press 9 10 11 15
Elsevier Science 4 19
Malcolm Emery 17 25
Harcourt Brace & Company Ltd 8 21
Her Majesty's Stationery Office 27 28
Professor Roland Gustavvson 32
The Royal Society for the Protection of Birds 22 26
The Scottish Agricultural College 1
Sinauer Associates 18

All photographs are by the authors.

Preface

Definitions

It would be nice to begin the book with a clear definition of terms and subject matter but like many aspects of landscape work the boundaries, both biological and cultural, of what may be classed as 'urban nature' blur at the edges and defy neat semantics.

The very concept of **urban nature conservation** in itself can seem like an oxymoron. Nature conservation does not imply a blanket desire to care for or direct resources into promoting the survival of all and any other living species. Conservation needs to be a focused activity that addresses those species which are under some sort of threat or decline. In the majority of cases such threats are ultimately attributable to human activity including habitat destruction and urbanization. Those species that have been able to find a niche in urban areas are normally tolerant of human disturbance and are experiencing an increase in habitat range rather than a decline.

Nevertheless urban nature conservation has grown in importance and richness as a theme over the recent decades. From origins earlier this century as a Cinderella subject, largely ignored by professionals, scientists and policy-makers, we now see a widespread interest in the topic as well as an established body of information that has arisen from a few active academic researchers and more widely from committed individuals and urban naturalists. Many of the organizations, governmental and non governmental, charged with biodiversity protection now include urban programmes in their work.

The managers of urban land need to understand the priorities and issues that have driven this expansion of concern, and which set implicit and explicit goals for the management systems. Much of this book therefore is a review of what nature conservation really does mean in an urban context, and what the implications are for the professionals.

What about the terminology that is used to identify those areas where this aspect of landscape management has a priority? A recent definition by some of the leading UK researchers in the field classifies **natural greenspace** as:

Land water and geological features which have been naturally colonized by plants and animals and which are accessible on foot to large numbers of residents (Harrison *et al.*, 1996).

Since this definition neatly excludes completely man-made landscapes, even the most advanced examples of habitat creation, and excludes land which may have important influences on urban wildlife and the urban environment even if not accessible, some other terminology is needed.

The origins of the term urban countryside are not clear, although early in the 1970s Richard Mabey coined the term the 'unofficial countryside' to describe those wild spaces in town that were often appreciated more by local people than by professionals (Mabey, 1973). Decades on it is certainly untrue to suggest that professionals are still neglecting this resource. In this text the term **urban countryside** is therefore used as an all encompassing term which is nevertheless a convenient means of separating out those areas of urban landscape which have:

- semi-natural origins *or* appearance;
- where maintaining wildlife interest is one of the objectives of the management;
- where the ecosystem is made up of complex and changing communities that need to be managed (where management is required) with an understanding of their dynamics and of the interactions between plants and between plants and animals.

The use of the term 'countryside' allows for interesting parallels with the rural landscape. It allows a focus on land which is not **natural** (since it is dominated by human intervention in terms of which species are found there) but which because of the setting or visual characteristics may appear to the public as if it has not been deliberately created. Part of the value that such sites have lies in the extent to which they are perceived as relatively natural or uncontrolled areas, reminiscent of more natural environments but surviving in an urban setting. This perception is important even if at times it is superficial and inaccurate.

A related term that has sometimes been used is **ecological landscapes** (see for example Ruff and Tregay, 1982) and this will also be used here, particularly to describe man-made designs that are intended to appear natural. However as an umbrella term the phrase is perhaps best avoided since it seems to invite confusion with **landscape ecology** which has been adopted by geographers for a specific field of study (see Chapter 5).

Technical challenges

On the technical level urban countryside sites can present new challenges for the landscape managers. Because of their specific complexes of plant and animal species or because of the objectives and goals of the managers and users, these areas often need to be looked after through the application of ecological rather than horticultural techniques.

For much of its history landscape design and management has been based on horticultural principles which rely upon study of how individual plants grow and the factors which encourage them to grow better. Monocultures or very simple mixtures have been created, where weeding is often the most important management tool, to reduce competition, and where human organization of the vegetation structure and patterns is paramount.

We are being asked increasingly to produce or conserve for society complex populations and mixtures of different species living in intricate communities where weeding in the traditional sense becomes a meaningless task. In these settings we can not possibly dictate the fate of most individual plants but must attempt broader and more subtle management operations that re-direct community dynamics to get the desired results. It is essential therefore to learn a new set of tools, based on ecology, that influence the competitive balance rather than directly manipulate populations and species mixtures. There is a focus on processes of plant interaction as much as on the pattern of the finished effect.

Challenges to policy formulation

The issues involved in the urban countryside go far beyond that of maintenance procedures. The re-introduction of wild areas to the urban environment is, for many people, a means to compensate in part for the disappearance of nature from everyday experience. The interest in ecological landscapes reflects concern for the loss of the aesthetic, spiritual and recreational values characterizing the natural environment. They represent an opportunity to explore and address some of the most fundamental concerns about environmental protection and social philosophy. In many cases ecological designs, therefore, provide one of the most effective (but of course not the only) means of exploring the development of stronger relationships between human beings and nature. Again this can be achieved often by focusing on the **processes** of community involvement in landscape projects instead of having an over-riding concern for the product.

This focus on human values adds another layer of complexity to the management issues. The urban countryside is also characterized by the complex diversity of goals and objectives that may need to be reconciled. In contrast to the objectives within traditional amenity landscapes in parks, it is not enough, or sometimes not even particularly high priority, that these landscapes are attractive or functional. Often they need to be managed to promote wildlife or to meet other needs, and unlike some rural areas conflicting land uses can not be easily accommodated by zoning. Everything that happens in urban areas may be exposed to the scrutiny of large numbers of interest groups, and developing a clear perspective on what should be done is often the hardest task facing the manager.

The presumption of much nature conservation policy is, and has to be, that attempts are made to protect biodiversity **regardless** of whether that protection is acceptable to the majority of politicians, business people or even the public. But anyone who has worked in nature conservation usually quickly realizes that the subject area is not in any sense an objective science.

For example, data gaps are an inevitable problem, and make the task of setting policy priorities a matter of professional judgement. Often therefore, decisions are made on the basis of subjective preferences by the conservation staff. Wider issues of global biodiversity protection are substituted at a local level by a debate about the type of wildlife that the nearby community will value contact with, so that fierce battles can be fought over the protection of species which, in national or international scientific terms, have very little conservation significance. Of course it can be argued that by promoting contact with and awareness of local wildlife, the wider cause of global nature conservation is served. By extension local authorities and other organizations need to be seen to be acting in a local way with the same ethics of care that we would want to see globally.

With very few exceptions urban nature areas **are** devoid of species that are in any way endangered or that justify direct protection. (There are certain notable exceptions which will be discussed in more detail later.) Urban nature conservation therefore presents a particularly interesting distillation of certain aspects of the biodiversity conservation debate, where priorities and interests, successes and failures, are fought out in an arena devoid of clear indication of what really **is** the best thing to do. Discussion of these aspects too will form part of the substance of this book.

Finally, by focusing this book on ecological types of landscapes there is no intention to underrate the importance of the more formal and more ornamental parts of the urban scene such as traditional flower borders; these areas are an equally fundamental part of town and city greenspace, they give great pleasure to many people and, at their best, they are works of art. They are also not as devoid of wildlife interest as is often assumed, although this dimension is rarely taken into account in the management objectives. In places the text will discuss the relationships and potential conflicts between these two paradigms of open space management.

A tremendous amount has been done to raise the understanding of the need for wild areas in towns, but in many cases local authorities still seem to feel that designating certain areas as reserves or ecoparks is sufficient. The reality is probably that the basic framework of the urban landscape should be managed along naturalistic lines, with formality and intensive maintenance being reserved for areas where it seems clearly appropriate. A Groundwork survey of the St Helens area found that half of all the greenspace in the area consisted of fertile but species poor, regularly cut, rye grass swards (Figure P.1). Another quarter was fertile grassland that is uncut and becomes a coarse tussocky sward dominated by grasses like yorkshire fog and prone to summer fires. Director of the Trust at the time, John Handley, pointed out 'no one denies the need for traditional amenity grassland in Knowsley, but there is just too much of it' (Handley and Bulmer, 1987).

On the other hand it is essential that the supporters of ecological landscapes recognize when the style is not appropriate. They need to respect other people's tastes and identify the valid role for ornamental landscapes and exotic plants in society. The development of an ecological approach need not mean that the other functions of open space have to be sacrificed.

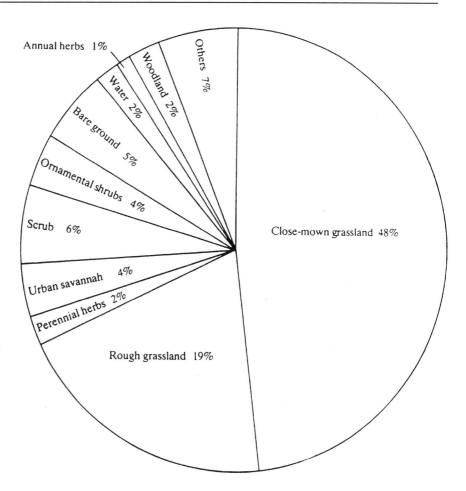

Annual herbs 1%

Water 2%

Woodland 2%

Others 7%

Bare ground 5%

Ornamental shrubs 4%

Close-mown grassland 48%

Scrub 6%

Urban savannah 4%

Perennial herbs 2%

Rough grassland 19%

Figure P.1 The make-up of urban greenspace in St Helens (Handley and Bulmer, 1987). This chart illustrates the degree to which featureless grassland dominates the urban landscape.

The role that land plays in our lives can be very complex; it can fulfil many needs.

Our ancestors began gardening by making small changes to the natural landscape they saw around them. A move towards ecological styles should not mean turning our back on everything that we have learnt since then; it means using that knowledge and that understanding in a way which is just as sophisticated as any other style of cultivation, combining the lessons of horticulture with those of ecology.

Open space should bring joy and delight, an extra, and very special, dimension to the urban environment. There should be sunlight and shade, colour and flowers, sounds, scents and perfumes. Turning a park into an ecological area should not mean that we have to compromise these pleasures. It should provide all of these things and more. It should be a place where there are more delights, more sounds, more colours and more scents – not just the scent of flowers but of hay and the fallen leaves, the sight of dragon-flies dancing in the sun, the colours of fungi emerging from the litter beneath the trees, the sparkle of spider webs in the fog, the sound of bees humming around heather.

Excellent texts already exist which detail the richness of the urban countryside and also address the techniques available for protection of the habitats that are found or created, and there is no need to reproduce the detail of these here (see for example Gilbert, 1989; Baines, 1986a; Goode, 1986). However, with a few notable exceptions much of this research and information is still at the stage where people are documenting what is there, how it has developed and what are the maintenance options rather than attempting a synthesis of principles that will guide landscape management and policy formation at a more strategic level. This text attempts to move towards such a synthesis.

1 The urban estate and the 'urban countryside'

Firm, quantified, data about the urban countryside do not always come readily to hand. We know surprisingly little about the open spaces that we live among. Even local governments, charged with responsibility for management of much of the land, have until very recently been able to get by with an amazingly vague picture of the land they look after.

Certain changes have occurred in recent years in the UK that will lead to better information supply, most notably the development of land registers, local authority environmental strategies and the requirement for Compulsory Competitive Tendering in local authority departments. Obviously work can not be passed to contractors without some documentation of the nature, objectives and size of the urban estate that is to be managed. However even this data-gathering process will leave us with a very incomplete picture for several reasons.

- Much of the land which is essential for urban wildlife survival lies in private hands (although this is not always beyond the scope of local authority influence through designations such as Tree Preservation Orders).
- It is a characteristic of much of the 'wild' landscape of towns and cities that it has developed on land which is neglected and overlooked.
- There are areas where the ownership may not be clear (local authorities often own land that their staff are not aware of), and in many cases the land may be temporarily unused but may be classified by the planning and development control system as something very different to open space.

It has been found that the actual areas of greenspace in urban areas can often be nearly double that of previous official estimates when such sites are taken into account. It can even be a matter of debate whether urban nature is only found on 'green sites' since 'in time all urban plots are capable of supporting natural assemblages, even derelict buildings and car-parks (Harrison *et al.*, 1996).

Not surprisingly, different urban areas show different patterns when surveys are attempted. In a land-use survey for Leicester formal grass

counted for about 20%, agriculture, semi-natural land and other miscella-
neous accounted for just over 15% and residential and commercial areas
accounted for 65%. In the Tyneside/ Newcastle conurbation formal grass
accounted for less than 10% of the land whereas agriculture and other land
uses accounted for nearly 40% and the residential/commercial component
was only about 50% (Carr and Lane, 1993). These figures seem to
completely overlook gardens as a separate land use. Brussels has about 50%
built surface, with 20% open space, 20% private gardens and 10% sports,
nature reserves, agriculture and other land uses (Gryseels, 1995).

In the heart of the City of London open spaces make up approximately
7.5% of the urban landscape. Of this nearly half the area is regarded as
'green', but of this green space over a third is closed to public access
(Plummer and Shewan, 1992). This distribution of spaces is however influenced by the local economy and land use. The West End, has less than a
quarter the number of open spaces and a much lower percentage of green
spaces; Tower Hamlets has fewer open spaces but the shortfall is mainly
because of limited 'hard spaces' and the proportion of green is much higher.
Vacant land is effectively non-existent in the City reflecting the strength of
investment, but such open areas are quite prevalent in the Tower Hamlets area.

The quality of the green space also varies. There is frequently a correlation between site size and vegetation diversity, but this is also affected by
the regional economy, for example most spaces in the City of London are
highly formal and seen as extensions of the local architecture.

As well as difficulties in comparing because of the different survey
criteria and methodology, the figures often depend on arbitrary city or town
boundaries which may incorporate more or less greenspace and countryside.
Vegetation cover in Berlin ranges from 32% in the built-up areas of the city
through to 95% in the outer suburbs (Sukopp et al., 1979).

Depending on the location within the urban framework there can be huge
variation in site size. Heavily developed areas and particularly the more
historic areas are frequently characterized by very small sites. In the UK the
influence of post war planning has often been to preserve larger tracts of
land for recreation or amenity, although these tracts are frequently not
managed in a way that supports much wildlife. They form the 'featureless
green deserts' that are widely criticized (Elliott, 1988).

Obtaining figures for urban wasteland is in many ways even more difficult. UK Government statistics on officially abandoned or derelict land can
be obtained. (Derelict land in the UK is identified as 'land so damaged by
industrial or other development that it is incapable of beneficial use without
treatment', but excludes sites where the existing developers have planning
commitments for restoration.) However it is less easy to identify vacant sites
which are technically still in ownership and regarded as 'operating' or
awaiting development, even though in practice these sites may be effectively
devoid of use for decades. It certainly is known that these areas can be
substantial. In the town of St Helens in 1989 it was estimated that more than
a quarter of the land to the south and east was either derelict or unmanaged
(Handley, 1996).

A survey by the UK government of urban areas with populations over 10 000 people suggested that out of a total in England of approximately 940 000 ha, some 50 000 ha could be regarded as derelict or vacant (DOE, 1992) although some non-government agencies would still regard this as an underestimate. However it is also important to recognize the difficulty of value judgements when deciding whether such sites are truly harmful or 'incapable of beneficial use'. Vacant land can be seen as blighting and corrupting, reducing local environmental quality, reducing economic health and inciting vandalism, all of which leads to a downward spiral of urban quality. However the UK survey mentioned above included an estimate of some 28 000 ha of land which has remained vacant and has never previously been developed. Almost certainly much of this would meet Mabey's (1973) definition of the unofficial countryside. Many such sites are regularly used and usage levels can be increased to match that of urban parks with the addition of paths and some attention to safety (Handley, 1996).

Despite the complexity of data analysis we are able to recognize that the urban countryside is remarkably diverse and surprisingly capacious. A somewhat easier task is to begin to categorize the main types of urban land that may be of particular interest to conservationists.

Origins of urban open space

There are several locations which are often particularly important components of the urban nature matrix, and these are discussed in more detail below. Their origins are diverse but two main classifications can immediately be identified which will have a huge implication for the existence and allocation of resources for management.

Some are **open spaces maintained or created as a deliberate land-use decision**. This may include parks, recreation grounds and private gardens as well as sometimes quite substantial areas of landscape associated with large organizations or public buildings such as schools, hospitals and industrial parks. It also includes the non-specific open space, the land that acts as a filler or buffer in housing estates and alongside roads, railways and other transport corridors. Some sites have patches of land that are very diverse and have complex histories such as canals and riversides. It can include encapsulated countryside sites, such as commons, which have become absorbed and maintained as parks.

Despite their historic protection these sites can still be under threat. The privatization of public utilities and the rationalization of health authority and education properties are all likely to lead to the 'disposal' of unwanted land. Even parks authorities have been under pressure over recent decades to sell land for development to compensate for falling budgets. None of these bodies has a formal duty to maintain an estate for public or wildlife benefit and the changes in their structure may lead to a dramatic decrease in the proportion of open land in many urban areas.

Some sites have been protected by accident as land that has **somehow**

fallen outside of the development and planning cycle. This could include zones of derelict land, either reclaimed or spontaneously colonized by vegetation, and land which is temporary vacant awaiting development but has in some way survived and become accessible to the public. Sometimes this land becomes formally recognized as a recreation resource. In the UK the Gunnersbury triangle is probably the best example. This is an area of land that was isolated by railway tracks and became gradually colonized by pioneer woodland and other habitats. After a planning battle over a proposed development the land has been retained as a nature reserve for use by the local people.

This neglected land may also include areas of relict countryside that have been incorporated, through an accident of geography or history, into the urban fabric but is too difficult for building (Figure 1.1). It may survive because of steep slopes, difficult topography, poor drainage or for administrative reasons such as complex, unclear or communal land ownership. Many of these areas have no official status.

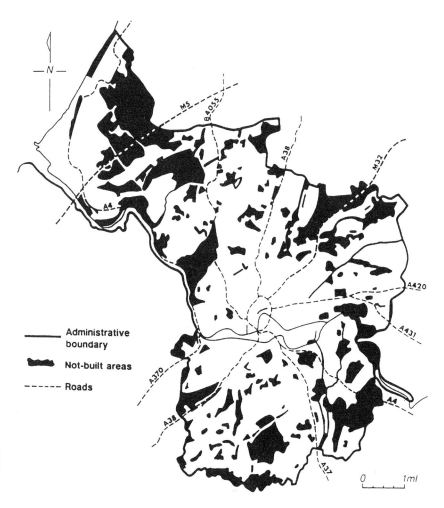

Figure 1.1. Areas within the city of Bristol which have not been built up (Bland and Taylor, 1991).

Obviously these two broad categories of 'unplanned land' may differ significantly in that the former is likely to have a preponderance of young, skeletal habitats while the latter can, in some instances, include some very ancient ecosystems. It is the latter that is likely to be seen as the most important in traditional conservation terms although there are exceptions as we shall see later.

One key characteristic that links these latter sites is that their day-to-day survival in urban areas has been dependent on neglect rather than on deliberate policies of land use. Indeed much of this land would be officially categorized as 'waste' or functionless. This does mean that the sustained existence of these sites can be fragile and threats may easily arise. For example in the UK local authorities are being encouraged to promote development activity on 'forgotten sites' that they own. It is not surprising therefore that, from time to time, local communities become involved in battles to protect these areas, and that many benefit from formal recognition as areas of local open space.

Even those sites which have been protected by their physical nature may now be threatened by increased development pressure supported by improvements in technology such as 'raft' foundation construction techniques for building on poorly drained sites.

Urban sites of particular importance

Churchyards

Churchyards and cemeteries are recognized as being among the most important urban nature reserves (Gilbert, 1989). Many of the oldest represent a direct link to historic countryside. Some areas of turf have never been disturbed or fertilized and therefore may contain important relict communities of wildflowers. Many such sites also contain very old trees and the stone features such as gravestones can provide an important habitat for lichens and mosses. Cemeteries, as opposed to churchyards, have frequently undergone dramatic changes in habitat status since once they have become full, revenue sources to pay for management rapidly declines. Many of the oldest have therefore become overgrown and dominated by invading scrub and trees, together with those ornamental species that were able to maintain a competitive place in the plant community.

As well as their natural history interest such areas also have high importance in terms of their social impact. All good landscapes speak to our feelings, and cemeteries must be potentially among the most emotionally charged places we ever encounter. People's feelings when faced by death are inevitably complex, and the challenges of producing a landscape that encompasses and responds to these feelings should not be underestimated. Wild landscapes seem to be relevant in at least part of these areas because they can create a sense that 'life goes on' or that nature finds new life in death.

This is of course the same sentiment that lay behind the use of evergreens in churchyards for centuries and reached a peak in Victorian times. However today we have more complex associations with many of the evergreens that the Victorians loved and we cannot read the same messages in the landscape. Conifers are 'aliens' associated with afforestation and with dingy grime-covered shrubberies lining urban streets. Today we need new landscapes that evoke the same feelings for our own generations and objectively natural landscapes seem particularly appropriate; if carefully designed, long grass and wildlife can present a powerful message of the natural cycle and of renewal. Evergreens will play a part, but they should be used as a small element of a more natural habitat, not as the dominant focus.

It seems particularly ironic that new cemetery designs are among the most uncomfortable, sterile and mawkish mish-mashes of structureless and often over-maintained planting imaginable, embodying the worst of municipal ornamentalism. Angular hybrid tea roses sit awkwardly in beds carved out of close mown grass in a setting that seems devoid of an appreciation of any spiritual and cultural dimension. The justification given for such styles is usually that people want and appreciate these plants, and that wild landscapes are equated with a lack of care. Leaving grass uncut is interpreted as an insult or at least a shocking dereliction of duty on behalf of the management authority. (Although it needs to be recognized that there is a growing interest in 'ecoburials' where people choose to be buried in natural surroundings, so stylistic preferences for cemeteries may change in the future.)

In a way, therefore, cemeteries and churchyards embody a philosophical, almost spiritual, debate that lies at the heart of the urban conservation movement. For many people, allowing nature more freedom within the cemetery is corrupting and somehow equates with a lack of human care, or worse a complete moral abandonment. The value of wildlife as a positive factor in the landscape, and the need for and value of human involvement in the management of nature is poorly recognized.

Nevertheless this cannot be tackled by attempts to 'ban' exotic plants or force people to live in more natural surroundings. At present anyone who does favour more natural settings in cemeteries will find their choices reduced by a vociferous lobby, and there is nothing to be gained by replacing this with another extreme stand. The need is to encourage more choice through promoting more positive associations of nature in urban areas, and more examples of good naturalistic designs but also to recognize that these will always need to integrate with more formal and ornamental areas.

Gardens and private open space

Outside of the urban heartlands of shopping precincts, offices and the most intensely developed workers terraces, where hard surfacing and concrete are dominant, towns and cities retain a remarkably large percentage of green, and this remains the case even when looking at housing estates and urban layouts from many different social periods. However, the pattern and content of the land often changes dramatically as does the division between private and public land. As a consequence the importance of the land to urban conservation and the potential for wildlife support also varies.

The patterns of land and land use in urban areas is inevitably closely influenced by social and historical factors. Most of the towns in Europe have grown organically over centuries. There are many different layers of urban development – a medieval core in some cases but nearly always areas of Victorian and Edwardian development as well as phases of planned urban expansion carried out in almost every decade of the twentieth century. It is a fairly simple task to date zones of the urban fabric by looking at the architectural style of the buildings and road patterns. What may be less obvious is that the nature of the landscape also follows certain predictable trends and can also be dated from its appearance and content.

Early urban cores are often fairly deficient in open space, unless there has been significant redevelopment since (or because of) the last world war. Although the original developments may have incorporated more open land, centuries of infilling during times of population pressure have almost entirely eroded this resource. Notable exceptions are often associated with powerful landowners of the past, such as the church or colleges.

Victorian residential developments are characterized by relatively large gardens for certain privileged classes whereas the majority of workers' housing had little associated ground. In compensation the Victorians invested in allotments and large urban parks; the former to be used to provide a healthy diet and the latter to contribute to health and social well-being by providing resources for fresh air, recreation and also beauty to refresh the spirit and to civilize the working classes. The Victorians therefore anticipated many of the ideas of the multiple benefits from urban greenspace that we still hold dear today. In many ways it was only their limited grasp of issues such as the nature of pollution and plant ecology that limited the sophistication of their projects. It was also an age where there were relatively few controls over development. Social reformers could have an impact in very specific instances, but were unable to dictate that what we would now call 'environmental issues' should be given consideration in wider development.

The inter-war years were characterized by the increasing influence of planning in town development. Housing areas were influenced by the 'garden city' philosophers who wished to place more emphasis on gardens for all dwellings and also on the provision of more greenspace around and between buildings. Grass verges and avenues of trees were often provided. New parks were still created but these were smaller and less ambitious as there was less need for all of the benefits of open space to be met by them.

Both of these phases showed quite high levels of investment in the landscape. That this investment was predominantly targeted at the ornamental shrubberies and exotic trees that were the fashion should not detract from the attempt to produce something of quality in the green environment.

The 1950s saw a revolution in philosophy in town planning, one of the major tenets being that the various functions that were fulfilled by different parts of the town could be improved by separation and concentration. Housing areas were separated from industrial and retail and on a smaller scale residences were aggregated together such that the open space was not 'wasted' by dispersal into private gardens but could be assembled to form a 'park' landscape into which the buildings were set.

The epitome of this approach was of course based on Le Corbusier's vision of apartment life where people resided 'in the sky and above the park'. The reality, in much of post-war Europe and certainly in Britain, was that this vision was degraded by economies and perhaps by poor appreciation of the technical problems that needed to be solved. The buildings were often obvious failures: the landscapes were as well. However in both cases many of the problems related directly to inadequate funds which made it impossible to ensure quality. For whatever the reason, urban housing landscapes began to take the form of the infamous 'green deserts' – large tracts of uniform mown grass stretching between windswept towers and with a light peppering of standard trees. Gardens were reduced to minimal vestiges and where large proportions of the site were kept in public ownership there has often been a predominance of mown grass and standard trees, a style often favoured more by the building architects than by landscape architects. Conversely in other areas and at other times land was allocated more freely to residents who were able to have more direct control over the content of the landscape.

More recently housing landscapes have undergone another transformation. The philosophy behind 1950s and 1960s developments had been discredited. There was something of a 'return to traditional values'; with new houses having their own private space as well as integrating a significant presence of public land. Land values mean that the size of these new gardens are often regrettably small, but planners are able to insist on quite significant areas of new tree and shrub planting in association with the developments. Perhaps of greater importance has been the increasing emphasis on 'planning gain' whereby new developments are sometimes required to fund the establishment (and sometimes maintenance) of some sizeable new public parks. Many of these have incorporated areas of countryside in a largely unchanged form; others have had some significant investment to improve their nature conservation value.

This is not the place for a review of the social attitudes and ebb and flow of fashions in town planning that both contributed to and arose from these different styles. However a simple truth is pretty obvious. The division of land into small parcels, each of which attempts to meet the aspirations and interests of individuals, means that urban areas dominated by private gardens often have an incredibly diverse and structurally rich vegetation. Much of it is dominated by exotic species and there is disturbance always present from humans and their pets, but for species which can tolerate these factors there is access to what is one of the most beneficial habitat types imaginable. Gardens represent a fine grained matrix of habitats, with an intimate inter-relation of open space and shelter, that would never occur or be sustainable in public landscape.

In contrast public owned land is often simple, even structurally monotonous. Attempts to relax the intensity of maintenance, letting grass grow longer, raise problems of equipment and also opens the authority to complaints from public intolerant of 'untidiness'. (Anyone who has ever shared the rental of a house or flat will know that people vary enormously in their thresholds of tolerance for untidiness and in taste. It is similarly a characteristic situation in public landscaped areas that the 'clean and tidy' lobby are vociferous and ready to complain when the standards of maintenance do not meet their expectations, whereas it is much harder for people with different aesthetic standards to complain that areas are 'too tidy'.)

The one major advantage that might be expected on larger areas of public landscape would be the freedom to plant large forest trees rather than smaller, or 'garden', varieties. Unfortunately the use of such large species has gone out of fashion as a result of increasing worries about the maintenance costs and possible harmful effects of such specimens on the urban fabric (shade, leaf litter, road and pavement damage, damage to foundations, property or physical damage if part of the tree falls etc.) We have therefore seen a dramatic shift towards small species and varieties (what Peter Thoday refers to as 'pet' trees) in professional planting programmes associated with housing land (Land Use Consultants, 1993). Garden infilling by additional development is not a new phenomenon and is likely to have been a key process in the urbanization of inner cities. Particularly under threat, therefore, are the large old existing gardens with big trees associated with periods of generous land allocation to development.

The importance of the garden estate is therefore huge in terms of urban nature conservation. Yet this importance is an issue that many conservation planners have a rather confused and almost schizophrenic attitude towards. It gets pointed out regularly that urban gardens collectively have an area that is far larger than our designated national nature reserves for example (Owen and Owen, 1975). Yet the distribution of such gardens is widely ignored and not usually presented in assessments of urban wildlife sites.

Confusion also reigns concerning the degree to which the owners of such gardens need to change what they grow and how they grow it in order to improve the wildlife quality of the garden. In particular there seems to be general uncertainty about whether most gardens are really havens for wildlife or actually hostile deserts poisoned by 'huge armouries of chemicals' (a stock phrase that seems to have become one of the clichés of the wildlife gardening journalists). This emotive rhetoric simply does not bear close examination since most people simply can not be bothered to make any 'chemical inputs' into their garden. Certainly it is actually a rare exception to find any gardener who makes regular use of broad spectrum pesticides, with the possible exception of keen allotmenteers and even these are being increasingly influenced by 'organic' ideals.

A far more significant factor that reduces the wildlife value of gardens is the constant disturbance that comes from the proximity to housing and people and most of all the artificially high populations of predatory pets, especially cats (Jarvis, 1990). The latter problem is particularly difficult to find a solution to. Technological developments may also have an influence. For example strimmers allow gardeners to 'tidy up' corners easily that would otherwise have remained neglected.

The desirable content of a wildlife garden is also something that people tend to get confused over. The issue of restricting plants to natives only will be given a more detailed discussion in this book but certainly for many animals structural diversity and a wide range of flowers and other food sources is probably more important.

Also widespread is the mistaken belief that any one garden, within its own bounds, needs to attempt to meet all of the life requirements of a myriad of species when this is patently not possible. There is a fundamental distinction that needs to be made between creating a complete habitat and 'attracting wildlife' into the garden. For the vast majority of urban species no one garden alone can meet all of the territory and food requirements. Birds, hedgehogs and most flying insects need to roam across a wide area and the suitability of a location for them will depend on the composite value of all of the gardens they can gain access to, together with the wider matrix of public and industrial land. If the intention is to increase their population numbers then the best wildlife garden for these species is one which addresses the limiting factors for their survival and removes that limitation.

Therefore it follows that if someone's house is close to some waste land rich with stinging nettles, then there is no particular need to add yet another colony to the garden when a hot sunny glade with abundant nectar sources for the adults may be far more beneficial. (In a twenty-minute walk from my own town garden through allotments and rough ground I counted between 100 000 –150 000 stems of stinging nettle.) What would be of more value is stinging nettles established on freshly manured ground which are frequently coppiced in rotation to maintain lush foliage.

Exotic species **do** have value. A rich variety of well-chosen exotic plants with a wide season of nectar supply in an intricate design is probably preferable to a few isolated native trees in uniform rough unmown grass. Similarly birds may benefit most from evergreen shelter and berrying shrubs that are in fruit during the hardest winter months.

In many natural habitats animals are widely dispersed at low densities and are hard to see; there are countless people who have spent a whole day in quite good rural habitats without seeing any significant animal activity whereas the wildlife experience that can come from having a non-native *Pyracantha* shrub in the garden during a hard winter can be extraordinarily rich. The design goal in a wildlife garden is therefore to try to find that missing component in the landscape which will best meet the animal's needs. In so doing we can temporarily concentrate the local population where they can be more regularly seen and enjoyed. Conversely these high activity locations, where many animals pass through, make rather poor permanent bases and most individuals would then choose to retreat to quieter locations elsewhere.

The message that should be promoted to wildlife-keen gardeners is that they should be preserving old features of value, such as trees and walls and should also be lobbying for more sensitive management of the wider landscape, promoting nature parks, turning parts of the green deserts around schools and factories into scrub and rough grass for example. Sometimes more intensive management may be useful in some places, for example ensuring that the local wasteland nettle patch is cut back occasionally to provide the rich young growth that butterflies need.

Ultimately, the main value of a wildlife garden relates to the psychological significance to the people who own and develop it. Gardens are where we shape the natural world into patterns that we desire. As such they mirror our beliefs, over-riding concerns and needs with regard to nature. The increased interest in wildlife gardening is a barometer of people's feeling about the disappearance of habitats from the world around, and a measure of their wish to establish a new and more positive relationship, but again it is vital that these changes are approached and promoted in a way that builds on what is already positive, rather than focusing on areas of unnecessary potential conflict.

Parks

Approximately one hundred years after the movement for their creation was at its strongest urban parks are now widely recognized as being in the middle of a crisis of funding, political support and perhaps also of direction (Holden, 1988; Elliot, 1988).

Most of the Victorian parks reflected the fashion for high-quality ornamental horticulture; a few preserved a somewhat different character that reflected perhaps common-land origins. The majority of use was focused on rather formal low-key recreation activities, such as walking and carriage riding, that was to be conducted in a civilized and decorous manner.

However, since then the 'official' provision of recreation space has become increasingly dominated by the sports lobby, a group that placed ambitious targets for local authorities to meet which were usually expressed in terms of the provision of numbers of playing fields in relation to heads of population. Within this lobby there was a relatively narrow perception of what sports and forms of recreation were worthy to be promoted (i.e. mainly those which appealed to young, fit, men). The other benefits and interested parties that the landscape should serve tended to be overlooked (Elliot, 1988). Aside from the sports council and similar bodies there were very few lobbies that actually existed at the time to put pressure on parks departments. Nobody else seemed to have a clear opinion or goal for the future of open space. The result was that all investment became targeted towards these developments. New parks were rare; new 'recreation grounds' added to the acreage of mown grass that had begun to completely dominate the landscape.

This philosophy continued to dominate through the relative prosperity of the 1960s. When financial constraints hit local authorities in the 1970s the

Table 1.1 *Record of landscape features lost from two post-war parks in Knowsley Borough, 1974–86*

Feature lost	Webster Park	Wignall Park
Ornamental flowerbeds	17	28
Rose garden		1
Rustic pergola	1	
Peat garden		1
Rockery	1	
Garden for the blind		1
Sand pit	1	
Paddling pool	1	1
Tennis courts	4	8
Crown bowling greens	2	2
Putting greens	1	

Source: Handley and Bulmer (1987).

target for cuts were costly provisions including some resource-hungry sports but mainly the remnants of the 'horticultural' landscape that the Victorians and Edwardians had introduced to the parks. Flower beds with plants such as annuals and roses were removed as being 'too costly' to maintain (Handley and Bulmer, 1987) (see Table 1.1). The publicly maintained land estate was growing, but the contribution it could make to the quality of life of the urban population was rapidly shrinking. Many of our parks began to be less and less popular and unattractive, paving the way for development threats and the potential loss of the land resource.

By the 1980s a more balanced view of the possible role of public open space was beginning to emerge. The wildlife lobby in particular presented a strong counterpoint to the sports movement. However the new finance for such developments was often limited. A few new parks did sometimes come into existence as a result of land reclamation or inner-city refurbishment programmes. Some of these were even of high quality and some of these had a strong emphasis on urban wildlife, e.g. Camley Street.

There was also a trend to sell off existing areas of 'underused' greenspace for development. These areas may be important as reservoirs of wildlife which are feeding into the surrounding land, and as such their value was not necessarily related just to direct use.

The need to get people with different interests and backgrounds back into parks is of high priority. The design solution that would almost certainly be adopted for these areas by landscape professionals today would place great emphasis on native plants and on habitat creation, although it is of course vital that a balance is preserved with the needs and interests of other groups. In some European countries the focus on the value of parks for wildlife has become so dominant that it has become difficult to see where people fit in (Wittkugel, 1988). The obvious danger is that one lobby group may be substituted by another.

Sports and recreation interests, those that appreciate traditional flower designs, arts and community activity groups and even those who see in parks the historic legacy of Victorian art and endeavour that is part of the heritage that needs to be preserved – all form legitimate interest groups that need to be integrated. Even among people who simply value the park as a green landscape for relaxation, there are some groups who will not relate to the paradigm of naturalistic planting and would rather see more overt order and control in the design and management approaches. Some people find ecological styles disturbing or potentially threatening. Even here, however, there may be room for technical compromise, for example creating shelved edges and islands in the middle of what remain essentially ornamental ponds.

Another issue that frequently gets raised in terms of parks development is the widespread belief that ecological management of landscapes is bound to be cheaper than traditional intensive maintenance. This issue is in fact complex and is dealt with in more detail in Chapter 8. However, suffice to say here that it is not always the case that ecological designs are cheap. There needs to be careful consideration of the use of such rhetoric, as ill-considered promises regarding the potential for budget savings can be dangerous. There is a risk either of a loss of credibility as the projected savings fail to become realized, or there is a likelihood that the park remains under-funded and that critical inputs, which may be necessary for ecological as for formal designs, will not be sanctioned.

A problem that comes up regularly with regard to ecological management styles within urban parks relates to the apparent lack of sympathy shown by some traditional local authority maintenance staff. Nearly every ecologist seems to have a ready anecdote about how wildflower grasslands were close mown to the point of destruction, or how a dead-wood habitat was tidied up and burnt. At times this is attributed to 'horticultural training' among the maintenance teams but the reality is of course that many of the people working for local authorities have had little training of any kind, nor indeed did they always have clear work objectives set for different areas by the higher management or guidelines on desirable practice. Baines (1986b) has argued that if the subject was approached in the right way most maintenance staff would welcome the chance to practise many different types of mainte-nance which would add to their job interest and complement traditional methods rather than threaten them.

However these issues may have become largely irrelevant today. Probably the most significant development regarding parks in the UK in recent years has been the introduction of compulsory competitive tendering legislation whereby local authorities have become obliged to offer parks maintenance work to the private sector for tender, and to use these private contractors wherever they are shown to be cheaper than in-house labour. The full impli-cations of this change are complex, and not surprisingly there are negative as well as positive components. In some areas maintenance standards have fallen; in others they have been maintained or have improved. There has been a loss of some of the job functions that permanent local-authority staff carried out, since these functions were not often formally recognized in the job description. These losses include the ability to liaise closely with the public as users, or to provide a permanent presence which helped to make the parks feel safe. There has also been a dramatic increase in the amount of bureaucracy and paperwork associated with even the most simple of maintenance operations.

Conversely in order to issue and police contracts local authorities have had to produce, often for the first time, a full and detailed inventory of the landscape estate that they are maintaining, and to set formal management goals and performance standards. For many local authorities the separation of client responsibilities (i.e. setting objectives) from the day-to-day running of the parks has provided an opportunity to stand back and assess their overall directions and aims.

The implications for the transition, if wished, towards a more ecological style of management are also complex. New impediments exist; there is a huge exercise in contract preparation that needs to be undertaken whenever a revision in management is proposed and this presents an administrative hurdle to change. Conversely some previously existing hurdles have disappeared. Traditionally a simple matter such as a change in mowing regime in a park may not have been acceptable because of the existing stock of mowing machinery and staff deployment patterns. Now a change in the contract can be introduced and it is the responsibility of those contractors who wish to tender to ensure that they have the appropriate machinery, labour and staff skills to do the job.

Of course, some problems may still remain. There may be an absence of appropriate machinery for some tasks within the region; because of this, or simply because of unfamiliarity with the tasks, many contractors may give unnecessarily high bids; there may be difficulty in writing or policing contracts in a way which is flexible enough to meet with the demands of ecological management (for example it may be desired to delay hay cutting until most of the wildflowers have finished blooming, but the actual date of this can be very climate dependent from year to year). These problems are primarily associated with transitional periods during the move towards a different style, and they should gradually disappear.

Probably the most likely vision of the future for parks is for the wider fabric of the landscape to be designed and managed in a more natural and relaxed style, but with a clear role for intensive management to allow for sports and activities and also with areas of traditional horticultural planting, albeit probably more concentrated and strategically positioned than was often the case before.

Industrial sites and institutions

Large components of urban land are in the ownership of factories and institutions such as hospitals. These share the common characteristic that usually the primary interests of the landowner are elsewhere. It is also likely that improved public access will not be welcomed. The sites are often typified by a woefully low concern for the quality of the landscape. In many cases land is seen as a liability rather than a resource; the only recognized function again being organized recreation. There are of course exceptions in the cases where the landscape of an earlier age has been preserved – some hospitals contain surprisingly large estates which may have a semi-rural character that has survived largely through indifference. The newly privatized authorities such as water boards or power generation utilities also often have surprisingly large land holdings. Traditionally the concern they have for the landscape they own is often dictated most strongly by the extent to which it will be an asset for planning permission.

Since the 1950s private-sector landowners have come under increasing pressure from planners to ensure that new developments are accompanied by quite a large investment in the landscape. The most prestigious and costly new landscapes to be created in the UK over the last 30 years have been associated with industrial parks. In scale and quality, developments such as Stockley Park near Heathrow Airport are the nearest equivalents we have today to echo the grand power statements of historic landscapes such as Versailles, Chatsworth or Stourhead. However the over-riding concern that the companies have for prestige and image, and the relatively limited opportunities for people to interact with the landscape, has meant that there is almost always an emphasis on ornamental qualities.

Nevertheless many landowners may be interested in maintaining the landscape for use by the employees or clients, or through general social responsibility. In such circumstances the work of advice (and sometimes even volunteer labour) is often co-ordinated by quangos such as the Groundwork Trusts or NGOs. It is not uncommon, however, that periods of activity may suddenly come to a halt when the company or institution faces budgetary restraints (or undergoes a management change) and chooses to consolidate on their core activity.

For example hospital wildlife gardens were a fashion promoted briefly by the organization UK2000. These were small areas of naturalistic planting put in place in the hope of encouraging more wildlife activity near to the wards (Avon Wildlife Consultants, undated). Unfortunately the wider value of the hospital landscape, which often contains vast areas of grassland and woodland as a legacy from the adoption of large estate buildings, is frequently still overlooked.

Progress in encouraging a more positive utilization of hospital (and even factory) grounds may be achieved through research into the wider health (and perhaps productivity) benefits that may be obtained from contact with nature (see Chapter 9).

Schools

Schools are another institution type which own a huge land estate in urban areas. Traditionally this has also been largely shunned and neglected, with a focus placed primarily on sports use, with some small fragments of land put over to rose beds or similar features near the entrance to improve the public image. However, in recent years great success has been achieved in promoting to schools the educational and developmental benefits that access to a positive landscape can provide. The organization Learning Through Landscapes has undertaken many studies illustrating the ways in which school grounds can be utilized to promote both the formal and informal curricula.

Certain difficulties are associated with the successful utilization of school grounds for complex objectives. The majority of the grounds will be maintained by either contract or local authority labour. The temptation to remove sensitive areas from this system is difficult to avoid, but the onus then falls on the school community to ensure that adequate and timely maintenance is undertaken. This is particularly difficult during the vacation periods, but it can also be difficult when demands of the teaching programme become too great.

Perhaps the most common problem with regard to school landscape development is the fluctuation in skills, commitment and interest that is seen as the teaching staff within a particular school change. It is far too common to discover neglected school ponds or overgrown wildlife corners which are remnants of a forgotten or unsustained initiative. It is vital for long-term success that the initiative is promoted beyond individual staff members to the point where the majority of the school community understands and has a stake in the continued exploitation of the grounds. The long-term prospects for success may be increased if there is an organization that can act as enabler, perhaps working with many schools helping to co-ordinate necessary work and to continue to promote and encourage volunteer work or other support among the staff, pupils and particularly the families of the schoolchildren.

Schools can also suffer from particularly strong outbreaks of health and safety panic, where access to the natural world is suddenly classified as so dangerous that practically every possible spontaneous initiative of the children is suppressed while fences and gates separate different parts of the landscape. Campaigns against poisonous plants inevitably flounder against the realization that, since hundreds of plants have developed biochemical protection systems, it is actually impossible to guarantee that there is no risk (see Chapter 8).

Waste and derelict land

Industrial wastelands can develop a great richness of unusual and interesting plant and animal species for several reasons:

1. They are often heterogeneous with a range of different substrate types, each with different physical and chemical characteristics. Drainage ranges from poor to very rapid, pH and fertility also varies. Each type favours different species. This means that the overall site diversity can be high even when individual patches are relatively poor. Some patches of substrate may be very different from the typical soil type of the region, which can encourage locally scarce species. It is possible to see close

combinations of different communities that are normally never found adjacent (Box, 1993).

2. A common characteristic of the substrate is low fertility and this encourages a sparse open vegetation that can support many plant species of low competitive ability.

3. The land is often structurally complex with varied topography and also with large areas of hard standing and rubble which creates good shelter and basking spaces.

4. Access is sometimes difficult and human disturbance may therefore be low once industrial activity has ceased.

The species which are particularly successful on derelict industrial land are those that have good dispersal characteristics, are tolerant of extreme conditions and are poor competitors in more productive habitats. The plant groups tend therefore to be categorized as stress tolerant ruderals *sensu* (Grime, 1979). Pollution levels can restrict diversity, and on contaminated sites it is often the case that there will be just one or two plants species (or ecotypes from within a species) that have unusually high tolerance.

The interesting flora that can be found on ex-industrial sites has been well documented by Gemmell (1982). Particular botanic richness is often associated with alkaline and moisture retentive but infertile subsoils and wastes which typically accumulate many orchids and rarities. This flora has parallels with that found on limestone grassland and particularly with the plant communities of alkaline dune slacks and coastal areas where similar pH, high levels of certain salts and deficiencies of other nutrients and a high disturbance status, are found. Where site conditions on derelict land are favourable some of these species can rapidly expand their numbers to the point where local or regional populations are heavily represented by the individuals found on post-industrial land (Williams, 1995; Lunn and Wild, 1995). More recently the invertebrate fauna of such sites has become more widely studied, with many uncommon species being found (Eyre and Luff, 1995); (these are probably also 'ruderal' species that need open, complex, early successional sites). Some sites are of such interest that they have been designated by the government as protected sites on nature conservation grounds.

The development of biological richness on such sites can be a comparatively slow process, it typically takes something like 15–20 years before an orchid flora can develop for example. This may be a function of the time required for colonization, but is more likely to reflect the need for gradual amelioration of the hostility of the substrate, through leaching of pollutants and gradual accumulation of nutrients (even species that prefer infertile soils of course have some nutrient demand and can not grow in soils that are completely devoid of nitrogen). This delay prevents the development of diversity on many potentially valuable sites, since the land is often recycled to other use much earlier. (It is a difficult philosophical question for planners to be asked to take into consideration potential conservation importance, even if they can be convinced that there is a very high probability that it will develop.)

One of the most valuable characteristics of the urban flora is therefore that each town or region frequently displays a unique and characteristic assemblage of early successional communities that are the result of a rich combination of industrial and cultural human activity interacting with the regional ecology. Some of these industrial activities can be regarded as essentially non-recreatable and some sites in the UK have been designated as National Nature Reserves (Box, 1993).

Unlike many traditional, rural, reserves the plant and animal communities associated with ex-industrial sites have developed following disturbance and without management intervention. However even though they have been created without purposeful human intervention, they often will not survive unless such intervention is introduced. It is quite typical that as the succession progresses and a scrub and tree canopy develops, many of these sites lose their uniqueness and turn to rather ordinary young woodlands, probably dominated by *Acer pseudoplatanus* in the UK (although we rarely have any idea of the result of undisturbed succession beyond the period of a few decades). On some sites this may be acceptable but across the whole range of locations it would be undesirable. In some instances, therefore, rotational soil disturbance is required to restore the early successional stages. It can look bizarre to some people to see the vegetation being destroyed by bulldozers in the name of conservation, but this is precisely what is required.

Even when sites clearly have biological interest there can be a problem of incorporation in urban conservation strategies, since the land ownership or planning status may put priority on other land uses. Indeed the potential conflict arises at least partly from the widespread definition of derelict land as 'land incapable of beneficial use without treatment' (Bradshaw and Chadwick, 1980) which encourages people to assume that there is nothing of value there. In fact there are many instances where derelict land of great inherent conservation interest has been converted to urban open space through what has been seen as a pointless, expensive process of traditional landscaping which has produced a site of far lower quality and interest.

Popular appreciation of the recreation and wildlife value of derelict land can develop despite a lack of official recognition. This is particularly likely on sites that develop a good cover of secondary woodland in a mosaic with grassland. Attempts to develop and recycle such sites may meet with great local opposition, and some bitter planning battles may occur. One of the most famous in the UK was a dispute over the future of the Gunnersbury triangle, an area of railway land which became scheduled for development but was valued by local people as an informal recreation space (Johnston, 1990). The site was saved from development and this was a great urban conservation milestone that set precedents for planning recognition to be given to secondary, undesignated, sites where they were of exceptional local importance.

One of the attractions for such after-use solutions is that there are substantial possible financial savings. Unlike restoration for agriculture, for example, there is less need for topography to be modified, drainage schemes to be implemented or soil fertility to be improved. Studies have shown that the restoration costs of nature conservation can be typically a quarter of that of agriculture (Land Capability Consultants, 1989). However new challenges have now been presented to planners as a result. Where developers have to undertake land reclamation as part of their clean-up obligations on a site, the planning officers need to be able to evaluate the feasibility of the restoration proposals. It is essential that a credible and politically acceptable criteria for assessment of proposals should be developed.

The problem is that it is relatively easy to identify areas where natural colonization has lead to 'interesting wildlife' on derelict land; it is far harder to develop this recognition into a predictive tool suitable for guiding planning decisions. Simply allowing reclamation sites to 'go wild' or to develop rank vegetation may be cost effective but is of limited value to conservation and in the long term would simply undermine the concept of this form of after-use. There is already evidence that where planners are encouraging conservation after-use they are allowing completely the wrong methodology to implement this.

The methodology of revegetation of land that has developed over the last 40 years has been implicitly targeted towards the goals that would be set by agronomists, notably maximum productivity and uniformity, with the resulting soil types judged against an agricultural norm. To develop conservation value environmental variability and low productivity are the key.

Many sites that have superficially been reclaimed to 'conservation' in fact consist of poor vegetation communities. There are political and social pressures that require any reclamation programme to show early results, yet it is essential that these early results do not compromise the long-term development of natural communities of interest. 'Minimal amelioration' is required, which involves initiating carefully controlled site improvements that overcome the major limitations to plant growth yet do not raise productivity too high.

Wetlands

Urban areas are often rich in waterbodies, partly because of historical settlement and economic expansion patterns which have favoured towns on estuaries and near to rivers. New artificial features such as sewage works, industrial lagoons and flooded pits, reservoirs and canals, have combined with amenity lakes and garden ponds to make for a richness of water distribution that is often unrivalled in the surrounding countryside. Some of these have become exceptionally important for wildlife, particularly waterfowl.

However, the following two constraints have reduced the quality and value of these sites.

- Industrial pollution is often very severe, exhibiting as either the presence of direct toxins such as heavy metals, nutrients which lead to eutrophication or highly reactive organic materials which have an excessive biological oxygen demand.

- Urban areas are proportionally devoid of wetlands, by which is meant the areas where wet soil and water is found in close conjunction. For a combination of reasons including access, an engineered approach to drainage, ease of construction, safety and a dislike of some wetland pests the tendency has been to sanitize waterbodies by surrounding them with concrete and hard surfaces, while the land around is drained. A quick review of the local names of many estuary-based towns and cities, such as London, will quickly show how dramatic this change has been.

Pollution controls have begun to have a noticeable effect on many major urban waterbodies, with sensitive fish species returning to rivers such as the Thames. This process has been accelerated by the decline of many traditional manufacturing industries in such areas.

Increasingly awareness has also spread of how urban water features can be modified so that their wildlife value is enhanced. Topographical variation below the water level, the modification of shorelines and the creation of islands have all been researched with the result that it is possible for some industries, such as sands and gravel extraction companies, to leave behind created wetlands which are almost immediately suitable for a wide range of species. New approaches to sewage treatment may also be significant, with more and more attention being given to natural treatment processes such as those based on reed beds. In rural areas efforts are being directed towards a more natural approach to the engineering of rivers, with flood plains being tolerated, or even being re-opened. Such steps are unlikely within an existing urban framework but the likelihood will be of improved water quality with rivers carrying less silts and nutrient loads.

Development does of course continue to be a threat and as technology advances new options become significant, such as the creation of barrages or wave power interceptors. Perhaps the most significant growing threat to the wildlife value of urban waterbodies is the development of recreation interest and especially the range of powered high-speed craft now available which can lead to significant water turbulence, physical destruction of vegetation and bank erosion. Restoration of historic waterways such as canals for recreational access by such craft can lead to the decline of habitat value in several ways, such as the dredging of shallows, construction of engineered bank edges and the clearances and disturbance of tunnels that have been colonized by bats. Such conflicts of interest are complex with many short- and long-term implications yet to be resolved (Byfield, 1990).

The urban fringe

The urban fringe, the interface between the town and the countryside, has long been recognized as an area with unique character and unique problems. Low land prices and opportunities for expansion attract certain types of development, notably housing estates, schools, factories and business parks as well as landfill and refuse receptor sites etc. The characteristics of the urban fringe may be particularly strongly influenced by the presence of a green belt policy, as this can constrain most but not all types of development.

The problems of the urban fringe include the impact of the urban community on the surrounding farmland; vandalism, theft, dog worrying (or the expectations of these) can discourage farmers and lead to land abandonment. The land itself may be more attractive to families owning horses, although again vandalism is a worry. Therefore remnant habitats in the urban fringe may initially be of high quality but are prone to degeneration through the change in land use and breakdown of the continuity of management.

Although the urban fringe may represent the point where true countryside meets the town there may, ironically, be few opportunities for access and enjoyment of the land. Public transport or parking access may not be extensive and there may be few focal points. The layout of the outer edge of the town itself can often be introverted and unwelcoming. Factories, landfills and the like do not allow easy access to the land beyond, while the functioning farmers in the surrounding land may be highly sensitive to intrusion.

These challenges therefore often inspire the need for proactive strategies, such as that run by the Groundwork programme in the UK. They are increasingly the site of woodland planting initiatives, using predominantly native species to create borders and buffer zones rather than to produce the fastest rate of timber production (see Chapter 7). Planners may also need to take special steps to reduce fragmentation of green areas that cross from the rural to urban zones.

Characteristics of urban countryside

It is not always easy to identify the characteristics which unite these possibly very different sites together as the urban countryside. Their style, content and the owner's approaches to management (or lack of management) are all different. The extent to which these function as a mutually supporting whole can also be a matter of great debate.

In addition to this variation in types and management objectives there are several ideas that are prevalent among observers and also some professionals concerned with urban ecological landscape management that are probably myths, but which are based on enough truth to lead to a confusion of objectives:

- that only an ecological style of management favours wildlife;
- that only native plants favour wildlife;
- that ecological management is cheaper than 'formal' landscape design and management.

These ideas among others will need to be discussed in more detail in later chapters. But for now if it is accepted that they are not always true, it makes it

1 Traditional urban landscape design is often seen as 'sterile', lacking the richness of experience and the complexity of vegetation structure and texture that naturalistic designs may produce for comparable cost

even harder to identify and define the essential characteristics that make 'urban countryside' or ecological landscape sites worth creating or preserving.

We will see that it is not enough to say that these are landscapes that are similar to or even reminiscent of rural countryside. Rather, it seems that our focus should be on places where complexity and richness are favoured over simplicity, where human control over ecosystem development is less deliberate and where plants and animals are free to interact and to compete. For the purposes of this text therefore it is the internal ecosystem function and the methodologies of landscape management (which can include deliberate non-intervention) that help to define the urban countryside rather than any poorly conceived images of what the end result should look like.

The urban countryside is also, at least in part, determined by the attitudes towards the level of control we want to have over the land and the species on it. Usually in any landscape design and management programme following horticultural principles there is a frequent (if seldom explicit) assessment and evaluation of the species present. Their value and function is recognized even if they are only intended for aesthetic effect, and clear choices are made by the designer and manager concerning which ones should be present in which places.

In more natural landscapes, whatever their origin, there is usually a presumption that the communities present will be more able to develop according to their own internal processes, and that part of the pleasure arises from the diversity and unpredictability that results. Of course management control may still be imposed, and it may certainly still be the case that individual species are encouraged or attacked, but in general the framework of the community may not be rigidly specified.

This atmosphere of relaxation of control, of a tolerance of natural processes and vagaries rather than the imposition of rigid human direction, may have great psychological importance which can be one of the greatest justifications for and benefits of urban ecological landscapes. This is discussed in more detail later.

The three main functional classifications of 'urban countryside'

As we have seen, urban countryside comprises landscape of very different origins, ownership, history of use and composition. Nevertheless to aid management and priority setting these can usefully be categorized into three main types according to their content and history of intervention. Of course the divisions between each is not always clear and there are many levels of interaction.

1. Relict countryside

The expansion of the urban fabric often leads to the encapsulation of pockets of countryside that, manage to escape development because of land owner-ship constraints (e.g. common land), soil, topography or poor accessibility (steep, unstable land or land prone to flooding for example). In the former case the land often has very well developed patterns of access and recre-ational use and may even have become formalized as local authority run naturalistic parks.

Many of these areas that they have become divorced from the manage-ment patterns and inputs that maintained them originally. The extent to which these areas retain their original nature and the original plant and animal communities depends on many factors:

- their dependency on sustained traditional land use which may no longer be viable or may simply be forgotten;
- the dependency on larger land mosaics, habitat ranges or interconnected features which may be interrupted as urbanization progresses around;
- the new management, land use or disturbances that are imposed;
- the presence of invasive species in the surrounding land;
- the vulnerability of the species to diffuse urban impacts such as tempera-ture or hydrology changes, dusts or gaseous pollutants.

In the UK, the surveys of the London Ecology Unit have demonstrated a remarkable resource of such land within the capital, including a surprising number of sites which are still of reasonable quality (see bibliography). At their best these patches of encompassed countryside may contain complex semi-natural communities characteristic of times before the agricultural revolution put many plant and animal communities under threat. It can be argued that in some ways urban land can be less hostile to wildlife than rural areas where widespread use of agrochemicals and modern farming techniques can be so damaging to biodiversity (Baines, 1986c).

Of course it is usual that the relict patches that have survived in the town will have been in some way changed or degraded from their original form. Woodlands, particularly those which have not been managed on a relatively intensive management system such as coppicing, are most likely to have survived moderately intact in their macro-structure and composition. Nevertheless there are likely to have been significant changes in those species sensitive to climate and pollution, such as bryophytes, those which are intolerant of light, noise or disturbance or those that are dependent on a wider territory of rural habitats. Typically urban species such as escaped garden plants will have established within the habitat. Often drainage systems may have become blocked over time, while run-off from surrounding hard surfaced land may have increased, leading to waterlogging and tree death in some areas. The scale of this may or may not be acceptable and the evaluation of 'quality' obviously also depends on how long the woodland has had to adjust to the new circumstances.

Grassland habitats may also survive in relatively good condition but there will usually have been a change in the type of management from grazing or hay cutting to more regular mowing. The degree to which this will harm the flora found there is dependent on specific circumstances. Gang-mowers tend to over-ride much of the original variation in height of a sward that may be found when low-intensity grazing occurs. Patches of heath or meadow vegetation will have been converted to something which is much closer to an intensively grazed pasture.

Nevertheless many such mown grasslands are certainly richer in species than is often suspected. Many grassland species are able to survive as dormant seed or rhizomes, or even as very small stunted plants, but never growing or flowering, and with barely any leaves showing. Much greater damage may have been done by the ploughing of parks and ornamental gardens during periods of social adversity such as the Second World War campaign to 'Dig for Victory' or even earlier in the Napoleonic wars. The impact of the management change on other aspects of the biota, such as invertebrates, may be greater.

It is also possible to identify urban sites which were once open grassland but because of less intensive grass management are reverting to more extensive scrub cover (Hampstead Heath in London, for example, is far more heavily dominated by scrub and woodland than it would have been a century ago). Some grassland or heath sites may have turned almost completely to secondary woodland. Increasing shade beneath the canopy, linked with recreation pressure in urban commons, has in many cases led to the almost complete loss of the ground layer vegetation.

It is likely that relatively unchanged 'urban' habitats will in fact be found within the urban fringe where the period of isolation from traditional land use is shortest and where the magnitude of the urban influence is least. These sites sometimes merit conservation for many of the same reasons that rural examples do. They may have a complement of species that reflects centuries of gradual colonization and competitive balance. They may contain species which are so immobile, or unable to cross intervening landscape types, that they may never again appear in an area once lost. However, most often these relict areas may be of no great nature conservation significance in either national or regional terms, but have a very great importance in terms of their accessibility to people. Even if they are not the best of their type they provide an opportunity for many town dwellers to visit habitats and see wildlife that they would otherwise be unfamiliar with.

Not surprisingly, relict areas are popular with urban wildlife trusts, naturalist bodies and local authorities; they meet our preconceptions of nature very strongly. Some sites of great quality can survive close to city centres, such as the ancient woodlands on the Avon Gorge which runs through Bristol.

However, the evaluation of habitat 'quality' by these organizations may be too heavily coloured by the criteria that would be used in rural settings (Gilbert, 1989). The best examples of such relict landscapes in the urban fringe may not in fact be particularly accessible since they are often surrounded by various industrial developments and poorly served by public transport. They may also merit poor comparison with better preserved examples in the nearby rural surrounds that can be reached with relatively little extra effort.

> Their apparent high status is in fact an artefact produced by the contrived limits of the (urban) survey area. The idea of urban wildlife groups and local authority ecologists devoting scarce resources to promoting slivers of countryside at the edge of towns is alarming. They would do better to concentrate, as a priority, on the special . . . communities that occur in heavily built-up areas; no-one else will (Gilbert, 1989).

However, one of the most important characteristics of the encapsulated countryside lies in its obvious cultural link with the rural past. There are, therefore, social as well as biodiversity reasons for focusing on those sites which have successfully maintained their initial status.

The increasing interest in conservation oriented land management inevitably raises the question of whether traditional management patterns should be re-introduced, perhaps linked to a habitat restoration programme. Although desirable from many perspectives there are always some consequent problems, most notably a commitment to management costs that were previously being avoided, the need to restrict public access during the vulnerable re-establishment phase and the need to communicate effectively to the public the reasons why trees are being cut down. Many of the issues discussed with regard to the contract management of parks will also apply to these areas.

In the case of overlooked habitat remnants, access may not be well established; indeed in some cases the land may be well hidden by development and not noticed by the communities that live around it (with the usual exception of some of the local children). Identification of a site is often followed by investment in access, assuming that the landowner is agreeable, or that the land can be purchased.

There is a temptation in many of these areas to maintain them as urban nature reserves with very controlled access. This reflects the limited human impact that the sites would have received. Aside from initial capital-intensive investment, many secondary woodland sites have been without management inputs for so long that non-intervention is a viable option, at least in the short to medium term. It is not uncommon for paths to be kept away from particularly interesting areas, or for access to be time-limited. The tendency is also for the management of such sites to be undertaken by non-government organizations who do not have such over-riding commitments to public access as would be seen within a local authority.

2. Man-made ecological landscapes

It has been estimated from surveys that approximately 60–70% of urban vegetation is deliberately planted (Gilbert, 1989). Although this planted landscape is likely to include many different styles, including high formality and dominance in some areas by exotic species or highly bred cultivars, it is increasingly the case that significant areas of the land are being designed and managed in a form which echoes the assemblages and dynamics found in semi-natural vegetation. Although they are artefacts they have many parallels with other landscapes dealt with in this book because they:

- are composed of complex mixtures of species living in close conjunction;
- are often intended to encourage a wide range of biota, including birds and invertebrates, rather than just the plants;
- are managed in a way that allows a dynamic of interaction and competition to operate (sooner or later) between the individuals planted such that the objective is to maintain the community rather than the individual plants;
- may have a long-term viability that is comparable to longer established relict countryside, if managed correctly. (Of course the plant communities superimposed on the land may not actually be a good match for the site or the management programme. In such circumstances they are not sustainable and a change in composition will occur.)

Hitchmough (1994b) identifies certain potential values of naturalistic or ecological styles of landscape design:

- potentially low-cost, sustainable landscapes may be created;
- the landscapes may reflect an intrinsic sense of place;
- they provide a valuable contrast of experience to ornamental style designs;

- they do not require excessive maintenance inputs (specifically irrigation in the Australian context);
- they may be of value as conservation, education and recreation resources.

Of course the latter advantage encompasses many complex themes that will be explored in more detail in this book. Perhaps one aspect that should be added is that they provide scope for participation in, and use of, the landscape in ways that traditional landscapes often do not. The detail and resilience of natural plantings may make them particularly suitable for children. The opportunity for community and volunteer management may also be greater than with formal horticultural treatments, although this is not proven.

The style of landscaping that is represented here largely dates back to the 1970s in the UK, when an interest grew in the techniques and methods that were at that time more widely adopted in continental Europe, primarily in Holland and Germany, intended to emulate nature. The story of this developing movement and the campaign to introduce what were seen as innovative styles and techniques to the UK are discussed further in Chapter 3. The focus for much of this activity was the north-west of England with its spiritual home residing somewhere between the Liverpool organization Landlife, Warrington New Town and Manchester University School of Landscape (Ruff, 1979; Ruff and Tregay, 1982; Laurie, 1979).

It is also possible to trace the development of some components and elements of the ecological landscape style much earlier through UK landscape history. Some elements are characterized by the work of Capability Brown, the subsequent architects of the picturesque movement and of course the wild garden styles of William Robinson. In fact the style is characterized by a complex web of ideas and attitudes that deserves closer examination, and the differences and similarities between different approaches will be discussed in more detail later.

A strong theme that played a part in this developing style involved the search for landscape solutions that met complex goals such as community involvement and environmental education and also more cost-efficient establishment and management. Again, these concepts are so fundamental that they are dealt with separately.

So influential has the fashion for man-made nature become in some countries and in some circles in the UK and so zealous are some advocates that it becomes worrying that the role of more traditional landscape styles has been forgotten. Sometimes it is necessary to question whether the theme has as much acceptance with the general public as it does with professionals. Nevertheless it is clear that on some levels an interest in naturalistic landscapes has spread to the amateur and the subject of wildlife gardening is now a well-established theme in garden magazines and books with principles based on many of the same concepts as in professionally designed schemes. In fact in the popular gardening press there is often a better coverage of some of the detailed and small-scale options of habitat design that get overlooked on large-scale professional projects (e.g. Gibbons and Gibbons, 1990).

2 A range of native plant communities have been established surrounding English Nature's offices in Peterborough, England.

Naturalistic landscaping has also become mixed up, usually under the heading 'habitat creation', with the issue of mitigation or compensation for loss of land of conservation value for development. The principle of such mitigation is becoming well established in planning law and guidance such as the procedures for Environmental Assessment. Because there are some similarities (but also many important differences) between habitat creation for mitigation and for ecological landscaping these issues are addressed in more detail later (Chapter 6).

One of the key elements of the man-made ecological landscapes found in most developments is that, although modelled on comparatively stable communities, the majority of them are relatively immature. The creation and establishment of such communities sometimes requires the use of techniques that are not completely compatible with long-term development of the landscape and the challenge of management is to steer this transition. The most obvious example is the question of spacing and species composition in tree and shrub mixtures. The choices made by the landscape designer in order to give rapid impact may require careful thinning and selection to achieve an optimum balance in medium age and mature woodland stands. Unfortunately, contemporary systems for landscape design and creation place so much emphasis on the initial creation stage at the expense of long-term creative management that there are many examples where opportunities for positive development have been overlooked.

One of the major advantages of man-made sites rather than existing areas is that the full range of opportunities for exploiting human contact with nature can be maximized. They can, at least in theory, be sited where they can make a strong contribution to the survival and maintenance of diversity in other locations through landscape scale interactions (see Chapter 4). (However, in practice the establishment of new urban landscapes is frequently a response to opportunity and may reflect accidents of land use and ownership as much as does the survival of relict countryside. In attempting to integrate these various issues Johnston (1990) proposed the following design considerations for nature areas:

- retention of existing vegetation;
- utilizing available opportunities such as aspect and gradient;
- provision of variety and interest through landscape design, vegetation structure and colour;
- consideration of physical characteristics and underground services;
- providing for a variety of uses;
- separation of sanctuaries and sensitive wildlife areas from those with greatest activity;
- promoting links to other open spaces;
- providing for special needs in the community;
- anticipating changes in the vegetation as it develops;
- siting of facilities, such as notice boards, fencing and a nature centre;
- locating access points and paths on desired routes as far as possible;
- consideration of management and financial implications of the design.

3. Spontaneous urban flora and fauna

Urban regions are characterized by several unique environmental and biotic factors, all originally caused by human influence, which lead to the formation of specific plant and animal communities. In the vast majority of cases the species that are found are not those that would traditionally be regarded as having any conservation importance. None is rare, many are exotic (denigrated by terms such as 'alien', 'casuals' or 'garden escapes'), many are tolerant of disturbance and positively seem to flee from the pristine sites of great botanical interest. Historically, therefore, they have been ignored or even vilified by many ecologists and landscape professionals.

However, scientific and cultural value can reside in unique assemblages of common species. The urban communities of plants and animals are the result of the action of a complex dynamic of interacting forces and hence are as valid a subject for study as any semi-natural plant community. Urban flora and fauna are widespread, robust components of the urban landscape and need to be recognized and incorporated into policy.

A presumption that runs through much of traditional conservation management of land is that native species are intrinsically worth more than alien. So influential has this concept been in the determination of landscape policy that the rationale and justification of this stand is discussed more fully in Chapter 4. However, for many urban residents who lack the prejudices of professional ecologists the presence of colourful aliens and garden escapes may make them more attractive. Perhaps more importantly urban plant communities often reflect the complex cultural and industrial history of the region. They can therefore vary dramatically from site to site and between towns and this cultural dimension is something that should be valued.

The keystone work on recognizing and studying these urban communities must be that which was carried out in Berlin by Professor Sukopp and co-workers (Sukopp and Werner, 1987). There ecologists were forced by political constraints to study 'nature' in an urban setting rather than the countryside. In the same spirit a detailed review of the ecology of truly urban plant and animal communities in the UK context is given in Gilbert's *The Ecology of Urban Habitats* (1989). This is probably the most balanced and enjoyable treatise ever written on the subject in the UK and must be required reading for any urban ecologist or landscape manager. It would be pointless to duplicate much of the work here (although brief reviews of the various different plant communities are of course referred to as an essential precursor to discussing their management).

There are four main factors that contribute to the unusual assemblage of species that are found in urban areas – the climate and the edaphic conditions of the site (both of which are influenced by pollution), the disturbance patterns imposed and the huge inoculation pressure from the intentional or unintentional release of exotic organisms imported or grown for human use or pleasure. These are addressed in more detail in Chapter 2.

The unique problems of urban climate and soils are of course also an issue in any area of landscape development and management in towns and cities. However, it is arguable that the influence of urban conditions is more clearly seen in the locations where the full range of potential colonists are free to compete and form communities without any direct human influence.

A further major characteristic of the urban environment is its variety and heterogeneity. Despite the shortage of open land there can actually be a greater plant biodiversity in urban than rural areas (Gilbert, 1989). This can arise because of the very wide spectrum of habitats that may be present over very small distances and because the relatively limited flora of the UK is boosted by the presence of exotics. However, much of the value lies in early successional stages and the mosaic of different conditions. As a long-term sub-climax vegetation, individual spontaneous plant communities on urban sites are usually woody and characterized by a low diversity.

The importance of the urban estate

The importance of urban wildlife and even of urban landscapes is obviously relatively limited when considered according to the priorities of traditional

3 A stunning community of evening primroses and other flowering exotics and native plants bring colour and beauty to railway sidings.

scientific nature conservation. It has already been argued that with a few possible exceptions (to be discussed later) few of the species found in urban areas are under any significant threat or merit any redirection of conservation resources.

Certainly the pressures on the biota of the natural world are enormous and most acute where human influence is encroaching strongly into areas that were previously rich in species and moderately undisturbed such as the surviving forests of Asia, Australasia, southern and even northern America. By putting time and energy and funding into conserving peculiar urban fragments and man-made simulations we could even be accused of indirectly hastening the decline of species that may otherwise have been saved.

However, urban conservation does have a clear justification. It is becoming increasingly apparent that any global fight to preserve biodiversity **on the present terms** is already lost. The areas of protected natural lands, hard fought for as they may be, are just too small and too vulnerable to a constant attrition of exploitation and abuse that they will do no more than slow the rate of decline of species.

> Protected areas are a seductively simple way to save nature from humanity. But sanctuaries admit a failure to save wildlife and natural habitat where they overlap with human interest, and that means 95 percent or more of the earth's surface. Conservation by segregation is the Noah's Ark solution, a belief that wildlife should be consigned to tiny land parcels for its own good and because it has no place in our world. The flaw in this view is obvious: those land parcels are not big enough to avert catastrophic species extinction by insularization or safe enough to protect resources from the poor and the greedy. Simply put, if we can't save nature outside protected areas, not much will survive inside; if we can, protected areas will cease to be arks (Western *et al.,* 1989).

In the light of this hard reality it has become increasingly obvious that solutions lie only in a fundamental change of attitudes, aspirations and priorities in human society. The entire thrust of global conservation strategy has been forced to undergo a rethink, and to pursue objectives of sustainable development whereby human goals are recognized, integrated and accommodated into a new paradigm of living that provides for the survival of nature just as strongly as for economic gain and social equitability (IUCN/UNEP/WWF, 1991)).

The role that the urban ecology movement and urban wildlife can play in this revolution is obvious. It has been highlighted several times in recent seminal works (Nicholson, 1987; Nicholson-Lord 1987; Gilbert 1989). An urban wildlife park in the heart of the inner city is the place where the purest distillation of traditional human aspirations and goals can be confronted by the natural world, where positive contact between the two can be re-established and where the germs of a new sensibility of coexistence can be fostered.

Rural dwellers may feel that they have a greater understanding of countryside and the natural world than those in town, indeed it has become almost a truism of response for those who resent some proposed change in their lives (cf. attitudes towards possible bans on fox-hunting). Yet in a democracy, that fight also has probably been lost – urban public opinion ultimately influences rural policy and also international conservation policy through sheer weight of numbers. Attitudinal and policy change must begin in the city, and the challenge to conservationists is to recognize this and to begin a process of connection between the living world that people do contact, the trees in their own backyard for example, and the broader needs of the global environment. The fight for the future of the countryside, not only in Britain but in the world, is taking place in the towns.

2 The urban environment and urban species

It is well understood that urban areas differ from rural in certain fundamental characteristics. Normally attention is drawn most strongly to the peculiar characteristics of urban climate and, increasingly, to urban soil. 'Pollution' is usually regarded as a climatic factor, although there are serious problems of chemical contamination in urban soils. The key points of these various topics are reviewed below, not with the intention of again recapping information that already exists in many texts, but to draw attention to the particular design and management challenges and opportunities presented.

Urban environments are also dominated strongly by a myriad other forms of human influence which have a determining factor in controlling plant and animal distribution and ecology in towns (Gilbert, 1989). The impact on ecological processes, propagation, establishment, survival, competition and so on are all complex. Urban areas also have unique characteristics when considering the feasible management and maintenance possibilities.

It is often tempting to identify the particular environmental characteristics of urban areas differences as 'problems', and in many ways they are. For conventional procedures of plant establishment and landscape creation, soil factors in particular can cause major challenges, but it is important to remember that these stresses and hostilities are also the factors which produce the distinctiveness of urban habitats and dictate the nature (and in many cases the richness) of the plant and animal communities we see.

The urban climate

Urban climates differ from rural partly because of the heat energy produced by human activity. Sukopp and Werner (1987) suggest that this can be equivalent to 25–50% of irradiated solar energy. In addition the reflection and thermal properties of the large areas of tarmac, concrete and stone and the overall low rates of evapotranspiration which arise from limited vegetation cover and from the tendency for water to pass rapidly into sewers rather than being recycled contribute to a warmer urban climate.

Significant urban conurbations in temperate countries usually have annual

Table 2.1 *Average changes of climate parameters in built-up areas*

Climate parameters	Characteristics	In comparison to surrounds
Air pollution	Condensation	10 times more
	Gaseous pollution	5–25 times more
Solar radiation	Global solar radiation	15–20% less
	Ultraviolet radiation	
	winter	30% less
	summer	5% less
	Duration of sunshine	5–15% less
Air temperature	Annual mean average	0.5–1.5°C higher
	On clear days	2–6°C higher
Wind speed	Annual mean average	10–20% less
	Calm winds	5–20% more
Relative humidity	Winter	2% less
	Summer	8–10% less
Clouds	Overcast	5–10% more
	Fog (winter)	100% more
	Fog (summer)	30% more
Precipitation	Total rainfall	5–10% more
	Less than 5mm rainfall	10% more
	Daily snowfall	5% less

Source: Horbert (1978).

mean air temperatures some 0.5–1.5 °C above that of the surrounding countryside. The temperature is warmer than the surroundings on most days and nights and can be much higher on still, clear, nights when radiation losses from the land are minimized by high building density (see Table 2.1). The differences between town and rural areas are least in windy and cloudy weather. The urban 'heat island' effect is therefore certainly stronger in stable continental climates than in maritime areas such as the UK with a complex and windy weather system.

Although it is clear that means and averages do differ, it is characteristic of meteorological records that patterns of minima and maxima, and variations about the mean, are less clear and much harder to interpret even when data are presented. Equally low minimum temperatures may be attained in urban areas and the rural surrounds, but with a reduced frequency. On the other hand it is likely that higher maximum temperatures are experienced in some urban spots than are typical in the countryside (Bernatzky, 1979).

For the ecology of some plant species it is likely that these extremes are more significant than the means, but the effects are unpredictable as the physiological processes that control aspects such as plant hardiness are extremely complex. As a general rule we can predict that many plants will experience earlier growth, a longer growing season, earlier flowering and so on. Some species may survive that are not hardy in rural areas; some may set viable seed that would not ripen in rural areas. However other species, with absolute intolerances of certain temperature minima, may do no better in towns unless they are in very sheltered micro-climates, which can also occur in rural settings.

It is equally possible that summer temperatures may be too high for some species but the effects are likely to be more complex as they will interact with water availability in the substrate and with the relative phenology of competing plants within the community. Others may be limited by an absence of adequate winter chilling.

Wind speeds are on the whole lower in the town, but there is a much greater likelihood of eddying and violent wind damage, and there may be effects of wind concentration into the inner city zones as a result of rising hot air, which can concentrate dusts and other air pollutants and prevent them from escaping.

Subtle modifications of regional climate can therefore occur which can dictate which species are likely to dominate natural systems (Gilbert, 1989). In particular the climatic differences may allow naturalization of species that could not compete in the rural surroundings. The significance of these species is discussed later.

Air pollution

The historical effects of air pollution on vegetation are quite well understood. The dusty smogs of London and similar cities had their most severe effect on evergreen trees, and on those with very finely divided leaves and a large leaf surface area. The group most severely effected were conifers which were completely excluded from some inner city areas and replaced by known pollution tolerant species such as London Plane. There was also difficulty in growing species with high light demands. In extreme conditions all trees were hard to establish (see Figure 2.1).

Following the introduction of clean air legislation air pollutants in cities today are often less visibly damaging but can be just as harmful. Conifer exclusion is likely still to be occurring in some areas as a consequence of high SO_2 levels. However, it is more common today for gas-emitting industries to exploit high-level chimneys to lead to distant dispersal of pollution, so that the areas of consequential damage may be far from the area that generates the problem.

The impacts on lower plants, lichens and bryophytes which have a comparatively large surface area and absorb materials freely from the air, is well understood as is the suppression of some fungi such as black spot on roses. The species range of bryophytes and lichens may therefore be limited in urban sites, but these groups are rarely completely eradicated and many of the sensitive species are now returning where air quality has improved.

Also well documented is melanism in invertebrates through the selection of sooty coloured mutants, although again with declining pollution the endemic forms are beginning to give place to the normal. Other more subtle impacts on ecosystem ecology, and particularly on fungi which have a poorly understood distribution, are likely to be unrecognized. It is widely recognized that human health can suffer dramatically from air pollutants and

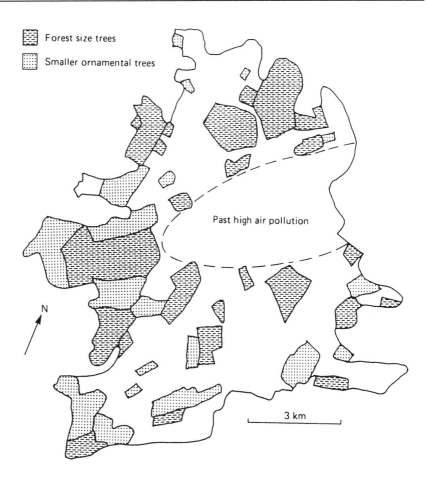

Figure 2.1 The distribution of trees in Sheffield shows an area to the middle and east of the city where high levels of air pollution prevented successful establishment (Gilbert, 1986).

it is more than likely that the same is true for some urban mammals but the effects are hard to quantify. Certainly animal pathogen dynamics can be very dramatic in urban areas, and we probably have a very limited understanding of the relationship between the different factors.

A form of urban pollution that is becoming increasingly recognized is that of light escape. The direct problems for people that can arise from excessive or poorly focused lighting include a loss of the ability to see stars, and a general confusion of landscape identity and character. However for many other species, and especially invertebrates, light can cause disorientation, interfere with mating (glow worms are becoming scarce in the UK for this reason) or attract animals into areas where predation rates can be high.

Interaction between plants, climate and pollution

Vegetation can provide many improvements to the urban climate, but the effects are strongly dependent on the nature and patterning of that vegetation. It is rare that opportunities exist, or are exploited, that maximize the full potential. It is of course equally possible, although much less widely discussed, that vegetation can have locally adverse effects, perhaps by preventing the dispersal of polluted air, by channelling winds or, probably most commonly in cool and cloudy climates such as the UK, by shading areas excessively.

To be most effective it is desirable for the shade cast by the tree to be matched to need, both in terms of the degree of light interception and also the timing, or phenology, of leafing. Late leafing species such as *Fraxinus excelsior* may be preferable to evergreens in countries where spring sunshine is greatly missed.

Shelter from winds can be very important in ensuring the use of grounds and open areas. Trees can also be used to disrupt the fixed patterns of air flow in cities. The transpiration and shading effect can also lower high temperatures and raise humidity. Winds are worst in the winter, so there is value in an evergreen component of the tree flora, although more people may be outside in the summer.

Partly permeable trees are of course widely recognized as preferable to solid barriers for wind control, as eddying and gusting is less likely and the beneficial effects are more widespread. However, successful windbreaks normally need to be carefully planned. It can be a difficult challenge to achieve an adequate layout of trees on patchy and fragmented land to cope with the varied and often severe gusting that results from the presence of the buildings. Ambitious plans are sometimes forwarded, such as using concentric rings of trees to improve town climate on a large scale, but the opportunities for this sort of rational urban design are rare (Bernatzky, 1978).

Impacts on air quality may be achieved at a much more local level. There is often 200 times as much dust in towns as in the purest countryside air and 30 times as much as in typical countryside containing some industrial activity (Bernatzky, 1978). Despite recent improvements in terms of obvious smokes and soots smaller, less visible pollutants are still widespread and there are concerns about possible health effects.

Research in Germany has shown that trees, because of their huge surface area, can reduce over 50% of the dusts in the air. A large tree can be holding 100 kg of dust, which is washed to the soil in rain. The optimum patterning is similar to that of windspeed reduction, with lots of trees moderately spaced so that the air filters through rather than being diverted (see Figure 2.2).

Dust is primarily a dry weather problem. Deciduous species are therefore perfectly suitable and may in fact be preferable as the annual leaf-fall may play a key role in keeping the plants healthy. In cases of severe dust pollution only particularly tolerant species are likely to survive. The effectiveness of dust control is enhanced where the vegetation allows air to penetrate but has a high enough leaf density to ensure adequate filtration. Again something approaching 50% porosity is probably ideal. Although species with small leaves will absorb pollutants most effectively, they are as a consequence often more prone to damage and conifers in particular may be killed sooner than deciduous species in areas of high dust pollution.

The effects of trees on gaseous rather than particulate pollutants and on air ionization are less well understood. The most obvious gaseous 'pollutant' that

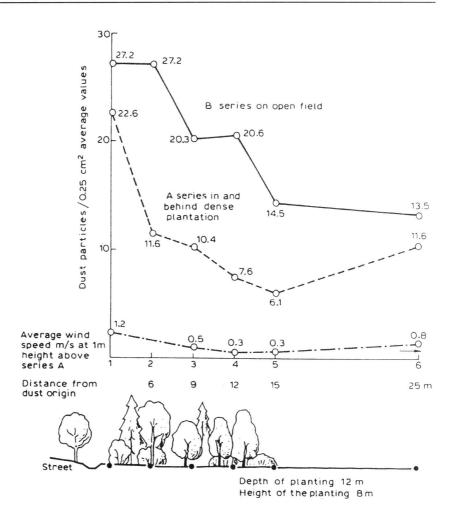

Figure 2.2 Dust sedimentation on a dense planting and on an open field (Hennebo, 1955 in Bernatzky 1978).

may be of concern is rising carbon dioxide contributing to global warming.

Of course the carbon fixation properties of vegetation are only effectively functioning while the plants are growing and increasing biomass. It has been calculated that it needs approximately 140 mature trees to compensate for the carbon emissions of one driver (Bradshaw, Hunt and Walmsley, 1995). Over-mature trees may be respiring nearly as much as they fix, and decaying or dead vegetation will probably be releasing CO_2 as micro-organisms digest the stored carbon. Long-established woodlands containing mixed age trees are therefore probably carbon-neutral with as much being released as is being fixed. However, such woods are still a store of much carbon which will be released if they are destroyed.

A mature beech tree produces as much O_2 as is needed by ten people a year, but a young transplant may produce 3000 times less. The need to preserve a mature population of trees is obvious. In practice something like 30–40 m^2 of typical greenspace is needed to supply O_2 for each person and it is unlikely that urban vegetation will do much to compensate for the O_2/CO_2 imbalance (Bernatzky, 1978). On the other hand urban vegetation may play a key role in focusing greater understanding of environmental issues and of the role of global vegetation in maintaining a healthy planet. The key importance of urban trees is therefore their role as a focal point for awareness and environmental education.

Whether trees can absorb meaningful quantities of other toxic gases is hard to establish. Noise pollution control by vegetation is often less effective than people wish to believe, with plants performing much less efficiently than solid barriers (Coppin and Richards, 1990). Plants can have a positive effect in the following areas:

- they play a role in screening some noise frequencies effectively;
- they can screen the source of noise, which is sometimes said to be beneficial;
- they can screen physical noise control barriers, such as walls, fences or earthmounds;
- they can mask noise by making more pleasant sounds (aspen leaves rusting in the wind).

Noise is rarely a seasonal problem so evergreen species are often desirable.

The urban soil

Patterns seen in long established semi-natural plant communities may reflect the geology closely. Slight competitive advantages gradually manifest over time and dictate the pattern of plant communities. New habitats on urban soils are often raw and skeletal. There is a much greater random factor controlling what grows where. The correlation with plant type and soil may be less rigorous, but it will still exist given that many urban soils are also extreme and may not be physiologically suitable for some plants.

The soils that we encounter in urban areas have highly variable and sometimes very hostile characteristics (Ash, 1991; Craul, 1992). The substrate material in urban areas can include almost any soil type or even waste or spoil, encompassing almost any extreme of physical or chemical qualities. Of course most sites are very benign even if they are made of materials such as waste, but unusual conditions can be found and often lead to the most interesting areas. The pH may range from 2 to 12; the nutrient content may range from excess to almost non-existent; there may be little or no buffering capacity; there may be almost no organic matter; many sites may carry a pollutant load (Dutton and Bradshaw, 1982). Every textural class and soil classification can be encountered, including some which have never been properly described. The profile may be extremely complicated, with many mismatched soil types overlapping, and there may be many buried obstacles. Large areas of the soil may be covered with variably permeable hard surfaces. Often there is very great variability on

Table 2.2 *The problems to be expected in different types of urban planting site*

	Physical					Nutrient			Contaminants				Total
	Stability	Structure	Compaction	Drainage	Drought	Nitrogen	Other macro	Micro	Metals	Organic	pH	Other	
Housing clearance	2	0	1	1	0	2	0	0	0	0	0	0	6
Factory clearance	0-2	0	2	2	0-1	2	0-2	0	0-2	0-2	0	0-2	6-17
Transport disuse	0-2	0-2	1	0-1	0-2	2	0-2	0	0	0	0	0	3-12
Quarry/borrow pit	0-2	0-2	2	0-2	0-2	2	0-2	0	0	0	0	0	4-14
Mine waste	0-2	2	1	2	2	2	0-2	0	0-2	2	0-2	0-2	11-21
Industrial waste	0-2	2	0-2	0	0	0-2	0-2	0	0-2	0-2	0-2	0-2	2-18
Gas works	0	0	2	2	0	0-2	0	0	0-2	2	0	0	6-10
Refuse disposal	1	0-2	1-2	0-2	0	0-1	0	0	0-2	0	0	2	4-12
Neglected land	0	0	0	0-1	0-1	0	0	0	0-2	0-2	0	0-2	0-8
Old parkland	0	0	0	0-2	0	0-1	0-1	0	0	0	2	0	2-6
Farm land	0	0	0-1	0	0	0	0-1	0	0	0	0	0	0-2
Roadsides	0-2	0	0-2	2	0-2	0-2	0-1	0	0	0	0	0-2	2-13
Street sides	0-2	0	2	2	0-2	2	0-1	0	0	0	0	2	8-13

Notes

0 = rarely a problem, 1 = moderate, 2 = severe problem

For totals <6 few problems to be expected; >12 problems likely.

The difference between figures indicates potential variation.

Source: Bradshaw *et al.* (1995).

just one site. The situation is then often complicated further by the deep soil compaction and denaturing that occurs during development. The conjunction of these problems can lead to very difficult conditions which limit plant options (see Table 2.2).

Table 2.3 *Soil conspectus for urban soils*

---

1. Man-made humus soil. A thick (>40 cm) man-made A horizon resulting from bulky amendments of manure, mineral matter or domestic rubbish. Allotments, old gardens, small holdings, rubbish dumps.

2. Topsoiled sites. A/C or A/BC soils created by spreading topsoil of variable quality over raw, disturbed mineral soil. May be compacted at one or more levels. The evolution of these rankers to brown soils is helped by cultivation. Recently landscaped sites.

3. Raw-lithomorphic soils. Initially these consist of little altered raw mineral materials often of man-made origin, at least 30 cm deep, and show no horizon development attributable to pedogenic processes. With time they evolve into lithomorphic soils as a distinct humose upper layer develops. Two subdivisions can be made in each group.

   (i) Soils with only one layer that is not humified topsoil.
   (ii) Soils with at least two layers including a humified topsoil.

   (a) Brick rubble. Man made raw soil evolving into pararendzina. Brick rubble often mixed with a little old soil and subsoil. Building demolition areas.

   (b) Furnace ash, slag, cinder. Man-made raw soil evolving into humic ranker. A coarsely textured non-calcareous soil associated with railway land, particularly old sidings, heavy industry etc.

   (c) Chemical wastes. Man-made soil evolving into a range of lithomorphic soils. The raw material may have an extreme pH or contain highly toxic substances. Of limited occurrence, associated with the chemical industries and electricity generation (pulverized fuel ash).

   (d) Disturbed subsoil. Man-made raw soils evolving into profiles that have affinities with ranker-like alluvial soils in which the humose layer passes down into an unconsolidated C horizon which may show stratification. These soils form from a stratum of artificially arranged or transported material >40 cm thick consisting predominantly of mingled subsoil horizons (B, B/C or C). Found in some recently landscaped sites, some landfill sites.

   (e) *In situ* subsoil. Raw skeletal soil evolving into a variety of lithomorphic soils. Unconsolidated or weakly consolidated mineral horizons, sometimes partly stratified, which have weathered *in situ*. Found on steep banks associated with transport corridors or sites benched for major buildings. Also widespread in non-urban areas.

   (f) Hard surfaces. Tarmacadamed, paved and concrete surfaces. Roads, pavements, floors of demolished factories, angle between pavement and wall etc.

Source: from Gilbert (1989).

4 Urban land is likely to contain a complex mixture of polluted sites and areas where the substrate has no resemblance to a rural soil profile.

It is notable that on most soil maps urban settlements are left blank and no attempts are made to make predictions about the soils that will be encountered. More recently attempts have been made to rectify this, such as the urban soil conspectus proposed by Gilbert (1989) (see Table 2.3). However, the results of such work are inevitably limited by our lack of detailed knowledge of these soils and in particular of how they are likely to age and mature. We don't really know enough about the long term development of a biologically active soil over PFA for example.

For new sites we have the technology to undertake manipulation of the soil environment with a great deal of sophistication. In practice, however, the status of the site soil often remains completely unaddressed by landscape professionals. In new plantings there are always a few hopeful phrases in the specification along the lines of 'the contractor shall ensure good drainage at all times', but the designer often shies away from a detailed investigation or assessment of the soil. Not only does this approach lead ultimately to the failure of many designs, but it also represents a wasted opportunity – in many ways the soil can be the key to the creation of a landscape of great originality, vitality and interest.

Plant growth is, for good or ill, intimately linked to the soil. Whether we ignore it or not, the site drainage, fertility, pH and other characteristics will manifest in the performance and appearance of the vegetation it supports. The relation with soil type can be obscured in many traditional landscape plantings, which use plants of a broad physiological niche. Management is geared up to establishing plants in a way that avoids excessive competition and we find that nearly all species can be grown in nearly all places. However, in the case of ecological plantings we may need to be much more conscious of the way that soil type will influence the end results.

Compaction

Soil compaction affects plant growth in many ways. It can lead to poor water use, restricted nutrient uptake, lack of oxygen, accumulation of carbon dioxide, or root impedance (Craul, 1992).

Compaction is not necessarily damaging. In certain soils a small amount of compaction may actually increase plant growth by producing a better balance between air space and water retention. However, the scale and severity of the damage caused by heavy machinery on development sites means that the effects are nearly always detrimental. Direct damage may take the form of plant losses through drought or waterlogging, poor plant or seed establishment or a general reduction in plant vigour. There are also many possible forms of indirect damage including increased aggressiveness of certain diseases, or increased disease susceptibility where plants are growing poorly, increased likelihood of unintentional herbicide damage because of low vigour and surface rooting, and possibly increased suscepti-

5 Urban soil may be characterized by extreme compaction and loss of structure.

bility to climate extremes. Managerial problems can include greater difficulties in working the soil, greater time required for irrigation and greater inputs of water and nutrients required.

Compaction in agricultural systems, which is where most research has occurred, is usually the result of machinery running over *in-situ* soils causing surface compression and pan formation. Obviously this can happen on urban sites as well, however the practices of topsoil removal and respreading may mean that the pan layer can be much deeper than usually expected. As well as deep pans caused by construction traffic, there may often be multiple pans resulting from deliberate compaction during soil movement. The standard mound building technique can lead to a situation where a pan is encountered at 150 mm intervals (Coppin and Richards, 1990).

Soil pans inhibit rooting, but can also have an influence on soil behaviour outside of the compacted zone. Poor drainage can lead to water build-up in wet conditions and shallow rooting and drought in dry conditions.

Topsoil, which may have initially been in good condition, can undergo several degradative processes when stored (Craul, 1992). Organic matter degeneration under anaerobic conditions in the middle of the heap leads to nitrogen loss and the possible development of toxins, although these are usually short lived once the soil is respread. There is also a decrease in the structural strength of the soil clods making the material more prone to damage either through the pressure of its own weight or during re-spreading. Biological changes can also be profound with dramatic and long lasting changes to the micro-organisms found in the soil and also the build-up of massive populations of weed propagules in the soil.

Finally large areas of the site may be covered with variably permeable hard surfaces which can restrict aeration although the precise consequences can be hard to predict (Bernatzky, 1978).

The above soil effects are a major problem for situations where attempts are being made to establish plants, for example new woodland planting schemes. Amelioration options may need to be considered to achieve reasonable rates of plant establishment.

The problems associated with soil compaction are complex although not all of these need to be long term and some can be avoided completely. Lack of aeration and poor drainage are perhaps the most serious. Other effects can be eased by various means, for example if nutrient deficiency or unavailability is reducing plant growth then fertilizers can be applied; if there is a lack of moisture then irrigation may help.

Where a simple deep pan exists as a result of soil traffic then deep subsoiling or chisel ploughing of the soil may be all that is required. An alternative approach where such treatments are logistically difficult is to use manual cultivation or to sink sumps or 'vertical drains'.

If conditions are not too poor, improvements to soil structure will eventually occur over time due to the action of plants, animals and the weather. A grass ley can lead to a rapid improvement in soil structure, although it can still be years before the soil improves to anything like an undisturbed soil. The formation of a good soil structure is also encouraged by worms and by soil drying and cracking (which in turn is encouraged by roots). Frost cracking is also helpful although it does not happen on all soils as it needs the correct moisture conditions together with a slow freezing process. Frost only affects the surface of a soil and does not help with deep drainage problems.

Unfortunately plant root growth or worm colonization is unlikely to be effective if compaction has occurred at depth. Subsoil damage may be particularly difficult to resolve. These natural remedial factors are also unlikely to help where the soil is poorly drained or has such a high bulk density that nothing can easily penetrate.

Subsurface mole or tile drainage systems and the like will be inadequate and water will continue to sit on the surface. There may simply be too few large soil pores to allow water to move at an adequate speed through the substrate. Any other form of cultivation that does not create a system of deep drainage will simply open up the soil allowing more water to infiltrate and aggravating waterlogging.

The solution lies in the use of deep cultivation equipment that causes pores to open, such as rippers or subsoilers or high-pressure air injection devices. However, even these treatments will not work when soil moisture conditions are wrong. Very wet, plastic soils can not easily be fractured. There may need to be some initial remedial work to encourage soil drying to occur. This is best done by reducing water infiltration by creating a topography that encourages the water to move off site or to open drains.

The sort of large pores, separated by amorphous, impenetrable clods, that such treatments create will still be sub-optimal compared to undisturbed soil systems. Large areas of the potential soil resource will remain unavailable, while the large soil air spaces created will be more like normal atmospheric air than ordinary pores. They will be relatively dry and may harbour more pests and disease. However, they will allow the soil to dry to the point where other pedogenic processes can start which will eventually improve the tilth. Oxygen will move more easily through fracture planes and the roots will follow these networks. In the long term, therefore, the roots will help to stabilize these cracks and keep them open.

Cultivation may help in such situations. Cultivation replaces the natural balance of soil crumbs and pores with an artificial structure. Although such a structure may not be long lived, it may improve conditions to the point where natural soil forming processes can begin to function.

Soil contamination

As well as physical problems urban soils may be characterized by chemical contamination (see Figure 2.3).

Urban soil contamination may take many different forms including:

1. heavy metal ions, organic contaminants or other materials which can be directly toxic (these are sub-classified into phytotoxins, materials which

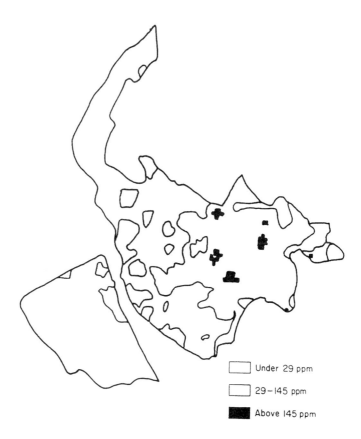

Figure 2.3 Available copper in Merseyside soils (Handley, 1984).

☐ Under 29 ppm

☐ 29–145 ppm

■ Above 145 ppm

are harmful to plants at concentrations far below that which pose any risk to humans or other animals, and zootoxins where the reverse is true);
2. salts, such as those arising from road-de-icing procedures, which primarily have a harmful impact through their effect on the osmotic potential of the soil;
3. materials which modify pH to extremes or which lead to induced nutrient deficiencies;
4. materials which influence the physical status of the soil, e.g. by leading to deflocculation or acting as an oxygenation barrier.

These materials present a stress on the plants and reduce growth and vigour. At low levels it may be that they can act as factors which encourage species diversity according to the principles of Grime (1979), although there are few clear examples (this would certainly be true for materials which raise pH). In acute concentrations it is more likely that the effect will be to depress diversity, since there are likely to be few species adapted to tolerate the conditions present.

However, the distribution of the contaminants in soils is often highly heterogeneous, with extremely localized deposition. Over a few metres it is possible to pass from soil which has no contamination through to soil which is toxic to all but a few specialists and back again. This presents problems for site survey, as it is almost impossible (or highly expensive) to undertake soil analysis with enough rigour to be sure that all possible contaminants are identified. There are obvious risks for the success of standard landscape schemes in such circumstances, as local patches of vegetation failure will not be acceptable.

Conversely for naturalistic landscapes such variation may be acceptable and may even have advantages. Even though species richness in localized patches will probably be low, the contaminated areas may favour tolerant species which add to the overall site habitat diversity. Even areas which have only a sparse vegetation cover may be favoured by some fauna as basking or burrowing spots.

Where zootoxin contamination is found, there may be local environmental health issues which force a site clean up (depending on the concentrations). The same urgency is less likely to be encountered with phytotoxins.

De-icing salt contamination is a common phenomenon alongside roadside verges, and this often has the obvious effect of leading to a change in vegetation cover, with sometimes halophytic coastal plants dominating in sites miles from the sea (Gilbert, 1989).

Nutrition and pH

Urban soils that are derived from wastes and rubbles are likely to be lacking in some critical plant nutrients. In particular any substrate that has not previously supported plant growth, a primary substrate, will be devoid of organic matter. This in turn means that the soil will almost inevitably be deficient in nitrogen. This is the nutrient required by plants in the largest amounts and yet it has no normal mineral source and is only stored in organic forms.

Nitrogen deficiency may also be seen in materials that were once reasonable topsoils, secondary substrates, but which have had their organic matter load diluted by mixing with subsoils or through processes of soil breakdown during long-term storage. The evidence of such deficiencies is often apparent in sparse, yellow, poorly established grass, with strong green patches found wherever there have been nutrient inputs, e.g. from dogs.

Of the total nutrient stores typically only a small percentage are available to plants at any one time. Conversely small amounts of nutrient, if present in a plant available form, can support growth and mask any longer-term deficiencies. Soil disturbance, which is typical in urban soils, is one of the means by which the rate of nitrogen release, or mineralization, is temporarily raised and it is not uncommon to see vegetation responding to nutrient flushes on soils which are generally infertile.

Problems of nitrogen deficiency can be resolved by fertilizer addition, but this is at best a short-term solution since the amounts that can be added without environmental damage represent a small fraction of the total store that an ecosystem would require. Even if all added nutrients were taken up by plants and incorporated into soil organic matter, it would typically take

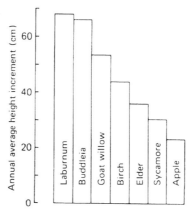

Figure 2.4 The growth rate of a selection of trees on urban wastes shows the particular capabilities of nitrogen fixing species, and also others which seem to have other mechanisms for low N tolerance (Gilbert, 1989).

many decades of feeding before a highly deficient system could become self-supporting.

A more complete solution can be achieved by the addition of organic matter at rates comparable to ordinary soils. However, this material should not be too carbon rich or it may actually depress nitrogen availability in the short term.

Soil nitrogen levels can also be raised by growing nitrogen-fixing species of plants. Such nitrogen fixers are at a competitive advantage in nitrogen poor soils and frequently outperform other species (see Figure 2.4). A second group of plants seems to have a tolerance of low nitrogen even though they have no fixation abilities, such as pines and scrub willows. The mechanisms of nutrient harvest and use have been less well studied in these species but they seem to have very efficient nitrogen scavenging properties and may develop enormous root:shoot ratios (Kendle and Bradshaw, 1992).

Nitrogen fixers sometimes form a high proportion of the colonists on deficient soils. For example, large colonies of clover are frequently found invading nitrogen starved grasslands on rubble sites (Dutton and Bradshaw, 1982). However, their arrival may be limited by:

- An absence of other required nutrients. (Legumes often have a higher than average demand for calcium and phosphorus).
- Poor seed dispersal. (The plant forms a symbiotic relationship with bacteria which actually do the work of nitrogen fixing. Until the plant is large enough to make such a link and to provide food to the bacteria it needs to live on stored resources. Nitrogen fixing plants therefore often have large seeds that limits dispersal.)
- An absence of the necessary symbiots. (Very little is known about the patterns and colonization rates of micro-organisms into urban soils. However, many practitioners recommend the inoculation of efficient strains of bacteria when sowing legumes which suggests that the natural distribution of such forms is sometimes limited. Certainly on skeletal mineral urban soils with very low organic matter content the initial biological activity of the soil may be low.)

6 Nitrogen deficiency in urban soils is often revealed by darker patches in grass associated with clover or dog mess.

Counteracting the trend for nitrogen deficiency is the high rate of deposition of nitrogen in the form of air pollutants, particularly arising from NOx gases emitted in exhausts. The annual inputs of such nitrogen in some heavily polluted areas can come close to meeting the entire available nitrogen demand of some species. Such nitrogen contamination may indeed be a problem where the aim is to keep soil fertility conditions low.

Absolute deficiencies of nutrients other than nitrogen are less common, particularly given the widespread distribution of dusts and other ion-rich pollutants. Indeed many of the trace nutrient elements are encountered in near-toxic concentrations on urban sites. However, unusual substrates arising from industrial processes may again show exceptional problems.

Plant uptake of phosphorus, which is a very immobile nutrient, can be limited by poor root growth in conditions where the total soil levels are not actually low. Phosphorus deficiency therefore may be seen in young transplants more frequently than in mature specimens. The efficiency of root uptake of phosphorus in some species is greatly increased by the presence of mycorrhizal fungi. Again the appropriate symbionts may be missing from some skeletal urban soils. (It has sometimes been found in tree-planting experiments on degraded land that tree performance can be variable and only those trees with mycorrhizae are successful whereas those without are not. This is usually attributed to the effect of the mycorrhizae in boosting nutrient supply and is given in evidence of patchy mycorrhizal distribution. However, this may not always be an accurate indicator: it has to be remembered that again the relationship is symbiotic, and there may be instances where trees which are already under-performing, for example because of poor handling or locally limited water supply, may be unable to form an appropriate association with a fungus even if it is present.)

Nutrition and pH issues are closely related. Except at pH extremes where some direct effects of acidity or alkalinity may be seen, the soil pH is primarily of significance to plants because it modifies the availability of plant nutrients. Plants which are 'lime haters' for example are adapted to the high availability of some ions, and in particular tolerant of the excess of aluminium, found in soils of low pH. Under high pH conditions they may suffer from nutrient shortage.

Although industrial wastes can be encountered with extreme characteristics, it is most common in urban areas that the soils have a higher than average pH. This is largely because of the incorporation of mortars and other calcium rich materials in rubbles and wastes. However, long-established grasslands on base-poor soil can become extremely acid as a result of a combination of leaching, removal of vegetation in clippings and mowings and a failure to replace the bases by liming. The effect can be aggravated also by acid rainfall deposition.

Of course the natural world contains a wide diversity of species with many adaptations and growth strategies. It is rare that even a combination of pH, nutrient and soil physical problems will completely prevent plant growth. Problems arise more often because the type of vegetation that is desired, or the vegetation rates desired, cannot be achieved. It is impossible therefore to separate definitions of good and bad soils from value judgements about the form of landscape that is desired.

What are good soils therefore?

It is already clear that soil 'problems' which may be disastrous for traditional plant establishment may be less problematical or even actually be of advantage when we are trying to produce ecological designs or are involved in habitat creation. The theoretical background for understanding how poor soils can give desirable results can be found in the work of the NERC Unit of Comparative Plant Ecology (Grime 1979; Grime Hodgson and Hunt 1988) (see Box 2.1).

Our basic concept and definition of a 'good' soil has its roots in agriculture and horticulture. These are systems where the goals for vegetation growth are relatively easy to define. Crop producers need maximum productivity and maximum ease of workability from the substrate. The plant communities they work with are also extremely simple and attempts are made to control all unwanted invading species.

This horticultural soil ethic, the search for the 'deep, well drained but moisture-retentive loam' that pervades garden books, has also pervaded professional landscape work even though sometimes the goals are more complex and harder to define. The temptation is always to equate the most fertile soil with the best soil. Nature, of course, does not agree – vegetation can adapt to a very wide range of soil types and often some of the most diverse and distinctive communities are found on the most extreme soils.

As well as horticultural criteria we therefore need to recognize ecological soil criteria that must be applied whenever we wish to grow complex

Box 2.1 Grime's theoretical basis of comparative plant ecology

Grime considers the relationships of species within a plant community, and classifies species on a functional basis as competitors, stress tolerators and ruderals. The classification allows a prediction of the relative success of established specimens of each species in any particular environment.

Table 2.4 *Some attributes characterizing primary plant strategies*

Competitors – high potential relative growth rate
- tall stature
- densely branching or tussock forming allowing extensive and intensive exploitation of the environment
- dense litter formation reflecting high productivity.

Stress tolerators – low potential relative growth rate
- morphological reduction
- evergreen with long-lived root and storage systems in roots and shoots
- sequestration and slow turnover of carbon, mineral nutrients and water, often uncoupled from vegetative growth – infrequent flowering
- low palatability to unspecialized herbivores.

Ruderals – high potential relative growth rate
- high commitment to seed production.

Source: after Table 3.3, Grime *et al.* (1988).

The C-S-R model proposes that plant communities reflect the equilibrium between stress (constraints on production such as nutrient deficiency or extreme pH) and disturbance (physical damage to vegetation). In situations with low stress and low disturbance, competitive species dominate plant communities, with high stress and low disturbance, stress tolerators dominate, with low stress and high disturbance, ruderals dominate. The combination of high stress and high disturbance presents an unviable habitat for plant establishment.

Table 2.5 *Primary environments and plant strategies*

Intensity of disturbance	Intensity of stress	
Low	High	Stress-tolerators
High	Low	Ruderals
Low	Low	Competitors
High	High	(No viable strategy)

Source: from Grime (1979).

Secondary strategies have also been defined reflecting equilibria between competition (C), stress (S) and disturbance (D). The primary and secondary strategies are listed below.

PRIMARY AND SECONDARY PLANT STRATEGIES
- Competitor
- Ruderal
- Stress-tolerator
- Competitor – Ruderal
- Stress-tolerator – Ruderal
- Competitor – Stress-tolerator
- Competitor – Stress-tolerator – Ruderal

7 Urban soils which may be disastrous for traditional landscape use, such as here where a grass sward is to be established on a rubble-rich waste soil, could be effective or even desirable for the development of diverse plant communities.

These strategies could provide a baseline in the selection of plants for the creation of artificial plant communities or dynamic plant associations. Grime also considers the possibility of using the C-S-R model to derive a competitive index for species providing further refinement of the primary and secondary strategies.

It is argued that there is an equilibrium between competition, stress and disturbance in relation to the development of species-rich plant communities. Plant communities remain species-poor in situations of very high stress or disturbance, and in circumstances allowing dominance by highly competitive species. Communities are species-rich in intermediate situations.

The environment can also be looked at in relation to the equilibrium between stress and disturbance. This explains the value of hostile sites since they restrict both productivity and competition. Very extreme sites may only be colonized by a few species, but these may be unusual and of interest in themselves. The diversity can also be expected to increase as these conditions gradually become less hostile.

The triangular model has also been used to cast light on the range of habitat conditions normally found within cities (see Figure 2.5).

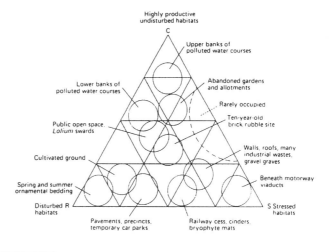

Figure 2.5 Grime's C-R-S model converted to illustrate the range of habitats present in cities (Gilbert, 1989).

communities or wild gardens or undertake habitat creation or conservation. Above all, the fertility targets applied must be substantially different. The case was put succinctly by Green (1986):

> if the amenity land manager is ever in doubt as to his best course of action, he has merely to think of what a modern farmer or forester would do, and do the opposite. His objective is to make one blade of grass grow where two grew before.

Many of the activities that are undertaken as part of 'horticultural vegetation management' – such as feeding, watering plants etc. – are exercises aimed at overcoming the limitations to growth imposed by the environment. In other words, we deliberately minimize stress. However, stress is one of the factors which limits the growth of dominant, competitive, monocultures and which leads to the development of diversity. For naturalistic landscapes therefore we need to create it deliberately. This was identified by Tregay and Gustavsson (1983), Baines (1986a) and Roberts and Roberts (1986) but the principles have only been slowly adopted since then.

Once the decision is made to explore the potential of soil stress rather than attempting to overcome it, another obvious approach which can be adopted is to resolve poor drainage and compaction problems by making the soil so impervious that it begins to function as a wetland, although clearly there will be areas where this would interfere unacceptably with the function of the landscape. Conversely there may be advantage in making areas so arid and drought-prone that they become re-vegetated by xerophytic species, such as many mosses. The options for proactive soil manipulation are discussed in more detail in Chapter 6.

Of course, although high fertility is seen as a problem in ecological plantings, it is possible to encounter soils which are so infertile that they simply cannot support any plants, or at least only specialists. Typically under such circumstances fertility will gradually increase by natural processes, or the effect can be speeded by additions. However it is important to know how far to drive the system without undermining the objectives for species richness. This will be discussed in more detail in Chapter 6.

Human disturbance

Although intangible, disturbance is another factor that characterizes the ecological status of the urban environment and the ability to tolerate disturbance is a requisite for urban species. The term embraces a wide range of processes that vary in their frequency, intensity and nature. Grime (1979) regards disturbance as any factor which destroys biomass once formed, although a clear distinction is sometimes required between those disturbances which completely kill the organism and those which lead to a reduction in size. Main (1993) distinguishes between physical disturbances such as drought, flood and fire, and biological disturbances such as herbivory in

Table 2.6 *Species richness related to disturbance*

Kind of disturbance	Frequency/intensity/size of disturbance		
	Rare, infrequent or slight	*Moderate*	*Frequent, intense and extensive*
Physical e.g. death from windstorm, drought, flood or fire	Low: dominated by long lived plants	High: patches of different size and post-disturbance ages; great differences between patches	Low: widespread occurrence of a few disturbance-tolerant, e.g. grasses in fire induced grassland
Biological, e.g. herbivory, predation	Low: dominated by rapidly growing space occupying organisms	High: within area richness high	Low: grazed or predated species infrequent; mostly unpalatable species present

Source: Main (1993).

determining the patterns of diversity seen and the life form of the successful species (see Table 2.6).

Although short term perceptions therefore often suggest that disturbance is primarily a negative influence which limits the behaviour or excludes some species from the system, for those species which are adapted to disturbed habitats, disturbance may be a key component in limiting competition from other species and enabling poor competitors to survive. If correctly timed and targeted, disturbance can therefore extend the range of biota that can survive in a given location and increase potential species diversity. Stochastic disturbance events may also play a key role in providing colonization opportunities for species which may be able to maintain themselves but not reproduce under normal conditions.

Indeed the beneficial effects of managed disturbance is easy to appreciate when it is recognized as one of the main strands of gardening where it is used to establish and maintain a huge diversity of plant species way beyond their natural competitive range.

Strong parallels are sometimes seen in woodlands which are actually surprisingly open habitats – the amount of bare ground that is present is often as much as 70%. This obviously provides many regeneration opportunities for woodland herbs. The limiting factors that may reduce such growth may be the litter layer, the root competition from trees and shrubs and the shade that is cast. However, these limiting factors can be relatively dynamic over the life-cycle of a woodland – as trees grow the amount of shade and litter they produce can become greater and greater, and the spread and demand of the roots will also change. It is also known that many woodland herbs depend on the presence of gaps in the canopy to provide additional, valuable light. What this means is that the herbs associated with woodland, even very stable woodland, often need to have some ruderal qualities; the ability to be able to move around even quite small distances may be the key to survival.

The amount of disturbance that an established grassland receives from grazing animals can again be surprisingly high. Germination niches also arise from the activity of worms, moles or other burrowing creatures. These may help to maintain diversity in the plant community, favouring short-lived or mobile species.

Of course not all forms of disturbance can be tolerated by different species. Hodge (1995) identifies the positive effects of disturbance in woodland management as:

- control of unwanted aggressive species;
- arresting succession;
- manipulating shade levels;
- providing colonization niches.

However, some habitats are vulnerable and are not tolerant of disturbance. Biodiversity may be degraded either directly or indirectly as a result of colonization by undesirable species. For example, open ground in woodlands can be the result of the damaging effect of trampling which the plants are often unable to tolerate. However, even here it is a question of degree, since many individuals are found alongside paths where they clearly benefit from the reduced competition and slightly increased light levels.

Disturbance, involving physical damage to vegetation or plant community structure, therefore provides the basis of many management and maintenance operations. On the other hand incorrect or uncontrolled disturbance can lead to habitat degeneration either directly through destruction of desirable species or indirectly by modifying processes such as nutrient cycling or by opening systems to invasion from competitive or alien species. The challenge is to match the degree and nature of the effect against that which the system can tolerate.

Understanding the value of disturbance and characterizing the likely effects of impacts is therefore a critical aspect of the task of the landscape manager. Indeed we have more ways of achieving this effect than ever before. The historical activities of cutting, grazing, burning, pruning and coppicing are now supplemented by other options, such as massive soil disruption or the use of selective herbicides to change competitive relationships. The sensitivity and risk involved in experimentation makes it difficult to be advantageous in traditional systems, but in urban areas and man-made habitats there is a strong argument for experimenting with different types of disturbance inputs to clarify their effects.

A rural reserve, where the managers are struggling to maintain what may well be a sub-optimal population of different species, is not the place where research or innovative techniques can easily be assimilated. However, there is in consequence a tendency to sanctify areas and to attempt to protect them from apparently excessive damage when in fact such damage may have been typical of the original ecological processes that originally created the habitat. We often greatly underestimate the extent to which old habitats are really highly dynamic ecosystems which have a high turnover in the plant populations and which rely to some extent on disturbance in order to allow the necessary regeneration.

Consider this scenario for example: it is possible that a water meadow community may be influenced by gap formation processes due to flooding and silt deposition that may have only occurred once in several decades. These occasional, unpredictable events are difficult to identify or integrate into land management programmes but may be key to long-term ecosystem health. In more recent years land-use changes and river engineering may have completely controlled natural flooding and the species present will begin to modify as recruitment opportunities or soil conditions change. Even if the manager were able to identify the need for some sort of intervention, the interactions of the timing of the gap formation and their size or severity with the presence of propagules of desirable species, of undesirable competitors and even with pathogen behaviour can be difficult to predict. Experiments also need to be replicated many times. There may be the correct timing and type of disturbance undertaken, but it may happen in a year where, because of climate or lack of dispersal agents or pollinating agents, very little seed germinates.

It is generally accepted that disturbance favours species which have invested more in reproductive and dispersal strategies than in competition or tolerance of unusual adversity (cf. r-K life strategies and Grime's C-S-R theory – Grime, 1979). Therefore the colonists of large open gaps will favour species with small wind-disturbed seeds, or ones that travel in car slipstreams etc.

Periodic disturbance also favours some perennial herbs (e.g. *Rumex crispus*) which seem to be unable to take advantage of undisturbed conditions; this is probably due to a poor competitive ability or a preference for disturbed soils which differ in their chemistry from more stable conditions in organic matter content and rate of mineralization. Their spread is primarily vegetative, but they can travel large distances as a result of transport of soil or wastes.

If disturbance is defined as some factor which tends to destroy biomass (cf. Grime, 1979), and disturbance-tolerant species as those which have adaptations which allow them to avoid or survive this destruction and exploit the opportunities so formed, then herbicide treatments could also be included in the definition. In many industrial areas characteristic plant communities can form of species which are able to tolerate the chemicals used.

An assumption is often made that since disturbance is a common result of human activity, disturbance-tolerant species are common and rather uninteresting, whereas intolerant species tend to be rare. However this is not necessarily always the case. There is a class of plants and animals which seem in fact to be 'ruderals' in much of their ecology, in that they are uncompetitive and need disturbance to provide niches, but that are also uncommon and seen as important for nature conservation. This rarity may reflect weaknesses or inefficiencies in their reproduction or dispersal. Examples among plants include many terrestrial orchids. A possible example among fauna could be great crested newts. Both are frequently associated with old and stable, open and often low productivity habitats, and yet also seem to have an amazingly frequent link with naturally revegetated post-industrial wastelands for example (see Chapter 4).

In new landscapes selection of species appropriate to a disturbance regime

Table 2.7 *Disturbance and biodiversity interactions on ex-industrial sites*

| Disturbance/management | Relative biotic diversity | | |
	Low	*Medium*	*High*
Low	Grossly polluted areas	Old disused mineral workings (except those in column 3)	Older chalk and limestone, colliery subsidence flashes
Medium		Urban waste land; grounds of power stations and hospitals etc.; urban waterways and reservoirs; rubbish dumps	Flooded gravel pits (with recreational use); railway land; old fashioned sewage farms; larger parks and golf courses etc.
High	Active quarries and mines; urban centres and dense housing; heavy industrial areas, refineries etc.; stations, ports, depots etc.; urban roads	Formal parks, sports fields and airfields; allotments	Suburban areas

Source: Davies (1976).

may be desirable. If extreme disturbance is repeated regularly then only ruderals will be favoured, and it is important to recognize their potential value rather than dismissing them as 'weeds'. Ruderal plants are sometimes recommended for greening temporarily derelict sites (Baines, 1989). In Holland ruderal species are utilized in median strips along roads, requiring annual soil disturbance to renew the display.

The role of disturbance is therefore complex. It can be a factor that may both support or undermine diversity and a sound paradigm is needed to understand which activities are desirable and which are not. Davis (1976) has attempted a classification of artificial environments of urban and industrial origin according to their relative biotic diversity and the degree of disturbance or management to which they are subjected (see Table 2.7).

Inoculation pressure and urban species

Despite a general focus on rural plant communities, studies on urban fauna and flora have been carried out by naturalists for many years. For example, the distribution of alien and exotic species around centres of importation such as railways yards, certain factories importing foreign products etc., is often mapped. In unique cases these combine with extremes of environment to produce truly bizarre clusters of plants and animals, such as tropical species surviving in canals in the heated waste water from factories (Gilbert, 1989).

These exotic species survive and live among a framework of natives which are themselves either relics of other land use or are species which have invaded and shown themselves to have the ability to prosper in the particular soil and climatic conditions encountered.

The more urban a setting becomes, the more intense this inoculation pressure may become, the more disturbance there is to original species, the more fragmented the landscape becomes and the more the soils and climate will deviate from the norms of the region. There is therefore a greater likelihood that exotic species or foreign genotypes of native species will begin to dominate, or at least complement, the flora and even fauna. This helps to explain why there is apparently a higher species diversity in larger urban conurbations than in smaller. However, at the same time, the number of species and range of landscape types declines moving from the urban fringe to the centre, with the inner areas dominated by highly synanthropic species and exotics surviving in either what tends to be long-established areas of greenspace or on waste ground or other early successional sites.

Even so, the potential value of these species should not be overlooked. Sukopp and Werner (1987) argue for the development of new green areas by total or partial removal of pavement from surfaces, tolerating weed invasion in cracks and planting of courtyards, rooftops and façades. They also see a need for mechanisms which prevent newly available fallow land from becoming developed before the potential use as green space is explored. Loss of wasteland is also seen as undesirable, and potentially equivalent to loss of green space.

Some of the exotic species that establish in the city may subsequently go on to invade semi-natural communities in the adjacent suburban land. (It is common that species that normally never grow alongside each other are found in new combinations in urban areas, and an occasional result can be the production of vigorous hybrids which, if fertile, may extend their range.)

Urban plant communities may also be characterized by certain deficiencies. Some plant types are highly unlikely to be present in urban situations, notably those lichens and bryophytes which are particularly susceptible to pollution and nutrient build-up. Gilbert's (1989) analysis of the floras of urban areas also shows a deficiency of the ground flora species associated with deciduous woodland and native scrub species. (Scrub in urban areas is often dominated by exotic species such as *Buddleia.*) Also uncommon are oligotrophic habitats and mature habitats characteristic of long succession. Among urban trees there are relatively few mature specimens, and those which are decaying to the point where they may be valuable habitats for other wildlife are frequently removed as hazardous. In a recent survey of urban trees only 9% of specimens were above 50 years old, and only 1% above 100 years old. 'Considerably' diseased or damaged and dead or dying trees made up less than 5% of the sample.

Like urban landscapes themselves, the flora and fauna of towns and cities are composed of many different groups of widely disparate origins and characteristics.

- There are species which really have no particular affinity or tolerance of urban conditions, but which have become incorporated within patches of land which are large enough and undisturbed enough to give them refuge.
- There are species which rely upon a wide dispersed habitat range – they

may be primarily rural creatures but exploit urban settings temporarily during their lives. It is frequently seen that the size and species range of urban fauna increases in adverse winters, and this may play a role in their learnt adaptation and exploitation of urban life (Baines, 1986c). This group may also include species found as 'casuals', i.e. without a self sustaining community within the urban area alone, but constantly replenished by spread from a population situated elsewhere. Their presence in urban areas may be dependent on the existence of other habitat types in the surrounding rural areas.

- There are species which are as much at home in urban as in rural settings, and which are sufficiently tolerant to disturbance and of urban conditions that some populations are able to survive entirely within towns as well as in the countryside.
- There are synanthropic species which are urban specialists, with populations which show strong affinity for the environments which are heavily manipulated by man. They are often non-native species reflecting the environmental changes (in aspects such as climate) which urban areas show compared to local countryside (Gilbert, 1989). There are many such species which seem to be common between different cities in the same climatic zone, but there may also be regionally unique components that reflect different land-use histories.

Of course even for these species there is still the influence of the dynamic and immature status of many urban habitats. Stochastic factors influence colonization strongly, to the point where not all species that could be expected will be found in each place. This variation contributes to some of the interest, and confusion, that arises when urban communities are studied. It also creates opportunities for species introduction which will be addressed later.

Urban fauna

Many of the most successful urban specialists, especially animal species, have predictable characteristics:

- disturbance tolerant – only those species that can accept human presence, or that do not have key life-cycle processes that are interrupted by urban influences, are even candidates for urbanization (an example of a species in the UK that has little chance to adapt is the glow-worm which suffers disruption of mating patterns where artificial night lights are too abundant);
- adaptable and flexible in their requirements;
- broad food range – omnivores and seed eaters among birds, scavenging habit among mammals;
- tolerant of hard landscape settings, e.g. some cliff living species of birds have adapted to urban settings;
- a nocturnal habit among mammals (although species intolerant of night light will not succeed);

Table 2.8 *Causes of animal death in London*

Mode	Animals affected
Impact	
Vehicles	Foxes, hedgehogs, squirrels, weasels, rabbits, deer, songbirds, snakes, insects
Structures – glass windows, TV masts, tower buildings, power lines	Songbirds, particularly migrants, waterfowl, owls
Drowning	
Sewage canals and tanks	Hedgehogs
Ornamental pools	Owls, squirrels
Rainwater pipes and gutters	Sparrow chicks, sand martin chicks
Electrocution	
Railway lines	Badgers, rabbits, otters, foxes
Power transmission lines	Raptors, swans, geese
Neon display signs	Sparrows
Poisoning	
Pesticides	Foxes, badgers
Baits	Hedgehogs, birds
Heavy metals	Invertebrates, rodents, songbirds
Confinement	
Litter — cans and bottles	Small rodents, insects
Netting	Blackbirds
Predation	
Cats, dogs, man	Rodents, rabbits, hares, foxes, reptiles
Kestrel, tawny owl	Songbirds, amphibians
Crow, magpie, jay, jackdaw	Pigeons, doves
Fox, weasel, stoat	Waterfowl

Source: Gill and Bonnett (1973).

• low or reduced territorial sensitivity;
• social structure that tolerates casualties.

For those animal species which are able to adapt, urban areas can provide a ready supply of food from waste, are relatively warm, shelter is easy to find and there may be an absence of the predators or harmful agrochemicals that are found in the countryside. In areas where their populations are low, there may be only one or two missing environmental factors and if these are provided population numbers may rise, e.g. following the introduction of shrubby plants that provide cover beneath trees.

Often these animals may still show high death rates, and in some cases their life expectancy may be lower than that of those rural individuals which survive from infancy, but high food availability and hence successful reproduction may compensate for this. Gill and Bonnett (1973) identify the causes of animal death in London as shown in Table 2.8.

An aspect of mortality that is not yet well understood in an urban context relates to animal disease epidemiology. The spread of disease in populations relates to many factors such as population density, feeding behaviour, breeding and genetic patterns and health and age profiles and these may be very different in urban animal populations compared to rural. In Bristol in the UK the urban fox population, perhaps the best documented in the world, has undergone an almost complete population collapse following the spread of mange (Harris, 1986; 1996).

One fascinating aspect of urban ecology is the tendency of animal species to develop greater levels of tolerance over time to urban conditions. In the UK foxes, badgers and increasingly often muntjac deer are known to have undergone such an urbanization process in recent decades; the phenomena is likely to have been occurring ever since cities were first created, and many of our now familiar town-dwelling fauna (including some major pest species) are likely to have undergone similar waves of adaptation. Of particular interest, however, is the speed with which the contemporary invasions seem to be happening, with colonization and behavioural change progressing rapidly over a few decades (Harris, 1986).

Sometimes the animals may have specific habitat requirements that correspond in fascinating ways to the cultural history of urban development. For example in Bristol the urban fox population distribution best matches the spread of 1930s housing with large gardens, whereas the urban fabric built before and since has smaller areas of suitable territory (Harris and Woolard, 1991). Although these animal invaders may sometimes be restricted to habitats that parallel their rural origins, they can also be surprisingly capable of exploiting new opportunities (see Table 2.9). The urban fauna includes many species that are non-natives, and certainly many species which are not regionally native or that have moved outside of their traditional habitat types. Cliff-nesting pigeons and coastal gulls are now dominant components of inner-city bird communities. The ability of these species to move into very different conditions provides interesting information about the nature of habitat constraints for species.

Some of the components of the fauna are introduced by man as pets or working animals. These can have huge population numbers that are bolstered by artificial food inputs to levels far higher than the area could reasonably support otherwise. The impact of cats as predators on urban animal diversity is enormous, but of course their effect is offset by the behavioural changes that regular feeding and domestication have introduced. The impact is greatest in areas where large feral populations have developed which find enough food from people to stay alive but which also have to hunt for additional resources.

Of course it is inevitable (although not always remembered) that nature conservation activity represents the integration of ecology with value judgements. People are incredibly selective in what they appreciate, or even recognize, as wildlife. Once urban animals become too common they often lose their charm and are increasingly seen as pests. Any animal which does too well in the urban context and thrives too much from human contact will

Table 2.9 *The number of badger setts associated with different habitats within the city of Bristol*

Habitat	No. of badger setts
Wooded banks, woodland	143
Waste land, scrub, disused gardens	65
Gardens	42
Fields, sports grounds, paddocks	21
Rubbish tips	13
Golf courses	11
Disused quarries	11
Under sheds, buildings	11
Allotments	6
Hedgerows	6
Factory sites	4
Under walls	4
Railway banks	3
School grounds	2
Old drains	2
Ditches	1
Cemeteries	1

Source: Harris and Cresswell (1991).

generally not be favoured by landscape policy. Therefore although the most common urban mammals include feral cats and dogs as well as rats and mice, the focus in much urban wildlife literature is on foxes and on species which are just commencing the process of becoming urbanized in some locations.

The synanthropic species can therefore be further categorized into those that are popular, or at least neutral, in people's opinion and those that impact undesirably on our lives, such as rats. Management problems sometimes arise when attempts are made to encourage the former and not the latter, compounded by the possible interactions between these groups. At times even species normally seen as attractive can cause potential conflicts by their behaviour (see Table 2.10).

The success of many animal species depends, of course, on the provision of habitat factors and food supplies that they require. Animals may be either specialist or catholic in regard to the plants they need. Many may have such specialist feeding or habitat structural requirements that the absence of a particular plant will automatically mean that the animal species will never survive. Some insects, e.g. caterpillars, depend on certain plant species. However, they will most often be found where the food plants are also growing in a particular spatial context (Kirby, 1992).

In many cases therefore the wider the range of plant species the more likely that a variety of food plants will be present for insects with specific nutritional requirements, and also the more likely it is that a continuity of food will be available through the year (see Figure 2.6) (Andrews and

Table 2.10 *Number of households in Bristol, excluding flats, which have suffered nuisance or damage from badgers (sample size 1596)*

Type of damage	No.	%
Rifling dustbins	262	16.4
Breaking fences	161	10.1
Digging holes in lawns	59	3.7
Digging dung pits in gardens	41	2.6
Digging in flower beds	36	2.3
Digging in compost heaps	16	1
Damaging fruit cages	10	0.6
Breaking gates	5	
Digging up rockeries	4	
Digging out bee/wasp nests	3	
Damaging bird tables	2	
Digging up drains	2	
Digging under sheds	2	
Attacking pet cats	2	
Attacking/killing pet guinea-pigs	2	
Taking cat's food	1	
Taking dog's food	1	
Catching fish in garden pond	1	

Source: Harris and Cresswell (1991).

Rebane, 1994). In a low-diversity sward dominated by aggressive perennials there is also likely to be less structural diversity than with a species-rich vegetation, although this is a gross generalization since many insects respond positively to small-scale variation between different plant communities.

Sometimes shelter rather than food is the limiting factor – this is seen in many uniform habitats. Add a mound of rocks to a garden or a pond and almost immediately animals start to move in. As an experiment I left a small pile of twigs in the middle of the lawn in our garden. Within an hour various spiders were building webs. Within two days the twigs had become colonized by a range of other invertebrates including snails, woodlice and beetles and a red ant colony had started to extend their nest upwards by building a soil pile around the twigs. This was clearly a successful exercise in habitat creation.

Many insects need warm temperatures and often prefer protected yet open situations, such as edge habitats bordering scrub and woodland or glades. Invertebrates may also appreciate the warm microclimate associated with thin, poorly vegetated ground, together with the structural and species diversity that is often seen in early successional colonizing plant communities. These provide small, sheltered areas, where the sun freely penetrates and where the vegetation produces many showy flowers. Small birds too may prefer shelter where they are able to hide and where their energy loss can be more successfully controlled. The development of a natural undergrowth beneath shrubs and woodland again favours the breeding of many bird species.

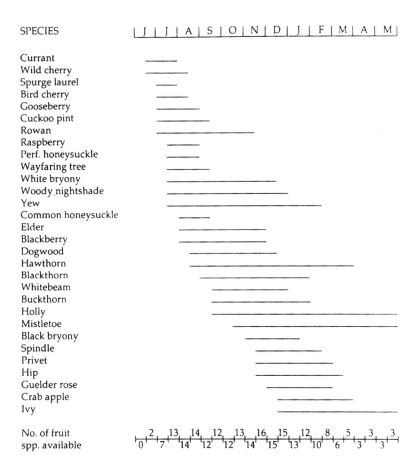

Figure 2.6 The ripening dates of berry-bearing shrubs in the UK (Snow and Snow, 1988).

Many animals therefore respond to different factors of the habitat, such as the architecture and complexity of the vegetation stand, stability and disturbance. Many are able to exploit any productive, nutritious (and often botanically dull) plants. Animal conservation interest can therefore arise in habitats where there is no particular botanical interest, such as in long rough grass. Where grass is maintained more intensively it is usually accepted as valuable if every year a small area of rough herbaceous vegetation is left unmown to allow insects to over-winter. However Wiren (1995) showed through survey that short grass in parks, if linked with a mosaic of scrub (and especially of thorny and berry-bearing shrubs), was widely used by birds and was far from being the 'biological desert' that is frequently claimed. He also identified the value of short grass as a habitat component that brings many birds into view, increasing the value of the landscape for human users.

Being mobile, animals are able to meet different aspects of their life requirements across a wide spatial area, but ultimately they may be constrained by the absence of any one factor within their normal travelling range. Animals may also have wide territory demands, so that if the habitat needs are not present in large enough amounts for a viable breeding population they may not be able to establish or maintain a presence.

This issue is of particular relevance to small-scale habitat creation projects, since it is rarely possible in a small area to produce sufficient resources to change the population size of many larger animals. Often what can be achieved is to attract in to the site species which are actually exploiting a much wider territory. This does of course has value, since it helps to make some species more obvious to the human visitors, stage managing their visits in effect.

If a net increase in urban wildlife really is required, the habitat created should attempt strategically to remove the main limiting factor to population growth within the site, complemented with a strategic overview of the wider needs of the species across the landscape.

Bird tables, bat boxes and 'artificial' sources of food are a simple way of encouraging wildlife. They are particularly valuable if the vegetation is insufficient to support a viable population unaided. Their careful location also helps to 'stage' feeding displays and make certain they are visible from windows. Designs of bat boxes and the like can be found in Emery (1986). Often the biggest problem with food sources is making sure that they remain accessible to desired species but do not favour undesirable ones and complex designs for feeding devices have been produced.

Animals of course can be found that will exploit almost any phase in habitat succession. For example some ground-nesting bees are eager to exploit bare and open ground. But the number of species will increase as habitat complexity and food sources increase. Developing a complex community with complete food webs therefore tends to favour more species. It is valuable to encompass the full cycle of growth and decay. For example, dead wood should be allowed to lie rather than being tidied away.

Predatory animals of course feed on others, and while this is a natural aspect of the food web, it can cause distress sometimes, for example when people watch predatory birds such as magpies gradually robbing a nest.

Hunting of mammals does happen in urban areas, sometimes for pelts and sometimes to capture animals for baiting. Unlike rural hunting, there is not the possible advantage that an interest in hunting will convince landowners to change their land-management practice.

Birds are the wild species most widely observed in urban areas, and in many heavily built-up areas they may represent the only form of wildlife that people see. Their effective mobility means that sometimes they may be found in inner cities, and yet may not be completely urban species at all. Some may feed in rural areas or exploit urban warmth and freedom from predators during certain periods (Plummer and Shewan, 1992), but there are also species that have become completely urbanized and may even prefer inner-city to suburban conditions (Bland and Taylor, 1991).

Birds can be good opportunists. For example, population numbers can increase near to lunch time, reflecting the extent to which they are used to scavenging for food scraps. However, it is not always easy to know what behaviour they are following, and attempts to monitor the distribution of species is also complicated by competition between different birds.

The density of the majority of vertebrate species tends to fall off towards the inner city as the areas of open green space fall. Exceptions are those which feed on human wastes and obtain shelter almost entirely within the built urban framework, such as mice and pigeons. However, although complex urban green spaces may decline, frequently water and grass are still found, and even in very hard areas vegetation is still present in the form of trees. Some bird species may therefore maintain high populations, and can even become pests through direct damage, messing (which can amount to tonnes of mess on some buildings (Bland and Taylor, 1991) and through association with some diseases.

One of the major problems with inner city locations, therefore, is not that they are devoid of nature, but rather that the species which can adapt are able to develop large numbers and operate in an environment that is largely free of competition, such that they cross the boundary from infrequent and desired wildlife to common and undesirable nuisances.

Urban flora

It has already been noted that spontaneous natural plant communities in urban areas comprise many aliens together with natives. As with animals, these represent species that have been deliberately or accidentally introduced by man, and which find opportunities in the dynamic and climatically atypical urban ecosystem. Even where there may be a low probability that these species will survive in the long term, the populations may continually be reinforced by new introductions.

These 'aliens' should not be regarded as too serious, unless objective damage is clear. The rhetoric of traditional nature conservation often assumes that these 'aliens' are threats to some assumed 'perfect community', but they represent a substantial, but rarely harmful, percentage of our national flora and in an urban system they may be a key part of the diversity and richness and completely appropriate as a component of what is ultimately a human dominated situation. Of the 4000 or so broadleaved exotic taxa which are recorded as having established naturally somewhere in the British Isles, the vast majority are clearly localized, perhaps establishing through vegetative means or thanks to a very high local seed rain, but with little genuine competitive ability (Clements and Foster, 1996).

In fact, less surprising than the number of naturalized plants is the fact that out of so many different species and varieties of cultivated plants that we grow in cities (approximately 60 000 taxa currently available in the nursery trade in the UK (Lord, 1996), most of which are hardy as mature plants, there are so many which fail to naturalize successfully. This is even more surprising when we consider that many set at least some viable seed, that they may lack large populations of natural pathogens or pests and when you also consider that the British flora is really artificially depauparate because of isolation from continental Europe, with many potential niches possibly not filled. Sukopp *et al.* (1978) note the introduction of 3000 species of woody plants to cultivation in Central Europe since 1500, and Kunick (1982) observes that of this total only 114 woody species native to Central Europe and 118 non-native species occur spontaneously in a survey of 10 different cities.

Kunick (1982) found that native species dominated on relatively undisturbed sites, especially sites with a high nutrient status and high humus content whereas non-native species dominate on highly modified sites, such as building rubble and disused railway tracks. This suggests that it is really very difficult for new plants to gain access to closed communities – an issue that will be returned to later when considering habitat creation in Chapter 6.

Again as we have seen with regard to animals, the presence of non-natives in the communities is not always welcomed by people. Some species are identified as weeds because of the direct damage that they do or because of the potential safety threat that they may present (for example Giant Hogweed is often identified as a matter of concern in the UK because of the harmful sap).

There is also a general assumption and concern that non-native species as a group are undesirable and harmful but it is important not to get mislead by the rhetoric of rural nature conservation. Within a city these 'aliens' are not threats to some assumed perfect community, they are a key part of the unique urban flora. The issue of the perceived greater desirability of natives is a complex matter that cannot be understood without looking in more detail at how value judgements are placed on different species within a nature conservation context. This aspect of the urban flora is therefore considered in more detail in Chapter 4.

3 The history and development of ecological landscape styles

S. FORBES, D. COOPER and A.D. KENDLE

People shape gardens and landscapes to provide the sort of environments they most strongly yearn for. Changes in landscape design and landscape management inevitably arise out of changes in our attitudes towards Nature and changes in our understanding of how the natural world functions. Garden history, and the history of naturalistic landscape styles in particular reveals a progression of ideas that gives a better understanding of present fashions and points to likely trends in the future.

In this progression it is possible to trace the development of three themes:

- nature perceived as a pattern – an image and an artistic goal;
- nature perceived as a process – the science and understanding of ecology, or interrelationships and cause and effect;
- nature perceived as an inspiration – the positive spiritual force of life, the need to find ways to co-exist in a positive relationship with the natural world.

The challenge to the environment professions of today is to bring the science and the art together, to use our understanding of ecology to create and manage landscapes that meet society's emotional and spiritual needs and which serve the demands of nature conservation.

What is an ecological approach to planting?

Ecology is the study of how organisms relate to each other and to their environment. It can be applied as much to a formal *Dahlia* bed as to a wildflower meadow. The science is a tool for creating designs that are as rich or as simple as we require. However the interpretation of which designs are 'ecological' or 'natural' reflect wider preconceptions and value judgements in the minds of professionals and the public that they work for and with.

The involvement of ecologists, landscape architects, landscape and countryside managers, garden designers, urban and countryside planners, and social scientists in environmental design has compounded jargon through subtly different definitions and issues of concern. As a result the terminology describing ecological landscapes is often confusing.

If we take it that all manifestations of flora and of the living landscape are aspects of nature, ecological planting could be taken to describe almost any form of planting from strictly native communities to mass bedding or shrub ground cover. Even though the latter are intended to be static, disclimax associations stable only for the functional lifespans of the component species, they still embody and reflect certain ecological processes. The principle for maintenance of disclimax associations is dominance, the process by which the resources in certain habitats are monopolized by one species or by a small number of species (Grime, 1979). The use of species with similar ecological or physiological tolerances simplifies management and maintenance by allowing application of extensive techniques including mechanization, and may reduce management inputs to a level comparable with those for semi-natural plant communities.

The ability of established plantings to dominate a site by monopolizing resources and restricting invasion presents a straightforward application of ecological principles in landscape design. However, when most practitioners refer to ecological styles of landscape they clearly have in mind a pattern and a process that to a greater or lesser extent reflects the behaviour of semi-natural plant communities. Bradshaw (1983) describes the ecological approach thus:

> The essential characteristic of an ecological approach is to copy with understanding what nature achieves by blind natural processes, i.e. to maximize the adaptation of species planted to their environment, to simulate natural conditions in their management, and so to create integrated and harmonious ecosystems.

However, this definition is also open to many different interpretations. Even before the formal development of ecology as a distinct science, designers frequently professed to follow natural principles or the laws of nature, but the variation as to which natural principles were focused on and how strictly they were adhered to is enormous. Ecological planting, as we shall see, has had very different interpretations. Some people see it as a strictly naturalistic philosophy, involving native communities very close to those found in natural and semi-natural areas. Others have taken these biotype models on board, while introducing appropriate non-natives into the community. A further group are fascinated by the study of almost entirely non-native groupings, and the way they interact in an essentially foreign environment. The latter is still legitimately argued as an ecological approach, as it encourages designers and managers to use ecological principles of competition and plant community interaction when formulating their policies.

The terms and ideals of the ecological approach are therefore clearly in need of further clarification. Before we can approach this clarification it is worth trying to understand the way in which ecological planting has developed historically. The following sections aim to identify the roots of the movement, and show how various influences have resulted in a rich diversity of ideas.

The historical origins of the ecological style

1. The English Landscape Movement and the Picturesque style

Even though there were earlier manifestations of interest, such as the medieval gardens in which flowery meads were a popular feature containing a wide variety of grassland perennials, the revolution in garden design characterizing the English Landscape Movement provides a convenient starting point for the analysis of the origin of a naturalistic style in Western culture. Indeed modern Nature-like designs sometimes consciously reflect an adaptation of the goals and methods of the English Landscape Movement to the requirements of modern developments (Tregay, 1988).

The English Landscape Movement was already established when William Kent (1685–1748) 'leaped the fence, and saw that all Nature was a garden' (Walpole 1771/1780). The style initially developed within the confines of the formal garden, as at Stowe, but the development of the English landscape park and pleasure grounds soon overtook and swept away the formal garden in a complete transformation of style. This change is usually attributed to a fundamental philosophical reassessment of the relationship of Man to Nature, and of Nature to the garden, as part of a contemporary Classical revival (Jacques, 1983). The clients of the landscape gardeners sought Arcadian ideals at a time of cultural upheaval in philosophy, literature and the arts, the desire being to present an altered attitude towards man's dominance over nature. Clearly echoes of similar philosophical readjustments can be seen today (Forbes, 1989).

While forests were valued for recreation certainly as early as Norman times a distinction had always been maintained between Nature and the garden. The acceptance of Nature in the garden required a redefinition of what gardens were as much as a re-appraisal of Nature. However, this was not simply an adoption of the existing agricultural landscapes, forests and woodlands; Nature in the English Landscape Movement remained distinct from the countryside, reflecting a civilized and idealized view, Nature 'rescued and improved, and art decently concealing herself under her own perfections' (*The World*, 1755 quoted in Hunt and Willis 1988). Nature in the garden was distinguished from the countryside by design – the hand of man had to remain obvious, making more beautiful what nature alone could not perfect. This approach had a great impact on the style of the design; although the appearance of the landscape could be said to be broadly modelled on the wider landscape, it had to have clear design influence and nothing was left to occur spontaneously.

This relationship of Nature and Art developed as the principal consideration in the continuing debate on garden design. The Picturesque controversy of the late eighteenth century reflects a reaction against the artificiality of the 'natural' style of the English landscape park and concern for applying contemporary artistic principles to landscape design. Today, both styles appear mannered and clearly artificial, so it is hard to realize how much of a step towards truly natural patterns the Picturesque movement represented. It marked the origins of an appreciation of natural scenery in the wild and was significant in influencing both garden design and attitudes to Nature (Andrews, 1989).

DESIGN IN THE LANDSCAPE MOVEMENT

The principal natural elements in the composition of the English landscape park are landform, water, grass and trees. The secondary elements within the composition include shrubs, used as evergreens in woodlands to define spaces, and as flowering species on woodland margins to provide diversity, colour and seasonality at a fine scale. The explicit use of flowers was restricted, often surviving only in separate gardens and greenhouses although there may have been quite diverse populations of native perennials present in the grass and woodland.

The development of the ha-ha was also significant to the natural design, 'the capital stroke, the leading step to all that has followed' (Walpole, 1771/1780, quoted in Thacker, 1979). The ha-ha was significant for development and management as well as for design, and allowed the estate to be maintained as functioning countryside, while still contributing to the visual objectives of the designer. Clearly a philosophy of multiple-use could be applied to the landscape garden which could not be applied to the formal garden, and although development of an English landscape garden was undoubtedly expensive (and even crippling as the dissipation of the fortunes of Charles Hamilton at Painshill and of William Beckford at Fonthill illustrate), some return on investment, at least from the park, could be expected and was at times instrumental in the acceptance of the style. The development of gardens on large estates was of course primarily driven by social and political objectives, but the move towards more naturalistic styles allowed at least some of the costs to be kept within bounds.

DEVELOPMENT, MANAGEMENT AND MAINTENANCE IN THE
ENGLISH LANDSCAPE GARDEN

The foundation for many modern management techniques was clearly established by the eighteenth century, reflecting the fact that ecologically sound principles work before they are scientifically recognized. The incorporation of existing meadows or pasture within the park clearly provided the most cost-effective option. However, the commercial availability of grass and clover seeds at the beginning of the eighteenth century also allowed for the moderately cheap establishment of new pasture (Rackham, 1986).

We know surprisingly little about the detailed management programmes on these estates. At Painshill, around the figures representing the Rape of the Sabines, Robertson (1795, quoted in Kitz and Kitz, 1984) noted:

> This little spot is ornamented by clumps of the most beautiful evergreens and deciduous shrubs, thrown into different forms, the green sward gently waving among them.

This suggests that grassland management, by grazing or cutting, was less intense than today, as modern swards in such parks certainly do not 'wave'.

Certainly, many of the landscape parks incorporated existing features that would today be regarded as of great conservation interest. For example the presence of massive pollard oaks associated with faint earthworks and around the platforms of vanished cottages at Ickworth and at Sotterley is noted by Rackham (1986). The ancient pollard oaks at Blenheim Park provide evidence of the inclusion of the Royal Park of Henry II within 'Capability' Brown's landscape (Moggridge, 1983). These preserved mature specimens and woodlands were of infinitely greater wildlife, conservation and aesthetic value than the newer plantations.

New tree planting was undertaken on an unprecedented scale both within the landscape park and in plantations. For example, tree planting was encouraged by the Society for the Encouragement of Arts, Manufactures and Commerce through the institution of gold, silver and bronze medals first awarded in 1758. Wood (1913, quoted in Henrey, 1975) reckoned that as a result of the Society's campaign to promote afforestation, at the very lowest estimate this number must have considerably exceeded 50 million, of which some 20 million were firs and larches, and some 15 million oaks.

It is likely that to a large extent the woodland blocks and species were patterned in a way that was pleasing to the eye, with the use of designed woodland mixtures and specimens where they were most visible – a process which echoes modern landscape treatment of afforestation. The use of conifers was not necessarily perceived as detracting from the naturalness of the scene.

Evelyn (1662) advocates using stock established by direct seeding:

> First, because they take soonest. Secondly, because they make the straitest and most uniform Shoot. Thirdly, because they will neither require staking nor watering (which are two very considerable Articles.) And lastly, for that all transplanting (though it much improves Fruit-trees) unless they are taken up the first Year or two, is a considerable Impediment to the growth of Forest-trees.

His advice is often consistent with modern applied ecological practice including Bradshaw and Chadwick (1980) and La Dell (1983, 1988), including the use of nurse plants to protect the seedlings from grazing and the need to control grass competition:

> if you mingle among the Acorns the Seeds of Genista spinosa, or Furs,

they will come up without any Damage, and for a while needs no other Fence, and will be kill'd by the Shade of the young Oaklings, before they become able to do them any Prejudice.

Removal of competing species is advised, particularly where watering is necessary, which is better poured into a Circle at some Distance from the Roots, which should be continually bared of Grass. (cf. Davison, 1983, Insley and Buckley, 1986).

Evelyn is, however, equivocal about the role of legumes in establishment:

whether the setting, or sowing of Beans near Trees, make them thrive the more . . . I leave to Experience.

Use of legumes as a nurse for nitrogen fixation is well established when planting poor soils (Bradshaw and Chadwick, 1980). However, Evelyn lacked the scientific understanding that would indicate which soils were worth trying the experiment on (a distinction that some latter day tree researchers still have trouble recognizing). He quotes Theophrastus as the source of the idea of using beans as a nurse. Interestingly the Latin name for lupin, another good legume nurse, comes from the Greek word for wolf. In a superb example of a misconception of cause and effect, the Greeks, noting that lupins were common on nutrient poor soils, believed that the plant was responsible for the depletion in fertility, rather than being the only species that could tolerate it.

The role of management in controlling successional processes was also observed by Humphry Repton (1802):

However we may admire natural beauties, without some degree of art and management it is impossible to prevent the injury which the vegetation itself will occasion. There is no medium between the keeping of art and of nature, it must be one or the other, and this practical part of the management forms one of the most difficult points. We must endeavour to imitate the causes by which Nature produces her effects, and the effects will be natural.

In the absence of ecology as a science, the design and management of the English landscape garden could only mimic the patterns of nature without ensuring that underlying processes worked to enhance and preserve the effect. Nevertheless, contemporary countryside management and close observation of nature allowed some aspects of the planning and management to proceed in close accord with a modern ecological approach. Where the practitioners differed so clearly from modern approaches was in their lack of a preoccupation with native species, and their clear commitment to the idea that nature's patterns alone are not beautiful, but need the input of the human eye to perfect them. In some ways therefore, the landscape movement still expressed a philosophy that put man in a dominant relation to the natural world.

2. The wild and woodland garden

Nature leaps back over the fence – the rise of
the Open Space Movement

The rapid urbanization of England in the eighteenth and, especially, the nineteenth centuries, resulting from the Industrial Revolution, produced chronic overcrowding in the cities. Concern for the social and physical conditions of the urban working classes and disillusionment with the Industrial Revolution resulted in calls for reform and for social justice. These were exemplified in the Open Space Movement and the Arts and Crafts Movement of the later nineteenth century.

The Open Space Movement encompassed concern for the conservation of the environment. However, this increasing concern for Nature beyond the garden was influenced by a prominent Romantic view. This directed the Open Space Movement towards nature preservation rather than conservation. These attitudes suggest a naive perception of Nature, and especially the role of traditional management skills in maintaining the qualities that were desired. For example, at Brantwood, John Ruskin

> would have his coppice cut no more. He let it grow, only taking off the weaker shoots and dead wood. It spindled up to great tall stems, slender and sinuous, promising no timber, and past the age for all commercial use or time-honoured wont. Neighbours shook their heads, but they did not know the pictures of Botticelli, and Ruskin had made his coppice into an early Italian altarpiece (Collingwood, 1903).

The acceptance of naturalism in the English Landscape Movement and in the Picturesque was in part driven by the accelerating enclosure into regular fields of existing arable land and pasture and the disappearance of wild landscape through agricultural and silvicultural improvement during the Agricultural Revolution. The accompanying changing attitudes to Nature are discussed in detail in Thomas (1983).

The later rejection of naturalism in the Gardenesque movement in part reflects a social environment dominated by the 'industrial spirit' and the urbanization accompanying the Industrial Revolution (see Wiener, 1981), but also in part reflects an artistic environment regarding the reproduction of Nature as neither Art nor an improvement of Nature – 'Nature "improved" was Nature destroyed' (Constable, 1822, quoted in Thomas, 1983). The love of Nature had not disappeared but rather its place and validity within a garden, even a garden of several hundred acres, had been challenged. This increasing regard for Nature in the wild therefore characterizes the Romantic movement, and is influential in the decline of Nature as a model for garden design, but an increase in the conservation of Nature as a social concern. Today these concerns are still being acted out as designers and ecologists disagree about the extent to which 'created nature' loses its authenticity.

The Open Space Movement inspired the establishment of many organizations for the provision or protection of public land for public access. The formation of the Commons Preservation Society was especially significant. This later incorporated the National Footpaths Society and became the Commons, Open Spaces and Footpath Preservation Society in 1910.

The concerns of the Commons Preservation Society was to promote land access for all. This was in contrast with some early parks which effectively precluded the working-classes (and often specifically excluded children). Land prices surrounding Birkenhead Park (dating from 1847) established a middle-class suburb and effectively contained working-class access. Despite the limited concessions of the Recreation Grounds Act of 1859, concern for the rights of the working classes (and especially children) to open-air recreation was only generally conceded in the 1870s in response to the publication of Octavia Hill's essays on urban improvement (see Hill, 1956).

NATURE CONSERVATION OR PRESERVATION?

The distinction between conservation, involving management, and preservation, involving only protection, is of course recognized as important today but the Open Space Movement was, initially at least, principally concerned with protection of the status quo. The necessity for management of grasslands and heathlands is self-evident as invasion by scrub is rapid in the absence of management. However, systems for achieving such maintenance without relying on the vagaries of agriculture were largely unaddressed, nor was there recognition of the way in which subtle changes in the quality rather than extent of grasslands could result from practices such as fertilization.

Of course, recognition of the necessity for management to maintain semi-natural plant communities was apparent to some extent in the nineteenth century, and is implicitly recognized by the Open Space Movement in endeavouring to protect commoners' rights at law. Forest improvement by the conversion of coppice to high forest, the decline in coppice management and grassland and heathland burning, cutting and grazing, and an intrusion of arbitrary aesthetic considerations during the nineteenth and twentieth centuries nevertheless resulted in changes to a system of management documented for at least the previous 700 years (Rackham, 1986).

While management operations within grassland and heathland, including grazing and burning, require relatively short-term planning and unsophisticated craft skills, woodland management requires both long-term planning and sophisticated skills. In addition, the maintenance of woodland depends on the demand for forest products, which in turn requires sophisticated craft skills. Peterken (1981) observes that during the Industrial Revolution apprentices could not be recruited to the underwood crafts in the face of competition from better wages in industry.

EPPING FOREST – 'THE NATURAL ASPECT'

As the first natural area protected primarily for amenity and conservation values, Epping Forest provides an early example of the problems of conservation management in Britain.

As a result of lobbying by the Commons Preservation Society the Epping Forest Act of 1878 abolished the rights of the Crown and transferred the freehold of the Forest to the City of London. Although the Act required the Conservators of the Forest to protect the timber and other trees, pollards, shrubs, underwood, heather, gorse, turf, and herbage growing on the Forest (see Ranson, 1978), the Conservators' view of the natural aspect of the Forest, and including the view of pollards as maimed relics of neglect, resulted in the suspension of lopping rights, and thus the cessation of a management system of pollarding and coppicing, and in the replacement of old pollards with maiden trees.

Modern surveys of the forest indicate changes since the Act, including an increase in beech (*Fagus sylvatica*) and hornbeam (*Carpinus betulus*), at the expense of oak (*Quercus robur*) and understory species including *Primula veris*, *Ruscus aculeatus* and *Polypodium vulgare*. In the absence of pollarding Rackham (1978) predicted the eventual loss of beech and inevitable colonization by silver birch (*Betula spp.*). As Rackham (1978) notes, Epping Forest was one of the first 'wild' public open spaces and the Conservators had no precedent for the establishment of management policy. The application of an ecological approach, utilizing traditional management practice, was only becoming recognized fifty years after the Act (Ranson, 1978). Trials on the reinstatement of pollarding and coppicing indicate that some reversal of these trends is possible and traditional woodland maintenance is now a common feature of work within the Forest.

The contemporary view expressing dissatisfaction with the Conservators' management of the forest immediately following the Epping Forest Act was principally concerned with the desire for a return to the Wildwood and the creation of a forest of Picturesque trees (see Burrows and Boulger, 1883). The discrepancy indicates the dominance of a Romantic perception of Nature and a misapprehension of the role of management (see Rackham, 1978). William Morris's criticism of unsympathetic management also reflects the Art and Crafts Movement's view of the relationship between Art and Nature (Vallance, 1897).

The impossibility of this objective is clear and the results were counterproductive. The problem arose out of an inability to use ecology to predict the effect of management changes even though the role of coppicing in the response of the understory was clearly observable and understood empirically. Collingwood (1903) notes in discussing coppicing at Ruskin's Brantwood, Cumbria.

This clearance is always a sad thing for the moment, when the leafy thicket is rased [*sic*] away, leaving bare earth and hacked stumps and the toppings strewn about to rot into soil; but next spring there are sure to be galaxies of primroses, if not daffodils and bluebells to follow, and foxgloves as the summer goes on; and so the kindness of nature heals the wound. Next year there are shoots from the stubs, a miniature forest which might even attract a Japanese; and as the saplings grow the flowers thin out, until in two or three seasons the children wonder why there are no primroses in the primrose-wood, and cannot believe they are gone to sleep for ten years.

These years, therefore, signify the development of a much more reverential attitude towards nature, but also a failure to recognize fully the extent to which the British countryside depended on human management. Human intervention to some extent corrupted the beauty of the picture. Hence wilderness had no place within controlled landscapes such as parks.

THE ARRIVAL OF THE GARDENESQUE STYLE

The Romantic vision of the nineteenth century focused on Nature in the wild, while within the garden, 'the reign of Nature', characteristic of the Georgian garden, was gradually eroded. Some aspects of a Romantic vision in the garden were evident in the cottage garden and in woodland gardens, such as Ruskin's garden at Brantwood but in general the Victorian period was marked by a new vision of the garden preoccupied with the formal designs, plant collecting and exotic styles collectively called the Gardenesque Movement.

The Gardenesque style was characterized by its eclecticism. The Victorian fascination with technical innovation and new introductions, together with an expanding vision of design through trade and a colonial empire, when blended with established traditions resulted in a pastiche. The return of formal areas, loosely derived from the Italian villa gardens, was notable as the best means of integrating and accommodating the exotics gathered from around the world.

Economics again placed a limitation on the extent of the style. On most estates the survival of the English landscape park was rarely in question. However, the integrity of the park was often eroded by the establishment of arboreta and plantations.

The influence of John Claudius Loudon (1783–1843) on Victorian horticulture is especially significant and Loudon's publications dominate the period. Loudon was influenced by Quatremere de Quincy's thesis that gardens in the Picturesque style were indistinguishable from wild Nature, and that 'what pretends to be an image of nature is nothing more nor less than nature herself' (Quatremere de Quincy, 1837, quoted in Turner 1982). It is worth contrasting this feeling with modern debates about the 'validity' of habitat creation schemes.

Loudon therefore introduced the term Gardenesque in direct opposition to Picturesque, to define a planting style developed without reference to Nature (Loudon, 1834). Loudon considers;

> There is not a single writer, as far as we are aware, from Shenstone to Knight, Price, and Gilpin, who does not adopt the imitation of nature as a principle, and who has not, at the same time, forgotten, or failed to see that, in so far as landscape-gardening is to be considered one of the fine arts, the principle of imitation of nature must be rendered subordinate to that of the recognition of Art. . . . henceforth it may be considered as an established principle, that there can be no landscape gardening in the natural style, where only indigenous trees and shrubs are used. Where no foreign trees are to be obtained, recourse must be had to the geometrical manner of disposing of the local ones.

It is a sign of how far the wheel has turned that such a statement would today be seen as lunatic heresy by most ecologically minded designers. However, in its purest form the ideals of the Gardenesque movement are no different from those of highly respected modern designers such as Preben Jakobsen who uses plant material from all over the world in artistic and often formal ways. It is a result of a degeneration of the style in private gardens, and of the gradual piecemeal erosion of Victorian features in local authority parks that makes us think today that Gardenesque is synonymous with a style of garden layout characterized by a lack of artistic unity.

THE ARTS AND CRAFTS MOVEMENT

Despite moving from centre stage, principles of natural design did not completely disappear from gardens but were kept alive largely within a movement of arguably eccentric visionaries collectively termed the Arts and Craft Movement. Their rejection of the 'industrial spirit' is embodied in a wish to return to the integration of design and craft.

The philosophies of John Ruskin (1819–1900) and William Morris (1834–96) both profoundly influenced the development of the Arts and Crafts Movement and the Open Space Movement. Both expressed concern for the relationship between Art, Nature and society. While Ruskin's views and Ruskin's own woodland garden at Brantwood in the Lake District indicate a Romantic vision of Nature and a naturalistic approach to garden design (see Collingwood, 1903), Morris's idealization of medieval traditions and values required a return to enclosed architectural spaces, reminiscent of the English Tudor garden and involving a re-assessment of the integration of man and Nature.

The showy displays characterizing contemporary Victorian carpet bedding illustrate a movement away from both Nature and tradition, and were an anathema to Ruskin and to Morris:

Many plants which are curiosities only, which Nature meant to be grotesque, not beautiful, and which are generally the growth of hot countries, where things sprout over quick and rank. Take note that the strangest of these come from the jungle and the tropical waste, from places where man is not at home but is an intruder, an enemy (Morris, in Vallance, 1897).

The rejection of both the 'naturalness' of the English landscape and Picturesque styles and the 'unnatural' Gardenesque led to varying reactions. Despite the return to 'architectural' gardens, an important theme within these was the development of informal planting styles derived from the Romantic traditions of the English cottage garden. This style characterizes plantsmen and plantswomen associated with the Arts and Crafts Movement, the two most influential of whom must be William Robinson (1838–1935) and Gertrude Jekyll (1843–1932).

WILLIAM ROBINSON

The publications of Robinson, and of Gertrude Jekyll were as influential on late Victorian and Edwardian garden design as Loudon's on early and mid-Victorian garden design. In particular the publication in 1870 of *The Wild Garden* presented the crystallization of a new school of design thought. The use of guiding principles drawn from Nature and Art rather than the attempt to recreate specific patterns from Nature illustrates a new perception of Nature as primarily a process which leads to a pattern; this was a crucial leap in understanding which foreshadows much of the subsequent development of ecological landscapes.

The term 'ecology' was coined in 1850 and hardly recognized as a distinct branch of science when Robinson's *The Wild Garden* was published in 1870. While Robinson's approach to the wild garden was largely intuitive, he was able to draw on his own observations from extensive travel through natural and semi-natural areas in Europe and North America.

Robinson encouraged the placing of perfectly hardy exotic plants under conditions where they will thrive without further care. While native species are included for beauty and rarity, Robinson made no attempt to recreate the native plant communities with which he was familiar, preferring to establish new combinations of species.

This was no pretence to be an exercise in conservation. He was keen to stress that the life strategies of many wild perennials from northern and temperate regions made them ideal for naturalization here. Robinson was not alone in his thinking. In a book entitled *Flower Fields of Alpine Switzerland*, published in 1911, G. Flemwell devoted an entire chapter to the creation of alpine fields in English countryside (Crozier, 1992). Reginald Farrer, the plantsman and explorer, combined the picturesque with the native flowers of other countries, through his naturalistic approach to alpine gardening.

Apart from his romantic, overzealous and sometimes rather vague approach to writing, Robinson's ideals suggest a much more holistic approach to planting than many of his contemporaries. On his own estate at Gravetye Manor in Sussex, his garden extended to the hedges, woodlands and meadows of the surrounding countryside, his aim being to lift the passerby's soul with enriched visions of natural beauty (Robinson, 1894).

In addition to species already in cultivation, Robinson considered the flora of the whole northern world eligible for naturalization:

the Roman ruin – home of many flowers, the mountains and prairies of the New World, the woods and meadows of all the great mountains of Europe; from Greece and Italy and Spain, from the hills of Asia Minor; from the alpine regions of the great continents – in a word, from almost every interesting region the traveller may bring seeds or plants, and establish near his home living souvenirs of the countries he has visited.

A dynamic quality in the compositions is essential in Robinson's view:

If in a spot where a wide carpet of grass spreads out in the sheltered bay of a plantation, there be dotted blue Appenine Anemones, any Snowdrops, the Snowflake, Crocuses in variety, Scillas, Grape Hyacinths, many Narcissi, the Wood Anemone, and any other Spring flowers, liking the soil, we should have a picture of vernal beauty, the flowers relieved by grass, and the whole devoid of man's weakness for tracing wallpaper patterns where everything should be varied and changeful.

Species are arranged in natural patterns and drifts:

If the Wild Garden is to be carried out on the old dotting principle of the herbaceous border, its charming effects cannot be realized. To do it rightly we must group and mass as Nature does (Robinson, 1894).

While the English Landscape and Picturesque movements were concerned with idealized Classical landscapes or an ideal illustrated by 'landskip' paintings suggesting a static view of landscape design and Nature, Robinson had a dynamic view of Nature as a process. The principles embodied in the wild garden may therefore reasonably be considered as the genesis of a 'process-oriented' ecological approach, where a natural style was more concerned with species and population dynamics rather than just form and picture, but with inevitably the patterns in the landscape coming to reflect the process.

Indeed Robinson (1894) rejected any revival of the English landscape movement:

worrying Nature into a resemblance of Claude. The wild garden and the woodland garden were intended to retain a faithfulness to the landscape setting, creating a harmony between Nature and the garden, while landscape gardening was seen as contrived, and creating only an illusion of Nature which lacks any dynamism.

Some of these arguments are still levied at many of the designs of today's professional landscape architects, particularly by the ecological parks lobby.

However, as subtle as they were, to modern eyes these early attempts look as though the emphasis was much more on the 'garden' than on the wild. This is because Robinson lacked the perspective of the conservation ethic which today underpins the imperative to use native species, and to see more beauty in our own flora than in similar but slightly more showy exotics. This difference in perception can seem so incongruous today that many of the other sound ecological principles that Robinson developed tend to be overlooked.

For example, Robinson was aware of the relative competitive ability of different species:

Such plants as Heracleum, Willow Herb, and many others, which not only win, but destroy all their fellows, in the struggle for life, should be planted only in outlying positions, islands, hedges, and small bits of isolated wood or copse, where their effects may be seen in due season, and where they might ramble without destroying.

The Wild Garden also stresses the relationship between environment and plant performance in selecting species for a site. Robinson considers water availability, light levels, soil group and fertility and shelter in general terms to relate environment to naturalization. He hardly considers modification of the environment as species are supposed to survive and naturalize without cultivation. Establishment of certain species in the wild garden may nevertheless necessitate soil preparation, as with heather beds, planted in large masses in well-dug ground, but

once established (left alone, and allowed) to grow together in their own way ... As to soil, the best way is to avoid the trouble of preparing it; the point is to adapt the plant to the soil – in peaty places to place plants that thrive in peat, in clay soils those that thrive in clays, and so on (Robinson, 1894).

Robinson also puts forward the opportunities for reducing maintenance costs in support of the wild garden. The management principle for the wild garden in grassland or wood-pasture was often for a single hay-cut in midsummer:

Mowing the grass once a fortnight in pleasure grounds, as now practised, is a costly mistake. We want shaven carpets of grass here and there, but what nonsense it is to shave it as often as foolish men shave their faces! There are indeed places where they boast of mowing forty acres! Who would not rather see the waving grass with countless flowers than a close surface without a blossom? Think of the labour wasted in this ridiculous work of cutting the heads off flowers and grass. Let much of the grass grow till fit to cut for hay, and we may enjoy in it a world of lovely flowers that will blossom and perfect their growth before hay time; some who have carried out the ideas of this book have waving lawns of feathery grass where they used to shave the grass every ten days; a cloud of flowers where a daisy was not let peep (Robinson, 1894).

Robinson also considered control of slugs and snails unnecessary as

the swarming plants of the woods and copses exist in spite of the slugs.

In this he could be said to have failed to appreciate the degree to which the predators were influencing which plants were growing in the woods, or rather which plants were not growing, but the principle of selecting plants to match environmental pressures is sound.

EXPLOITATION OF ECOLOGICAL ADAPTATION IN THE WILD GARDEN

Two principles are apparent in the use of plants in the wild garden. Firstly, the use of transplants, especially bulbs to confer a competitive advantage at establishment, allowing them to succeed and establish where seedlings would not survive, and secondly, the selection of plants appropriate to generalized habitats or management regimes. On limiting habitats in particular (such as on dry and gravely soil in Robinson's classification), plants appropriate to specific habitats are necessary.

Robinson uses an early form of a habitat classification for selecting hardy exotic plants for the wild garden. The classes in Table 3.1 reflect habitat preferences or functional attributes.

In more specific ways the success of individual species is impossible to predict and Robinson's own experience suggests that development of the wild garden was largely trial and error. Although analysis of a species' autecology may assist in predicting success in cultivation, the difficulty of isolating the principal factors determining the natural distribution limits this approach. Such limitations were clear to Robinson (1900):

> Then, as regards the soil and natural habitats of plants, there is no doubt that it is useful to know where they come from, whether plains, valleys, or rocks, and what soil they grow on; but it is a knowledge that may sometimes mislead, because rainfall and elevation and other causes may lead us to suppose results due to soil which are really owing to accident of position. Many of the beautiful plants of the mountains of the East, such as Aubretia, and a number of rock plants which grow in any soil, would do no better if we tried to imitate their actual conditions of life in their native habitats, which are often absolutely different from the soils of our lowland gardens in which many rock plants thrive and endure for years.

Table 3.1 *Classification of environments and species for plant selection from* The Wild Garden

---

a. A selection of plants for naturalization in places with dwarf vegetation, on bare banks, and in poorish soil.
b. Plants of vigorous habit for the wild garden.
c. Plants for hedge-banks and like places.
d. Plants for naturalization beneath trees on lawns.
e. Plants for very moist rich soils.
f. Plants suited for peat soil.
g. Plants suited for calcareous soil.
h. Plants suited for dry and gravely soil.
i. Selection of plants for growing on old walls, ruins, or rocky slopes.
j. List of plants for naturalization in lawns and other grassy places.
k. '. . . among the most rabbit-proof plants'.

Source: Robinson (1894).

In conclusion, *The Wild Garden* illustrates an understanding of the importance of Nature as a process. The use of ecological processes, including the use of dominance in shrub-beds and of naturalization in the wild garden, indicates a new vision of the relationship between design and management.

GERTRUDE JEKYLL AND THE WOODLAND GARDEN

It was largely Gertrude Jekyll who was responsible for firming up many of Robinson's vague concepts for design and plant association (Bisgrove, 1992). The woodlands and glades which Jekyll designed combined ecological principles with an artistic eye for colour, and an appreciation of space. Jekyll's attitude to the wild garden is considered, and contrasts with Robinson's unbridled enthusiasm.

In particular Jekyll felt concern about the degree to which exotic plants could be integrated into a naturalistic design before it begins to lose meaning, although it is clear that she refers to poor implementations of the style when, in *Wood and Garden* (1899), she writes,

> Even the better ways of gardening do not wholly escape the debasing influence of fashion. Wild gardening is a delightful, and in good hands a most desirable, pursuit, but no kind of gardening is so difficult to do well, or is so full of pitfalls and of paths of peril. Because it has in some measure become fashionable, and because it is understood to mean the planting of exotics in wild places, unthinking people rush to the conclusion that they can put any garden plants into any wild places, and that that is wild gardening. I have seen woody places that were already perfect with their own simple charm just muddled and spoilt by a reckless planting of garden refuse, and heathy hillsides already sufficiently and beautifully clothed with native vegetation made to look lamentably silly by the planting of a nurseryman's mixed lot of exotic Conifers.

While borrowing freely from Nature, the composition in Jekyll's woodland garden is neither a reflection, nor an idealized view of Nature. In this sense it is distinct from the wild garden. Jekyll acknowledges this borrowing,

> And so it comes about that those of us who feel and understand in this way do not exactly attempt to imitate Nature in our gardens, but try to become well acquainted with her moods and ways, and then discriminate in our borrowing, and so interpret her methods as best we may to the making of our garden-pictures.

Development of the ecological style in the twentieth century

From 1930 onwards the new ideas of naturalistic garden design became subsumed into the strong and diverse garden tradition of the country. The days when private clients had the wealth or area of land to commission large garden schemes were already numbered and new projects took on more modest proportions. In public parks and gardens Victorian formality reigned relatively unchallenged, and any ideas of naturalism were confined mainly to landscape park style layouts, woodland walks, and occasionally rockeries.

All this was to change after the Second World War, when a plethora of new policies and concepts paved the way for extensive ecological planting. This was accompanied by rapid advances in mechanization, allowing the management of much larger areas of land. During this time modern attitudes to, and perceptions of, Nature resulted in a more scientific interpretation of a natural style.

While the early naturalistic styles primarily recognized a pattern, and the wild garden recognized a process, modern ecological approaches reflect both aspects. At its best the modern ecological approach is concerned with the re-creation of functioning systems. Nevertheless the vision of what types of plants are acceptable in 'natural' landscapes has also changed in many ways. The perception of a need for 'improvement of nature', characterizing both the Georgian garden and the wild garden, has become much weaker and native plants are given pre-eminence in most, but certainly not all, manifestations of ecological planting. The wild garden looked for a natural pattern which was predominantly beautiful; today we put higher priority on authenticity of pattern.

The developments of the style in this century owe much to the influence of ideas from Holland and Germany, and also from the United States of America. The origin of these developments will be looked at before we look again at the recent implementation of ecological plantings in Britain.

1. Germany

Germany has almost certainly had one of the strongest traditions of natural landscaping in Europe, and through a few prominent figures in the field has dominated new thought. Ecological styles have become the over-riding theme in most contemporary landscapes in the country, and the ideal of encouraging local wildlife is sometimes pursued with such enthusiasm that there hardly seems to be room to consider the place for people. In some cases strict control is imposed over the species that could be used in landscape schemes, such that ecological styles are enforced.

One of the earliest roots of such a style can be seen in 1887 when Gamboeck's book *The Interpretation of Nature in the Garden in Theory and Practice* put forward ideas of nativism with a clear appreciation of phytosociology and ecology (Wittke, 1994), principles which had not been formally developed at the time.

In 1906, Willy Lange designed his own garden under the influence of new scientific achievements in the world of phytosociology and botanical geography, using their inspiration to design vegetative pictures and associations (Hottentrèger, 1992). Yet Lange's involvement introduced a sinister edge to the movement. German heath and German forest became the epitome of what was desirable in German landscape design, and this led to

8 In Berlin secondary woodland that developed on abandoned urban sites became of great interest to ecologists.

frighteningly nationalistic and racist ideologies at the time of the Third Reich, casting a shadow over the profession (Hottentrèger, 1992).

Lange's design ideology suggested that it was necessary to match the plant with its preferred ecological requirements and plant associations. Copying natural patterns was seen as less important than copying processes, but nature could also be enriched by human choices and manipulation since it was this which could transform a beautiful picture into what was considered a work of art. Plant associations could be created which included 'foreign' as well as native species as long as the plants were from compatible habitats (Wolschke-Bulmahn and Groning, 1994).

In some ways Lange's views would be seen as being naive today. He was concerned with putting plants in positions where 'they would like to grow'. However species distribution is driven primarily by competitive exclusion and plants rarely occupy a niche which provides their physiologically optimum conditions – most things therefore grow at the edges of their tolerances. Nevertheless his attitudes would be familiar to many people today, and they are particularly important for recognizing that process and pattern are both elements that need to be considered.

Today landscape planning policy throughout Germany is very supportive of ecology and vernacular planting styles. The rigorous surveys carried out by landscape planners have been instrumental in the formulation of regional plant lists. Munich, like other German cities, is well known for its strong enforcement of the ecological approach. Lists of plants which are native and naturalized in that area are produced and have to be followed where planning permission may be required. Even where two or more family houses are to be built, a separate freespace plan (Freiraumplan) must be produced, showing that development will be accompanied by enough trees, a high percentage of which must be native. Only in certain cases, such as private gardens, entrance areas and courtyards, where there is distinct isolation from wider nature, may exotic species be permitted.

Like many other German cities, Munich is also gradually adopting methods for changing the type of planting in streetscapes. The most extreme and dramatic development in Germany is arguably that of the encouragement and tolerance of 'spontaneous vegetation', i.e. those species that arise on a piece of land which is left without any planting. In Stuttgart, for example, blocks of roadside verge which were once ground cover planting are now composed of colonies of grasses and wild herbs that have established themselves (Koch, 1995). Inevitably these communities, at least initially, are dominated by those common and aggressive perennials characteristic of disturbed land, in other words 'weeds' such as *Rumex* and *Cirsium*. At Bonn, the Bundesforschungsanstalt fur Naturschutz und Landschaftsokologie accepts spontaneous colonization of site-works surrounding building foundations for the landscape.

This shows the ultimate evolution of the adjustment of the relationship between man and Nature which began in the 1700s. With an acceptance of spontaneous vegetation people have the perspective that everything Nature does is somehow beautiful, and indeed the landscape is dignified and made more desirable by the very absence of human intervention to 'perfect it'.

THE USE OF NON-NATIVES

In contrast to the strong native plant ethic that dominates much public landscape in Germany, there has also been an interesting and strong subtheme exploring the use of non-natives in ecological approaches. We have seen that an important theme in the development of design approaches has been to explore the processes of plant response to its environment and ecological relationships between species rather than to put value judgements on the content of the communities. In some ways these designs are more 'valid' than the Landscape Movement patterns which created a superficial appearance of naturalness but in fact relied on static designs which were dominated by human influence.

When the German government sent the great architect Herman Muthesius to London in 1900, he returned excited at the way in which the house could be extended into the midst of nature (Joyce, 1989). This was not the nature of Gamboeck and Lange, but a romantic and structured interpretation using lush plantings of non-natives, as well as natives, often within an architectural framework.

Not only did this influence the Bauhaus, but it also initiated a fervent proliferation of breeding and selection in the perennial world, improving on native species and providing the material required for the garden rooms of the day (Joyce, 1989). The list of great nurserymen is extensive, but Karl

Foerster stands out as Germany's guiding light in these early years. Not only did he lead in the field of hardy herbaceous perennials, but during his life he influenced garden design through his partnership with Hermann Mattern and Herta Hammerbacher (Hottentrèger, 1992).

Foerster, who was deeply opposed to the nationalist ideals of Willy Lange and his associates (van Groeningen, unpublished), was throughout his life an inspiration to a new generation of enthusiasts, notably Richard Hansen. Post-war, he continued to write, and students of landscape design made pilgrimages to his nursery. Foerster had, however, become somewhat stranded behind the Iron Curtain, and though this did not entirely inhibit his work, the torch was handed over to Richard Hansen who began his career at Weihenstephan, Munich's Technical University, in 1947 (Wittke, 1994). His interest was in harmonizing artistic ideals with the natural habitat requirements of plants. The garden he created at Weihenstephan still has self-sustaining plantings dating back to the 1947–54 period when he began (Wittke, 1994). This style, breaking down the divisions between formal and wild, ornamental and native, has resulted in naturalistic gardens and exotic meadows of striking beauty and appeal (von Schoenaich and Rees, 1994). In Germany the generations of landscape architects educated during the last 40–50 years have been strongly influenced by his pioneering work and this is demonstrated by the popularity of the approach among professionals. Hansen has many distinguished and well-respected followers, such as Rosemary Weisse and Urs Walser, all of whom have formulated their own interpretations based on his work.

Figure 3.1 Example of Hansen's approach to ecological planting (Hansen and Stahl, 1993).

Hansen examined the life strategies of individual species and then trialed

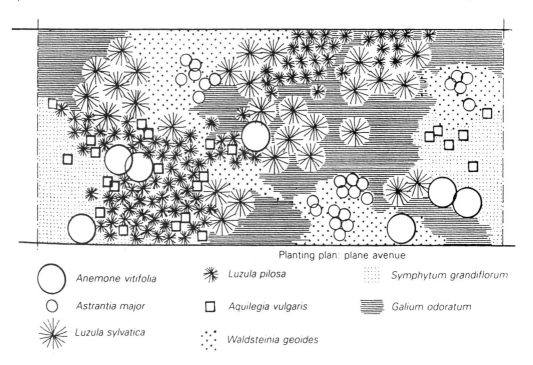

Planting plan: plane avenue

○ Anemone vitifolia   ✳ Luzula pilosa   ⬚ Symphytum grandiflorum

○ Astrantia major   ☐ Aquilegia vulgaris   ≡ Galium odoratum

✳ Luzula sylvatica   ∴ Waldsteinia geoides

seemingly appropriate groupings. Though a native planting contains plants which are normally found together in nature, Hansen's perennial planting is made up of plants which may only be linked by their abiotic or climactic requirements, and even then these may be manipulated to control their behaviour. For example, nature has shown us that species such as the yellow globe flower (*Trollius europaeus*) and *Polygonum bistorta Superbum* can form a stable association in damp European mountain meadows (Chatto, 1989), but what interactions might one expect when a Mediterranean species such as *Iris unguicularis* is grown in close association with a Californian species of lupin? Plants may also exhibit very different sociability when, for example, the climate, degree of shade or substrate is altered.

With so many possibilities, the scope for research would appear limitless and the results difficult to assess quantitatively. However, Hansen believes that enough pieces of the ecological jigsaw are in place to formulate some preliminary principles. The aim has not been to create a set of hard and fast rules, or to become a slave to ecology, but simply to suggest and demonstrate a sound basis for successful, sustainable and attractive plantings. An example of the style is shown in Figure 3.1.

Plantings of the Hansen school rely strongly on the beauty of development found in perennials throughout the season, creating an ever-changing sequence of pictures. In design, aesthetic goals require that consideration is given to selecting species which maximize flower display across the growth window before the summer hay cut (Hitchmough, 1994c). Extending the display into the latter parts of the year can be a problem for the designer if only the native flora is used, since many British natives have completed their flowering by this time (Kingsbury, 1994).

Groupings are also allowed to vary annually via natural methods of reproduction. Here again, plant life strategies play an important part in the design, some species persisting and spreading vegetatively for some years and other short-lived perennials regenerating spontaneously from seed. As well as creating attractive variation, these interactions are essential in allowing plantings to respond to changes in surrounding conditions. For example at Weihenstephan woodland edge plantings have successfully adapted to increasing shade and woodland conditions without significant human intervention (Hansen and Stahl, 1993).

While interaction within a community group is acceptable, there is also the possibility of invasion of weeds from outside sources. Most of these, particularly annuals, are tolerated, the density and informality of the style reducing the impact of any alien species. Pernicious weeds are usually treated very seriously indeed before planting. Since herbicides are not allowed in Germany, it is not unheard of either to hand weed an area, replace the topsoil, or sterilize the whole area using steam. The latter treatment has caused almost as much controversy as Hansen's acceptance of perennial weed species such as ground elder in established plantings, his solution being to plant something equally competitive and let them fight it out.

Hansen's ideal could therefore be seen as a vastly more sophisticated distillation of the ideas embodied in William Robinson's writings. By many

Box 3.1 Physiological and ecological species requirements

In a complex community where there is less latitude for deliberate control and management, plants must compete on a much more equal basis with their native neighbours. This requires a detailed understanding of ecological fit between planting site and the plant itself (Hitchmough, 1994c). While it is relatively easy to assess the optimum conditions for a species in isolation (the physiological response), once subjected to competition it may be forced to occupy a niche at the extremes of its tolerance the ecological niche.

Ellenberg (1988) demonstrated these issues clearly with regard to the distribution of tree species across central Europe relative to soil acidity and moisture levels. Many trees are found in environments which are at the very edge of their tolerances and certainly outside of their optimum growth conditions (see Figure 3.2).

The broad-hatched area shows the physiological range of tolerance of each species. The fine-hatched

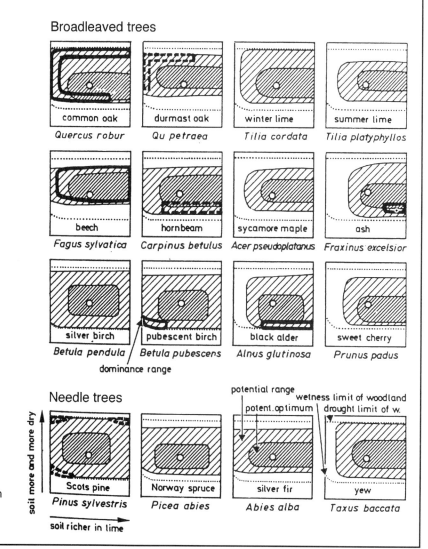

Figure 3.2 The effects of moisture and soil acidity on the growth of tree species in Central Europe (Ellenberg, 1988).

Figure 3.3 Ellenberg's (1988) ecogram showing the resulting pattern of dominance of tree species in woodlands in Central Europe, depending on the response to soil moisture and acidity. The larger the type, the more important the species is in woodlands undisturbed by man.

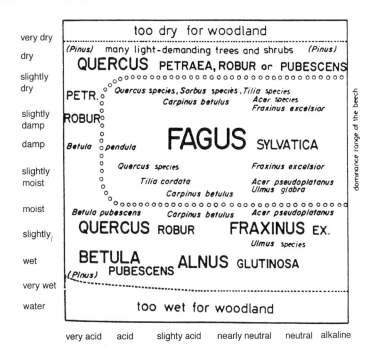

area shows the physiological optimum of each species. The dark borders show the typical ecological affinity of the species, i.e. the circumstances where it is normally found. A solid line denotes that the species achieves dominance under these conditions, a broken line denotes that it is a co-dominant.

It is obvious that most tree species are relegated by competition to conditions which are far from optimum for their growth (see Figure 3.3).

Although establishment and survival in cultivation reflect environmental tolerances, competitive interference and husbandry inputs, the usual horticultural classifications for genotype reflect morphology, phenology and environmental tolerances. Sometimes (or even usually) morphology and phenology override considerations for environmental tolerances in selecting species for decorative plantings, and an increase in husbandry (as site preparation, management or maintenance) allows the species to survive.

Thomas (1990) considers the selection of plants according to environmental tolerance a significant style in modern garden design, and distinguishes 'ecological gardening' as studying the needs of each plant and ensuring that it is as nearly suited to the prevailing conditions as possible.

A distinction between the ecological amplitude of species within a natural distribution, and the environmental tolerances of species in cultivation presents difficulties in the use of autecological data. The distinction reflects the complex of environmental, biogeographical (including interspecific competition) and historical factors determining a natural distribution.

Hansen and Stahl (1993) present an example of a comprehensive systematic classification of species for ecological gardening. While the natural habitat is inadequate to characterize environmental tolerances and competitive strategies in cultivation, the classification provides a significant practical contribution to ecological gardening. By establishing species in environments similar to natural habitats, Hansen and Stahl (1993) aim to establish attractive artificial plant communities and reduce maintenance. All efforts and the correct choice are rewarded, when the perennials develop and spread. That means they are able to retain their new position in the garden by their own efforts rejuvenating and colonizing.

Hansen has structured his findings into different garden habitats or *lebensbereich* (literally translated as living spaces) in which perennials may be planted according to their wild nature. These are:

1. Woodland,
2. Woodland Edge,
3. Open Ground,
4. Rock Garden,
5. Border,
6. Marshland and Water's Edge,
7. Water.

Under each heading can be found a number of subheadings which further refine the choice of species according to increasingly specific criteria. Plant selection was an important aspect of Hansen's work, stemming directly from Foerster's exhaustive research. Only species and cultivars suitable in terms of growth habit, durability, fertility and ease of maintenance in that particular situation are included in the lists. The lists can be used in a similar way to a key, the resulting information being a selection of perennials ideally suited to a specific habitat (Von Schoenaich, 1994) and to the formulation of ecologically sensitive plantings.

Though these plants may have similar origins and requirements, they will not form a stable and long-lived community together unless laid out according to their strategies for coexistence. To assess the dynamics of different associations would clearly be a task of monumental proportions, and while Hansen's book goes some way towards establishing a basis for grouping, the trial gardens at Weihenstephan remain the most extensive demonstration of phytosociology among cultivated perennials.

definitions his approach could be called 'ecological'. Nevertheless for many traditionally minded urban conservationists, the very idea of promoting non-natives in meadow design would be seen as almost shocking.

2. Holland

In Holland as in Germany, much ecological planting design has had a focus on native species. In the early days of the twentieth century, teacher and biologist Jaques P. Thijsse began to experiment with the idea of an instructive landscape garden, partly in response to the rapidly disappearing countryside around cities such as Amsterdam, and partly because he believed that existing parks failed to demonstrate the significance of natural beauty (Ruff, 1987; Joyce, 1989).

The first garden, Thijsse Hof, opened in 1925 and contained woodland, heath, dune and water habitats (Joyce, 1989). At the same time the Amsterdam Bos was created, a 400 ha native woodland designed specifically for the urban public (Goode and Smart, 1983). By the late 1930s the idea had taken root and further development saw the foundation of the Heempark movement in Holland (Joyce, 1989). The first, Thijssepark, was the brainchild of Chris Broerse (Hayter, 1995) and opened in 1940 in Amstelveen near Amsterdam. The aim was not to mimic nature, but to utilize the charm of wild species in an artistic setting, again with echoes of the perfected nature of the English Landscape movement. Whereas the Amsterdam Bos is today criticized for its lack of diversity and detail (Tregay, 1986), Thijssepark has developed into a tremendously successful, varied and beautiful landscape (Hayter, 1995).

A number of the ecological landscapes in Holland had the primary objective of introducing Nature into the urban environment, and while creating the best of all possible recreational and aesthetic values, there was a high priority on encouraging the participation of people.

Community involvement with landscape design and construction characterizes developments at The Kennedylaan, Heerenveen and the Gillis Estate, Buitenhof, Delft. Le Roi's creation of an 'alternative landscape' at The Kennedylaan, Heerenveen integrated the environmental and social concerns of the 1960s and 1970s. Le Roi argued that public open space should be returned to the public for the creation of nature reserves and 'People's Gardens' and for small-scale food production. He considered that the architects and planners lacked the necessary vision and had lost touch with the people for whom they planned and the land they managed (Le Roi, 1973, quoted in Ruff, 1987).

In rejecting landscape planning Le Roi relied on the use of a diverse range of plants, and the development of spontaneous plant communities. The role of the community in elaborating the design and in determining management and maintenance was supposed to result in a dynamic landscape. However, problems resulting from the ecologically naive selection of species and a diminishing community involvement have marred the development at The Kennedylaan.

After the experience at The Kennedylaan, Le Roi worked at Lewenborg, a new residential development in Gronigen. Ruff (1987) observes:

Lewenborg is possibly one of the most exciting projects to come out of the 1970's and could prove to have a profound influence on the future of green space planning and management. At a time of less state involvement, community responsibility for the greenspace is an attractive alternative.

The Gillis Estate in Buitenhof, Delft, was begun in 1968 and

finally established the distinction between the social landscape and the gardenesque park (Ruff, 1987).

H. Bos, the Director of Parks in Delft, considered the use of the countryside for recreation (especially play) and favoured the dynamic and spontaneous attributes of Nature that were to be included in housing developments. The design and management of areas within the Gillis Estate became the responsibility of the community, with the parks authority providing support. Species selection was primarily concerned with providing a dynamic and spontaneous environment, rather than a stable and diverse environment (Ruff, 1987).

Another 'social' value that may arise from ecological style designs puts a focus on education. In Holland Heemparks (and other instructive native plant gardens) and nature gardens present varying balances between ecological, design and social objectives. Habitat construction to demonstrate native plant communities, as at, for example, Madestein, Den Haag, Westerpark, Zoetermeer and Presikhaat, Arnhem, present a laboratory for ecological and horticultural research.

Another designer of great interest is Dr Gerd Londo. In his work in Heemparks and nature gardens he prepares the site and soil in complex ways which produce an environmental palette onto which the design is painted by Nature through the processes of natural colonization. Although the site preparation can be said to be highly artificial, the fine detail and process of the design is purely natural and in some ways therefore akin to spontaneous revegetation of urban wastelands and disturbed sites.

As with Germany, most of the work in Holland has been pre-occupied with the use of native species but a non-native school also exists. In the 1970s, Henk Gerritsen and Anton Schleppers began to combine wild and exotic species according to phytosociological principles, achieving strikingly free and spontaneous plantings (Koningen and Leopold, 1992). The flood of new cultivars from nurseries was utilized in loosely but deliberately composed plant combinations, and seedheads and dead stalks were allowed to remain throughout the winter. Their compositional style can be seen at the Priona Gardens in Schuinesloot, Holland (Koningen and Leopold, 1992).

Today Ton der Linden, in a way very similar to Gertrude Jekyll, has refined earlier ideas, perceiving naturalness not so much in an ecological, as in a pictorial sense. An accomplished painter, he is said to achieve an almost unknown quality through his spontaneous, yet elaborately conceived perennial plantings (Koningen and Leopold, 1992).

The rise in interest in exotic and ornamental solutions to landscape design, while still retaining some of the ecological understanding and methodology developed over the previous decades, presents an interesting twist, and one that provides many social benefits. Despite the enthusiasm of the professionals and generally overriding commitment to one style, a large proportion of the public remain faithful to more traditional gardens in their own plots.

Many people live in a city because they want an 'urbane' experience – the idea of walking into a landscape that gives a complete rural experience has not proved universally popular and for some it is frightening, alienating or at least just uninspiring. Even among some of the most celebrated examples of ecological design in Dutch housing areas, corners are now being converted to more traditional gardenesque elements.

3. United States of America

While in Europe the crisis between space for human development and the countryside was acute, this was not the case in the USA. The freedom of a new canvas on which to work and the vast scale of the landscape provoked a

9 A naturalistic woodland and wetland community established within the framework of an urban housing estate at Bijlmermeer in Amsterdam.

desire to exercise control over the overwhelming wilderness, and formality became closely allied with success and affluence. Eighteenth- and early-nineteenth-century gardens adopted the elaborate layouts of English, French and Italian gardens from previous eras (Griswold and Woller, 1991), often resulting in grossly opulent pastiches created in the name of good taste. The influence of Robinson and Jekyll had reached America, affecting the work of blossoming designers such as Beatrix Farrand (McPeck, 1989), but the gardens remained heavily structured and costly to maintain.

As the landscape architecture profession emerged between 1850 and 1900 so too did a new naturalistic or landscape style of design (Tishler, 1989). When Calvert Vaux and Frederick Law Olmsted were commissioned to design parks in a number of American cities, it was not an Italianate, but a pseudo-English Park style which they thought most appropriate (Joyce, 1989). Casual, sweeping informality in many respects echoed the freedom and openness of the American landscape; the style was visually modelled on natural landscapes, but there was no attempt to look for native integrity in the species used (Cramer, 1993).

Despite the early fascination with imported styles, in the New World the combination of response to a new environment, a search for identity and a rejection of the European gardening tradition led to a much earlier application of a scientifically ecological approach. The work of Danish-born landscape architect Jens Jensen, who pioneered the planting of native trees, shrubs and flowers was instrumental in the founding of the Prairie School of design, encapsulated by the architecture of Frank Lloyd Wright and Richard Neutra (Joyce, 1989). By 1905 in Garfield Park, Chicago, Jensen was constructing a public conservatory with re-creations of the prairie plant communities in various stages of geological development (Eaton, 1964). One of Jensen's finest surviving works, the Lincoln Memorial Garden in Springfield, Illinois, was begun in 1933 (Christy, 1989). Here a network of lanes divides a series of meadows, each providing a home to a single species or natural association. Like Thijsse in Holland and Lange in Germany, he wisely noted that while you cannot hope to copy nature you can, by careful observation, learn its motives and its aesthetic essence using these to create successful designs (Morrison, 1989).

All this occurred at the turn of the century, a time when enormous expanses of wilderness landscape were being ploughed up for agricultural use. For example, in Iowa, 30 million acres of perennial prairie were lost between 1850 and 1930 (Thompson, 1992). Jensen soon came to be seen as a landscape restorationist as well as a landscape architect, many of his landscapes being hard to distinguish from the real thing. This established a native ethic for the naturalistic school which has a strong following up to the present day. Parallel work involved Aldo Leopold at the Wisconsin-Madison Arboretum who was trying to re-establish working models of prairie ecosystems (Eaton, 1964; Jordan, 1989). The ecological understanding of many prairie species is particularly well developed due to prairie reconstruction research (Thompson, 1992) and the concept of urban prairies as a landscape treatment is now well developed in the States (Wilson, 1992).

Between 1930 and 1970 modernism and the functional, easy-to-maintain, Californian style took over, but homeowners quickly grew weary of low-maintenance gardens (Johnson, 1989). The environmental movement of the 1960s and '70s evoked an interest in the aesthetic pleasures of perennial gardens using ornamental grasses and native flowers. This has been seen as something of a breakthrough, being the first consistent departure from classical and European models (Johnson, 1989). (Of course the richness of the natural flora in the USA, compared to the relatively subtle, or even depauperate, UK vegetation influences the potential social acceptance of natural landscaping enormously. The wildflower trails promoted by Ladybird Johnson in Texas can sometimes echo the worst excesses of gardenesque half-hardy-annual bedding; they even contain many of the same species in roughly the same density and with similar tendency to form 'a riot of colour'.)

Such a strong allegiance to native planting, conservation and restoration has resulted in a very black or white, nature or artifice view of planting and the middle-ground ideas of planting non-native perennials among natives in a dynamic framework has yet to be widely explored or accepted. There are some notable exceptions, such as Jim Wilson who has promoted the establishment of many types of native community, particularly prairie, and freely advocates their enrichment with non-natives to prolong flowering season, prevent untidiness and generally maintain their attractiveness.

Also significant are Wolfgang Oehme and James van Sweden, who have a practice based in Washington DC and have been credited with returning the garden ethic to the public landscape (Oehme, van Sweden and Frey 1991). Oehme and van Sweden follow Karl Foerster's personal principles closely, using bold brushstrokes of plants in opposing and complementary colours (van Groeningen, 1994). Dramatic grasses are used as emergent, dominant elements, which hold the tension of the scheme; nevertheless their design ethic owes more to the likes of Jekyll than to the matrix plantings of Hansen and their plant associations are, by their own admission, far removed from the German traditions from which they stemmed to the point where it could be argued that the ecological integrity of their approach has been lost.

In common with Hansen, plant selection is rigorous. Most schemes use a very similar base palette of plants which includes improved forms of many US natives and many exotics, particularly species from China and Japan. Plants are chosen very much for their suitability to the existing environment, but also for toughness, versatility and seasonal effect. However, although they claim to allow interaction, any major movement or invasion of weed species would be highly disruptive in such polished designs. The reliance on clumps and drifts would make any alien weed species look incongruous. Having said that, stylistically their plantings have a lot in common with German schemes, both of which have a certain fluidity and feeling of freedom and fantasy.

Contemporary styles in the UK

The origins of the contemporary ecological approach in urban planning and landscape design are therefore diverse in comparison with earlier movements, and several different styles can be recognized.

Ruff (1979, 1987) discusses the origins of an ecological approach in terms of a redefinition of the relationship between Man, Nature and the garden. In considering the problems with terminology he coined the term 'ecological landscapes', to include a spectrum of approaches ranging from the reconstruction of semi-natural vegetation, and the utilization, or directed succession, of spontaneous vegetation to landscape compositions using native plants (e.g. the Jacques P. Thijsse Park, Amstelveen, near Amsterdam). The ecological landscapes also include the gardens which incorporate native and exotic species for habitat creation and amenity values, (in contrast to the direct reflection of semi-natural plant communities), and the work of Londo (1977) in the creation of habitats to control spontaneous colonization.

The later acceptance of ecological landscapes in twentieth-century Britain compared to North continental Europe may reflect the wider survival of the historical countryside. Ruff (1987) highlights the nature of the industrial expansion of Dutch cities and the disappearance of the countryside, especially after 1945. Post-war industrialization (including agro-industrial-ization) in Holland radically altered the landscape. These changes in the physical and social environment may be contrasted with both the earlier industrialization and less complete transformation of the countryside in Britain. The UK may also have had a sense of complacency due to the early successes of the Open Space Movement and The National Trust. It is also possible that landscape development may have proceeded more rapidly if it were not for the nineteenth-century revival of formalism in response to a huge influx of exotic plants.

During the 1970s, 1980s and 1990s there have been many new develop-ments in the UK with roots as diverse as eco-art, new-age philosophy and most importantly greatly heightened environmental awareness. Yet again, designers and the public alike are beginning to seek a new purpose in the landscape, finding natural principles a refreshing and necessary antidote to what many see as an over-powerful civilization (Beckett and Parker, 1990; Wilson, 1992). This time an ecological approach is not seen as an expression of taste, applied in one's garden, but rather as a necessity, based upon sound ecological understanding (Ruff and Tregay, 1982), to be used as a model for the whole landscape.

Many modern ecological landscapes in Britain are an adaptation of trends in Holland (Ruff, 1985), but it would certainly be unfair to say that the ideas are new. A recognition of the role of ecology in landscape design in Britain was apparent as early as 1946 in the Presidential Address to the Landscape Institute (Jellicoe, 1946, quoted in Ruff, 1985), and in the syllabus of the entrance examination for the same year (see Ruff, 1985). Nevertheless there was traditionally a great deal of opposition from local authorities who were more concerned with tidy or glamorous landscape projects. Outstanding examples are therefore comparatively recent. These include the William Curtis Ecological Park, London from 1978 to 1985 (Cotton, 1982; Cole, 1986) and the Camley Street Natural Park, London, from 1985.

The development of such designs can be put into the context of the rising tide of interest in urban nature. Landmark planning battles were being fought to preserve wildlife areas within towns in places such as the Gunnersbury Triangle. The Nature Conservancy Council were showing the first major signs of widening their interest into cities with studies such as *The Endless Village* (Teagle, 1978). Local authorities began to employ ecologists on the staff. Urban wildlife trusts were established as a counter-part to the long-established rural naturalist trusts.

Important texts were produced that documented the extent of urban wildlife (see London Ecology Unit, 1985) and also defined urban conserva-tion as a popular movement with a strong human focus. These included Mabey (1973), Nicholson (1970), Fairbrother (1970) and Laurie (1979) in the 1970s and Emery (1986), Brooker and Corder (1986) and Nicholson-Lord (1987) in the 1980s (the latter in particular presents an excellent detailed review of the rise of urban ecology as a land-use philosophy in the UK).

In the 1980s there was also a proliferation of groups associated with urban wildlife, such as the Trust for Urban Ecology and the Fairbrother Group (ecologists and conservationists being famous for their tendency to splinter into different sub-groups). Local authorities have begun to compete for Environment City status, and for many urban nature has become a component of planning. Urban Nature Conservation strategies are now common, and some authorities have open-space management woven into proposals for Local Agenda 21 and for holistic environmental health programmes.

Wildlife gardening has also developed as a strong and regular theme among amateurs (as any casual visit to a local bookshop's garden shelf will show), but this too has been encouraged by professionals such as Chris Baines (1985) who has put a high priority on developing popular political support for conservation by encouraging an interest in garden wildlife.

The new towns

The rise in interest and commitment to the ecological style of landscape coincided with the implementation of the last wave of the UK's new town movement, such that naturalistic planting forms the pre-eminent style in large areas of Swindon, Milton Keynes and other settlements. Each has an interesting story to tell, but by far the most influential was Warrington which lies between Manchester and Liverpool.

The objectives and practice for design, management and maintenance in the Oakwood residential development in Warrington New Town are considered in papers by Ruff and Tregay (1982), Tregay and Gustavsson (1983),

10 Planting in Swindon uses native species producing a stylized version of the forms and patterns seen in the UK countryside. The parallels with the English Landscape Movement are obvious.

Moffatt (1986), and Tregay (1986). These emphasize the philosophical and technical aspects of the construction of Nature-like plant communities (plant selection, species mix and planting density), and emphasize the site preparation, management and maintenance rather than design *per se*. Allowing natural processes to dictate obviously restricts design and much of the landscape debate of the last few decades has focused on ways to optimize the balance (e.g. Tregay and Gustavsson, 1983; Tregay, 1986).

The distinction between the relationships of plants and plant communities to environment as the province of the plant ecologist, and the relationships of Art and Nature to the requirements of the community as the province of the landscape designer results in differing perspectives on design. The involvement of plant ecologists in landscape planning has been treated with some suspicion by landscape architects who are sometimes concerned that their approach may undervalue social and aesthetic concerns.

As an ecologist Moffatt (1986) provides objectives for a phytosociological approach at Oakwood, Warrington that is clearly distinct from the landscape architects working on the same project:

1. to unify and link the existing semi-natural landscape elements to provide a back-drop into which the development would fit;
2. to restore habitats which had been lost or severely reduced in extent in the area and in the country through industrial, residential and agricultural development;
3. to provide a style of landscape on a large scale that was substantially cheaper to implement, maintain and manage than traditional styles;
4. to provide a landscape that was robust and would stand public pressure, vandalism and use for such activities as adventure play;
5. to provide a landscape that had ecological/ wildlife and educational spin-offs;
6. to create a landscape that did not look planned or 'designed' and to develop a structural diversity at an early age;
7. the desire to adopt a more natural approach was also brought about by a dissatisfaction with the artificiality of the traditional, more formal, approach to structural open space.

Moffatt's objectives for the 'natural approach' recognize the role of Nature-like vegetation as a solution to low cost structure planting, linking recreational, residential, industrial and service areas. The first six objectives are concerned with wildlife conservation and management, and only the final objective, which appears as an after-thought, relates to style. The contrast in perspective between the plant ecologist and the landscape architect are compatible but the distinction in emphasis is immediately apparent.

Tregay (1986) questions the relevance of wild nature to urban landscapes, and attempts to develop a coherent structural design language reflecting the historical and modern environment. The structure of the vegetation, including a complexity of form and process, and formality and naturalism, allows for the expression of design within the urban landscape. The hope is to reinforce the social and landscape history of the site to develop a 'sense of place'.

Within residential developments green space is usefully subdivided into three primary units for landscape planning. Gardens and curtilage plantings surrounding dwellings; structural plantings on service areas; and, plantings in recreation areas. Design objectives for these units may be quite independent.

The emphasis on semi-natural style woodlands and grasslands at Warrington (and in other ecological landscapes) has been interpreted as a substitute for design. The potential conflict (in this case within landscape architecture) was anticipated as early as 1959 by Clark (quoted in Ruff, 1985),

> as landscape architects we sometimes made mistakes when being scientific about the landscape. On these scientific moments – we must study the landscape in terms of plant communities which have, as the biologists teach us, structures, activities and laws of their own, each depending on the relationship of its individual members to one another. In such natural communities all is well until these communities are affected by climatic or soil conditions or by anthropogenic factors. In other words, by human activity. This dualism, leads us in our profession to an attitude towards ecology which forgets that it exists as knowledge which it has gained for use in the service of mankind. So often, in our efforts to preserve the balance of nature, we eliminate mankind and its needs as being too much of a heavy weight which might tip the scales in what we might erroneously think is the wrong direction.

Gustavsson (1983) distinguishes three views in the analysis of vegetation, and while representing extreme positions, the views illustrate the components of modern design.

1. The physiognomic view. Vegetation is seen as a group of individuals with special colours and individual forms related to their growth as isolated specimens.
2. The species combination and the plant community view. Vegetation seen as groups or communities, and interest is focused on the species together with the soil, water, nutrient and climatic conditions.
3. The structural view. Vegetation seen as groups of individuals where the structure or the 'architecture' that individuals form together is most relevant. The relationship between the individuals and how they grow in different situations in the group is important.

These can be identified with different professional perspectives. The physiognomic view reflects the perspective of garden designers, the phytosociological view the perspective of ecologists and the structural view the perspective of landscape architects. Nevertheless the objectives, to achieve or create a varied environment that is adapted to urban living conditions, so that direct experiences with natural elements in the environment will become part of daily life for city dwellers suggest a common goal.

Tregay (1986) looks for a reconciliation of the perspectives identified by Gustavsson:

> No longer, in designing with ecological approaches, with conservation and habitat creation in mind, need we be hampered by the need to express form and pattern in 'natural' terms. We need not, in other words, be limited to solely designing landscapes which 'look natural'.

Perhaps somewhere in this view is the beginning of a design approach which really is relevant to what society wants today: to be progressive, yet always to seek reference to the past, to its heritage; to control nature, yet to see it protected and expressed all around us in our home landscapes; to see in the landscape a precision, a formality, a design intent, yet to be able to discover the undesigned, the chance find, the unplanned expression of nature.

Ecological approaches utilizing non-natives in the UK

Currently gaining strongly in interest in the UK among many professionals is the scope for application of the Hansen-style of mixed plant communities that are composed of compatible species that may have arisen from many different countries around the world. Because of the need to work outside of the ideological constraints of 'nativism' the main proponents of such styles are usually from landscape design or horticultural rather than strictly ecological backgrounds. Rather than follow existing habitat paradigms, the aim is to maximize flower colour and create an intimately mixed Persian carpet of bloom (Hitchmough, 1994c). As we have seen, this style shares many themes related to the need to understand the ecological functioning of plant communities rather than the behaviour of individual species under horticultural cultivation (for example many communities created by Hansen and his intellectual descendants require infertile soil conditions).

The inability of Robinson (and subsequent writers) to predict, rather than simply observe, the fate of species in the wild garden limits the selection of species for naturalization to only a small proportion of those available, and there have been notably few advances in this field since his time. As examples, the successful naturalization of species such as *Lilium martagon*, *Galanthus nivalis* and *Narcissus spp.* contrasts with the difficulty of naturalizing species such as *Sternbergia lutea* and *Tulipa spp.*, and equally with the behaviour of invasive species such as *Fallopia japonica*, and of course *Acer pseudoplatanus*.

Inter-specific competition is incompatible with a strictly Gardenesque style; however, in garden and landscape design, even beyond the wild garden, the desirability of mixed plantings (or polycultures) with varying phenologies and morphologies co-dominating a site usually invites inter-specific competition. The possibility of predicting species survival in

Table 3.2 *A suggested categorization in terms of Grime's strategies for a number of familiar herbaceous plants*

Stress tolerators
Helleborus orientalis, Iris x germanica, Polygonatum multiflorum, Primula helodoxa, Scabiosa columbara

Stress tolerant competitors
Acanthus mollis, Bergenia spp., Geranium spp, Hosta spp., Romneya coulteri

Competitors
Anemone x hybrida, Filipendula ulmeria, Monarda didyma, Petasites spp., Polygonum campanulatum

Ruderals
Aquilegia vulgaris, Campanula alliarifoloia, Meconopsis cambrica, Polemonium caeruleum, Silene dioica

Stress tolerant ruderals
Digitalis purpurea, Echinacea purpurea, Eryngium giganteum, Linaria purpurea, Lychnis coronaria

Competitive ruderals
Anchusa azurea, Foeniculum vulgare, Impatiens glandulifera, Oenothera biennis, Salvia sclarea

Source: from Hitchmough (1994a).

polycultures by considering competitive strategy (*sensu* Grime *et al.*, 1988) is possible, although data for decorative plants is extremely limited. Initial efforts have been made by Hitchmough (1994a), although the categories originally utilized by Grime *et al.* have been somewhat modified here to represent trends among herbaceous perennials, none of which could be strictly called ruderals, for example (see Table 3.2).

Data useful in assessing competitive ability in addition to a competitive strategy interpreted from established natural and semi-natural plant communities including life-form, phenology, height, seedling relative growth rate, established strategy and regenerative strategy is rarely available. Even if it were, the success of exotic species in a previously unavailable site may be largely unpredictable. Restrictions operating on a species through competition (including competitive exclusion), and environment in a native habitat are replaced by new restrictions in a new habitat. Nevertheless the scope for relating environmental tolerances in cultivation to niche in a native habitat is explored by Hansen and Stahl (1993) in developing a classification of herbaceous perennials and garden habitats. Although less revealing than the comprehensive accounts of Grime, Hodgson and Hunt (1988) the relationship between native and garden habitat, and between native habitat and competitive strategy may still allow useful predictions of success in a new environment.

On a garden scale, Christopher Lloyd has been looking at this idea for some time. His garden, Great Dixter in Kent, is one of the few successful demonstrations of wild gardening existing in the UK today.

Some interest in artificial plant communities is also seen in the 'Prairie'

Table 3.3 *Species for 'Prairie' experiment to diversify productive grasslands on urban wasteland*

Aster novi-belgii
Hypericum calycinum
Inula helenium
Lupinus polyphyllus
Lysimachia punctata
Oenothera erythrosepala
Solidago canadensis
Tanacetum vulgare
Verbascum thapsus

Source: Ash *et al.* (1992).

experiments established in 1988 by The Groundwork Trust at Knowsley, Merseyside (Ash *et al.*, 1992) with funding from the Nature Conservancy Council and Knowsley Metropolitan Borough Council. Competitive herbaceous species have been used to diversify areas of neglected coarse grassland on high-quality sites. Species utilized are listed in Table 3.3 – Robinson includes all of these species, apart from the native *Tanacetum vulgare*, in the lists for naturalization in *The Wild Garden*. Some limited success is reported in initial establishment of all species other than *Oenothera erythrosepala* (which was totally unsuccessful). After 130 years of the wild garden in practice, the establishment of experimental trials represents an interesting development.

A sociological perspective

An alternative perspective on the purpose (and hence desirable form) of ecological landscapes would put more emphasis on their value as a means of social improvement. Ruff (1979, 1987) emphasizes the distinction between the social context of ecological landscapes in Holland and early approaches in Britain. In particular the concept of community involvement in landscape design and management is stressed:

> it is important . . . that along with the vegetation we also create not a complete environment but one which is in a constant state of change. If residents are to appreciate their immediate environment, they should not be presented with it as a *fait accompli*, but should be allowed to help create it. Planning for care and change in the vegetation of a housing area could hopefully be a means for assembling residents for regular discussion of common problems in the external environment (Bengtsson and Bucht, 1973, quoted in Ruff, 1987).

It is intriguing that the ecological style has often become strongly associated with social involvement. On the surface there is no more reason why an ecological approach to planting is any more likely to attract or require community involvement than any other style. Indeed it could be argued that since scientific and aesthetic arguments are already complex and intangible it is already all too easy to ignore people, whereas formal garden styles explicitly as well as implicitly require human participation in their creation and management.

Certainly the development of ecological styles of land use have co-incided with the rise in community lead design and management of land. In some cases grass roots activity has been focused on developing or protecting areas of urban land that the professionals had no interest in. This level of community action has also been instrumental in the development of community gardens and city farms (Nicholson-Lord, 1987).

Perhaps one argument for greater public involvement in ecological landscapes concerns the likelihood that the public may not always be as keen on what is happening as the professionals. Despite the fact that experts cite the lack of contact with nature as a major reason for urban disquiet (Nicholson-Lord, 1994) there are several problems involved with mixing nature and urban man. Where wildflower meadows have been created in residential areas, individuals commonly complain of fire risk, untidiness, weed banks, vermin and mosquitoes. People in cities have been subjected to the neat and tidy approach of rosebeds and mown grass for some time. Long-term explanation and education will be required to bring about any change.

Naturalistic styles as a whole have sometimes been accused of being impositional and very much an interest of the middle-classes with time on their hands (see Gilbert, 1989). As successful as the landscape at Amstelveen was, it was very much imposed upon the community. One solution has to be community involvement.

Of course there are inevitably links between these different perspectives. In Britain Baines (1985) emphasizes the nature conservation aspects of the

11 Art in the environment can help to focus on or add value to landscapes. This earth sculpture was created at Ebbw Vale, Wales.

nature garden but also considers these primarily as 'political' habitat creation schemes where the greatest value lies in their education and recreation potential (Baines 1989).

Perhaps a more positive argument is therefore that the growth in the focus onto process as well as pattern in landscape has created wider recognition of long-term goals, and of the value of landscape creation as a positive activity in itself. For many professionals the act of creation and environmental improvement is the main reward and incentive for the work and this value can be passed to the local communities who are to benefit from the landscape. Involvement also offers many benefits, such as opportunities for the development of greater environmental awareness.

It is also important that many styles of ecological landscape are more resilient and able to withstand play and interaction than are formal horticultural designs. For example in Swindon, UK, coppiced willow have been deliberately planted near to play areas with the expectation that kids will be tempted to snap off branches without doing the shrubs any harm.

The new towns also helped to pioneer a new vision of park ranger whose role was in part to encourage the public to get actively involved with landscape in contrast to the traditional parks warden with a 'keep off the grass image'. In Kirby where large areas of new wildflower grassland have been created the local people are positively encouraged by the organization Landlife to come and pick the flowers, since 'positive use' is recognized as a vitally important step towards helping people recognize the value of green areas to their lives (Drury, 1992).

Ecological parks

The first high-profile ecology park in the UK was probably William Curtis park which was developed by Lyndis Cole of Land Use Consultants on land which was temporarily vacant near to Tower Bridge in London. Although designed and created with almost no money the site contained many components that are familiar in ecological parks today including a field centre and lots of miniature habitats. The park was very actively exploited by local schools using it as a visit and resource for children with very limited access to the countryside.

The argument for the use of temporary sites made some sense. Derelict and unused land may sit around for years, blighting a region and providing no benefits to the local community. It seemed quite reasonable to use these, for what could be a large proportion of someone's childhood, in a positive way. There was also the advantage that the sites were often made available for a peppercorn rent. However, inevitably when the time comes for the sites to be developed it can be very traumatic, especially if there has been a large amount of community labour and effort in the construction of the site. The landowners may find that they get a bad public image for carrying out a development which was always planned and endorsed by the local authority.

Inevitably therefore the idea that permanent ecology parks are required quickly took root and several of these have been created in major cities and

12 City Farms can help to provide a form of contact between people and nature, and lead to improved environmental awareness.

especially in London, despite the high 'book values' of land in the inner city. The most famous is undoubtedly Camley Street near Kings Cross, and it is therefore particularly ironic that this site too was threatened with destruction by development as a result of railway developments associated with the Channel Tunnel.

In another bitter planning battle the developers associated with the site forwarded proposals whereby substitute sites could be provided, with a net gain in area when development was complete. It was fairly easy to obtain expert evidence that nothing found on the current site would not be expected to arrive on a substitute location, or had such ecological importance that the development should be opposed on those grounds. Nevertheless, even though Camley Street had been created with a great deal of investment of finance by the local authority and professional skills (the hand of trained designers is immediately obvious to any professionals who visit the site) there was still a strong local commitment to the site from people who had developed a sense of ownership and who felt that the current landscape owed much to their efforts. It was therefore effectively irreplaceable and could not be substituted by a new site, no matter how much more improved it may be.

The issues concerned with the value of urban nature to people, including the importance of participation in process, are discussed in more detail in Chapters 8 and 9.

Defining ecological planting today

The twentieth century has seen a dramatic growth in both ecological understanding and in an awareness of the magnitude of threats facing the environment. Both of these have contributed towards what has become a fascination
with ecological process as a means of determining pattern, with many
attempts being made to minimize the overt human influence in the design.
We seem increasingly to value the spontaneous, unplanned or uncontrolled
in the landscape. Despite superficial similarities therefore, it is possible to
trace a clear progression from the Pattern focused naturalistic designs of the
English Landscape Movement, through to the Process focused approaches
such as the encouragement of spontaneous vegetation in Stuttgart streets.
This progression could be said to echo a changing perception of human
appreciation of nature, from a stance where nature was improved and
enhanced by human effort and spiritual sensibilities, through to one where
nature as it is can be valued as needing no improvement, and indeed even in
some cases degraded by human interference.

Certainly many conservationists today put greatest value on landscapes

13 (left) Deadwood and wet patches are particularly valuable for invertebrates. Here the two have been combined at Camley Street Nature Park, London.

14 Designs can be composed of native species, but may not necessarily mimic natural patterns or ecosystem dynamics.

and plant communities which appear as close to 'natural' as they can be. However, it is only necessary to look a little below the surface to see that there is still often great emphasis on what is legitimate pattern. The 'natural order' that is strived for is one which belongs to a world where human impacts are largely denied. Certain manifestations of nature are classified by many professionals as illegitimate and unwelcome. This is most obvious where ecological landscape styles have become confused with, and confused by, issues of 'nativism' in the use of plants.

Inevitably with a subject that is already complex, when different value judgements become involved there is a proliferation of different styles and opinions. It seems worthwhile therefore to conclude this chapter with an attempt to clarify the different components of what may be seen as 'ecological landscape style' of today.

It is a truism that ecological design requires some consideration to be given to the content and pattern of the plant community but this seems in many ways the least important aspect. Certainly it would be a mistake to confuse ecological styles with the use of native plants. Not only does this exclude many of the most important and interesting spontaneous communities (Smart, 1989; Gilbert, 1989; and Kunick, 1992), but it also is a distinction founded on some questionable and arguably damaging premises within the urban context.

The early proponents of naturalistic planting, such as Capability Brown, merely included native species as an element in an artistic composition. Even where patterns echoed nature, the schemes were highly managed and interactions were only permitted where this was beneficial to the intended result. Equally it is possible to conceive of formal designs (topiary and close mown grass, for example) that are composed entirely of natives and yet which would not be remotely plausible as ecological landscapes.

Ecological styles are often claimed to be those which minimize maintenance because they are less artificial and are closer to the natural conditions that would be prevailing on the site. Clearly, however, where the patterning is complex and the management operations are unusual, costs can still be high, whereas many 'formal' or ornamental plantings can be low maintenance.

It is also not satisfactory to see ecological plantings as styles which are reproductions of the rural landscape patterns. The establishment of plant species and communities native to a given area, with due respect to the prevailing conditions of natural distribution, patterning and complexity, while permitting and encouraging natural interactions as far as possible, forms part of the discipline of ecological restoration (Bradshaw, 1983). The ultimate aim is to create plantings which have the nature and properties of a similar community in nature and as such may be barely distinguishable. This is certainly part of the spectrum of ecological landscaping, but is too narrow a concept to represent the whole movement.

Even today it would be completely unrealistic to argue that designers and technology are sophisticated enough to produce accurate reproductions of semi-natural plant communities in all but a few locations, nor would this be desirable. In both rural and urban landscapes it is necessary to meet certain user and aesthetic requirements. What is required is a synthesis of human needs and values with nature. In some places this may allow simpler and more idealized reproductions of natural communities (such as floristic swards which are actually comparatively simple in composition); in other cases it may allow the naturalized mixes of native and exotic perennials produced by Richard Hansen.

It would be stretching matters to an implausible degree to insist that ecological designs are those which have a strong sociological perspective and are characterized by high levels of community involvement. It would also be unfair to other landscape styles and initiatives which are just as strong, or stronger, in their community focus (such as city farms or community gardens). Yet it is certainly the case that some of the most interesting and important developments are those which have a strong focus on exploring the relationship between humans and nature and which contribute towards a stewardship ethic.

However, what contemporary styles seem to require most is that the plants are part of a more or less dynamic community. Plant groupings are not merely chosen on the basis of aesthetics, function and suitability for the site, but they are expected to coexist and interact with one another, utilizing natural processes to create a balanced association that is nevertheless free to change. Stability and dynamism are both achieved, not by looking only at the plant as an individual, but as part of a community in the context of its environment including the associated fauna and the prevailing site conditions. This contrasts with horticultural styles where interaction and change may not be high priorities.

Selection of amenity plants in relation to competitive strategies allows a distinction in planting schemes between static and dynamic plantings. In static plantings species maintain a limited pattern, and as a result retain a design plan. In dynamic plantings species colonize and retreat in a fluid pattern within a design element, and design plans relate the relationships of these elements. Vegetative spread or seed recruitment is an essential attribute in dynamic plantings. Such a design stresses the nature of the plant associations, and utilizes the relationships of the varying associations to one another (Chapter 5). Consideration of competitive strategy is less significant in static plantings, whereas in dynamic plantings consideration of competitive and reproductive strategies is essential. While similar reproductive strategies may characterize both stress tolerators and competitors, the rate of colonization distinguishes competitors and results in dominance on productive sites. An ecological approach is relevant to static and dynamic plantings, although especially important in evolving a dynamic approach. The distinction between static and dynamic plantings represents a continuum beginning with an example such as shrub massing utilizing *Viburnum davidii* and ending with habitat reconstruction. In between, examples range from the use of a few 'wandering plants' such as *Verbena venosa* and *Oenothera* spp. to the wild garden.

The ecological approach to planting may therefore vary in the degree to which native or exotic plants are used, the extent to which they mimic natural communities and the amount of human intervention applied in steering the development of the resulting community. However, they share the scent of 'naturalness' that comes from allowing the component species the room to function as a community and to a certain extent to determine their own destiny in reaction to the environmental framework imposed. They avoid sterility in design, reflecting more clearly the cycles of seasons and the patterns of life, death and decay.

Ecological landscaping is not simply a rehash of old design and management themes using wild plants instead of exotics. At its best it requires a change of philosophy. The effects are achieved in a fundamentally different way – through encouragement and not through domination. It is the landscape manager's job to create the right framework for wildlife to operate, to provide the canvas on which nature paints in the details. Not

Table 3.4 Some features of planting design and management as attributed to a cross section of practitioners

	Brown (1715–1783)	Jenson (1860–1951)	Thijsse (early C20)	Lange (early C20)	Wilson and Druse	Robinson (1838–1900)	Foerster (1874–1970)	Hansen et al.	Oehme and van Sweden	Jekyll (1843–1932)	Chatto	Hitchmough
The use of mainly native and naturalized species	*	**	**	**	**							
Plant communities from that region deliberately copied or increased	*	**	**	**	**							
Plants regarded as a community	*	**	**	**	**	**	*	**	*	*	*	**
Plant life strategies used to influence design		*	*	**	*	*	*	**	**	*	*	**
Interaction and spontaneity allowed			*		*	**	*	**	*	*	*	**
Acceptance of invading weed species	?	?	*	?	*	*		**			*	**
Minimal intervention		?			*	*		**				*
Minimal or no environmental manipulation	?		*	*			*		*	*	*	*
Use of native and non-native species mixed	*				**	**			*	*		**
Layout as a stylised imitation of nature	**	**						*	*		*	
Manipulation of plant populations to maintain a balance	**	**	**	**	**	**	**	*	**	**	**	**
Plant communities from other regions replicated		*	*	**	**	**		**	*	*	*	**
Artistic principles strongly influential	**	**	**	**	*		**	*	**	**	**	*
Use of mainly non-natives							*	**	*	**	*	
Layout not recognizably following natural patterns							*			*	*	
Major intervention – plant populations maintained almost static							*		*	*	*	
No acceptance of weed species	*								?	**	**	
Use of highly hybridized plants			*				**	**	*	*	**	

** A deliberate feature, which is strongly associated with their philosophy and approach.

* A common feature, not always true of their philosophy and approach, or sometimes occurring by default.

? Information unavailable, but likely to have been a feature.

everything is ordered and controlled, it is a place where spontaneous and unpredictable things happen, and these things bring their own kind of pleasure.

On the other hand an ecological landscape isn't just a place where nature has taken over. More than any other, city open spaces are the symbol of the partnership between mankind and nature; they are the place where people and the green environment come into closest contact. The human hand has not only a place, but it plays an essential role in maintaining and encouraging the wild species that may come to live there. The urban landscape is therefore somewhere for us to play and experiment with our relationship to wildlife. In so doing, we may learn some ground rules that will help in managing and conserving the broader environment.

Table 3.4 lists a range of features common to planting design, attributing them correspondingly to a representative group of practitioners described in the previous section, in an attempt to draw out some major trends and foundations for definition. The principles range from what may be regarded as strict, or pure ecological rules (such as those which might be applied to an accurate habitat recreation), through to rather artificial rules which have been employed in more traditional approaches to planting.

It has not been possible to mention all those involved in the ecological approach. Parallels may be drawn between the ideas of Jens Jensen and those of Rob Tregay. A comparison of some of the Groundwork Trusts' work, notably that of Ash *et al.* on the establishment of native and prairie style grasslands and the ideas of Jim Wilson and Ken Druse also shows many similarities.

4 The objectives of urban nature conservation

It has been possible to trace the development of urban ecological landscapes as part of an evolution of design philosophy influenced by social attitudes in the face of an environment that is rapidly degenerating and becoming more controlled. However, there are other perspectives that have an influence as well. In recent decades there has been an increasing interest in the theme of urban nature conservation. For example, many local authorities in the UK have been working to produce nature conservation strategies that identify their own commitments and intentions in regard to wildlife protection within their geographic range of influence. Sites (not always in local authority ownership) have been identified and evaluated as deserving of conservation and management plans have often been produced with those aims in mind. The mechanisms and approaches to these conservation strategies will be discussed in more detail later but first it will be of value to review the basic principles of nature conservation and the way in which strategic policy directions are developing.

Obviously the local authorities have a local vision of priorities, and land within urban areas will be highlighted by the regional agencies concerned as being of conservation interest. The urban landscape manager needs to be able to integrate conservation objectives into their planning and activities to complement (and hopefully not conflict with) other goals.

Nature conservation planning is a complex issue and it can lead to a confusion of objectives unless the value of urban nature is carefully placed into a wider context. Nature conservation is ultimately an activity that relies upon value judgements placed on animals and plants by humans. Some species and communities attract the attention of conservationists, some do not – what distinguishes the two?

Obviously objectively conservation interest and priorities must relate to those species which would be most under threat if we did not take an active concern in their survival. We do not spend time trying to conserve rats or ryegrass, because these are common, resilient and, if anything, have been excessively favoured by human activity. It follows therefore that conservationists must rate as most important those habitats or communities which are:

- demanding of highly specific environmental conditions rather than those which have a wide environmental tolerance;
- characteristic of extreme or unusual environmental conditions which can not easily be reproduced, rather than commonplace circumstances;
- the product of complex ecological processes, such as colonization, which can not easily be reproduced;
- under threat from trends in land-use change or exploitation which will lead to (or has already caused) severe damage or fall in population numbers.

Resources for nature conservation activity are invariably limited, and society often has legitimate other claims for land use. Allocation of protective mechanisms or management resources must therefore, ideally, be targeted towards examples of habitats or communities which are most vulnerable and most valuable, as well as viable and with a reasonable chance of survival if protected. Reconciling these different issues is a complex task.

The paradox is that usually the case is that there are few species found in urban areas which have any great vulnerability or risk of imminent disappearance. (While it is true that rare species are sometimes found in urban areas, there is always a question as to whether their rarity is in fact an artefact of poor understanding of their distribution or regeneration ecology.)

Why is it therefore that urban nature conservation as a topic has increasingly gained respectability over the last few decades and is now a recognized component of biodiversity protection strategies worldwide? Why should money be spent on urban initiatives when rural conservation work so often faces a funding crisis? This section is intended to address these questions by reviewing the broader nature conservation context. Hopefully it will highlight and clarify the genuine contribution that can be made by urban initiatives.

Why is nature conservation important?

To better understand and evaluate decisions that are made in the name of nature conservation it is worth briefly reviewing the fundamental purposes and reasons for biodiversity protection.

1. **Resource protection** The most common argument put forward for preventing the erosion of the genetic base of species on earth (i.e. for protecting a broad genetic range within each species) relates to the potential value of exploitable products such as medicines, new crops or breeding potential for inclusion into existing crops. The resources that are available may relate to needs which do not yet exist, such as cures for diseases which may not currently be significant.
2. **Ecosystem balance** There is a premise that all species interact in a network that forms the life support system of the earth. Various philosophical and scientific paradigms can be used to express this view such as the Gaia theory. Despite a consensus of support from many sources, they have a weakness in terms of a political lever in that the timing or magnitude of

threat is hard to quantify. An analogy that is sometimes presented is of a plane which loses a rivet from its wing. This is a bit worrying for some of the passengers but not significant. As it flies further another rivet falls out, then another and another. Eventually problems will occur, but it is almost impossible to predict when these difficulties will arise.

3. **Education/scientific** The loss of a species removes any opportunity to study or learn from its ecology or behaviour. Conversely some species and habitats may receive high levels of funding support because of their research potential.

4. **Human preference** A great deal of conservation effort is expended on causes which in one way or another motivate people to concern. The human emotional, spiritual or aesthetic wish to protect a species or area of landscape has been one of the most powerful forces in determining *de facto* conservation policy and the designation of reserves for much of the last century. The negative side of this motivation is that it can be obstructive to a more objective evaluation of conservation priorities, directing resources or concern to high-profile or attractive species which are not necessarily endangered and away from some 'less cute' groups such as invertebrates or micro-organisms which are more likely to be vulnerable, more likely to contain biochemical resources and arguably cumulatively more integral to ecosystem balance.

4. **Moral imperative** All of the above arguments are ultimately human centred. They place a focus on the value of biodiversity for our own survival, development or pleasure. However, there is also a moral argument that says that all species have the right to exist and complete their evolution regardless of human concerns. They need to be integrated into conservation policy even if, from a human perspective, they are regarded as completely pointless.

Most conservationists have been concentrating on the promotion of 'usefulness' of wildlife in areas of high diversity, such as the rainforests. This is understandable when faced with economic pressures for other land use. However, this runs the risk of undermining the conservation position for some species, especially as technology for gene identification and manipulation advances. We are trying

> to convince members of materialist societies to alter hyperconsumptive behaviour in the interest of an even bigger payoff later. Can this argument effectively protect whole ecosystems when it concedes that life forms for which no human use is identified are expendable? (Western *et al.*, 1989).

Battles over the resource value of wildlife will inevitably be focused on areas such as the Brazilian rainforest. The argument for the need to develop a way of living that values nature intrinsically needs to be focused on urban areas, and it is this that is arguably the most important thrust for effective conservation.

Setting conservation priorities

Globally the scientific community is attempting to encourage and endorse an objective approach to conservation. Rescuing as much of possible of the world's biodiversity is dependent on prioritizing effort and identifying those areas where the most benefit can be gained from limited resources. However, the reality of conservation protection systems, such as land designation, within any one country is of course often dictated by pragmatism, opportunity and political acceptability.

Given that designation of land for conservation purposes is really a political act, it is inevitable that there will be more support, and more chance of success, for the protection of land containing popular species such as butterflies, birds and wildflowers and that other groups such as flies get overlooked. Despite efforts to the contrary we can not avoid subjectivity when making land-use decisions.

Many people get confused between activities and programmes which are part of an objective conservation strategy and those which are generally good for wildlife, i.e. they promote greater numbers of diversity of wild species but are not necessarily targeted on organisms that are under particular threat. A great deal of popular conservation activity is in fact aimed at species that, in objective terms, may not be the highest priority.

Contrary to popular belief increasing biodiversity in a region is not necessarily complicated. There are very many possible approaches and mechanisms by which this can be done. What is of greater importance is that only some biodiversity carries significance with regard to nature conservation priorities, and also that some particular species and communities are so demanding in their habitat requirements that prescribing for their needs is difficult. In order to make logical sense of restoration techniques we need to examine what it is that biodiversity protection and enhancement aims to achieve. We also need to recognize that these goals are too complex to be easily evaluated by the rather imperfect biodiversity assessment tools that ecologists have available.

The diversity of lifestyles and ecological strategies that different organisms show means that it is difficult to state that any land-use pattern or activity is in itself harmful or undesirable, since almost inevitably some groups of species will benefit. In the UK the conversion of deciduous woodland to coniferous plantation has favoured previously uncommon species such as pine marten which has complicated the debate about the biodiversity impact. Gilbert (1989) presents details of the ecosystem of lower plants and invertebrates that develop on a concrete post. The more concrete posts we build, the more some species will benefit. Conservation planning must therefore involve value judgement; it is vital to target activity towards those species which are most vulnerable and most under threat. Rarity is therefore a motivating factor, and without some perceived threat it is difficult to develop a strategy.

Box 4.1 The value of rarity

Urban habitats are primarily made up of species which are common and often becoming more so as human influence becomes pervasive. They are therefore of no direct value relevance to biodiversity protection strategies. Nevertheless, there is very real value in working with 'common and garden' species as it is these that give each region its distinctive natural flavour, that create our own 'home landscape' and sense of place. It is also those common species that provide the 'bread and butter' for conservation education; that give us material to work with and to learn about. One of the most important steps in the beginning of education is that people learn to recognize things through reinforcement; recognizing the plants and natural communities that we see around ourselves everyday and learning how our own local environment ticks is an essential first step to a broader understanding.

Cole (1986) sets the following three main objectives for urban nature conservation:

- to conserve and press for the appropriate management of urban sites of intrinsic natural history value;
- to increase the habitat diversity of formalized areas of public open space;
- to create new wildlife habitats, either on a temporary or permanent basis, on downgraded and derelict sites within the inner city.

In each case the concern is as much for people as it is for wildlife and heavy emphasis is placed on public enjoyment, community participation and school activities. Ultimately urban conservation is concerned with the dispelling of any perceptual division between urban and rural areas.

Cole therefore places the subject firmly within the overall field of environmental education.

> Contact with nature should be the experience of the many, not the few. A clear understanding of, and concern for, nature is best instilled through direct and frequent experience – quotidian nature. Urban habitats are frequently managed for public enjoyment ... and are therefore not directly subject to changing policies in agriculture and forestry.

Of course it is the rare species that people often value most, as it is these that give the real magic to nature watching. But there is something to be gained from accepting that part of the reason that we are keen on them is because they are rare, and that their rarity is itself one of the greatest assets of the conservation movement. There is a strange intimacy between opposites that has always entertained the minds of philosophers – it is a truism that conservationists would have no reason to exist without the habitat losses and dangers that threaten nature.

It is also important that some species remain locally rare. Ask yourself, if it were possible to wave a wand and to make all habitats and all species common and safe from threat, would you, in your heart of hearts, want to do it, or at least would you do it with no regrets? Surely many people would feel a sneaking suspicion that something has been lost as well as gained. There is an unparalleled joy in stumbling across unusual plants or never-before-seen animals. It is this excitement that drives much of the conservation work that we do.

When untamed wildlife was common, people had a fascination with controlling the landscape and dispelling or taming the natural world. Early man-made landscapes were highly formal and ornamental in nature. It is only since nature has been put on the run that most people in society have become ready for the change in attitude that teaches us to value wildness. It is those countries that have lost most of their natural countryside, such as Holland, that are among the most enthusiastic in supporting habitat creation or global conservation.

On a more philosophical level, as long as wildlife remains endangered and under threat, we have the evidence, and a poignant symbol, that things are not all well between man and the natural world and that we still have some changes to make.

One of the fundamental problems of conservation planning relates to the sheer inadequacy of our understanding of species distribution. Currently there are approximately 1.4 million species recognized on the earth. The current best estimates for the total number are around 10 million, although this can range as high as 100 million (Western and Pearl, 1989). To cope with the uncertainty that results, it is necessary for planners to make certain assumptions and educated guesses about the optimum strategies for species protection. Global priorities must be focused on regions which have, for various reasons, large areas of undisturbed habitat, areas which are structurally complex and particularly on regions which are known to have been loci for species diversification and evolution.

Ancient habitats that have been under comparatively stable conditions for a long time are valued because they are likely to have accumulated a high complement of species suited to the prevailing conditions. Among the most vulnerable and important of these habitats are those which are refuges for species with low-colonization potential. This could be either because the combination of conditions they require is rare or no longer prevalent and itself irreplaceable, or because they have limited powers to cross intervening land barriers.

Perhaps the best example is the species characteristic of ancient woodland in the UK. Following the glacial retreat after the last ice age the majority of the UK land area was colonized by woodland species moving from continental Europe. As the tree colonization progressed, associated animal and plant species highly dependent on woodland conditions were also able to invade. Some of these are, however, unable to move across intervening habitat types. Ancient woodland with links to this primal forest are therefore among the most valuable habitats in the UK. As woodland cover has been removed and fragmented by changing land use, these highly specialized organisms have become increasingly endangered (Peterken, 1981). The habitats they live in are completely irreplaceable in that colonization of secondary woodland will be highly unlikely to occur (unless perhaps the new woodland develops adjacent to the old and the two co-exist for long periods of time).

Priorities in global nature conservation also favour natural habitats, i.e. regions which have developed without any human influence on species composition or distribution. The presumption is that these areas will contain those species which are most intolerant of disturbance and hence most vulnerable. It is argued that human influence on an area can always be added but can never be removed. Natural habitats are therefore a finite and shrinking resource (Ratcliffe, 1977).

In the UK and much of Europe there are no remaining habitats which have that status. Semi-natural habitats are hence seen as the highest quality resource, areas which have been influenced by mankind, probably by management, but where the species composition and patterning still reflect strongly the influence of natural processes. In countries where natural habitats are still found the term semi-natural is often seen as denigrating, a degraded resource of rather intermediate value.

Ancient semi-natural habitats will often undergo a period of loss of species and decline in diversity if the management influence is removed. Natural habitats do not so obviously need management. This distinction has lead to different perceptions in Europe compared to countries such as the USA concerning the role of human influence in nature reserves.

In contrast, urban ecosystems are of course recent and recreatable, highly unnatural, and tend to comprise species which are, by their very nature, tolerant of mankind and of factors such as pollution and disturbance. They are primarily, therefore, not endangered or vulnerable and in themselves they do not seem to merit significant conservation efforts on almost any of the above grounds beyond that of human affection and pleasure. There are of course rarities discovered in urban areas, but it is necessary to wonder whether these are really scarce or vulnerable, or whether there is a problem of under-recording.

In Leicester in the UK the entomologist Jenny Owen has been recording diligently the invertebrate species that have visited her town garden over 15 years. In this time she has found over one-third of the UK butterflies, hover-flies and bumblebees, with similar numbers of other insect groups including eight species newly recorded in England and two species new to science. Extrapolations suggest that the site may act as a habitat component for one-third of the total UK insect fauna (Owen, 1991). These sorts of statistics in other locations would justify serious consideration for designation as a nature reserve and a site of key importance for biodiversity protection in the UK, but it of course reflects our patchy understanding of the real distribution of invertebrates and the true species composition of most gardens.

The complexity of biodiversity means that we can probably never know the full range of species on our sites. Landscape managers addressing conservation issues therefore have to work with a data gap – sometimes it is necessary to act in a fashion that will be judged to favour organisms of whose actual presence there is no direct evidence. We may sometimes be driven by a pragmatic need to act without trying to establish what the consequences may be, since delaying action to await full surveys (which may never be achieved) may be likely to be more damaging.

This inevitably generates certain management tactics, such as to manage for diversity whenever no clear over-riding priorities argue otherwise and to follow any established management pattern with consistency. Managers must also have the skills to identify trends which may be indicators of potential problems. Monitoring is often forwarded as an essential component of any conservation activity, especially where there is uncertainty of the possible outcomes. As rational as this panacea may seem, it is sometimes a red herring, since it will never be possible to fund enough monitoring to give clear feedback on all sites.

Rare species and their significance in urban settings

Nature conservation policy in most rural locations must ideally be carefully targeted in order to ensure effective deployment of limited resources. This requires that value judgements are made about which wildlife is highest priority in terms of protection, and which conservation programmes are likely to be most effective. The scientific goal is of course to prevent the erosion of genetic diversity, but this is clearly easier said than done. Success is compromised by gaps in our knowledge of how much genetic diversity there is, where it is and the severity of the threat that is faced.

Finding the correct measures for indicating success may not always be easy. Species richness in a habitat is not necessarily significant if the individual species or the assemblages are common. On the other hand it is possible for certain unusual patterns or groupings of species to be seen as worth protection even if the individual species are not of much interest. Some sites may be very important if they contain just a few uncommon species and the overall diversity is low. Optimizing criteria for site evaluation is therefore a complex issue that has concerned many conservation scientists and planners for a long time (Usher, 1986).

As well as problems of identification of priorities, biodiversity protection may also be compromised by local political, economic and social realities which sometimes prevent the implementation of necessary policies, and in other situations demand the implementation of policies which suit the interests and needs of local people even if they have limited direct significance for biodiversity protection.

We have seen that urban areas are almost entirely characterized by species which are, practically by definition, tolerant of human impact and hence are not likely to be under significant threat. They are for the most part likely to find their habitat preferences increasing rather than decreasing, and it is the more vulnerable specialist species which need to be given highest priority. It can be argued that overall urban conservation initiatives run the risk of re-directing attention and resources away from other areas which are a higher priority. The answer of course is that urban areas are where political support, environmental education and above all care for nature must be fostered but it is still vital that the policy-makers and landscape managers appreciate these broader priorities and seek to maximize the value gained from investments in urban nature. Above all it is worth remembering the distinction between encouraging nature in urban areas and encouraging the value and appreciation of nature in urban areas – the latter should nearly always gain priority in any conflict of interests.

One issue that sometimes arises and complicates policy formulation is that there *are* some rare species that are found occasionally in towns and cities. Gemmell (1982, see Table 4.1) and Shepherd (1995) illustrate this for plants; Caradine, Page and Bullock (1995) for spiders and harvestmen; Lott and Daws (1995) for beetles; Andrews and Kinsman (1990) identify 24 species of butterfly which may be expected to appreciate the conditions in recently re-vegetated quarries.

These are sometimes plant species which are adapted to soils very different from the typical local types. The peculiar substrate of the wastes therefore allows colonization by species that are uncommon in the locality, but may not be very important elsewhere. Since the colonization process

Table 4.1 *Some uncommon Greater Manchester species colonizing ecologically curious industrial habitats*

Species	Principal industrial habitats
Blackstonia perfoliata	Leblanc process waste
Carlina vulgaris	Calcareous wastes
Centaurium erythraea	Calcareous wastes
Dactylorhiza incarnata	Calcareous wastes, clay pits
D. praetermissa	Calcareous wastes, clay pits
D purperella	Calcareous wastes
Epipactis palustris	Pulverised fuel ash, boiler ash
Erigeron acer	Calcareous wastes
Gymnadenia conopsea	Leblanc process waste
Linum catharticum	Calcareous wastes, clay pits
Lycopus europaeus	Calcareous wastes
Ophioglossum vulgatum	Leblanc process waste
Orchis morio	Leblanc process waste
Orobanche minor	Leblanc process waste
Osmunda regalis	Mining subsidence marshland
Salix repens spp. Argentea	Calcareous wastes, quarries and pits
Senecio erucifolius	Clay pits
Sisyrinchium bermudiana	Leblanc process waste
Stratiotes aloides	Old canals

Source: Gemmell (1982).

may involve species moving large distances and crossing many natural barriers to dispersal, the resulting communities may comprise unusual assemblages of plants that have adequate mechanisms of travel. The presence of some of these species, while perhaps of local and scientific interest, would not be given too much importance by conservation planners since the distribution has been influenced by an accident of artificial soil formation. (An analogy would be if a pile of chalk was dumped in the middle of a granite derived acid soil range. The resulting flora would be locally rare, but this would not justify major protection measures.)

There are also species of animals or plants found which are not just locally unusual, but which are nationally uncommon. To put their importance in context it is worth considering in more detail the nature and significance of rarity in natural ecosystems. Rare species can be identified from different groups, with a particularly important distinction being made between:

1. those which have declined nationally to the point where all individuals or small colonies are regarded as important; these may be surviving as a remnant of a pre-existing community in a relict habitat fragment;
2. those which are adapted to conditions which are uncommon either spatially or over time and which would probably have been rare even without habitat loss; these species may be well adapted to maintaining

themselves in small and fragmented populations, or surviving long periods of adversity where population numbers fall to very low levels (or even go through apparent extinction in the case of plants surviving as buried seed).

Some urban rarities may therefore be favoured by conditions which are uncommon in rural and mature habitats, but which have become more common in heavily disturbed inner-city areas or on post-industrial land (Eyre and Luff, 1995). Although in some cases these could be late successional and immobile species, it is more likely that colonization of newly disturbed habitats will be by species which have the ability to build populations rapidly when conditions suit and when competition is limited.

It is widely recognized that life strategies of plants and animals vary, and that two extremes may be identified. At one extreme are species which are adapted to stable but possibly highly competitive or stressful conditions. These may have low dispersal and reproduction rates. Others are adapted to exploit temporarily favourable conditions that occur following disturbance. These favourable opportunities may be spatially and temporally unpredictable and the species concerned often show a high investment in reproduction and in mechanisms for achieving effective dispersal or for surviving adversity in a resistant form such as an egg cyst or seed. These types are often referred to as 'ruderals'. For the most part they are common, and sometimes becoming more so since the disturbance they need to establish is a widespread consequence of human activity but there are some which may not be widespread.

It is a truism that when a species is rare there is something about its ecology that is in some way complex or unusual. Almost certainly our understanding of the natural history of many of these species is too poor to allow rational policy-making. Many of them may go through apparently dramatic population declines, or may even become apparently extinct, but will have strategies that allow rapid population recovery and even a 'boom' if conditions become favourable again. Therefore, rarity *per se* may not be an indication of threat to the survival of that species. Rarity among ruderals may arise when a species has such an uncommon niche that there are very few opportunities available at any one time, but this does not mean that the plant or animal is endangered or in need of conservation unless its strategies for reproduction and dispersal are too inefficient to match the prevailing patterns of niche formation or unless the particular habitat requirements become so rarely formed, for some reason, that they never have the required opportunities for upward population swings. These then become genuinely rare species characteristic of disturbed grounds.

The essential problem therefore is to try and identify those ruderal rarities that are genuinely restricted and endangered, because of poor reproduction or high niche specificity and which therefore need to be deliberately encouraged, as distinct from those which may be uncommon but which have perfectly adequate recovery potential.

It is not always easy to identify which species are ruderals. The great crested newt is a species which sooner or later attracts attention among urban ecologists in the UK. It needs water bodies with a good food supply but is a poor competitor and is unable to survive in ponds that have significant populations of fish (Andrews and Kinsman, 1990). It dislikes high levels of disturbance and is frequently dependent on old stable countryside, but also is frequently found in built-up areas, perhaps reflecting the fact that it needs to find suitable ponds at a high frequency. It has a preference for some shade within a generally open landscape, and has a preference for particular topographical features within the water, frequently (and contrary to what is often commonly assumed) preferring sharp transitions from water to land (MacGregor, 1995). On the other hand the newt seems to be capable of rapidly colonizing certain ponds and pools and of building up huge populations relatively quickly; observation suggests that it is very often associated with relatively new waterbodies such as are sometimes found in association with urban or industrial sites.

The issue has developed unexpected significance recently in a battle over the Orton brick pits in Peterborough. This urban site consists of flooded abandoned clay workings of approximately 30 years old which was found to have what may be the largest colony of great crested newts in the world after plans to develop the site for housing were well underway. Many of the ponds are directly threatened by development, and the future of other newt colonies may be more uncertain given the likelihood of anthropogenic fish introduction into the ponds. English Nature agreed a plan for habitat creation and translocation with the developers. It seems plausible that if colonization can occur in such a recent habitat, then habitat creation is a viable option. However, this decision has been challenged by WWF(UK) who see the procedure as untested and feel that the site is clearly so important that it requires designation and strong protection (Byng and Johnson, 1995). The fact that both perspectives seem plausible is a reflection of how little we really know about the colonization patterns and population growth potential of these species.

Strategic approaches for nature conservation

Species extinctions have of course been a characteristic of the natural world since life first evolved, but for most of history these losses have been matched or exceeded by the rate of speciation. It is not the fact of extinctions, but rather the estimates of the magnitude of biodiversity loss in the next two decades that is the main motivating factor for conservation strategy development. The rate of species loss may be anything up to 10 000 times that which would be happening under normal circumstances (Wilson, 1989).

Conservation can be tackled through *in-situ* or *ex-situ* approaches. *Ex-situ* will include zoos, botanic gardens and increasingly high-technology derivations of these such as seed banks, embryo and sperm banks etc. Although these are clearly important the limitations are quickly obvious and they have to be seen as a desperate last resort when other strategies fail. The resources in these institutions are inevitably limited and have to be targeted carefully. Zoos will only be able to make a significant contribution to the survival of a few hundred animal species. The priorities will best be given to keystone species, those which have a major controlling effect on the ecosystem. Even in botanic gardens, seed banks and other initiatives will also have to be selective and will probably be based around groups that have a clear resource or research value.

In either case higher priority may need to be given to those species which are not quite sustainable in natural conditions, but which may be expected to undergo a change of fortune if the degenerative factors on their habitat can be reversed. Species which have undergone significant decline may have too poor a genetic base, or too limited a range, to be ever viable again as self-sustaining populations.

Long term *ex-situ* conservation meets few of the fundamental goals or purposes of biodiversity protection outlined above. An animal surviving in an embryo form is making no contribution to ecosystem balance or human appreciation, while the quality of its existence is certainly not free from moral doubts and uncertainties. It is also impossible to make any provision for species which have not yet been identified.

In many ways preserving the relationship between species is as important as preserving the species themselves. *In-situ* conservation, through habitat protection, must therefore continue to form the keystone of biodiversity protection strategies. Yet this too is fraught with difficulties. It is becoming increasingly obvious that the existing system of reserve designation and protection is based on an outmoded understanding of the nature of ecological pressures and is completely inadequate for coping with the problems of the world into the next century.

Recognizing past and future causes of biodiversity loss

Public consciousness of threats to biodiversity often focus on development activities such as road building or mining. However, these are often only significant because of the fragmented and impoverished nature of the countryside. It is a change in the nature of agriculture and forestry which is at the root of most of the conservation problems that exist today.

These changes include direct habitat destruction of course, but probably more serious has been environmental change through drainage, liming and the increasing use of fertilizer and pesticide inputs to maintain high productivity together with the use of improved strains of grass and increasingly trees. These have tended to reduce diversity even where the overall biome type remains unchanged. These changes in the intensity and nature of management in some areas have been matched by a decline in some traditional land use practices and neglect of land in other locations. Traditional production systems such as grazing of lowland heaths and coppice have become uneconomic or have seen traditional markets disappear.

In semi-natural habitats, therefore, designating land as a nature reserve is in itself entirely inadequate to ensure protection of the species within. Provision has to be made for the critical management inputs that would have been typical of the traditional land-use system that created that habitat type

Figure 4.1 The degree of heathland loss and fragmentation in Dorset (Goode, 1984).

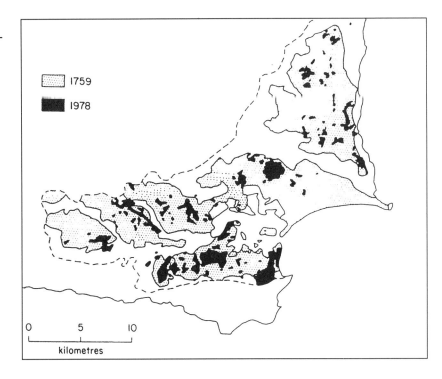

initially. However, the fragmentation of habitats has often led to excessive complications when attempting to do this.

For example, lowland heaths in England need to be maintained to keep a proportion of the heather in a vigorous juvenile stage and to prevent scrub invasion. If unchecked succession would lead to conversion to young woodland, a habitat type which has some wildlife value but is of vastly lower conservation importance than the heath it replaces (Figure 4.1 and Figure 4.2).

Figure 4.2 Tree colonization within heathland leads to habitat loss from within (Green, 1981).

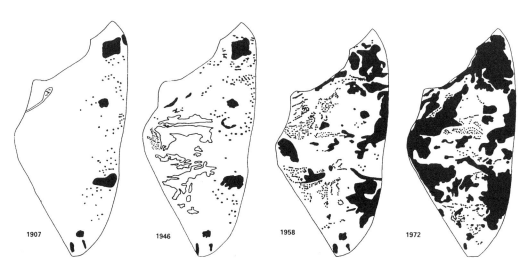

The most typical management options include grazing or burning, but the small size and fragmented nature of the sites makes it very difficult to undertake either. Individual locations are often too small to support viable herds, while burning (where there are not problems of proximity to houses etc.) has to be undertaken on a rotational basis so that animal and plant species can recolonize. This rotational management in turn reduces the area of land that is at any one stage in the succession, perhaps undermining the survival opportunities for any species that needs a large territory.

When species-rich habitats covered extensive tracts of countryside, sufficient variation in management stage, intensity and frequency would occur randomly, so that all species would be able to survive. The integrity of any particular habitat may also have relied upon ecological processes, such as perhaps periodic flooding which created regeneration niches. These processes in turn may have been interrupted by changes in the surrounding land use, undermining the integrity of the protected area.

Today on nature reserves the manager therefore has to try to balance and provide all such species requirements and this can lead to such complex patterns of intervention that there can only be parallels with wildlife gardening. Indeed levels of intervention are increasing all the time, including for example species recovery programmes to compensate for localized extinctions. Historically localized extinction would have been a common process, but would have been compensated for by a general flux of migration, re-invasion and re-establishment. Now we compensate by propagation and replantings.

Cumulatively this means that the management demands of the protected areas is at least equal to, and often far exceeds, that which the land originally had. Even areas which were originally 'natural habitats' and had previously received no management may require intervention to maintain optimum species balances in a small area, or to compensate for processes which have been disrupted. The result is a management crisis that is increasingly going to become the main constraint to biodiversity protection unless alternative incentives and mechanisms are found to achieve the goals.

Even if the required management can be achieved, the current system of reserve designation may still be unable to achieve its objectives for biodiversity protection. One reason is that it is clear that reserves and biodiversity protection currently are too low in political and economic priorities and the rate of attrition is often frighteningly high. The reserves function just so long as the political or economic interests that challenge them are not too powerful, but sooner or later conflicts do arise whereby nature loses out. The effectiveness of the policy for long-term protection clearly needs to be questioned.

Technical analysis of the size and population levels of many reserves has also highlighted that many of the areas originally thought protected are simply too small to support viable populations of the species in them, and that genetic paucity is likely to lead to decline. A greater understanding of species:area relationships and the impacts of stochastic catastrophes on small habitat units (Shafer, 1990) has also raised awareness that random events are likely to destroy areas of minimum size which have no buffering capacity (see Chapter 5).

The greatest threat to biodiversity in the coming decades must be pollution, particularly nutrient enrichment, and climate change. These are likely to modify the environment to such a degree that many of the most vulnerable species begin to simply disappear from the reserves despite the strongest policy. Climate change has of course occurred many times in the past and species have adapted or migrated, but the rate of the expected change in the next century will be unprecedented, while the level of habitat fragmentation will of course present almost impossible adaptation challenges to species with slow dispersal mechanisms. These influences are becoming so pervasive that it is threatening the very status of 'natural' landscapes, since there will be no landscape on earth which will be free from a human-induced influence on species composition.

Future directions for conservation strategies

The issues outlined above demonstrate the seriousness of the problems that need to be tackled over the coming decades. The outlook is obviously not good since many of our current conservation policies and strategies are not working effectively, and it is probably the case that the obvious failures to date are little more than a prelude for worse to come unless new approaches are explored (Wilson, 1989).

It is not surprising therefore that strategic policy formulation for the next century increasingly looks for radical new approaches and mechanisms for resolving or minimizing the problems. Probably the most important component of that change is a growing perception of the need and benefits of human intervention in natural processes and participation in conservation initiatives.

So rapid and far-reaching have these changes of attitude been, that it is sometimes hard to remember how entrenched opinions once were that human impacts were invariably negative and undesirable, and that the best thing that could be done for nature was to keep people out of its way such as in the National Parks of North America.

Today it is well understood that countless semi-natural habitats have developed their full richness, variety and beauty under some human management. We have even begun to recognize that many habitat types once regarded as 'natural' have been maintained by human activity. This is particularly the case where activities of aboriginal peoples have been overlooked. The prairies of northern America were probably deliberately burnt at frequent intervals. Even the tropical rainforests, popularly regarded as the last great wilderness, have been influenced by human selection of certain tree species.

With the incredible pervasiveness of factors such as pollution which are influencing species distribution and survival even in the remotest areas of the world it could be argued that strictly there are no 'natural' ecosystems left. But naturalness in the landscape is more than a condition which can be defined in technical terms. It is also an embodiment of a human attitude towards the landscape which has many positive aspects but also carries an overtone of a feeling that man and nature are somehow disparate things which can never be reconciled. Human presence in truly natural areas is in many ways still felt of as more degrading and corrupting than potentially beneficial.

The realities of nature conservation in the next century call out for intervention on all levels. Fencing off reserves and keeping people out will sign their death warrants as surely as a bulldozer. Direct management of the species and processes that are of value will become more and more necessary in all places. The scale and magnitude of this intervention may even extend as far as direct habitat recreation and species translocation; indeed we already see interventionist species recovery programmes forming an increasingly important part of biodiversity protection strategies world-wide.

But the most important step in such a revolution has to be the promotion of an ethic that sees human influence as a factor which is potentially positive and sustaining in the landscape; that encourages each of us to explore the positive steps that we can take to protect nature, and more than that to heal and restore nature. This is one of the key tenets of sustainability and as such forms a thread that runs through documents such as Caring for the Earth (IUCN/UNEP/WWF, 1991) and Agenda 21. It is also the fundamental principle that runs through dramatically different styles of land designation, such as the UNESCO Biosphere reserves which only become designated in areas where human exploitation of the landscape is present in a sustainable and positive form.

The key elements of a future conservation strategy are therefore likely to place emphasis on:

- the increasing reliance on *ex-situ* methods of conservation but with a realization that these are a rather pathetic substitute for *in-situ* methods, and that they need to be linked to recovery programmes wherever possible;
- habitat restoration and similar intervention techniques, to overcome fragmentation and isolation effects and to accommodate necessary species displacements;
- a focus on mechanisms and policies that move away from the salvation of small isolated sites and try to ensure better environmental quality in the wider landscape;
- environmental education and initiatives designed to gain greater public and political support for biodiversity protection; these will be focused less on developing knowledge in the public, and more on developing concern and a positive attitude to nature;
- exploration of methods of sustainable land use where human needs can be met with respect for and partnership with nature.

The necessary directions are becoming clearer, even though there is a huge amount of work that needs to be done to clarify the methods. What is clear is that increasingly the most important focus of such a new vision of the protection of the natural world has to be the town and city. This is partly because urban areas can be an experimental ground for new methods, such as habitat restoration. Mainly, however, towns and cities are important because that is where people are, and nature needs to be brought to them.

Conservation problems are caused by the cumulative decisions of all of society; conservation battles will never be won by conservationists alone. Reaching the public is the most important job there is for the landscape manager. People and popular support are the only real resources and assets the conservation movement, and particularly the voluntary sector, possesses. Conservation work is dependent on public interest in wildlife; we need people to generate funds, labour and above all the political pressure that will help to conserve threatened habitats and endangered species. Above all we need to remember that it is people that are the cause of the damage to the rainforests or the peatlands; ultimately it is only a change in the way that people behave that will be their salvation. The development of a sense of personal responsibility required for social change will only be won in urban areas.

In fact a great deal of conservation work has always been done for its amenity value – which means because of its importance to humans, not because of its importance to wildlife. Facing up to this reality with a clearer vision allows the opportunity to undertake a positive rethink of the goals of urban conservation management. We need to encourage people to come into contact with, and to enjoy, wildlife. In so doing we aim to improve awareness of the value of nature, to encourage respect for wildlife, to promote an understanding of how the natural world works and more importantly of how people work in it.

The real conservation value of urban nature reserves and ecological landscapes therefore becomes more apparent. They exist for environmental education in its broadest sense. This does not necessarily mean that they are intended to send people away with overt messages about the loss of the rainforest or threats to Antartica. The first step is that they are intended to make people care a bit more, to help them to understand a bit more clearly our necessary dependence on the natural world. To achieve this means seeing more value in the small places, rediscovering beauty and also 'naturalness' in the weeds that grow in the corner of a derelict building site.

Of course not everyone will be able to relate to naturalistic landscapes. Many approaches also need to be explored for promoting a more sustainable society with higher levels of environmental concern; these include community gardens and city farms through to traditional parks and botanic gardens. Different people see value in different manifestations of nature, and this is exactly as it should be. Each of these styles and land use systems will have a role to play. The key thing is that opportunities are recognized and seized that allow more positive involvement and connection with the natural world.

In pursuit of this goal it is also vital that the various manifestations of the environmental movement learn to be more co-operative and more tolerant with regard to the different aspirations and tastes of other interest groups. All sorts of strategies are going to be necessary to meet the challenges of the future, ranging from traditional approaches to preservation and conservation wherever they are required through to interventionist programmes when appropriate. In general this wider perspective is becoming more common, but there remain many areas where it seems difficult for the wider perspective of the true needs of nature conservation to be adequately recognized.

Identifying existing urban sites of value

In the UK the best known criteria for identification of nature conservation sites worthy of protection were outlined by Ratcliffe (1977).

In urban areas much of the rationale must of course be different. Aspects such as diversity are valid concerns, but on sites where the primary function is public enjoyment and education then sometimes areas with a very low species diversity can still be successful and a broader landscape evaluation is required. Other more pragmatic criteria may come to the fore, such as consideration of the extent of public access or feasibility of integration within a management framework.

Rarity of species within sites becomes of less concern than the dispersal of sites across the town, with many planning authorities anxious to highlight areas of wildlife deficiency and also to focus on areas of land which function, at least to some degree, as a mutually supporting network that facilitates species dispersal. There are problems with many of the assumptions made about wildlife corridors which will be discussed in more detail later, but in general the wish to see protected areas considered as part of a mutually supporting network is a sophisticated concept that has much merit.

The fragility and likelihood of long-term survival of the sites is important in some cases but certainly not in all. Many urban sites are young, early successional habitats that have developed any natural diversity over a comparatively short time span. In many cases it may not matter from an ecological perspective whether these sites remain ephemeral as long as there is an adequate turnover of urban land to provide for their replacement. However, in cases where the urban sites have developed great social importance, becoming widely recognized and valued by local community groups and schools, for example, it can be traumatic if they are lost and it may even be necessary to instigate management to preserve them in the early successional stages which are characterized by many interesting herbs and invertebrates.

It is clear therefore that established land designation methods would inevitably undervalue urban sites. Nevertheless, planning authorities in particular still feel the need to find ways to highlight sites of value. Particular problems that can be identified are:

- the need to develop a value system that recognizes local rather than international priorities;

Box 4.2 The Ratcliffe criteria for evaluation of nature sites

Size

Importance to nature conservation generally increases with size.

Diversity

Variety is better than uniformity, species richness is better than a poor species complement. Sites with a range of habitats are preferred (but rarity or interest need not coincide with diversity).

Naturalness

Sites which have been least modified by man are most valuable.

Rarity

Sites are more valuable if rare species or communities are present.

Fragility

Fragile communities are more valuable and deserving of protection. They may be vulnerable to internal changes, e.g. low population numbers causes die out, or successional change, or vulnerable to external change, e.g. by human action.

Typicalness

One objective is to maintain examples of all habitat types, good examples are as important as rare ones.

Recorded history

Sites which are well researched or documented are more valuable.

The position in an ecological or geographical unit

This relates to landscape ecology, for example a wood which is contiguous with other woods is more valuable than one which is not.

Potential value

Sites with diminished importance, but not irreversible decline, can have a potential value greater than present value.

Intrinsic appeal

This often applies more to species than habitats. Birds and flowers are more conspicuous and appeal more to people.

Most of these criteria can be complementary, e.g. size and diversity. Some are arguably in conflict such as rarity and typicalness or diversity and naturalness (a site can be managed to be more diverse but it becomes less natural).

- the need to come to terms with the diversity and real composition of urban nature;
- the policy and methodology challenges posed by early successional sites;
- the need to actively promote positive and restorative conservation programmes.

Criteria for identification and designation of urban sites have been put forward by the London Ecology Unit (1985). Some of these criteria relate most to those sites which have significance for biodiversity conservation *per se*, and may be expected to apply most to regionally important sites. These are:

- richness/diversity;
- rarity;
- presence of ancient habitats;
- size;
- presence of non-recreatable habitats.

Some of the criteria relate more to the human value of the site and pragmatic issues related to planning and promotion. These are:

- potential;
- existing protection and opportunity;
- public access;
- aesthetic appeal;
- proximity to urban areas;
- presence in areas of deficiency (see below and Chapter 4).

Local land designations

National and international conservation goals are met largely through mechanisms such as land designation which allow sites of recognized importance to be protected from development or destructive activity (although the need to develop systems which can ensure the required degree of necessary constructive activity is still extremely poorly addressed within conservation policy). Not surprisingly, the distribution of sites which have national or international importance concentrate on irreplaceable and unique habitats associated with rare species rather than those of regional interest. The lack of designation for sites of local but not national significance was in fact often a weakness in planning applications, where an assumption has been made that the sites can not really be that important, although conversely at least most urban development activities require planning permission, which is in contrast with farming activities in the countryside.

Until recently it was left to non-governmental organizations such as local Wildlife Trusts to pioneer the designation of areas as nature reserves which have primarily educational value or popular appeal, but in recent years the UK mechanisms for local authority involvement in this process have been extended through the introduction of Local Nature Reserve designation. These parallel National Nature Reserves but put emphasis on locally rare habitats or on sites of great importance to local people. They are normally under the direct control of the local authority.

More recently we have seen the development of designations such as Sites of Nature Importance or similar. A variety of terms are currently used to describe such areas. These parallel Sites of Special Scientific Importance in that the designated land remains in the hands of a private landowner. These new designations have no statutory backing and they do not allow the authority to control what is done to land that they do not own. They carry no penalties for destruction or land-use change and a site owner may, usually entirely legitimately, choose to destroy the wildlife value of an area in order to safeguard possible future planning applications. It would certainly be perfectly within the law for a landowner to change the management of the site to destroy the conservation interest if they have intentions to make a planning application some time in the future. Nevertheless, the consensus seems to be that more sites are lost through ignorance than through deliberate action and that the value of such a designation mechanisms outweighs its potential drawbacks (Barker, 1986). They are, therefore, used as mechanisms for signalling to planning authorities (and to local lobbying groups) when activity is proposed which threatens the survival of habitats of local importance. For this reason they are sometimes generically referred to as 'Alert Map Sites'.

Even though new and more flexible designations do now exist, there is still an issue of how to identify the sites that contain wildlife of value. Increasingly programmes of site survey are allowing a comparatively full inventory of valuable areas to be compiled. Many urban authorities and wildlife trusts are able to list many areas of local wildlife significance.

However, it is inevitably the case that potentially valuable areas can be overlooked. Sometimes these problems arise from simple problems of access, where habitat stretches are either unreachable or even unknown about. Amazingly it is also often the case that the value of areas of open space that are visited by thousands of people each year may still go unrecognized. This may arise because of a prejudiced assumption by naturalists that some areas simply can not be of value – short mown grass and strands of exotics such as *Fallopia japonica* are two examples of vegetation types which, despite appearances, may have very rich plant species assemblages in the right circumstances (e.g. Gilbert, 1992). Indeed short mown grass has far more chance of maintaining diversity than an area of grassland which has been devoid of any management for many years. It is also often the case that conservation value may arise from the presence of unusual invertebrates or lower plants which are not easily recognized by anyone except specialist naturalists.

Ideally, therefore, whenever undertaking the management of areas of green space a valuable first step is to commission a survey or review of the existing wildlife value. Areas already used by wildlife should be preserved in preference to the creation of new habitats.

Of course it is still almost impossible to develop a complete picture through survey and more information needs to be gathered as part of a long-term monitoring programme. To catalogue even a representative sample of the full biota would require surveys carried out at different times of year, at different times of day and over several years. However, a good naturalist should be able to identify that a site has the appearance of a potentially rich wildlife habitat even if the details must remain obscure. The greatest danger, as outlined above, is that prejudice and superficial evaluations may still be a problem. Ideally, therefore, the person undertaking such an evaluation should be well versed in the different priorities and dynamics of urban nature conservation.

Finally once the sites that have some biodiversity richness have been identified, there still remains the last and often the most complex step in the evaluation procedure. It has already been argued that the real conservation value of urban nature lies in its relationship to the people of the town or city, and in the potential this therefore presents for developing a land stewardship ethic. The essential balancing act of the urban countryside evaluation process is therefore to match the distribution of the habitats identified with qualities such as the ease of access of local people, the size of catchment area, the opportunities for recreation, the visual attractiveness of the landscape and so on (Barker, 1986).

New and innovative techniques for identifying such areas have begun to be developed. For example, the UK environmental charity Common Ground has promoted the idea of Parish Maps whereby local people produce a map of their surroundings that highlights the features that they most value. These maps can be a fascinating and artistic blend of the objective, subjective and historical values of the land. They help planners to recognize exactly which areas and features are most loved and appreciated.

The result of such an analysis may often be that highest priority and status must be given to sites which are not the most important in terms of biodiversity. High biodiversity sites which do not have public access may still be of value of course, since they can help to support the general wildlife presence across the urban habitat matrix, but the extent to which resources should be targeted towards the protection of areas that no-one can use must inevitably be limited in urban areas.

Particular management dilemmas arise when there are sites where whatever biodiversity value there is can be expected to decline if there is any significant pressure of use. In rural sites, where the biodiversity is of regional or national significance it is fairly clear what the priorities should be. The conservation of the resource must override the right of access to the resource. But in an urban situation the very substance of the importance of the site may be that it is valued by local people, so the challenge of restricting access can cause both practical and philosophical headaches.

Accepting urban ecosystems – reducing the antipathy to exotic species

The complex and sometimes negative attitude to exotic plants in urban areas has already been discussed. It is an unfortunate phenomenon that enthusiasts of wildlife gardens and naturalistic landscapes sometimes show incredible antagonism for these species and do not hesitate to criticize people for their choice of plants or aesthetic and design preferences. For example, in Britain the Royal Society for Nature Conservation has made a call for some exotic plants to be 'banned' from landscape plantings on the grounds that they are 'ecologically useless' (Anon, 1991a).

This intolerance is usually justified by reference to the need to support native wildlife, which gives a moral backbone to the crusade, but the hard

Table 4.2 *The number of insects associated with different trees and shrubs*

Tree species	Insect and mite species	Tree species	Insect and mite species
Willow (5 spp.)	450	Rowan	58
Oak (2 spp.)	423	Lime (2 spp.)	57
Birch (2 spp.)	334	Field maple	51
Hawthorn	209	Hornbeam	51
Poplar (4 spp.)	189	Honeysuckle	48
Scots pine	172	Sycamore	43
Blackthorn	153	European larch	38
Alder	141	Juniper	32
Elm (2 spp.)	124	Elder	19
Crab apple	118	Spindle	19
Wild rose	107	Sweet chestnut	11
Bramble	107	Holly	10
Hazel	106	Horse chestnut	9
Beech	98	Walnut	7
Norway spruce	70	Yew	6
Ash	68	False acacia	2

Source: from Andrews and Rebane (1994), amalgamating data from Kennedy and Southwood (1984) and Ratcliffe (1977).

truth is that there are no truly endangered species which are likely to have their chances of survival materially influenced by the use of more native plants in gardens and urban landscapes.

It is worth examining in more detail the arguments for the use of native plants, to see how valid they really are in towns and cities. The evidence cited to support the scientific case in the UK is nearly always based on the work of the entomologist Richard Southwood whose work on the insect preferences for different tree species must be one of the most widely disseminated pieces of ecological research this century.

In essence the study showed that in general native trees and shrubs supported much greater numbers of species of invertebrates than exotic or recently naturalized species (Kennedy and Southwood, 1984). The premise was that invertebrates were able to adapt to exploit species over time and the longer a plant had been a UK native the more invertebrate species would be found feeding on it. Broadly the point was shown to be true. The importance for conservation planning in the wider countryside is clear. However, there are many points which need to be considered to qualify the extent to which this theory should be applied to urban situations.

- The contrast that is almost invariably cited compares oak, the most important native species for invertebrate diversity, with an exotic such as sycamore, although it is worth remembering that the list produced by Southwood includes some native species which have an insect fauna much poorer than sycamore does, such as holly.
- Although invertebrate diversity is low on some exotic species, invertebrate

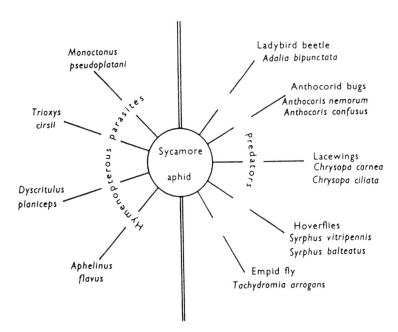

Figure 4.3 The invertebrates directly associated with the sycamore aphid in the UK (Gilbert, 1989).

biomass can still be relatively high. For example, *Acer pseudoplatanus* can carry high populations of aphids which are of course valuable for other species (see Figure 4.3).

- Very little is known about the invertebrate distribution in urban areas, but it is certain that many of the species of invertebrates that a species such as oak could support are specialists of certain habitats, perhaps rural woodlands of a certain stand type.

- The Southwood table concerns leaf feeders and not wood feeders, for whom the stage of decay of the tree may be more relevant (Key, 1995). Invertebrates are often highly dependent on habitat structure as well as food plant and many oak-living species are associated with ancient woodland conditions with many over-mature and decaying oak trees, precisely the sort of specimen that is absent from urban settings. Young trees will carry far fewer species (Table 4.4). Indeed it is likely that we'll not know the full range of invertebrates that a species such as sycamore could support in the absence of ancient over-mature sycamore stands in different settings across the country. Bland and Taylor (1991) relate bird diversity in cities with the presence of large gardens and mature trees and shrubs, rather than any association with native plants *per se*.

- Linked to this, the expectation is often promoted in people's minds that if they were only to look at an oak tree they would see this teeming with invertebrate life. This can be depressingly easy to disprove, as can be testified by many people who have attempted to study invertebrates as part of an environmental education programme. A broad range of invertebrates will often only be found in areas with good habitat structure.

- The relationship between natives and other plant and animal groups may

Table 4.3 *Important invertebrate habitat in woodland*

Major feature	Habitat	Microhabitat	Use by invertebrates
Woody plants trees and shrubs	Foliage	Canopy	Mainly as foodplants
		Understory	Mainly as foodplants
		At woodland/ride edge	*Foodplants/perches etc.*
	Flowers	*Sallow, hawthorn, sloe*	*Nectar sources*
	Bark Surface	**Rugosities**	**Niches for cover**
	Bark damage	**Loose bark**	**Saproxylics, cover**
		Sap runs	**Specialists**
	Living wood		A very few woodborers
	Damaged or	**Rot holes**	**Saproxylics, cover**
	decaying wood	**Heart rot**	**Saproxylics**
	on living trees	**Cavities**	**Saproxylics, cover**
	Water-filled rot holes		**Specialist fauna**
	Roots	Living	Mainly gall causers
		Decaying	**Saproxylics**
Herbs	Foliage	*In sun*	*Foodplants, perches etc.*
		In shade	Foodplants
	Flowers/nectar sources	***Especially composites and umbellifers***	***Nectar sources***
	Roots/storage organs	Mainly bulbous species	Foodplants
Bryophytes			Cover
Fungi	Soil fungi and mycorrhizae	Mycelium	Specialist mycophages
		Fruiting bodies	Specialist mycophages
	Dead wood	**Mycelium**	**Specialist saproxylics**
	fungi	**Fruiting bodies**	
		– Bracket	**Specialist saproxylics**
		– Gill	**Specialist saproxylics**
Plant litter	Leaf litter		Cover, saprophages
	Fallen dead wood	Accumulations of twigs	Specialist saproxylics
		Branches	Saproxylics
		Tree boles	**Saproxylics**
		Wood mould	**Specialist saproxylics** and soil fauna
Soil	Soil surface	*Bare soil in sun*	*Solitary bee and wasp nests* *Basking, thermophili species*
	Soil body	Woodland soil in shade	Specialist soil fauna
	Soil water	Seepage and flushes	Specialist 'squidge' fauna Different in *sun* and shade
Water	Standing water	Ponds and lakes	Different faunas in *sun* and shade
		Puddles (mainly in sun) on clay	*Temporary pool fauna*
	Running water	Rivers and streams in shade	A few specialist aquatics

Features particularly important to open space species italicized
Features particularly important to old forest species in bold (this latter group are particularly likely to be absent from urban woodland)
Source: Key (1995).

Table 4.4 *Association of lichen species with trees*

Tree/shrub	Number of lichen species	Tree/shrub	Number of lichen species
Oak (common and sessile)	326	Scots pine	133
Ash	265	Rowan	125
Beech	213	Alder	116
Elm spp.	200	Field maple	101
Sycamore	194	Holly	96
Hazel	162	Lime spp.	83
Willow spp.	160	Hornbeam	44
Birch (silver and downy)	134		

Source: Harding and Rose (1986).

not match Southwood's pattern e.g. lichen and bryophyte species are often seen on *Acer pseudoplatanus* (Table 4.4).

- Many exotic plants provide valuable supplements to the native flora by compensating for gaps in the species range or phenology of our natives. For example, late nectar sources of flowers are comparatively rare among indigenous species, and plants such as *Buddleia* and *Sedum spectabile* are widely recognized as excellent food supplements. Berries and fruits may also be produced with greater abundance or at unusual times of year by exotics. The UK flora also has few evergreen shrubs and many introduced species provide shelter for over-wintering birds.
- Even plants which have no recognized direct value as a food source or host may still create an environmental setting in which desirable species thrive. In areas in the UK where only sycamore trees develop reliably and rapidly, such as very exposed areas, woodland species will be dependent on those trees. In a review of which trees are most tolerant of urban conditions, Bradshaw, Hunt and Walmsley (1995) identified a list of mainly introduced species (Table 4.5).
- Another naive notion that is sometimes forwarded is that native trees 'grow better' or are hardier in the UK than imported plants would be. In reality many native plants are at the edge of their range and remain very vulnerable to climatic extremes; many only survive in favourable micro-climatic zones. In contrast, farms and forests are stocked with dozens of

Table 4.5 *Tree species adapted to extreme urban environments*

Acer platanoides	*Malus spp.* & hybrids	*Sambucus nigra*
Acer pseudoplatanus	*Platanus x acerifolia*	*Sorbus aria*
Aesculus x carnea	*Populus x euamericana*	*Sorbus aucuparia*
Ailanthus altissima	*Populus nigra*	*Sorbus hupehensis*
Buddleia davidii	*Robinia pseudoacacia*	*Sorbus intermedia*
Crataegus monogyna	*Salix alba*	*Tilia x vulgaris*
Fraxinus excelsior	*Salix daphnoides*	
Ginkgo biloba	*Salix viminalis*	

Source: Bradshaw *et al.* (1995).

taxa of exotic plants which are hardy in Britain; indeed many of them grow better here than they do in their own country. Most are chosen for no other reason than that they perform better than our own natives. *Acer pseudoplatanus* is particularly important for its ability to tolerate exposure and some poor soil types. In difficult conditions it is possible to get tree cover much more easily than would be the case with an oak.

The general validity of the importance of native species is not under question, but it is essential to achieve a balance and to allow room for other styles and other plants. The native plant ethic becomes dangerous when it is promoted, on what are actually weak ecological grounds, in a way which leads to unnecessary controls over people's initiatives or sends undesirable social messages.

For example, the real value of urban wildlife gardens lies in the way that they get some people to connect more with nature, to begin to care more. But when people are not tuned in with that style there is absolutely nothing to be gained by criticizing their likes. It is far more valuable that they value growing **something**, which may be an endangered species from another country, and that they don't learn to see the conservation movement as critical and antagonistic. Exotic plants are often well loved; they are familiar and easily recognizable to many people who do not want to hear that their gardens are stocked with plants that are in some way 'second rate' life forms, fit only for replacement by blackthorn scrub. Above all exotic plants are an important component of the culture of the UK; they have played a vital role in the development of our society and civilization and do not deserve to be rejected as 'pointless'.

The Black Environment Network has also drawn attention to undesirable rhetoric that accompanies 'nativism' which can be counterproductive when attempting to promote nature to a multi-cultural inner city population (Wong, 1997). The implicit assumption 'all natives are good, all aliens are bad' inevitably carries social overtones and builds barriers in areas where they desperately need to be broken down. At is worst the terminology may even carry overtones of racism. To some ecologists this may sound far-fetched, but it is worth remembering that in Nazi Germany there was a very strong ideology that promoted native plants and animals as superior to aliens, in parallel with their social beliefs (see Chapter 3 and Hottentrèger, 1992).

The constant focus on natives is certainly a position that may make it harder for ethnic communities to participate in environmental issues and environmental improvements, which can not be a good thing. The deliberate planting of exotics can be used to provide a focal point for interest, discussion and a point of entry for such groups into the broader environmental movement (Wong, 1997).

It can be argued that the very concept of 'native versus alien' as an issue is misguided or at best a misnomer. The true problems relate to invasive plants, which can be both native or exotic. Yet even invasiveness alone is not always a sufficiently sophisticated criteria. For example, in the UK the butterfly bush, *Buddleia davidii*, has become naturalized to such an extent that it is a rapid and sometimes very dominant colonist of urban open spaces. It seems to have a preference for germinating in rubble and waste dominated soils and even has the ability to establish on walls and on roofs to the point where it can begin to cause structural damage. Nevertheless, the plant is widely accepted and even welcomed as a sort of 'honorary native' that is even included in otherwise purist wildlife plantings. The reason is of course that its attraction to butterflies, and its contribution to their nectar food supply in late summer, is so obvious that all other faults are overlooked.

The focus on the value of native species undermines the importance of introduced plants to our well-being, and in particular underrates the spontaneous city habitats teeming with a mix of alien plants. Despite their origins the fascination and the wonder conjured by their ability to colonize and survive such hostile and artificial conditions gives them potentially important value as a symbol of nature triumphing over dereliction, and makes them a group that we need to promote (Gilbert, 1989).

More recently the debate concerning the value of natives has extended beyond the species to the ecotype level. There are increasingly calls for landscapers to use only regional ecotypes of wildflowers and native shrubs for example. The issue is particularly targeted towards wildflower seed producers. This is discussed in more detail in Chapter 6.

Conservation of early successional and changing communities

We have seen that the interest found on many of the 'post-industrial' urban sites arises from their early successional status. The unusual soil types are valuable because in part they allow locally unusual species to take hold and partly because they create conditions which are infertile or otherwise stressed and which can form the appropriate conditions for the development of a species-rich, uncompetitive plant community.

Early successional habitats have traditionally suffered from low status among conservationists who have tended to regard maturity and stability in ecosystems as equivalent to quality. They have, therefore, been largely overlooked in terms of research and policy formulation. In many ways the case for their protection is weakened by the presumed ease of their recreation but it is not always easy to be sure that recolonization will follow similar patterns.

The goal of protecting early successional communities is therefore complicated further by the greater degree of randomness that operates compared to late successional habitats. In stable conditions traditional climax theory states that the site will be inhabited by those plants and animals which are most successful and competitive under the prevailing climate and soil. In disturbed conditions competition between species is, initially at least, reduced. The mechanisms whereby one plant may outcompete another and exhibit greater fitness for the site environment do not become significant until the impact of the disturbance fades.

The extent to which this 'window of opportunity' can lead to the develop-

Table 4.6 *Lichens which may be encountered on a ten-year-old urban common*

Soil		Damp brick	
Cladonia chlorophaea	O-F	*Lecania erysibe*	R
C. coiocraea	R	*Scoliciosporum umbrinum*	O
C. fimbriata	O	*Trapelia coarctata*	C
C. furcata	R		
C. humilis	O	**Mortar, limestone chippings**	
Collema limosum	R	*Arthpyrenia monensis*	R
Peltigera spuria	R	*Bacidia caligans*	O
P. uliginosa	O	*B. chloroticula*	R
Vezdaea retigera	O	*Lecanora dispersa*	C
		Lecidella scabra	O
Wood		*Sarcogyne regularis*	R
Lecanora conizaeoides	F	*Sarcosagium camprestre*	O
Placynthiella icmalea	F	*Trapelia obtegans*	O
Trapeliopsis flexuosa	R	*Verrucaria muralis*	C
T. granulosa	O	*V. nigrescens*	C
Clothing and cardboard		**Rusty metal**	
Lecanora conizaeoides	O	*Bacidia saxenii*	F
Steinia geophana	R		

C – common; F – frequent; O – occasional; R – rare
Source: Gilbert (1989).

ment of ecologically interesting communities is often overlooked. Sometimes early-successional sites are even surprisingly rich in species that are normally associated with longer term and stable conditions (see Table 4.6).

In a freshly cleared site therefore there may be many hundreds of species which could invade and form a viable part of the early successional community. The ones which do arrive and establish are able to do so as the result of a compendium of chance factors such as the timing of the disturbance relative to the availability of colonizing seed. This means that almost identical early successional habitats may contain very different species depending on their location and the nature of the disturbance that formed them.

As we have seen, traditionally nature conservation priorities have favoured long established and comparatively undisturbed habitats on the basis that these habitats will have accumulated a full and representative range of species adapted to the conditions, and also that they may represent species assemblages that were able to colonize during very different conditions or climate or landscape pattern and which may never be able to recolonize again.

The 'locate, designate and protect' strategies that have been appropriate for these groups of stable habitats is clearly of less direct relevance to plants and animals normally adapted to effective dispersal in the search for temporary niches. To maintain such species on a particular site as part of a conservation programme requires the evaluation of areas which have had a high disturbance impact, and to continue to recreate that disturbance, probably on

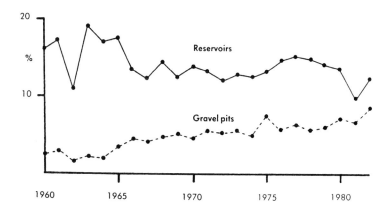

20

%

10

Reservoirs

Gravel pits

1960   1965   1970   1975   1980

Figure 4.4 The percentage of counted wildfowl in Britain on gravel pits and reservoirs (from Owen *et al.*, 1986)

a rotational basis, to maintain the favourable conditions. This is of course possible, but it is nevertheless the case that such 'disturbance' sites are really not irreplaceable and finite, in the way that long term stable ecosystems are. Even if scarce ruderal species are found in a certain locality, the degree to which that discovery must lead to long-term preservation of the site therefore needs to be evaluated with a large amount of caution and common sense.

A species that provides a good example of such behaviour is the sand martin bird, which builds its nests in open banks often associated with water bodies. This species is capable of colonizing newly created opportunities in quarries and banks, although its arrival can never be guaranteed, and it can build up large population numbers quickly, only to see these collapse again if successional processes destroy the open ground it needs. The colonization of newly created wetlands by birds has been so rapid and extensive that the value of new secondary sites as a conservation resource for all but the most sensitive species can hardly be questioned (Figure 4.4).

Another difficulty with early successional habitats is recognizing the optimum stage of habitat development and determining when ecosystem change has progressed so far that the net gain in species is worth less than those plants and animals which will be lost. Again conventional succession theory states that species richness increases as succession progresses, reflecting the increase in structural diversity and the increase in stability which allows more species to be accumulated and more niches to be exploited. Figure 4.5 illustrates this progression on a theoretical basis (Green, 1981) and Figure 4.6 shows how structural diversity can develop during a succession (Emery, 1986).

However, there are certain qualifications of this trend which need to be recognized for effective conservation. Firstly, as we have seen already, the value of the species present needs to be evaluated against their relative scarcity or vulnerability. Woody scrub for example is not an uncommon habitat in the UK; it has increased in response to a decline in rabbit

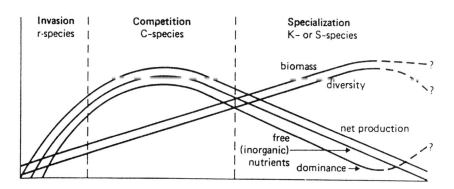

Figure 4.5 The theoretical changes in ecosystem attributes as succession develops (Green, 1981).

Table 4.7 *The numbers of species in scrub stands dominated by* Crataegus *on calcareous soils*

Canopy	Open	Patchy	Closed
Total	124	109	45
Grassland species	79	55	2
Marginal species	18	27	10
Woodland species	0	0	12

Source: adapted from Duffey *et al.* (1974).

populations and abandonment of some marginal grasslands over previous decades. Secondly, there is often a period of decline of species following the change from one biome to another (Table 4.7).

A grassland habitat which has accumulated a wide complement of species adapted to such conditions will degenerate following the transition to woodland, and it will take many years for the woodland to develop equivalent richness. A change in management or land use does not, therefore, necessarily mean a decline of nature conservation interest but the potential of the new conditions will not be able to be expressed in terms of the plant and animal communities until colonization and re-adjustment is again complete. The rate and extent to which this happens is dependent on complex factors such as the local species pool, the isolation of the habitat in question and the continuity of conditions.

The threshold of change from one biome to another can therefore represent a particular challenge to the manager; the initial invasion by components of a later successional biome can add diversity to an area. However, it is necessary to be conscious of the impacts on the species previously established.

A good example relates to lowland heathland which rapidly becomes invaded by scrub and trees if the management intensity is not comparatively high. The early stages of such scrub invasion can increase the diversity of flora, invertebrates and especially birds using the heath. However, as scrub cover increases, several environmental changes take place such as an increase in shade. This has been implicated in the decline of the natterjack

Figure 4.6 (facing page) Vegetation structure changes that are expected following the progression from bare ground to woodland (Emery, 1986).

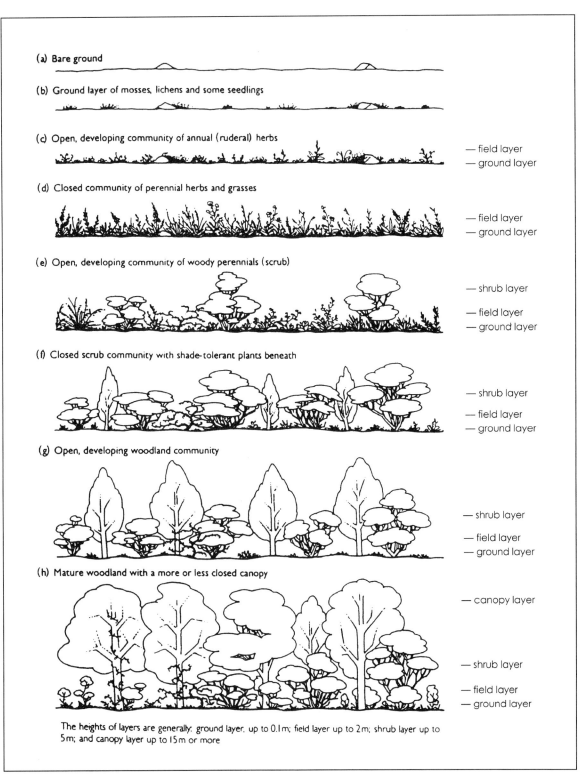

(a) Bare ground

(b) Ground layer of mosses, lichens and some seedlings

(c) Open, developing community of annual (ruderal) herbs

— field layer
— ground layer

(d) Closed community of perennial herbs and grasses

— field layer
— ground layer

(e) Open, developing community of woody perennials (scrub)

— shrub layer

— field layer
— ground layer

(f) Closed scrub community with shade-tolerant plants beneath

— shrub layer

— field layer
— ground layer

(g) Open, developing woodland community

— shrub layer

— field layer
— ground layer

(h) Mature woodland with a more or less closed canopy

— canopy layer

— shrub layer

— field layer
— ground layer

The heights of layers are generally: ground layer, up to 0.1 m; field layer up to 2 m; shrub layer up to 5 m; and canopy layer up to 15 m or more toad in the UK, as reduced heathland temperatures has allowed the spread of the more competitive common toad (Beebee, 1992). Assessment of the degree of loss of lowland heathland, among the most devastated habitat types in England, is therefore complicated by the need to make a judgement of when the habitat has actually disappeared – how much scrub invasion represents the moment of transition? At what point, if ever, does the decline in heathland habitat become effectively irreversible?

The different facets of this habitat decline conundrum are obviously sometimes subtle. As any one biome changes or fragments there may be a decline in the population size of component plants and animals that are intolerant of other conditions. This decline may be acceptable in the name of increased diversity as long as it does not undermine the long-term maintenance of the populations present. However, there is a recognized Minimum Viable Population for many species below which there may be many undesirable effects, such as an inability to reproduce effectively or an erosion of the genetic base of the population which decreases the fitness of the individuals in the long term (Wilson, 1992). In extreme cases, if the population falls beneath this low point then the species may not be able to recover easily, even if there is a subsequent improvement in the habitat status. The extent to which this is a realistic scenario for many ruderals and early successional species, which are adapted to huge population swings, is of course debatable, but it may certainly apply to some of the more vulnerable 'rare ruderals' discussed above.

As habitat decline progresses and individual species are lost there may also be consequential losses of other dependent organisms. For example, if an insect's food plant disappears then the animal will do so as well; similarly plants may suffer from the loss of key pollinators or animals that act as seed dispersal vectors, although the effects will be rather slower to manifest and populations can survive for many years looking healthy, even though in fact they no longer have a future.

In some cases the disappearance of a particular plant or animal may have a profound effect on many other species and can lead to a 'cascade of related local extinctions'. This relates to the concept of keystone species, which have a dominant and controlling effect over certain key processes which maintain the very integrity of the ecosystem. An example would be if a predator becomes extinct leading to a consequential increase in the population of herbivores, which in turn lead to disappearance or suppression of many plants and also of the invertebrates which depend on them and so on (Shafer, 1990). Of course predators, because of their position in the food web, often have a large territory requirement and, unless they are catholic in their habitat requirements, they may be particularly prone to habitat fragmentation.

Probably the most difficult aspect of habitat decline is when there has been the loss of key processes or management inputs which maintain the system in a healthy state. The example already given is where periodic flooding may be necessary for some wetland edge communities (providing nutrient inputs, or creating regeneration niches) and may have been removed because of flood relief schemes or river canalization. Another example is the suppression of accidental fires which are seen as destructive but are in fact important for the renewal of some ecosystems. In the case of systems where these effects are required on a low frequency it can be years before the negative effects of the loss of inputs are identified. The habitat may continue to appear healthy long after it has lost long-term viability.

In some cases it may be difficult to recognize that a key input was needed at all. Historical records suggest that grassland communities typically managed as hay or pasture may have had periods where the management types were mixed or confounded. Certainly it was likely that grazing after a hay cut was a common practice which often led to severe ground disturbance and poaching. This degree of disruption and production of bare ground may have been essential for preventing equilibrium in the long term and for encouraging the survival of certain components in the ecosystem. In general severe disturbance is now seen as undesirable in plant communities but there is a risk that landscape managers may severely underestimate the role of stochastic disturbance events in rural plant communities. More 'sensitive' management which attempts to reduce apparent damage may in fact undermine one of the processes which maintains diversity in the system.

It has also been noticed that some woodland perennials such as wood anemone do not spread rapidly and remain as indicators of old undisturbed woodlands (Peterken, 1981). However, horticulturists know that if these are dug up, divided and replanted the rate of increase can be relatively fast (a common growth response seen in many herbaceous perennials grown in garden borders). Again it may be the case that animals digging or disturbing the soil may have been important dispersal vectors in traditional communities.

Another aspect of the protection of early successional and post industrial communities relates to their image and poor appearance which may make it difficult for the public to accept that they should be protected at all (Eyre and Luff, 1995).

Restoration focused nature conservation policies

We have seen that long-established policies for nature conservation and biodiversity management in rural areas have been based upon a paradigm that sees human impact as ultimately undesirable and damaging. The need to manage 'natural areas' is still felt by many to be an oxymoron, and even when it is accepted there is often still a sense of regret. The focus on 'protected areas' is also to a large extent based upon such a paradigm with excessive intervention seen as undesirable; the role of management has been to suppress or compensate for undesirable impacts from outside the protected zone.

Over time, in countries such as the UK where land fragmentation and countryside change is well advanced, the need to manage protected areas more positively has been recognized. There was, not surprisingly, a recognition of the need to maintain plagioclimax communities by re-creating the management operations that would have formed and shaped the habitat in the first place.

The level of intervention was then increased by the recognition of a need to diversify habitats structurally. New management tasks have become necessary in nature reserves to compensate for the disappearance of similar species-rich habitats locally. At one time these would have functioned often as a network of inter-related sites with many species finding a niche somewhere even despite local extinctions and landscape change. Indeed, once the philosophical need to extend management beyond traditional activities became accepted, reserve staff began positively to relish the challenge of optimizing the species support value of their sites. As discussed earlier, many have developed a complex pattern of inputs that could be called 'gardening nature' if it were not that the staff seem to find such terms insulting. Patterns of rotational grazing have been introduced on some sites that have little in common with farming practice. Some sites have introduced artificial shelter or even food supplies to maintain populations of animals that may be functioning on sub-optimal territory range, or which are no longer competitive with invading species.

Despite this artificial activity, the main aspect of intervention that most reserve managers refused to accept was to directly introduce plants or animals, or to alter their patterns of distribution through planting. The psychology of conservation seems to be that humans are allowed to modify the environmental and management framework that allows certain patterns of species diversification to occur, but nature must be allowed to do the work of colonizing this framework. In this way a semi-natural status could be maintained.

Increasingly the new management challenges discussed above are encouraging a move to greater and more profound intervention in the form of habitat creation and restoration (Wilson, 1989). However, these new techniques have many possible drawbacks and limitations. They include elements that are expensive compared to traditional practice, and which are far from proven technically. They may therefore divert priorities and resources away from other areas and should only be undertaken where there is a clear recognition of their purpose and value, and a clear-sighted assessment of the appropriate techniques and methodology.

High-intervention policies also degrade any quality of naturalness that a site may have. We have seen that naturalness is one of the criteria valued for setting conservation priorities (Ratcliffe, 1977), and clearly the more there is deliberate control over the nature of a habitat the more its naturalness is compromised. There is also the problem of the disruption of opportunities for scientific assessment about the 'natural' distribution of a species.

Of course the counter argument is that naturalness probably is already irreversibly compromised by human impact, and we can't put a greater priority on saving naturalness than we do on trying to save the world's biodiversity. Plant and animal distribution is often totally controlled and influenced indirectly by people from the distribution and fragmentation of existing populations, the scope and the means of dispersal of seed, the viability of survival in a new site and so on. Yet such artificial restriction or encouragement of species behaviour would still be seen as natural, whereas planned influence on species distribution is argued to be artificial. If we do not allow positive intervention then there is only room for all of the destructive and negative forces which restrict the spread all over the earth. Is it more natural to allow a plant to be driven to extinction by man's activities than to provide the mechanisms by which it can re-find habitats which are suitable but are not easily reached?

(There are also spiritual and emotional values that arise from contact with 'naturalness' and which may be of great importance. Arguably these values need not necessarily be lost if positive intervention is approached in the right way. This issue is discussed in more detail in Chapter 6.)

It is clear, therefore, that interventionist techniques will develop rapidly as a key component of biodiversity protection strategies, but at the same time there needs to be caution in their wider application. They represent a fundamental change in both the methodology and philosophy of nature conservation and will not be implemented in highly sensitive areas until well proven. The potential drawbacks are, however, much less significant in urban areas, and these are where new technologies such as habitat creation will need to be developed and trialed.

As natural habitats disappear and, along with them, the opportunities for the establishment of new reserves within pristine habitat, our descendants will be faced with a surplus of degraded land and impoverished biotic communities. Thus, the scavenging and rehabilitation of degraded places may become the dominant activity of conservationists in the twenty-first century.

Obviously only a tiny fraction of such re-naturalised land will be returned to something like the conditions that existed before.... wildlife will have more lebensraum.

It is apparent that the emphasis in conservation biology will gradually shift from the protection of quasinatural habitat fragments (there will be none left that aren't either protected or doomed) to the opportunistic construction of artificially diverse landscapes (Western *et al.*, 1989).

Aspects of interventionist approaches to urban nature conservation are discussed in the following chapters, at a strategic level with regard to planning the urban countryside, and the role of landscape ecology, and at a tactical level with a discussion of the optimum approaches to habitat creation to increase opportunities for urban wildlife.

5 Biogeography and conservation planning in the urban countryside

It is becoming increasingly apparent that many of the assumptions underlying conservation planning have been too simplistic to guide management accurately, or to explain adequately all of the relationships seen between species and reserves. Slowly ecologists are developing an understanding of the ways in which broader habitat patterns, comprising shapes, sizes, internal structure and the spatial relationship between all of these and between the habitats and the surrounding landscape influence the diversity of species found within a reserve or wildlife area.

The discipline of landscape ecology has been defined by the UK branch of the International Association of Landscape Ecology as

> the interactions between the temporal and spatial aspects of a landscape and its flora, fauna and cultural components (Griffith, 1995).

In many ways it is a direct extension of the subject of biogeography.

The subject grew largely out of the interests of central European biogeographers in the regional and local scale patterns and processes in the landscape (Naveh and Liebermann, 1994), although the terminology inevitably has become entangled and confused with those aspects of work of the landscape professions which have an ecological orientation, such as have been discussed in earlier chapters regardless of their scale. For the purposes of this chapter, the term landscape ecology is used in keeping with the above definition – the objective is to review the interaction between the pattern and distribution of habitats and sites within the urban fabric and to consider how the relationships between them may affect their function.

The significance of such a study lies in its potential contribution towards strategic planning and the identification of areas where green space creation, protection and management strategies may be targeted towards regional benefits. It is increasingly the case that environmental planners across Europe are using principles of landscape ecology as guides for determining policy and in some countries such as Holland there are extensive programmes of proactive green space designation and habitat creation that are determined by the perceived benefits arising from improvements in the pattern and distribution of open land (see papers in Griffith, 1995). Many of these applications are focused on urban areas, where constraints on overall land availability mean that clear guidance is often needed for prioritizing site protection or purchase.

Many of the most challenging problems of modern ecology arise from attempts to quantify and more accurately predict processes and patterns within the natural world. Of course this objective is both understandable and desirable, but the temptation always exists to develop theories and paradigms beyond their role as conceptual aids to the point where individual elements can be studied in depth and measured. Much of the basis of landscape ecology and of conservation planning relates to the basic principles of island biogeography theory developed by MacArthur and Wilson (1967). There is clearly value in exploring these concepts in rather more detail here.

The basic concepts of the island theory

Island Biogeography Theory (MacArthur and Wilson, 1967) attempts to identify the processes which underlie equilibrium in species numbers on any island (not, directly, in the population sizes of each species) through studying the processes of immigration and extinction. The theory was inspired by three patterns which had long been recognized as part of island ecology:

- that larger islands tend to support more species;
- that remote islands tend to support fewer species;
- that there is often a turnover of species on islands, with newcomers replacing other species that become extinct.

Immigration rates of species (i.e. the rate at which the island is colonized by species not already present, and which become successfully established) is greater for islands which are near to a mainland (if this is seen as an unlimited 'source' of all potential species). Island area must have some affect on the likelihood of colonization occurring, but this is not usually seen as significant. Obviously the main process of concern is that dispersal becomes more difficult the further the island is from the species origins.

In addition, although colonization of individuals may be a continual process, the more species that are present on an island the lower the probability that any new species invading will be a genuine addition to the fauna or flora. Nevertheless, it could be the case that the population of a given species on the island may be too small to be viable in itself, and it may rely upon continual immigration to provide additional numbers or to maintain genetic health.

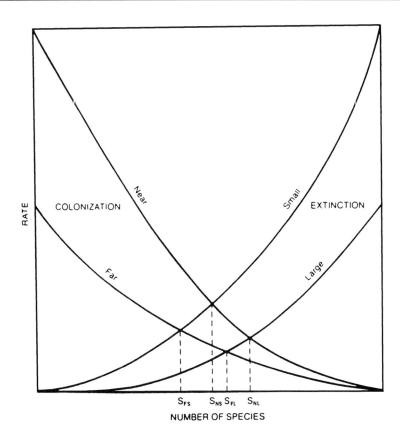

Figure 5.1 A diagramatic representation of MacArthur and Wilson's equilibrium model (Wilcox, 1980).

The extinction rate of a species is higher on a small island than on a large. The reasons contributing to this are complex:

- large islands are likely to consist of a wider range of habitats which can support more species;
- the smaller the range of habitats the more likely it is that any species that arrives will have to operate within suboptimal environmental conditions and hence be more vulnerable to adversity;
- large islands may support larger populations of a given species making it less likely to die out; this applies especially to species with large territory requirements such as predators;
- the larger the island the less the chance that stochastic environmental catastrophes such as fire or flood will affect the whole population.

The equilibrium that controls species diversity therefore is expected to be greatest for large islands near to the mainland and least for small islands far from the mainland (Figure 5.1).

Certain of the assumptions and relationships embodied in the theory are obviously in need of greater clarification when an attempt is made to apply it to a real-life situation:

- The 'mainland' source of species may not have a wide complement of species, or may not contain habitats or environmental conditions comparable to those on the island.
- Island clusters and intermediate islands will affect the relationships, but not necessarily in easily quantified ways.
- The shape of the island will affect habitat size and distribution and hence the potential diversity.
- The assumption that larger islands have wider habitat ranges, more diverse topography etc. is not always true.
- Over a long-enough timescale and given sufficient isolation, speciation will occur on islands. The rate and effectiveness of speciation will vary from species to species.
- Environmental catastrophe that reduces population size may not lead to immediate extinction but may increase the risk of genetic depauperization and long-term reduction in viability. Repeated colonizations by the same species may not directly influence the immigration curve but they may play a key role in maintaining genetic diversity and viability within the species.
- The actual dispersal curves proposed by MacArthur and Wilson are just assumptions and certainly can not be similar for all species types – cf. mammals with birds and invertebrates and cf. angiosperms with bryophytes.
- Different species are likely to be at greater risk than others of extinction. This may be because of more exacting habitat requirements, slow reproduction, large area requirements etc. Turnover rate and equilibrium will differ for different plant and animal groups.
- Some plants and animals have a symbiotic relationship with others and will not survive if their symbiots are not present.
- Some 'keystone' species play a key role in determining the function of a community and hence the extinction of one animal, for example, may lead to the disappearance of several others (Paine, 1966).
- The degree to which there really is a turnover of species on 'islands' which are at equilibrium is also a matter of debate. The principles are difficult to test in ordinary experimental timescales. Turnover of species, if it does occur, is a difficult concept for nature conservation as there is often a presumption that the species that are already present in a country are 'preferable' to those which immigrate.

The cumulative effect of these various problems is that some critics see the model as fundamentally flawed. ('One of the few models of community ecology that have been repeatedly and unequivocally falsified' (Brown, 1981, cited in Shafer, 1990)). Nevertheless, it is difficult to overestimate the tenacity and importance of the Island Biogeography model in most conservation planning. This probably arises because it is often impossible to build strategic decisions upon firm data, since the latter is either missing for many species, unreliable or conflicting when the likely fortunes of different organisms are compared. (NB: In some rural habitats where species of genuine national conservation significance are found, priorities can be easy to set; in urban areas decisions to favour certain groups of wildlife above others can seem rather more arbitrary.) The island theory may often not work as a precise prediction tool, but the relationships it proposes are essentially plausible if seen as trends rather than absolutes.

Application of island biogeography theory to nature conservation

One of the main applications of MacArthur and Wilson's theory (or of closely related concepts which pre-date it) has been in the planning of terrestrial nature reserve designation and management. When transferring the principle to terrestrial systems the key assumption that is made is that 'habitats' or reserve sites themselves can start to function as isolated islands if they are surrounded by land of a very different type that is hostile to the species living within.

The following concepts underpin many landscape ecology studies and are generally implicitly accepted in most nature conservation planning strategies:

- Related habitat types which are in close enough proximity are able to function as a related whole. For some species the cumulative area may be available for exploitation. For other species which appear to function as isolated groups there may be enough movement between sites to maintain an overall healthy population and to compensate rapidly for localized extinctions.
- The fragmentation of habitats which increases dispersal distances between similar communities will lead to a reduction in the species numbers that these isolated areas can support.
- Isolation of populations may lead to genetic impoverishment and inbreeding.
- Reduction in area of a given habitat will reduce the number of species that can be supported within it. Of particular concern is that many nature reserves were designated at a time when they were surrounded by land of perhaps lower quality but not completely hostile. The species within the reserve were in reality part of a wider population. As land-use change intensifies and the surrounding buffer land disappears the species content of the reserve may fall.
- Reduction in area will usually increase the ratio of perimeter to core, increasing the risk of perturbations or colonization by new species and leading to changes in habitat character which may influence specialists.
- There is a conflict between attempts to maximize diversity within a reserve by extending the range of habitats, and the increased risk that this will make any one species more vulnerable to local extinction as the area it can exploit begins to fall.
- There is a minimum viable area/minimum viable population size for isolated species below which the risk of extinction becomes unacceptably great.

PRINCIPES FOR DESIGN OF FAUNAL PRESERVES

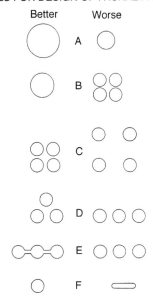

Figure 5.2 The SLOSS debate. The shape and distribution of habitat fragments is anticipated to affect the degree to which they can support biodiversity. Not all of the relationships are confirmed by research (Diamond, 1975).

• Corridors and habitat links between reserves are desirable as they may reduce the isolation and vulnerability of species.

Of course, in practice, much nature reserve designation is undertaken in an ad-hoc manner, often in response to opportunity or threat, and carried out in a climate of economic constraint and often political or social opposition. As a consequence there have often been strong pressures to minimize the land area protected, or to attempt to save interesting sites without a detailed analysis of whether the populations contained are really viable. This can lead to suboptimal situations, with perhaps the worst scenario being that a habitat designation and protection programme can be set in place which superficially looks viable but is in practice no more than a stop gap that delays inevitable species loss. For example, it has been suggested that for woodland birds habitat patches of less than 25 km^2 could lead to 10–50% extinctions within a reserve within 100 years (Wilson, 1989).

Inevitably issues become complex when attempts are made to move forward to a more rational and planned strategy. For example, one of the most complex aspects of conservation planning is sometimes referred to as the SLOSS debate – Single Large Or Several Small (Shafer, 1990) (see Figure 5.2). In other words if ten hectares of land can be purchased as part of a nature reserve programme is it better to create one reserve of 10 ha, two of 5 ha, five of 2 ha etc. Experimental evidence is conflicting – for some species groups a single large reserve is preferable (presumably those species which have large territory requirements), whereas for others (especially those dependent on 'edge' or boundary habitats) several small reserves will be preferable. The scale and likelihood of stochastic disturbances will also be an important issue, as will the distances between the several small reserves. The shape of the reserves created will also carry different implications for different species.

The SLOSS debate also has a human perspective – small and distributed sites may give best human value even if there is a limited wildlife value. There is some evidence that many environmental qualities improve rapidly as site size increases, up to about 0.5 ha at which point the rate of improvement begins to tail off but the relationship is weak and there are many exceptions (Plummer and Shewan, 1992). It is a yet unresolved issue whether people too have certain minimum size criteria for different experiences – can 'wildness' be sensed in a single weed plant as well as in a rainforest? (see Chapter 9).

Limitations of island theory

It is plainly obvious that the details of island theory contain many assumptions and many generalizations which do not and can not hold for all circumstances. It is even possible that there are no real life circumstances which are adequately explained by the model, but this need not undermine its value as long as a broader perspective is maintained. Ecological theories of this kind are necessarily generalizations that underestimate the complexity and variability of the real world – if they did not they would be unworkable. We need a means of modelling and understanding the broad trends and processes that need to be taken into account but it is also important to remember that attempts to stretch the application of the theory to terrestrial settings are likely to push the ideas to their limits. This is particularly true of urban settings where many of the relationships are simply too poorly understood to be reliably applied.

One of the fundamental assumptions made in island theory is that the sea acts as a barrier to colonization, and that the severity of this barrier increases with distance. It was already mentioned above that this assumption, while perhaps true as a general trend, is not necessarily valid for different plant and animal groups. Certainly as soon as the question is asked as to **which** species colonize islands it becomes obvious that there are some very different responses:

- some species will not cross the 'barrier' no matter how short the distance;
- some species do show a decrease in colonization ability closely related to distance;
- some species appear almost independent of distance in their ability to colonize, although there may be threshold distances beyond which their dispersal ability rapidly drops.

When attempting to apply island theory to terrestrial habitats the question becomes rather more complex as we need to identify which environmental changes really do act as significant barriers to species, and which they find largely unimportant. In other words is it a valid assumption that a nature reserve surrounded by, say, urban conurbations or farmland, really functions as an isolated island? The answer of course will differ for different species. The significance of habitat discontinuities will be influenced not just by distance and size, but also by the quality of the landscape between them. For example, it is likely to be very significant for some species where two woodlands are separated by a sterile field containing nothing but arable farmland, or by a diverse patterned and small-scale landscape of hedges, grass and mature trees.

Another issue of some significance is that it may not always be safe to assume that encouraging flux of species or individuals between different sites is necessarily desirable. In some situations habitat fragmentation and separation may be an aid to conservation as it can limit the spread of pests and disease or predators or safeguard against the impact of local disturbances.

Dawe (1995) found positive evidence for species-area relationships in relation to many urban species, but also noted that other factors were superimposed, most notably a decline in species density per unit area approaching the city centre and in relation to numbers of people. He argued that disturbance within a given habitat may therefore over-ride simple area considerations, and that there is little direct evidence that supports the basic assumed relationship between immigration, extinction and proximity of source of colonizing individuals. Despite these uncertainties the thrust of proactive environmental planning for nature conservation is clearly focused on the need to overcome isolation and fragmentation.

Another interesting discussion of the application of island theory to an urban conservation context is provided by Bastin and Thomas (1995) who found that within the Birmingham area the likelihood of survival of 22 plant species was influenced primarily by:

- site area (+ve effect);
- habitat age (+ve effect);
- distance from the nearest population of same species (-ve effect).

Less important correlations were found with:

- adjacent habitat similarity or buffer zones;
- increasing habitat number within a site.

No significant relationship was found with length of time of isolation (encapsulation) of a habitat within an anthropogenic matrix.

The authors, therefore, found stronger evidence for habitat pattern affecting colonization (or recolonization) rates than for the effect on extinction rates. They recommended, therefore, that attention be given to artificial introduction of species or to the provision of habitat corridors, i.e. an area of land that facilitates species movement between larger habitats.

The role of corridors in species dispersal

The potential value of corridors is increasingly emphasized in all aspects of conservation planning in response to the recognition of the limited effectiveness of traditional land designation and protection programmes (Kirby, 1995). Corridors are particularly seen as key components of strategies designed to allow wildlife to adjust distribution in response to climate change. The goal is to overcome the negative effect of land fragmentation, so that different reserves can buffer each other and localized extinction and random catastrophes can be compensated for by re-invasion of species from other areas. Effective corridors may thus allow several reserves to function ecologically as one larger unit.

However, although the theoretical value of corridors is easy to understand, there is a great deal of confusion about the desirable nature and layout of corridors. Many corridors are categorized on the basis of assumption and hope rather than as a result of any clear evidence that they function as such (see Dawson, 1994). It is therefore worth reviewing in slightly more detail the issues involved.

It is quite common that the need to preserve rural hedgerows is justified on the basis of the role that they may play in encouraging and allowing species dispersal. Hedgerows therefore would make a good case study for testing the plausibility of the corridor concept as currently formulated.

Let us consider the case of two areas of woodland separated by farmland but linked by a hedgerow. As we have seen, terrestrial habitats are not true islands, and the nature of the intervening land is not necessarily as hostile as is often believed. There are numerous species which are capable of passing between two isolated woodlands without the need for intervening hedgerow.

There are also species which have a high dependence on true woodland conditions; shade, high humidity and above all limited competition. These will be highly unlikely to travel between woodlands within a hedgerow. In order for effective movement of these species to be achieved, it is necessary for the corridors to be wide enough to create equivalent inner-woodland conditions in the centre. Many of these species may have very low rates of movement and dispersal and will in fact take several generations to travel between sites, so these woodland interior conditions will need to satisfy all of their habitat needs and may need to be maintained for many years without excessive disturbance. Some work in the USA suggests that to allow the movement of the most intolerant species, those which are probably likely to have the greatest conservation significance, it would be necessary to have corridors which are over 3 km wide (Shafer, 1990).

The hedgerow may still be valuable to a group of species that can move if it is there, but will not move if it is not. The next problem is to ensure that the hedgerow is of appropriate quality to allow this to happen, and to happen with enough frequency that viable colonizing populations can be established. For some plant species for example, this may mean that there needs to be consistent soil conditions along the hedgerow. Some species may need other species to be present in the hedgerow before they can survive (e.g. a bark beetle may move along the hedgerow if it contains the right host tree, present at the right age and size). It is also important to consider what size of gaps they will tolerate etc. Some animals may be unable or unwilling to move across even quite small gaps, such as a gate in the hedge.

Some aspects of the hedgerow may increase the vulnerability of the animals and plants moving in it. For example, they are areas which are very prone to pesticide or fertilizer drift from adjacent fields. It is also often the case that predatory species hunt preferentially along hedgerow bases, and some authors have suggested that species can even undergo population decline when hedgerows adjoin their habitat as individuals may be lured into situations where they are vulnerable to attack. Corridor establishment may also allow the spread of undesirable species and threaten the survival of relict communities that are surviving partly because of their isolation (Schmid, 1995). For example railways, canals and rivers have often been the route of spread of undesirable weeds.

This is not to say that hedgerows do not have conservation value, but rather it is often the case that they are linear habitats in their own right, possibly unique in their characteristics. They are very important for the support of those species which are adapted to live in them, but they may not be functioning critically as movement connectors between other patches of land.

In presenting this review it is not the intention to deny the potential value or importance of all connecting land between habitat fragments, but there are many circumstances where there needs to be a more sophisticated analysis of what the nature of such a corridor could and should be. If habitat isolation really does pose a threat for biodiversity survival, the restoration of links needs to be approached on the basis of a detailed analysis of the dispersal behaviour of the key species. It is also essential that the possible negative effects of habitat connection are taken into account (Dawson, 1994). Above all, it is essential that more properly structured research in corridor ecology is undertaken.

Of course pragmatic assessment of corridors does require that compromises are made, and they may be particularly of value as foci of improvement works. If doubt exists about whether corridors are inevitably of value, or at least if there is a lack of clear supporting evidence, it still seems intuitively to many conservation managers that they must be of value, and anecdotal evidence of their use by wildlife does exist. It is clearly better to protect existing connections between habitats than to assume that they are unimportant. However, corridors should not gain unjustified prominence in urban landscape planning at the expense of other options and other issues. Most significantly measures aimed at preserving the quality of existing landscape patterns, usually through better support for management of land, are poorly addressed by current environmental planning mechanisms.

Urban nature conservation strategies

As we have seen, the logical extension of the study of the influence of habitat size and distribution on integrity and function is to build many of the principles into the planning system such that land use decisions can be made which support biodiversity protection objectives. The last decade has seen a rapid growth in interest in the UK in the preparation of nature conservation strategies for urban areas. These strategies are usually spearheaded by the planning department of local authorities, but are often prepared in close consultation with central government organizations and many non-governmental bodies, particularly the local wildlife trusts (e.g. Greater Bristol Nature Conservation Strategy).

Barker (1984) identified the following elements that should be in a strategic plan:

1. identification of the main reservoirs of wildlife by systematic surveys;
2. identification of the main corridors for wildlife in the built-up area;
3. identification of the key linkages between different reservoirs and corridors;
4. protection and enhancement of the above;
5. identification of the main areas where semi-natural habitats are not available to people;
6. policies aimed at improving these areas of need;
7. policies aimed at ensuring that the public can enjoy wildlife in ways which are both responsible and informed;
8. insistence on design standards for building development which make the most of opportunities to add to wildlife habitats and which cause the least possible damage to existing wildlife habitats throughout the whole built-up area;
9. policies designed to encourage local initiatives to achieve 1–8.

Some of these aspects are self-evident, others will be reviewed in later chapters. Chapter 4 has addressed issues to do with the identification of areas of land which have local importance as wildlife sites. However, there are also important issues to do with the patterning of such areas. As well as aiding in their protection, the recognition of the local distribution of such sites also allows a strategic overview and planning for positive policies of wildlife enhancement and habitat creation. These issues of pattern are addressed in this section.

Urban wildlife corridors

Another important aspect of landscape pattern relates to the identification of urban wildlife corridors which are lengths or linear habitat, or strings of open space sites which are sufficiently closely connected to be assumed to function as a route for wildlife movement. These corridors often link to the urban fringe providing a connecting between the town centre and the surrounding countryside. The objective of identifying such areas is again to highlight sites which are worthy of protective consideration in the light of destructive planning applications, and also to encourage favourable proactive developments which strengthen the corridor function.

In urban areas it is rarely hedgerows which are promoted as important corridors, but rather attention is given to green road and railway verges, river and canal sides. In areas where these do not themselves form complete corridors they are often linked to areas of public open space such as parks and golf courses.

However, this corridor designation is again usually made without clear evidence of their function, and many doubts must apply. In particular there are frequently quite considerable gaps and hostile sections, such as roads or stretches of land with no vegetation, within the designated 'corridor', and it is far from clear which species may be able to cross these. Many may be simply too narrow or heavily disturbed to be attractive to many species. Where such gaps are not a problem, most urban corridors are still made up of a disparate mix of varying habitat types, for example with heavily wooded patches alternating with areas of intensively mown grass, over-used playgrounds and the like. The number of species which are catholic enough to travel along all of these is probably limited to those which are able to travel across a range of land types including built-up land. It is often the case that urban corridors are identified with no reference made to the surrounding private land. In particular, private gardens, which frequently form a far more plausible network of inter-linked habitats of great wildlife value, are often completely ignored.

Where coherent routes do exist there is again the danger that they may increase the vulnerability to predatory species, which in urban situations would be usually domestic cats (Jarvis, 1990).

The validity of narrow urban corridors of poor inherent habitat quality can therefore be questioned (Bastin and Thomas, 1995). On the other hand it is certainly plausible that urban wildlife corridors may have a heightened importance as a recreational setting for humans which allows maximum enjoyment to be gained from the wildlife present (e.g. urban pathways), and the linking of corridor designation with green walkways is particularly to be welcomed.

Identification of areas of wildlife deficiency

This is usually on the basis of distance from land which is felt to be valuable to wildlife and the objective here is to draw attention to opportunities for habitat creation, re-orientation of landscape management priorities on existing open space etc.

Again it is usually the case that these deficiency areas are identified through reference only to the public land holding. The contribution of gardens to wildlife movement is ignored and hence it is hard to be confident that there would necessarily be any true wildlife deficiency in the areas in question. However, the deficiency concept also highlights the need for people to have opportunities for access to wildlife enjoyment on land in these areas, so a combination of nature conservation and recreation planning strategies is encouraged.

One complication arises therefore. Accessibility evaluation requires an assessment of reasonable distances for travel, which is determined by social and personal factors such as gender, health and age. Where assessments attempt to encourage widespread access by people of varying abilities the desired distances between sites obviously decreases. Recent studies have suggested a target measure of 280 metres in contrast to the more usual figures of 4–500 m (Box and Harrison, 1993; Harrison *et al.*, 1996). For many people a journey of over 5–10 minutes seems to require a higher level of determination and intent, and therefore reduces the number of visits that are likely (Bussey and Coles, 1995).

Other aspects of landscape pattern – the habitat mosaic

One of the major failings of the Island Biogeography Theory was its inability to take account of variations of habitat quality as a determinant of species richness. Habitat quality has of course long been recognized as a key element in conservation site management, and there are many examples of where species are lost through changes in the nature of a site. In some cases these changes can be extremely subtle, for example a change in grass height from 1 cm to 3–4 cm can lead to the localized disappearance of large blue butterflies, *Maculinea arion* (Thomas, 1989).

However, conservation areas can suffer from conceptual fragmentation as much as physical. It is typical that conservation management is discussed on a habitat by habitat basis, for example, with limited discussion of the effects of a combination of habitat types on the wildlife in them or of the influences of patterns and processes that link adjacent but different sites together. Only recently has the characteristics of mosaics of habitats become a matter of more explicit concern among landscape ecologists interested in the relationship between landscape pattern and biodiversity.

Consider two habitats, a woodland and a grassland, adjoining each other. The woodland edge is frequently rich in species because of greater food supply (shrubs fruiting more successfully etc.), greater structural variety and often favourable climatic characteristics.

The overall diversity of the area will consist of at least:

- those species that can survive in the woodland;
- those species that can survive in the grassland;
- those species that are unique to the ecotone between the two.

There may also be a group of species that rely upon the conjunction of the two habitats. Perhaps certain birds utilize the woodland for nesting or shelter, but feed predominantly in the open. There may be insects which have very different environmental requirements at different stages in their

Figure 5.3 The pattern of distribution of habitats effects the amount of edge and the amount of core habitat and hence affects species response. Size, frequency and contrast between habitats all affect species response. A 400 ha landscape that is divided into 1 ha blocks will produce different response in species such as Warblers (A) compared to wide-ranging species (B). Fragmentation effects may be reduced by modifying the structural quality of different fragments (Harris and Silva-Lopez, 1992).

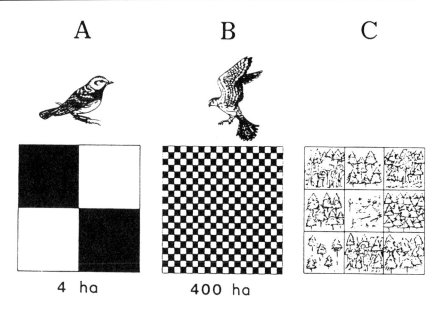

A   B   C

4 ha   400 ha

life-cycle, perhaps functioning as a woodland species when a larvae and a grassland species as an adult. The biodiversity of the grassland is therefore dependent not just on its size or internal structure but **also on the nature of the adjoining habitat types**. Many habitat types are of less value in isolation than when part of a complex mix of conjoining features (Falk, 1995).

Of course even this illustration is an oversimplification. The two habitats can exist together in a variety of ways, with sharp or subtle gradients, with complex or simple edges etc. Landscapes made up of a mix of 50% woodland and 50% grassland can still vary enormously in the way that these habitats are interlaced and patterned (Figure 5.3).

However, there may also be negative effects of such landscape complexity. Undesirable species may be favoured which can have a knock-on effect that degrades habitat quality, for example it is often suggested that an increase in small woodland cover in the UK is likely to increase problems of excessive deer pressure on woodland understory species (Harmer and Kerr, 1995; Ferris-Kaan, 1995).

Patchworks and patterns of species distribution in the landscape can affect biodiversity in other, more complex, ways. Some of the most difficult conceptual debates in plant ecology relate to the very existence of species richness in different systems. A fundamental tenet of plant ecology is the Competitive Exclusion Principle, which argues that under any given set of environmental conditions there will be one species that is physiologically and ecologically favoured and that would eventually come to dominate the community to the exclusion of all else. Diversity can only exist where there are factors that mitigate against the trend to monoculture.

Not surprisingly several theories have been developed to attempt to identify these factors, and many of them make reference to the relationship between spatial distribution and temporal disturbance.

Crawley (1986) identified the following main models, which he emphasizes are not necessarily mutually exclusive; indeed many are closely linked processes. The task of the ecologist is to determine which of these mechanisms have practical implications for the design, protection, and management of urban environments. Many of these models invoke mechanisms that prevent the plant community from reaching equilibrium, i.e. they assume that perfect competition is not possible in a community that is in some way disturbed. Environmental fluctuations allow species to grab transient opportunities before their competitors can reinvade or exert their full dominance. Other models attempt to identify processes or factors that can maintain species-richness within more stable ecosystems.

The Lottery Model assumes that establishment microsites appear randomly, and that colonization is opportunistic and random, reflecting the timing and method of propagation relative to gap formation. Once established, the individuals may remain for a long time.

Spatial Heterogeneity models suggest that apparently uniform areas do in fact contain many subtly different microsites that favour competition by different species. The idea is embodied in the Regeneration Niche ideas of Grubb (1977).

Niche Separation models argue that in many cases plants avoid or reduce the severity of competition by exploiting sufficiently different resources or sources of resources in the habitat. As with many such models, arguments that can easily be followed for one dimensional resources become very complex when attempting to understand interactions across all possible resources, as presumably direct competition for just one resource may be enough to lead to exclusion if that resource is fundamental to survival.

Selective herbivory may be important in some settings. Although in some cases herbivory may select against diversity, by eradicating palatable species, it may also be expected to increase diversity if the dominant competitors are edible. If nothing else, frequency dependent feeding may influence the strongest competitors most seriously and hence give an advantage to rare plants. 'Keystone' species may therefore be necessary to maintain a certain plant community (Paine, 1966).

Refuge models propose that species-richness will be enhanced if poor competitors have some locations where they can survive free from competition and can act as a source of propagules to exploit opportunities. Obviously the refuge does not need to be very close if the species have very effective dispersal (e.g. orchids). The survival of poor competitors may be achieved by many mechanisms ranging from ability to tolerate extreme conditions that others cannot and herbivore resistance, through to the existence of long-lived seed in the soil bank.

Disturbance models refer to the destruction of existing vegetation, often associated with soil disturbance that allows new species to invade. Obviously there are similarities with the lottery model, but the emphasis is on the effect of the rate of disturbance. At high disturbance only a few species will be adapted to survive, at low disturbance competitive exclusion occurs, but at intermediate disturbance levels species-richness can be high (Grime, 1979).

Grime (1979) also proposes that similar principles apply with regard to stress, or environmental adversity that limits plant productivity. He suggests that species-richness is often associated with moderately hostile conditions.

When considering the zoological components of the habitat, it must also be remembered that diversity is not always linked to the same criteria as is the case with plants (Chapter 2, also Kirby, 1992). Systems that may be very low in plant diversity may still be of high value for animals. No clearer example exists than the requirement of some ground nesting bees for bare soil. Effective habitat management from the bee's perspective may be rated as poor establishment by any botanist!

Some animals are specialist feeders and will only survive if their host plants are present. High plant diversity will therefore tend to increase diversity in these animals. However, insect diversity is often associated with diversity of physical structure as well. We also find that some insects may not be very effective at dispersal and may have less successful methods of surviving prolonged adversity compared with plants. Not surprisingly these vulnerable species are often the ones that are under greatest threat and hence rate highest in conservation terms. Because of their specialized life-cycles the concept of refuges becomes of acute importance for their survival. To encourage insect diversity, a management framework needs to be imposed that allows different plant communities to express a range of different morphologies and also allows the animals to avoid overall destruction.

For mobile species the concept of environmental heterogeneity takes on additional complexity, and the species that depend upon the existence of certain patterns within the countryside rather than any specific habitat are certainly the Cinderellas of natural science.

Nevertheless, the above ecological principles provide some pointers towards the necessary methodology for effective long-term habitat management focused on an understanding of process and pattern, although in many cases there is still substantial research to be done to convert concepts into practice.

A wider understanding is needed that shows the way that different habitat requirements can be integrated into all aspects of landscape planning. This is a field where many developments can be expected in coming years but ecologists are still a long way from being able to produce models which allow assessment of habitat mosaic to be accurately integrated into conservation strategies. I suppose that the key message, that habitats can not be considered in isolation, has been obvious for a long time, but it certainly is not typical of current land designation strategies to recognize so explicitly that the quality of biodiversity within a nature reserve will be affected by habitat changes around that reserve.

An understanding of the inter-relations between habitats therefore requires that an overall perspective is taken of land patterning and content across the whole of an area of concern. In urban situations much of the habitat mosaic that is encountered is usually extremely diverse and intricate, with a very fine-grained structure. The garden patterns of sheltered pockets of grassland, flower and shrub borders of a diverse structural range and a scattering of large trees provides an extremely rich habitat for some organisms. The major limitations are likely to be related to the high presence of predators and human disturbance, which are unlikely to be resolvable. Nor is it likely that the major habitat patterns found within gardens will change significantly.

Attention however can be turned to the larger blocks of urban land which tend to be rather more homogeneous in their design and content. Dominant in many urban areas are large tracts of grass which are mown with varying amounts of intensity. Opportunities for fruitful habitat diversification will probably best be targeted at areas where the grassland mowing regimes can be made more flexible, and also through considering the opportunities for scrub and woodland planting in areas where the grass is too dominant, such as around football and recreation areas.

Large tracts of woodland, wetland or other habitat types in urban areas are often the relict of some unusual historical land-use pattern, and are usually so rare or important that it would rarely be considered whether patterns of other habitat types should be created within them. Exceptions probably are large scale woodland plantings and also areas rapidly developing scrub cover through mismanagement, where consideration should be given to maintaining a mosaic of open areas within a wooded framework on the grounds that sensitive species requiring large areas of core habitat will be unlikely to arrive.

There are limitations to the sort of sweeping generalizations that should be made. The important issues are that an overview is needed of habitat distribution across towns and cities and that a new generation of nature conservation strategies would be desirable, based on a better understanding of what is there, what is missing and what genuinely useful options exist for amendments to landscape creation and management policies.

With the advent of technical developments such as GIS, the current interests in biodiversity and landscape ecology and the huge population of density in urban areas there really is no excuse for an absence of a very detailed information collection programme which could extend down to even the plant community level.

Box 5.1 Ecotones and boundary habitats

Ecotone is the term given to the transition zone between any two adjacent habitats. This edge or boundary habitat has long been known to contain more species than the central areas. The edge contains species which exploit the intermediate conditions as well as species from both of the main habitat types, and represents a meeting point for these.

Because of this additional diversity attempts have been made to modify the design of habitats to maximize the 'edge' effect, e.g. in restoration of gravel pits to wetlands. However, this is not always desirable. Increasing edge, e.g. by changing the shape of a reserve, can reduce the area available to those species that need undisturbed 'inner-habitat' conditions. Some authors have suggested that increasing edges may favour predators and parasites more than desirable species (Yahner, 1988).

Overcoming pattern constraints by planning and by management

Landscape ecology places emphasis on the way that pattern and process interact in natural areas, so that aspects such as species richness, population densities and flux of species and individuals can be understood better in their landscape context. The objective that planners often have in this regard is to influence, through zoning, incentives or control of consent for development, the pattern of the landscape.

Planners have few opportunities for initiating positive development. There have of course been an increasing number of cases where habitat creation is associated with developments, as part of planning gain. This can play a part in achieving the 'ideal' habitat pattern suggested by landscape ecology. The issue is discussed in more detail in Chapter 6, but a key objective should be to strengthen the viability of existing habitats. Nevertheless, planners are usually constrained by the need to wait for development proposals to be forwarded before such goals can be realized, and by limitations on the extent to which they can tell developers what form of scheme should be forwarded (Selman, 1992). Of course the powers to purchase land, and even compulsory purchase, do exist but these are rarely employed except for the protection of high-quality, existing sites of nature conservation interest since urban land prices are disproportionate to the benefits that may accrue from planned purchase of lower grade sites.

There is another strategic approach for maintaining diversity in fragmented systems, which is to influence process by direct management. For example the tendency for habitat isolation to increase the risk of localized species extinction can clearly be directly addressed by policies of species re-introduction. Similarly the population carrying capacity of small areas may be increased by provision of additional artificial resources such as nest boxes or even extra food.

Management control of habitat quality is therefore a key issue in the conservation of habitats, both urban and rural. The growing involvement of the planning professions in strategic conservation policy formulation is to be welcomed, but probably the greatest weakness in contemporary planning is that it is largely dominated by reactive and ultimately passive mechanisms that have little management dimension allied to them.

Ensuring the necessary management inputs for land quality maintenance is often extremely difficult. For example, when habitat creation is linked with development, it is rare for planners to be able to insist on more than five or ten years aftercare.

The long-term management viability of sites is therefore another layer of interest that could be addressed by landscape ecologists. New conservation sites will only have a future if they can be placed within a reasonably resilient and plausible land use framework, but this framework must also be diverse. At one time all of the myriad variations in management required to sustain species will have been achieved just by accident and inefficiency in the countryside. The more that habitats shrink in area, the more the precision of management input has to increase.

Tactical components of an urban conservation programme

It is clear that there are many strategic issues to be resolved in development of an optimal urban nature conservation resource. However, there are also tactical level issues to be addressed. It is from this sort of perspective that Johnston (1990) considered how local authorities can improve the provision and management of urban nature areas. Their suggested approaches included the following.

Assess the wildlife resource
- Undertake survey to identify areas valuable to wildlife.
- Identify areas of deficiency.

Use planning powers to protect sites
- Identify and incorporate nature areas in unitary development plans.
- Designate statutory Local Nature Reserves and non-statutory areas.
- Maintain a presumption against development on nature areas.

Make further land available
- Promote positive use of vacant land for the establishment of nature areas.
- Use planning tools to secure land for nature conservation.
- Require developers to incorporate nature areas into their designs.

Secure public access to nature areas
- Make areas safe by fencing, filling in dangerous holes etc.
- Arrange appropriate leases and licences for present or potential nature areas.

Manage council land for nature conservation
- Train staff to undertake appropriate nature conservation management on all public open space.
- Employ specialist wardens/rangers.
- Draw up management agreements with others to manage land in accordance with the requirements of nature conservation.

Establish an ecology centre
- Provide a focus for environmental education and public information.
- Use the centre as a demonstration project.

Involve the community
- Enable local people to make positive use of available land.
- Consult widely on proposals.
- React positively to suggestions for potential nature areas where appropriate.

Allocate sufficient resources
- Allocate sufficient resources for establishing managing and protecting nature areas.

- Employ specialists in ecology, countryside management, conservation planning and community liaison.
- Establish a separate budget for an ecological programme of work.
- Consider giving grant-aid to voluntary organizations.

Many of these issues and approaches are reviewed in the following chapters, which address in particular aspects of habitat creation (broadening the resource), finance and community involvement.

6 Ecological restoration and habitat creation

To recap the issues of concern outlined in the previous chapters, it is increasingly difficult to have faith in the long-established mechanisms of biodiversity protection and land designation for several reasons.

- The isolation of some reserve sites from the ecological processes, such as flooding in a river-side grassland, may lead to long-term species losses.
- The increasing fragmentation of habitats has isolated reserves to the point where reinforcement from surrounding habitats has become less common.
- Many reserves are too small to be viable in themselves and have no buffering capacity to safeguard against stochastic catastrophe. Management operations are also often made extraordinarily difficult by the small size.
- Some species have fallen to population levels which are too small to be viable.
- Climate change and other impacts threaten to undermine the long-term future of many plant and animal communities.
- Without a greater political and social commitment from all levels of society it is clear that many reserves are temporary refuges that will gradually fall to external development pressure.

To adjust to these new problems has required a complete re-consideration of the level and nature of intervention that will be appropriate in reserves that is founded on far more fundamental and far-reaching deliberate control over species and habitats.

Some of the components of this strategy are primarily based on management inputs within existing site boundaries to address the processes which sustain populations and diversity in the landscape. These include species recovery, whereby suboptimal populations are boosted by *ex-situ* propagation and re-introduction, or boosting resource availability, e.g. through nest box provision. Other approaches involve consideration of the pattern of habitat distribution, for example the acquisition of stretches of land adjacent to reserves for improved buffering or allow habitat restoration and a growing emphasis on corridor identification establishment to create links between isolated habitats and to allow species migration (Jordan, Gilpin and Aber, 1989).

Although these interventionist activities are as applicable to rural as to urban situations, many of them are politically and ethically contentious and technically unproven. (In fact many involve assumptions and judgements about likely outcomes that will always involve risk and can therefore never be 'proven'.) Experimentation with such activities therefore will inevitably be focused strongly on urban areas where disturbance has already been extensive, naturalness is an abstract quality at best and where the species involved are not too sensitive. It is also likely that the driving force for much habitat creation activity will be a link to development activity through planning gain, and this again will bring a focus onto urban and particularly urban fringe projects.

Urban areas are also the obvious focus for those habitat creation activities which are aimed at developing more opportunities for people to have contact with wildlife, rather than attempting to meet the difficult goals of restoration of complex plant and animal communities.

Also of importance are those habitat types which are characteristic of early successional processes on land which has been strongly influenced by human impact, such as the rich orchid communities that have developed on abandoned quarries. Obviously these habitat types can be recreated, and indeed they need to be; they have an ephemeral nature and as succession proceeds the valuable species are often ousted as commonplace trees, shrubs and animals invade.

Study of the temporal and spatial distribution of plant species and communities, including natural succession and the response of species to environmental variation, forms the basis of plant ecology and an extensive scientific literature. The establishment and management of plagioclimax communities *de novo*, is by comparison, a recent phenomenon. While some parallels are available from agricultural and horticultural studies on relatively simple monocultures, polycultures (or intercrops) and pastures forming disclimaxes, the methodology of restoration ecology is relatively new (Jordan *et al.*, 1987).

The theory for re-creation of habitats is derived from the fields of descriptive and analytical ecology – descriptive ecology provides a model for the reconstruction of plant communities, and analytical ecology suggests an appropriate methodology. The technical skills for habitat reconstruction and species establishment are, however, derived from agriculture, horticulture and silviculture but they often need to be applied in fundamentally different ways.

Terminology

The need for careful definitions in the field of restoration ecology is not a simple academic concern with detail, rather it is important to recognize that certain terminology is becoming increasingly standardized in the rest of the world, and the levels of attainment and obligations that are expected of people who use such terminology are also becoming more concrete.

People have been planting native trees, sowing informal grasslands and constructing ponds for centuries. If a true woodland is to be created rather than a plantation some degree of complexity, internal coherence and stability in the communities produced is implied particularly where they are proposed as mitigating measures for a development which destroys valuable existing habitats. These should also be linked to some defined and measurable goal. Goals in agronomy can be relatively easy to formulate; in nature conservation they can be complex as the interests of different species often conflict. In the absence of other criteria managers often aim to maximize species richness. Even this nebulous target implies greater than usual complexity of management and advanced appreciation of ecological principles.

Without such goals every re-vegetation or landscape project that uses native plants, no matter how ill-conceived or under-funded, could be given the label of habitat creation. It is relatively easy to create 'wild' or semi natural amenity vegetation, to create sustainable communities of value is much harder. The problems are complex, but a good place to start is with clearly understood terminology.

Habitat restoration or recreation is not used with consistency but an international consensus is growing that the term should be used for attempts to reproduce, as far as possible, a previously existing community or ecosystem. This area of work can be very sophisticated, becoming at best a rigorous scientific study of the way in which particular ecosystems function (see Jordan and Packard, 1989). Some of the best sites have accumulated years of research study. They may still be different to undisturbed systems but these differences are only apparent to ecological specialists.

The more precisely defined or sophisticated the target community is, the more difficult it will be to replicate. To match an original grassland we must do more than propagate a certain range of plant species. Ideally these species will have the desired population numbers, and also be found in the 'correct' mosaic and pattern of distribution. Above all, the species present should be capable of successful reproduction in order to maintain the community. There should also be an absence of any detrimental species that threaten the integrity of the system, e.g. invasive weeds. Of course as well as the higher plants all of the other components of the ecosystem would need to be present (invertebrates, fungi etc.).

Because target communities have been precisely defined, assessment of the success with which these have been restored is therefore in some ways straightforward. Obviously assessing feasibility will depend on analysing the reasons why the original habitat disappeared, and determining whether these factors can be controlled in the future. Targets may be easy to set but may still be demanding and hence technically difficult to achieve.

In the worst cases mitigation programmes are confused by the technology developed for popular habitat creation, which focus mainly on introducing plants and ensuring rapid, easy, establishment. For true restoration it is necessary to determine not just the biotic components of the system to be recreated, but also the parameters of the environmental framework, such as soil physics and chemistry, topography and nutrient cycles, as well as the macro- and micro-variation in these parameters. Most uncommon plant species for example are adapted to colonize uncommon environments. It is also necessary to consider the management patterns that, over centuries, created and reinforced these semi-natural communities. Restoration involves re-producing these management processes as well.

However, in some cases the fact that activity may be carried out on a partially degraded site, such as a ploughed farmland, at least implies that the soil type and climate is broadly appropriate for the target community. The ease of restoration therefore depends upon the degree and nature of disturbance. Some impacts, which may appear relatively minor, such as the addition of phosphorus fertilizer, may still have a profound enough impact to mean that 'true' restoration may never be possible. Most schemes therefore fall short of this goal and lead to partial or incomplete restoration.

Among the earliest and most famous examples of attempted restoration were based around the north eastern prairie grassland systems, with work focused on the University of Wisconsin arboretum in Madison, USA. This work dates back to the early twentieth century and is given extra import through the links with Aldo Leopold, one of the great early environmental visionaries and a man whose 'land ethic' has many parallels with today's philosophy of sustainable development.

More recently the best examples of success in habitat restoration have been associated with the repair of small island communities which have undergone gradual deterioration through the introduction of invasive and destructive alien species such as rats. Here the restoration approach has been based on the re-introduction of lost species and eradication of invaders.

Few other examples in the world can be said to be 'true' restoration successes in the sense that defined target communities can be shown to be reproduced. However, there are many examples where partial restoration has been achieved and the conservation value of a site has been clearly increased, where degraded plant and animal communities have been vastly improved and particularly where more has been learnt about the management and protection of the ecosystem in question.

Habitat creation is a much looser term, and is often applied to diverse activities with many different objectives. The nature of the work required must therefore be judged against the context of the activity.

Habitat creation usually implies the production of new communities which are modelled on existing semi-natural biotypes in broad terms. However, there need not be any particular clearly defined goals in terms of species persistence or abundance, nor any particular ecological, genetic or landscape link between the new habitat and what was previously on site. The following main directions can be identified which have different implications for the technology and design systems to be adopted.

1. Creation of 'popular' wildlife systems for maximum human enjoyment. Species diversity may actually be low but the appearance will usually be that of an attractive and natural-appearing habitat. Species richness in ecology is usually assumed to be desirable, however, species richness and diversity do not always mean maximum attractiveness or stability (Hitchmough, 1994c and Ash *et al.*, 1992).

   Wild grassland has a value in both amenity and conservation terms and it is important to recognize that visual effect (and also some conservation value) can result from the flowering of only a few species in a community that is not particularly diverse or botanically important. It is not even necessary for wild grassland to include a significant proportion of broadleaves in order for it to serve its function. Species-poor communities dominated by grasses such as *Arrenatherum*, *Festuca* or *Agrostis* can, in the right setting, appear striking and atmospheric especially as the grasses begin to flower and the flower heads wave in the wind. These 'monotonous' communities may also support some wildlife interest by giving cover to small mammals and invertebrates and, as a result, encouraging bird feeding.

2. Species-targeted programs, e.g. aiming to re-establish one, or a few, identified flowering plants with little detailed concern for other components of the system.

3. Creation of maximum diversity, with no specific species or community assemblages in mind, for example the production of a community that matches a certain NVC class. One option may be to aim for a system with similarities to the range and associations of species normally encountered together and appropriate to region. In other circumstances there may be fewer constraints (e.g. gravel pit restoration to wetland in a region where lakes do not exist; urban nature park).

4. Creation of populations of target species or defined community assemblages. Diversity could be subservient to the ideal of matching the correct assemblages. (This approach may even require a managed reduction of diversity where a system has been degraded by the invasion of exotic species.)

In Australia Hitchmough (1994c) has identified a spectrum of activities ranging from single-layer structurally simple vegetation of a native species, single or bi-layer plantings of defined phytosociological mixes through to multiple-layer formations of appropriate phytosociological arrangement and form. This spectrum represents increasing 'ecological integrity' and increasing technical challenge but for educational or recreational purposes it is recognized that 'even token communities may have value'. It is argued that the public read naturalness by consideration of vegetation structure and not content, whereas scientists tend to focus on the opposite criteria.

The management objectives of a site containing such vegetation may also vary (see Table 6.1).

Much early research into habitat creation in the United Kingdom was

Table 6.1 *Relationship between the management objectives of habitat creations and the technical challenge posed*

Management objective	Ease of attainment
To maintain a sense of 'naturalness'	NOT DIFFICULT
To perpetuate the visually dominant plant species	
To minimize the density of undesirable (weed) plants and animals	
To maintain typical structural diversity in vegetation	
To maximize faunal carrying capacity	
To maintain the typical diversity of native species in the community	
To facilitate adequate rates of seedling and other recruitment of desirable species to provide a stable, self-perpetuating vegetation community	
To maintain adequate genetic diversity and large enough populations of a species to allow natural selection to operate	VERY DIFFICULT

Source: Hitchmough (1994c).

specifically concerned with the first goal, creating attractive species-rich vegetation but using common, resilient plants in high-profile situations such as urban parks (Wells, 1987). Techniques concentrated on the methods required to get a generation of plants established into a habitat framework, albeit temporarily. The work was of indirect value to nature conservation in that it could alleviate pressure on existing semi-natural habitats, bring more people into contact with nature, and encourage support for wider conservation objectives. However, the use of rare species in such initiatives was positively discouraged.

Wells' criteria for selection of wildflowers

Wells' criteria for selection of wildflowers in habitat creation includes some pragmatic concerns aimed at making the plant community easy to establish, attractive and relatively robust.

- They should be perennial, preferably long-lived, with an effective means of spread.
- A high proportion should have colourful flowers and these should preferably be attractive to insects.
- Highly competitive species, especially those known to form monocultures in the wild, should be avoided.
- The seed should have a high percentage germination over a range of temperatures and should not have dormancy problems or special requirements.

Other criteria are clearly intended to avoid potentially damaging impacts on the distribution of species that are of high nature-conservation significance.

- The species should be regular members of the grassland community.
- They should not be rare.
- They should be relatively abundant in a variety of grasslands and preferably have a wide distribution.

In contrast to simple communities, mitigation or recreation work in rural areas often aims to rescue, or compensate for the loss of, species or communities of local or national importance. The methodology appropriate to this situation will fundamentally differ and must rely on restoring the correct environmental parameters and the ecosystem processes that reinforce the different communities that are to be recreated (Goode, 1993). However, landscape architects, ecologists, and restorationists working in mitigation have often been misdirected by the widely publicized technology developed for amenity vegetation development and have failed to address deeper issues associated with the development of habitats of conservation value.

A restoration approach to mitigation schemes, working to the goal of trying to put back what was there before, is clearly not always appropriate in an urban context. We know that many disturbed and degraded sites have, over time, developed fascinating and valuable plant and animal communities. It is particularly frustrating to think of sites turned into what may be poor copies of mature rural biotypes without consideration first being given to the way that they may develop their own unique habitat types (Gilbert, 1989).

There are many circumstances therefore where habitat creation is more appropriate in the UK than strict restoration. The methodology to use in different circumstances still needs careful consideration. It is worth remembering the fact that sometimes increasing biodiversity is very simple. For example felling a patch of trees in a large area of woodland will increase the range of species that are found. Habitat creation is easy; the professional skill comes from deciding what type of habitat is most valuable, appropriate, likely to survive and to make a contribution in the long term.

Incentives for habitat creation have been built into UK government countryside grant schemes such as the Countryside Stewardship programme. Under such initiatives farmers and landowners are given premium payments for attempts to re-establish traditional habitat types, such as species-rich grasslands. Despite superficial appearances, these are not true restoration schemes since they put no detailed emphasis on the nature and composition of the plant communities to be created, nor is there detailed assessment of the suitability of the soil conditions or the prospects for long-term survival. Their main value may lie in the encouragement of traditional management practices more than in the attempts to establish particular plant species.

There are several other terms which should perhaps be clarified. **Rehabilitation** is suggested as the best term for a partial re-establishment through human intervention of the original biota and/or ecosystem. **Recovery** may apply when a disturbed site becomes partially restored without any human facilitation.

Other terms which are developing a degree of international agreement are **revegetation**, **regeneration** or **reclamation**. These are used when establishing a form of functional vegetation cover on a denuded site but they do not necessarily imply any resemblance of the target to the original landscape present before destruction. These are therefore more closely related to habitat creation.

Habitat extension is a term which could be used where existing habitats such as nature reserves are expanded or linked through additional land take. This may be to provide a buffer zone that will protect the core habitat from adverse influences. It may also make small areas more viable. Traditional SSSI/Nature Reserve designation could not always preserve the size of estate needed for realistic management. Recent relaxation in rural land use pressures has provided opportunities to increase buffering and to make management programmes easier to implement. For example if patches of fragmented lowland heath could be re-united with similar re-created habitat then the problems of rotational management, or of keeping viable grazing herds, could be made much easier to resolve.

In such a situation the 'new' habitat needs to have a certain degree of functional similarity to the core landscape at the broad biome level (e.g. grazed grassland surrounding a pasture-land reserve), but it differs from 'restoration' because it may not matter if individual species are present or absent. It is, however, desirable to allow for species colonization from within the core – the preservation of open niches may be an important goal. Other ecological process links may need to be established, for example expansion of safe territorial ranges for animals.

Habitat extension therefore may apply in circumstances where there are no efforts made to introduce species, but where the management and land-use patterns are put into harmony with the requirements of the core plant and animal communities.

The above are therefore broad strategic categorizations that imply certain overall directions in the activity undertaken. Many of the following activities are more clearly understood as tactical approaches that will play a part in meeting these goals.

Habitat transplanting is usually carried out when existing natural communities are under threat from development. The objective is to preserve as much as possible of the former landscape by moving it to a new location. This work also implies that the target community can be well defined, and therefore success measured (although setting 'acceptable' levels can be hard). Ideally the entire original community would be rescued, so this is a technique aimed at habitat restoration as an overall strategy. Inevitably, however, there will be many losses. Implicit in the activity is a recognition that absolute restoration is not feasible but that even if only a few species are saved, this may be better than nothing. There is also the likelihood that disturbance vegetation is encouraged by the process, which sometimes give rise to data which implies that species diversity actually increases as a result of the process.

Habitat enhancement or enrichment refers to the deliberate managed diversification of an existing community. In many cases reserve managers are continually involved in this activity through variation in maintenance activities. However, enrichment can also involve deliberate planting or animal introduction. Species level activities that contribute to the process can be identified as follows.

Habitat diversification

This involves exercises aimed at increasing the species richness (usually floristic richness) of existing habitats through the introduction of previously absent species.

Species recovery

This involves the deliberate encouragement of populations of targeted rare or endangered plants or animals, aimed at extending their range or increasing the population density within existing boundaries. The work may also involve expansion of the genetic stock, e.g. by controlled introduction of new genes from external populations. The work often requires an assessment of the threat of genetic diversity collapse in relic populations because of reduced populations, self incompatibility etc.

Because of a collapse in mutually supportive metapopulations in the countryside, the continued re-introduction of individuals into habitat fragments may become a cornerstone of conservation policy into the next century.

Species recovery programmes usually only attempt to put a single species back into a community where it once existed. The likelihood of success depends on a realistic analysis of why the species first disappeared. Where this has been due to a major habitat change or environmental shift then simple re-introduction may not be valid. However, it is possible that some temporary adversity, change in management or even deliberate persecution may have left the habitat largely intact but with one or more key species missing.

In ecological terms this would imply that there is an unrealized niche in the community. The species there may have opportunistically extended their ecological amplitude to fill in the gap. The community therefore may be able to assimilate and integrate the re-introduced species. Another scenario is where the niche has been filled by an ecologically similar species which, once established, is strongly competitive. The outcome of the competitive relationship is far from clear, and there is evidence that 'possession is nine-tenths of the law' (Gilbert, 1989) suggesting that the re-introduced species may never oust the competitor; they may co-exist or the original species may eventually die out again.

In some cases a habitat may have shrunk below the viable territory size for a successful breeding population. In this case the supply of limiting resources at an artificially high rate, such as food or nesting boxes, may help to maintain population size.

Reintroduction

This is an activity closely related to species recovery, whereby a locally extinct ecotype is replaced by a closely related stock from a different area. Genetic differences may be inevitable unless a seedbank exists of the original types.

Species replacement

This occurs when a locally extinct species is replaced by one which may be taxonomically unrelated but which may have a functional similarity within the ecosystem. This is important where the extinct species was essential for effective maintenance of other aspects of the biota. Internationally this work may be carried out as part of a carefully defined restoration programme. An example may be where a given plant depends upon an animal dispersal agent for its seed, or where population levels of a herbivore must be controlled by a predatory species.

Species eradication

This is not normally considered as part of the same group of activities in the UK. However, it is seen as a fundamental mechanism for habitat restoration in situations such as island ecosystems where relatively undisturbed communities have been invaded by exotics which have threatened the integrity of the entire biota. Parallel activities in Britain, such as the removal of sycamore from a woodland reserve, are part of everyday management but it is rare to find full regional eradication attempted.

Species introductions

This would be the best terminology where an existing habitat type is diversified by the introduction of plants or animals which would be expected to survive but for which there is no evidence that they previously formed part of the community. This sort of activity would apply where there were unfilled niches in the community which the newcomers could fill. In relatively new secondary habitats this may be explained by limited dispersal rates; new habitats invariably take time to accumulate the species that can tolerate the environmental parameters imposed. Alternatively the introduced species may be one which has poor colonizing ability. For example it may be an obligate woodland species that cannot cross any other land type. The unrealized niche will remain open even in old habitats until deliberate introduction occurs.

   If a species is introduced into a community where there is no existing niche we would normally expect it to disappear, but some species may so modify the environment that they can reinforce their own survival and effectively create new niches. Introduction may create opportunities for permanent survival. Examples of such self-reinforcing species could be beech trees which now regenerate in woodlands that were originally planted far beyond their original distribution.

   Another interesting, if unproven, case could be made for the establishment of symbiotic species such as orchids. Perhaps one of the most intriguing questions about orchids relates to the number of superficially suitable sites that they are **not** found in, given that they have excellent dispersal characteristics. As obligate symbiots with fungi, orchid distribution cannot occur in fields where the fungi is missing. It is known that subsurface competition between fungi is sometimes intense, and it may be that orchids, once established, could reinforce the mycorrhizal species and allow a larger colony to develop, which in turn allows new orchids to establish. Many orchids also have specialist pollinating insects and a similar process of mutual reinforcement may occur once the system has been 'kick-started'.

Habitat or niche completion

Another situation may be where there is an incomplete species niche, or where there is some limiting factor on population development which can be overcome. For example a site may have sufficient food and shelter for birds, but there may be an absence of nesting opportunities. Alternatively there may be insufficient territory to provide food for a viable population of a certain species, so the provision of supplementary resources may be required. Perhaps the most common example comes from the creation of artificial reef communities, where presumably the only limiting factor for these species is one of sufficient anchorage. In terrestrial urban systems a good example of the sort of factors that may be limiting are the nesting and cover opportunities that may be offered to birds from holes in large over-mature trees. Artificial substitution of these by nest boxes and the like can boost populations.

American and European perspectives

The lead professional body in the USA, which has recently seen the formation of a UK chapter, has been the Society for Ecological Restoration (SER). The members have been responsible for many of the philosophical and practical debates in the literature which have formed the above definitions. They state that:

> Ecological restoration is the process of repairing damage done by humans to the diversity and dynamics of indigenous ecosystems.

Similarly the current president of SER states that the objectives are to 'upgrade the quality of existing natural areas and to augment the planetary inventory of natural areas'. On the surface these definitions seem to include habitat creation as easily as habitat restoration, but there is a clear assumption in the literature that the goal is to reproduce ideal pre-existing conditions.

One challenge is to define what those ideal conditions are. Debates take place about whether the goal should be to restore to the stage before any human impact (assuming this could be characterized), to restore to the stage before the more heavily and rapidly degrading impact of European emigrants, or to restore to some assumed stage which would be the development of some of these communities assuming that no high-level degradation took place.

It is worth remembering that for parts of the US landscape, the impact of human farming has been in place for less than one generation. The much longer and greater intensity of impact that human beings have had on the British landscape and the relative paucity of areas which allow a framework and baseline of 'natural' vegetation to be defined and studied make it harder to relate to some of these concepts. Indeed at times they seem almost baffling. As mentioned, most of the time the objective of work in the UK is to mitigate for a comparatively finite period of extreme degradation and attempt to return the site to the status prior to this disturbance event or sometimes to a slightly higher quality version of the same community type.

I believe that one positive aspect of the UK/European perspective is that we have much less trouble conceiving a vision of how humans and nature could co-exist in a harmonious way, rather than seeing all human life as some form of fall from grace for the world. In Europe so many of our traditional habitats are dependent on traditional farm practices that it is harder to distinguish between work aimed at habitat management and that aimed at restoration. Clearly the concept of 'pre-human' impact is not something we can endorse in the UK. Many of our most valuable semi-natural communities depend on human impacts and we would lose biodiversity if we ignored their needs. I prefer a vaguer definition of what my goals are, I aim to optimize the local biodiversity, or optimize the value of that biodiversity, on degraded land. Restoration is also a learning process at several levels and if this side is neglected it loses much value.

In reality the work of many American professionals does of course encompass both habitat creation and restoration. The society has many debates about whether the name is meant to be restrictive of simply a convenient umbrella. The broadest possible interpretation of the above definition allows for many strategies which can be used to strengthen human commitment to biodiversity restoration and much professional activity ranges into urban areas.

The ethical and conceptual challenges of restoration ecology

There are many technical and ethical problems associated with habitat restoration. For example restoration is invariably more expensive than conservation, and the results are more uncertain. It is important therefore that attempts to restore habitats do not redirect funds or energy from activities geared at protecting existing but degrading habitats in the region, unless the purposes and goals of the restoration process are carefully formulated.

The problems become especially acute when restoration or habitat creation is used in some way to formally compensate or mitigate for the loss of areas of nature conservation importance as a result of development. One obvious danger is that the idea that habitats can be replaced undermines the case for their conservation. Developers are increasingly aware of the potential value that mitigation proposals have for reducing the opposition to development proposals. It is now standard in the UK that significant civil engineering works for example will include what are often very expensive and elaborate compensation or works such as habitat translocation.

In some cases the quality of these proposals are difficult for the planning officer and public to assess. For example if we attempt habitat transplanting of ancient woodland we may be able to preserve:

- a subset (probably unquantifiable) of the plant and animal species that existed originally;
- at best, plant communities that broadly resemble those of the original woodland;
- genetic continuity with those species that existed before.

We would lose:

- some species;
- large and mature specimens of trees (and their epiphytes and fauna);
- the architecture and morphology of the woodland;
- the complex mosaic and inter-relations of species in the ground layer;
- archaeological characteristics and social links, e.g. place names;
- site patterns and links with the landscape.

Habitat creation proposals may be put forward that do not attempt to recreate previous conditions but instead substitute a very different type of landscape. They may therefore involve trade-offs of one habitat or plant and animal community type against another. How much new pond is of equivalent value to the loss of an old hedgerow and field system for example? How many songbirds compensate for the loss of certain invertebrate communities?

The last example is of particular interest since it reflects an argument that has been offered in development applications several times. It is fairly easy to demonstrate that new young woodlands or scrub can be planted that will support more species, and larger populations, of songbirds than do more ancient and purer habitats such as grassland or woodland (see Figure 6.1). This is because birds often show a preference for a mix of open and woody conditions on a fine grained pattern, with low woody shelter providing easy protection and nesting areas. To understand the equivalent importance of the two ecosystems requires some appreciation of the value of the wildlife found in each case (see Chapter 4).

From one perspective the development of restoration technology makes the evaluation of priorities in nature conservation simpler. The most valuable habitats are those which can not easily be recreated. Certain habitats simply cannot be reproduced within the timescales that human society works. In many cases the value of a landscape arises simply because it is old: some habitats contain species, or relationships between species, which will not be found in any new systems; sometimes of equal importance is the absence of species characteristic of new habitats; sometimes the very age and history of the landscape is a quality that we value. This puts the greatest value on ancient systems and especially those which were created under environmental conditions which no longer operate (such as ancient

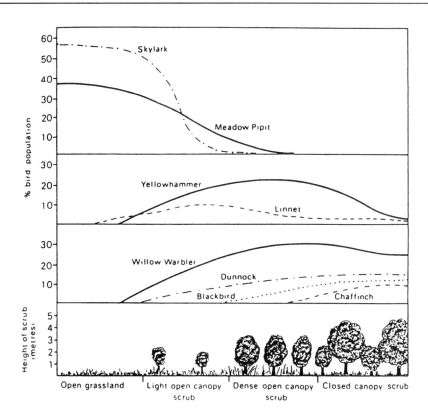

Figure 6.1 The change in breeding bird species following scrub invasion into downland turf (Fuller, 1982).

woodlands, limestone pavements etc.) However, in other ways the calculation of relative value can be complicated. Habitats may gain political, educational or social value if they are re-located or remade in areas where access by the public is improved, and this increase in importance may outweigh the significance of the loss of some species.

There are also many cases where the possible future of the habitat is already in doubt, such as where necessary management of a grassland can not be assured and where it is gradually turning to scrubland. Huge areas of existing habitat are in a management crisis. Translocation or restoration of this habitat following development may secure a better future for some components of the ecosystem than was the case prior to development. Even if there is a clear understanding that restoration cannot return the community that was there before, this does not mean that it is pointless to try, or to aim higher than you can achieve.

Even if technical and management problems could be overcome and if a perfect re-construction of a lost ecosystem could be made, there is another ethical challenge that faces the restoration ecologist. The sort of ethical question often posed is this: assume the Mona Lisa were destroyed by a motorway, but a perfect copy could be recreated elsewhere (such that no test could tell that it was a copy), is that good enough? The answer has to be that some quality has been lost, even if it is hard to define. It has something to do with the authenticity and the history of the site. Reference has already been made to the idea that the concept of 'naturalness' is often an important component of site evaluation in nature conservation. One of the greatest problems with restored sites, even if they are perfect copies, is that they have lost their naturalness because they have been put in place by the hand of man. In many people's minds a habitat that is exposed to human influence loses some spiritual quality, a touch of 'wilderness' perhaps, and is hence degraded. Not surprisingly therefore, the greatest limitation to habitat creation in the eyes of traditional conservationists is that the new or restored community, no matter how superficially successful and viable, is devoid of 'naturalness'.

There may also be cultural dimensions of the system which are lost, particularly following habitat translocation. Chris Baines once challenged restorationists that 'you may recreate the woodland, but you can't recreate the ghosts'. Certainly the whole archaeological and cultural history associated with managed landscapes, including associations with place names and ancient boundaries, is lost if the system is moved. The 'meaning' of the site has been damaged even if the component biodiversity has not.

Assessing restoration success

Assessing the success of a programme aimed at restoring a habitat presents many technical and conceptual problems. The most obvious is that to be able to measure successful restoration requires that we were able to fully measure or characterize the status of the system before disturbance. In the vast majority of cases this is simply impossible. To obtain a realistic picture of the biodiversity of a site requires intensive monitoring over every season of the year, and preferably over several years since some components may not be evident if the climatic conditions are unfavourable or if their population numbers are undergoing a cyclic decline.

Nature conservation is not about trying to retain diversity but rather retaining ecological value in a habitat. Restoration ecology can be seen as attempting to enhance value on a given area. There is a need to develop evaluation criteria that recognize what that value is, and to find ways in which we can quantify it. Indeed one of the most common misconceptions among many allied professions is that habitat creation or restoration goals can be met by 'encouraging wildlife'. If a project substantially increases the diversity of a system, but that diversity is composed of more unimportant species than were there originally then something has been lost.

There is also a need to consider the nature of the diversity measurement system to be employed. The more precisely defined or sophisticated the target community is, the more difficult it will be to replicate. Some restoration projects rely upon simple measures such as species composition before and after disturbance. However, to match an original habitat these species should also have the desired population numbers and also be found in the 'correct' mosaic and pattern of distribution. Species lists as a mirror on diversity are therefore far from perfect. Diversity indices are little better –

15 Wildflower mixtures from many different seed sources frequently stabilize around a much smaller range of species adapted to the site conditions.

they incorporate abundance measures but do not indicate much about the patterns, and nothing at all about the structural relationships on which many invertebrates depend.

Both are a very effective tool for baffling planners and the public, who are unable to judge whether the loss of 5% of the species (which may be masked by an increase in diversity due to an invasion of species, ruderals etc.) is significant or not or whether the value of the system is degraded as a consequence of the change. Focusing on certain aspects of the biota can be just as misleading, given that it is perfectly possible to favour different groups by developing different habitat types. As well as the desired species there should also be an absence of any detrimental species that threaten the integrity of the system, e.g. invasive weeds. Of course, as well as the higher plants all other essential components of the ecosystem need to be present (invertebrates, fungi etc.) and many of these groups are ignored, or are almost impossible to study, in site surveys.

In the most intensively researched examples it has been found that failure can be signalled by the fact that some superficially desirable components of the ecosystem seem to be too common or too successful. For example the presence of a grassland wildflower in proportions that are significantly higher than is the case in undisturbed systems may signal an absence of some other component, such as an invertebrate that is normally predatory on the seed.

Assuming that the restoration is only partially successful, as is likely, is the remainder likely to be viable? Under the prevailing environmental conditions and the management planned, will these communities continue to thrive, and if not how quickly will deficiencies in the restoration become apparent? This is a complex question which could cause sleepless nights to ecology theorists who have long tried to agree on the extent to which a habitat is defined and controlled by the species more than by the environmental framework.

Another question concerns the time period after which the restoration attempt is judged to be adequately successful. How do we know when a community is internally functional and capable of maintaining itself (with at least the same probabilities of long term survival as the undisturbed habitat had)? Restoration may fail from many causes. The main mechanisms of change would be as follows.

1. **Reproductive failure** Some species have a short lifespan and rely upon new generations. If there is a lack of correct regeneration opportunities these will show problems quickly, but others may survive vegetatively for over 100 yr before recruiting a new generation. The planning system requires rapid assessment methods, but we also need long-term monitoring programs to determine how stable created grasslands are. Ideally, experience will allow researchers to identify those species that occur early and that are good indicators of long-term success.

2. **Decline of species that have complex habitat requirements** This is particularly likely with species that rely on interactions e.g. orchids which may have obligate mycorrhizae and obligate pollinators required for successful reproduction. If these supporting species are not present, then they will not set new generations.

   Disappearance could also be expected with species that have low physiological amplitude and hence have little resilience in face of system fluctuations. Such fluctuations are known to be typical of new ecosystems. Similarly the arrival of an episodic climatic event can eradicate species. Disturbed soils may exhibit problems such as increased bulk density and reduced rooting volume which only manifest in the most extreme periodic drought but which could eradicate plants which would have survived in an undisturbed system.

3. **Invasion of new species not sown or introduced** These may be plants, predators or pests. Their arrival, or the sequence of their arrival, may be a matter of chance, yet if they do arrive they can fundamentally alter the development of the system.

   One of the very difficult problems of community ecology has been relating the community variants that we see, on what sometimes superficially seem to be very similar habitats, to the environmental differences that we see. Chaos-theory models of natural processes support the idea that relatively small differences in starting conditions can lead, through a series of complex positive and negative feedback processes that can not be modelled or predicted in detail, to widely different end points. This is in line with the developing contemporary concept of succession whereby the Clementsian vision of mono-climax communities has lost acceptance. Generally most ecologists believe today that succession can lead to many possible end points, although it may be the case that the probabilities for the development of one community may be higher than most.

In a restoration programme we know that if a certain community existed on a certain site, then at least it should be possible for it to survive there again, but also that there are many other communities that could probably be just as successful. Following disturbance several changes may have occurred that would be enough to send the system off into very different directions if succession is allowed to progress as before. A good example of a perturbation that is likely to do this is increase in soil phosphorus levels which may have a long-term influence on vegetation productivity.

Even if natural succession may have been deflected because of a change in probabilities for establishment, it does not necessarily mean that an imposed community will not be stable and self-maintaining if given adequate management inputs. There may also be a situation where a community could be imposed that survives in the short term but does not have enough internal coherence to be self-maintaining in the long term.

4. **Changes in management regimes** One of the major risks in a mitigation scheme is that there may be a relaxation of a management programme that had previously been rigorously followed. Of course this is equally possible in an undisturbed habitat. However, the risks are particularly high where management has been imposed as part of a condition of planning permission. This imposition can only be enforced for a finite period of time during which many developers will be happy to play at being land managers, but obviously their long-term business priorities will be elsewhere.

5. **Changes in ecosystem processes over time** There are many ecosystem processes which are dramatically altered following disturbance and which will change as the habitat matures. The most obvious is nutrient cycling. There are conflicting possibilities which will have an influence, such that the end result may be hard to predict.

The first is that disturbance increases the rate of nutrient cycling. Where the substrate is a nutrient rich material, such as a topsoil, nutrient cycling may be temporarily increased. This will tend to favour certain characteristic 'disturbance' species that will usually gradually disappear. (However, there are some disturbance species which can persist indefinitely in plant communities once they have become established. Many skeletal systems are vulnerable to these invasions in a way that mature systems are not.)

It is also possible that sites such as reclaimed industrial land may commence as nutrient poor systems, where the substrate is basically a spoil or subsoil. These typically accrete nutrient capital over a period of several decades, stabilizing at a point that is determined by the physical matrix of the substrate. There is a likelihood that the initial communities will therefore not be representative of a stable flora adapted to the site.

A third scenario is where a nutrient poor substrate has been used and soluble inputs of N fertilizer have been used to compensate for this. These inputs can become immobilized in biomass or lost through leaching. It is therefore possible to maintain cycling through management without fundamentally increasing the nutrient capital of the ecosystem. If this management ceases the system will rapidly degenerate.

The risk of failure is therefore high. Even if failure is not apparent it can be just as difficult to determine when success has been achieved. Some plants for example, surviving in perfectly viable natural systems, may not need to reproduce more frequently than once in a hundred years in order to replicate the population. If a man-made community also does not reproduce, is this a failure or may it just be waiting for the appropriate climatic or environmental event? The planning system requires rapid assessment of performance, but we also need long-term monitoring programmes to develop experience of how stable created grasslands are.

Measuring restoration success against a previously existing state also presents a conceptual problem in that this requires that an arbitrary 'snapshot' of previous conditions is used for evaluation, when of course all habitats are dynamic systems constantly open to change. All of the species exist in an intimate web of competition and mutual support, evolving and changing. This in itself gives rise to philosophical debate about whether the target for restoration should be the state immediately prior to the degradation or development that inspired the restoration effort, the period of optimum health or value of that system (e.g. prior to a period of long gradual deterioration), or the stage that the system would probably have progressed to if no disturbance had happened.

Of course the reality is that restoration can never be **proven** to have completely succeeded, i.e. that everything has survived and will continue to function as desired. Simberloff (1990) suggests a 'null hypothesis' for restoration, that as long as it is impossible to tell that a restored system differs structurally or functionally from an undisturbed system open to normal dynamic processes, we can, conditionally, accept that successful restoration has been achieved. Most projects will not achieve even this goal, and some loss of quality is likely. Although this does not remove the justification for the attempt, it makes it hard to assess what is reasonable for the mitigation program to achieve. However, the objective should be to produce a habitat of lasting value and importance.

Strategic methodology for habitat creation

There are three strands that go together to make up a natural landscape; the environment (controlled by site preparation), the plant species used (controlled by the design and the plant establishment) and management (Thoday, 1983). This distinction has long been recognized. Theophrastus in De Causis Plantarum also identifies the threefold distinction of the nature of the tree, the nature of the country, and the operation of man (Theophrastus c.300 BC, Einarson 1976, Plato c.410 BC).

Most habitat creation schemes put greatest emphasis on plant selection and methods of planting as the key operations and rarely consider the scope for environmental manipulation. In effect 'habitat creation' is often precisely the wrong term to be used, since it implies that attention has been given to the place where the plants and animals live, which is rarely the case.

Following species introduction there may be a period, perhaps a long period, when these introduced plants continue to grow and the created community appears to be a success. However, what has been produced will have the semblance of a natural community but may be incapable of behaving dynamically in the way that true natural communities would. Such plantings have more in common with a naturalistic design by Brown or Repton than with a 'habitat' – the designer of such shows no great advance on ecological understanding since the eighteenth century.

The long-term stability of a man-made habitat is controlled not by the planting and establishment, but by the ability of the component species to reproduce and establish new generations in the face of competition. This will only happen if the environment and the management is correct. If they are not, then throughout the second and subsequent generation the communities will drift further and further away from the original concept and the results are often disappointing (Smart, 1989). (Of course there are many scenarios where short term effects may be entirely appropriate, and where more important criteria would be the rapidity of effect and visual drama and beauty are more important than diversity and authenticity. These situations will be discussed in more detail later.)

Given the problems that exist with a simple pattern-oriented approach to habitat creation, despite the obvious appeal for managers and planners looking for concrete and rapid effects, it must be more important to address the processes and underlying environmental factors which support and maintain the functioning of the desired ecosystem.

It follows that there are three stages of importance in habitat creation:

1. the planning, design and preparation of the environmental conditions on site;
2. the introduction of species that may not colonize easily;
3. the management and aftercare.

Of these, introducing species is arguably of least importance since if the management or environment is wrong the grassland will never succeed. If they are right then natural colonization may do the work of developing the sward for you.

1. Building an ecosystem that has the potential for diversity

(A) LANDSCAPE PATTERNING AND HABITAT MOSAIC DESIGN

As we have seen above, the biodiversity and species content of a region will depend on the location, size and patterning of habitats as well as on the content of each habitat itself. Habitat creation therefore depends on careful design and assessment of which landscape features are to be created.

We are a long way from being able to develop consistent rules that can be applied with confidence in restoration projects. However, if this goal could be accomplished, the construction of a diverse mosaic of landscape types is clearly open to relatively easy manipulation. Landscape architects have great experience and great skill in controlling the structural relationships between different vegetation types, albeit primarily for aesthetic or recreational ends; this seems to be an area where further research is needed, and where a partnership between conservationists and landscapers may pay dividends.

One way to increase diversity is to develop habitats or biomes in a region where they did not previously exist, for example the diversity of a woodland ecosystem can be increased by creating areas of long grass. There is no challenge or complexity involved in creating such patches yet they will be popular with small mammals which in turn may attract more predatory birds. A great deal of successful work has been done by the UK Forestry Commission on the deployment of open space, glades and rides, in forest plantations. These are of great interest in facilitating recreation as well as making a key contribution to nature conservation interest and visual diversity. As with overall woodland design, these principles do not normally extend so far as to influence the actual woodland blocks which are created in accord with good silvicultural principles.

In woodlands managed for conservation similar glades and rides are important, but the division of open space and woodland blocks is sometimes less severe, grading into areas of more widely spaced specimen trees. Open space is often associated with other habitats which may be incorporated in the wood, especially ponds and streams. Wide rides are usually favoured since these allow enough light to penetrate to encourage a wide diversity of grassland species. However, variation in pattern may be critical. It has been found that dormice need areas where the canopy touches across rides in order to be able to travel between one woodland block and another (Andrews and Kinsman, 1990).

Of course when planning habitat mosaics it may be important that the components are assessed in regard to overall landscape character. An interesting example is the afforestation with exotic conifer species that has been the cornerstone of much UK government forestry policy throughout this century. Although exotic conifer species were predominantly chosen, and planted in a matrix which had nothing in common with ecological restoration, many are capable of supporting some of the wildlife that was adapted to native UK pine woodlands which are a degraded and threatened resource. It has long been an aggravation for some conservationists that the forestry lobby could point to increases in species such as pine martins and cross-bills at the same time that the planting encroached onto nationally valuable habitats such as raised mires.

Similarly it is fairly easy to show that planting trees in moorland will increase the net number of species that are able to survive there. However, the extent of the previous habitat will have declined, and even if some component plants or animals do not immediately die out, their existence will be more fragile.

Habitat size

Some nationally or locally scarce species may be restricted simply by a limited area of a given habitat, but their habitat requirements could nevertheless be very simple to define and to create. This means that species:area relationships must be considered. For example, the bittern is a scarce bird in the UK which requires a habitat of reed. Reed is not a scarce plant community, but there are very few contiguous areas which provide the scale of habitat that the bittern needs. Producing large areas of this habitat type is therefore a popular (and probably easily achievable) goal in some large-scale restoration programmes.

Ecotones and merging habitats

An additional source of diversity when habitat range is extended arises from the intermediate conditions found in an ecotone which will suit an additional group of species.

Environmental design to increase the number and length of ecotones is a commonplace technique in habitat creation. In the case of wetlands there can be advantages in increasing the shore edge through creating peninsulas and inlets. However, at its extreme such a development style can reduce the areas available for development of 'pure' habitat types such as open water.

Transition zones (or ecotones) between open areas and woodlands can have a major effect on the appearance as well as the conservation value of the planting. Sharp divisions can at times give dramatic visual effects, and may encourage people to venture more readily into the wood whereas woodland edge plantings can become dense and off-putting.

Habitat connections

The position of the new habitat in relation to the existing landscape should be analysed to determine whether it complements and supports or undermines existing plant communities. Reference has already been made to the concern for the development of corridors in contemporary conservation planning; it should be emphasized again that the evidence for the value of connections is complex and sometimes contradictory. Sometimes corridors may increase vulnerability of species by encouraging the movement of undesirable organisms.

Of course habitats do not need to connect to interact, but the degree of interaction will still be strongly influenced by spatial distribution and proximity.

Another way in which habitats may interact is through changes to the landscape that help to restore essential processes, cycles or resource transfers. For example, modifications to surrounding topography or river bank design may help to restore the necessary hydrological characteristics to a fragmented water meadow.

(B) CREATING DIVERSITY IN TOPOGRAPHY AND SOIL TYPE

Species-richness is a term which can mean different things in different areas, depending on the scale of assessment. One type of diversity is where there

16 Heterogeneity in soil conditions is a common characteristic of urban soils. This can be a key factor which helps to develop a complex patterning of different plant communities. The overall effect is that the area is species-rich even if any one patch has few plants.

are high numbers of species present within any one patch of vegetation in the community, such as is found in chalk grassland. However, another type of diversity is seen where the environment is very patchy and heterogeneous so that many different communities co-exist near each other in a complex mosaic. The overall effect can be an increase in biodiversity even where each patch is not particularly rich in species.

Restorationists often try to create communities with a high species diversity within each area. This is a great challenge and requires that the processes within the system are correctly tuned to support that diversity. However, most plant and animal community differences ultimately reflect differences in the soil, climate, management or other environmental factors. An alternative approach for the designer is therefore to create a mosaic of biomes, each of which may be comparatively species poor within themselves but which together create a rich landscape. This is often much simpler to do.

Aesthetic objectives are also worth considering for some purposes. In trials carried out at Reading University, wildflower seed mixtures were sown onto a range of different soil types. High ratings for visual preference were often most associated with the swards of lowest biodiversity (Marder, 1995). Aesthetically people seem to prefer situations where individual species have a strong visual effect as a result of forming large vigorous free-flowering clumps. These conditions are often characteristic of environments that show strong zonal diversity together with localized dominance by certain species and poor intermixtures of different plant types.

Gobster (1994) also found that people often prefer areas which have low naturalness compared to those with high naturalness. People do seem to have an appreciation for the broad structural components of naturalistic landscapes but truly natural systems were not appreciated, perhaps because they were too 'messy', 'unkempt' and 'overgrown'. At the same time activities such as brush and scrub clearance and tree removal are seen as negative, even where the long-term effects may be ecologically and visually desirable.

Obviously in a restoration project the appropriate patterning of species distribution should be determined and emulated for each target community, but it is worth recognizing that designing and engineering zonal diversity is relatively easy where technology can be used to maximize the diversity in the landform and the substrate – the analogy could be rather like a 'natural' herbaceous border where each species is growing in a patch of its own soil.

By importing and using a range of different soil types in a habitat creation scheme, differences in moisture retention, fertility, texture and even in the presence of seed within the soil itself will all affect the development of the different communities. Even 'wastes' such as brick rubble can be used – these are capable of developing their own unique and colourful flora (Gilbert, 1989). The value of environmental gradients also needs to be appreciated. Broad transition zones between different habitats (ecotones) are preferable to abrupt changes.

The potential of this approach has no better illustration than the work of Gerd Londo at the Rijksinstitut voor Natuurbeheer en Broekhuingen, Leersum, Holland. He has pioneered techniques of varying soil groups and water relations in habitat construction and in varying management practice to determine spontaneous vegetation associations (Londo, 1977).

Londo has developed extensive 'rules' for successful soil patterning. For example, alkaline soils should not be placed above organic rich soils as the migration of calcium will tend to increase the rate of organic matter breakdown and hence nutrient release encouraging competitive species. Conversely placing organic material over alkaline substrate echoes the conditions found in certain unique habitats characterized by orchids and other rare species.

Obviously alkaline materials should not be placed above acidic materials or there will be a tendency for calcium ions to migrate into the latter. Similarly fertile materials should not be placed above infertile. On south-facing slopes very free draining materials such as sand or gravel are likely to become too dry and too hostile to support much vegetation. Conversely on north-facing slopes clay soils may become too productive.

Landform will affect the aspect of soil, the drainage patterns and the depth to the ground water table. All of these factors will interact with the soil type in order to encourage slightly different communities. Ideally some areas of the site will be made poorly draining in order to encourage wetland communities which will reflect different frequencies, duration, and timing of seasonal flooding and the fate of the sediment load in any water which moves on the soil surface. The composition of the soil on which these patterns are imposed will also influence the community that develops, for example, free-draining loams can give a very different response to clays or silts under comparable flooding regimes, although we are only just beginning to understand the relationships between these variables. In some cases flooded habitats may be open to an engineered approach where landforming, water pumping and use of sluices are used to control community composition.

Inevitably a diverse topography may not be tolerable on all sites, and it is particularly important to remember the maintenance constraints such as working slopes for grass cutting machinery. In some cases it would still be possible to consider producing complex subsurface landforms which are then covered to an even grade by the top layer of the soil profile. This will be particularly effective where a subsoil is used with extreme drainage characteristics, such as a clay or a sand.

Dr Londo prefers to allow natural colonization to progress to see what species will naturally become colonists and dominants on the habitat matrix he has created. However, even sowing a standard mix over such a diverse mix of soil types and treatments will lead to the development of very different vegetation communities. Alternatively a complex mosaic of plant community types, such as woodland, scrub, grassland etc., can be superimposed. This will increase the likelihood that some valuable communities

Figure 6.2 Scrub conservation principles.

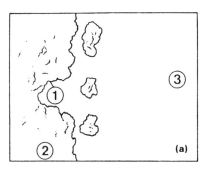 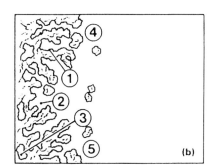

Block (a) is of limited value to wildlife:
1. Very little edge, with few sunlit clearings.
2. Solid blocks of dense scrub.
3. Grass

Block (b) is of much greater value:
1. Lots of edge, with intimate patchwork of scrub and grass
2. Approximately equal amounts of scrub and grass
3. Lots of sheltered holes, good for invertebrates
4. Dense blocks broken up, ideally over a few years, maintaining a diversity of scrub structure
5. Some patches left uncut – some rarities need undisturbed old scrub.

(Andrews and Rebane, 1994).

17 Rich aquatic habitats can be developed success-fully on old mineral workings such as sites for sand and gravel extraction. The key is good design of the sub-surface topography and the margins of the water bound-aries.

will find a niche somewhere. Often the more complex this patterning is, the more valuable it will be. This can be achieved by management (Figure 6.2), but such diversity can also be encouraged by soil manipulation.

Some wastes present the problem that initially they are too stress inducing and too hostile to support any significant vegetation cover. It is usually only after some decades of gradual improvement that their potential becomes evident. However, it is possible that mixtures of waste and subsoil or waste and small amounts of topsoil may significantly reduce the initial lag phase before a species rich vegetation can establish.

Interest in such approaches is developing among engineers concerned with developing environmental quality in schemes. In Holland 'ecological engineering' approaches to roadside re-vegetation and other large civil engineering works are increasingly common. Using earth-moving machinery, but using it in very different ways to what would previously have been typical, road engineers and their staff are exploring the potential for landform design, rough tilth formation, micro-topography and soil zoning to create habitat frameworks which then become colonized by naturally regenerating species. This technique is regarded as particularly suitable for the creation of wetlands and for habitats for associated mobile species such as orchids. Once the basic objectives have been learnt the approach has the particular attraction that no detailed plant handling procedures are required, and an ignorance of natural history is not in itself a disadvantage.

Problems seem to arise most often when small scale variations in micro-topography do not prove robust enough to withstand successional processes without intensive management; for example, silting and scrub invasion can rapidly erode small-scale wetland variation. This underlines the importance of having an appreciation of both timescale of target vegetation development, and also of the effect of scale on ecological processes, cf. landscape ecology, Chapter 4.

Ideally we would be able to work with and control edaphic variables with great precision in order to produce the vegetation we desire. Unfortunately we still have a long way to go before these criteria can be quantified and applied to different soil types. Habitats are extremely complex and soil factors inevitably interact with things like local climate or the presence of the appropriate animals to disperse seed or to create the correct germination niche at the right time of the year.

Soil amendment

In contrast to the approach of importing soil, it is of course also possible to consider altering or ameliorating the existing substrate to produce ideal conditions. Amelioration, by definition, implies some perceived desirable target characteristics and some perceived benefit of the amelioration chosen. In practice, however, we still only have the most basic understanding of the way that ameliorants can change soils, which ameliorants to use to resolve which problems, and what the relative cost effectiveness of different inputs are.

The methodology of soil treatment that has developed in landscape work has been implicitly targeted towards the goals that would be set by agronomists, with the resulting soil types judged against an agricultural norm where maximum fertility is desirable. Nature, of course, does not agree – vegetation can adapt to a very wide range of soil types and often some of the most diverse and distinctive communities are found on the most extreme soils. New objectives and techniques are required that meet conservation rather than agricultural targets.

Additives could be used in adventurous ways in order to 'design' soil conditions. In theory we could use additives to make soils drier or wetter, more fertile or more impoverished, more acidic or more alkaline – the full potentials have rarely been explored but may be particularly useful for habitat creation. However, the majority of experience in soil amelioration has been determined in situations where adverse soil conditions have to be improved, in a traditional horticultural sense, in order to allow the successful establishment of trees and shrubs. While, as we have seen, a traditional view of soil improvement is often **not** appropriate for habitat creation, there are also times when the success of plant establishment, especially trees and shrubs, will be compromised if adverse soil problems are not addressed.

One characteristic that many landscape sites have in common is that they are low in organic matter. This is especially materials that are not topsoils, such as brick waste, industrial spoils or subsoil exposed by building work, where an almost total absence of organic matter is not impossible (Bradshaw and Chadwick, 1980). The potential value of organic 'wastes' as amendments is obvious. On the other hand there seems to be an increasing trend for 'waste' organic materials to be packaged and labelled 'soil improver' without clear indication of the likely mode of action or probable value.

There is often considerable disagreement about whether ameliorants work or not. Great publicity was given to some Forestry Commission research work which showed that there was no benefit arising from the addition of peat to tree planting pits. Much less attention was paid to some research from Liverpool University published at almost the same time which showed small but measurable benefits from peat addition. Exactly the same situation exists with regard to research on water holding polymer gels. Some research has demonstrated that they do not work, and some research has demonstrated that they work very well (see Bradshaw *et al.*, 1995). The reality seems to be that under certain conditions, particularly where irrigation or rainfall is infrequent but not absent, they can make a substantial difference. Where there is plenty of water, or where there is none, they will not make any difference.

There are circumstances when certain amendments will be of value, and circumstances when they will not. The behaviour of amendments therefore cannot be judged in isolation and only has meaning when considered in terms of the soils they are used on. Very few of them are able to support growth in the absence of a suitable soil. It is a matter of great regret that many of the research results published do not recognize this fundamental reality sufficiently well.

A nutrient rich material may only have an effect on a soil that is nutrient poor; a crumb former will not work particularly well on a soil that is unable to develop such a structure, such as a sand; a material with a good buffering capacity would be extremely valuable on a sand but not necessarily on a clay. Sometimes additives may have complex or multiple effects; adding lime to an acid soil is not only likely to raise the pH and possibly help to flocculate the soil into crumbs, but it will also increase the rate of organic matter mineralization and hence lead to a flush of nutrients. Water holding gels remain as discrete particles in the soil – they will not directly improve soil structure but they can substitute for a poor structure by directly retaining moisture. 'Slimy', 'gummy' material such as alginures hold smaller amounts of water but they may have a profound effect on soil structure which in turn can greatly improve water relations in the soil.

It is possible to identify several different modes of action by which a soil ameliorant may modify a soil (Kendle, 1990). This include Sponge-like/Buffering Capacity by which the ameliorant directly holds moisture or nutrients, Textural Modification, Flocculation, pH modification, Soil Crumb Stabilizing Action, Nutrient Provision and Bulking Agents which may work by holding open soil pores even though the 'soil' lacks structure. Different ameliorants may perform different roles, and obviously this may explain the variability in performance reported.

Some soil ameliorants may have short-lived effects but these may produce a critical improvement in plant performance at the vulnerable plant estab-lishment phase. Other amendments may be slow to have an affect, or may even be harmful in the short term, but could lead to significant long-term soil improvement. Undecomposed organic matter may lead to anaerobic conditions when added to a soil, but after a few weeks or months there may be an improvement in structure which exceeds that from well-decomposed material.

Obviously the situation is complex and sometimes it is not possible to undertake a detailed soil investigation to allow a more rational approach to the use of ameliorants. This means that we may have to continue using general purpose materials as 'an insurance', but like any insurance we need to accept that there will be times when they are not actually necessary and the money spent will not lead to a return. Negative results need to be seen in that context.

At times many unanticipated effects may occur.

- Increased waterlogging may result from the use of organic material in planting pits on poorly draining land.
- Shrinkage and instability is sometimes seen when pits are filled with a very high percentage of organic matter. This can lead to poor rooting and drought even when the surrounding soil is good.
- Rooting barriers are sometimes said to occur where plant roots find the interface between rich organic matter and mineral soil difficult to cross. There is no clear evidence as to which circumstances, and in particular which soil types, make this effect likely.
- Rewetting is slow with some amendments, particularly peat, making them less effective at retaining periodic water supplies, e.g. summer rain.
- Nutrient Immobilization occurs when carbon-rich organic matter is broken down by bacteria. To achieve the correct balance of chemicals they require, micro-organisms may take N and P from the soil, which leads to nutrient deficiencies.
- Oxygen Depletion/Methane Generation may occur when reactive or undecomposed organic matter is used in waterlogged or anaerobic condi-tions. These materials should not be used at depth.

- Salinity levels are high in some materials, particularly nutrient rich manures and some sludges. In practice this is usually temporary and the salts soon disappear, particularly when the materials are used in winter, but it is best to be careful and to allow for a 'fallow' period if necessary.
- Toxins arising from industrial pollutants are a major problem in domestic refuse and particularly in sewage. These can only be controlled by very strict specification of the maximum permissible levels and policing by regular sampling.
- Plant and human pathogens are common in wastes but fungi, nematodes and bacteria should be killed by adequate composting/digestion. Even so, it is not uncommon to see weed seeds such as tomatoes surviving on sludge which has been composted. This suggests that cold spots have occurred and other organisms may also escape in such circumstances. Virus death is harder to ensure and spread of Tobacco Mosaic Virus from compost has been recorded. The situation with human viruses is complicated by a lack of knowledge of the possible vectors and levels of contamination likely to present a risk. No authority can guarantee that viruses will all be killed and the issue of possible media scares regarding materials such as sludge must be a problem.
- Weeds are very common in some amendments and are frequently seen sprouting with great vigour out of tree pits. By increasing competition and in particular water loss they can do much more damage than the unameliorated soil would have.
- Nitrogen uptake and immobilization may occur if carbon rich organic material is used. Availability of other nutrients may be reduced if very high pH materials are added.

It is obviously difficult to provide general purpose specifications for all soil amendments. Their use and the rates of application must be decided in the light of cost, the soil conditions on site, the species to be planted and the availability of other site treatments such as ripping. For maximum benefit amendments must be chosen by matching their effects to the soil type or soil problems encountered.

On heavy, slow-draining soils use amendments that have a humic, separating, crumb-forming or flocculant affect. On compacted soils use amendments that are good soil separators, crumb formers, and resource storers. Crumb formers and humus sources should be incorporated across the whole site. Soil separators should be ripped in to form drainage channels.

On light soils use amendments that are crumb-forming, nutrient sources, resource storage improvers or with a high buffering capacity. On organic matter deficient wastes and subsoils use amendments that are humic and are good nutrient sources. On contaminated land use humic and buffering amendments, those that are nutrient sources (if high in phosphorus) and calcium (to raise the pH and reduce solubility of the contaminants). These ameliorants are best if incorporated across the whole site.

Often the pattern in which an ameliorant is applied is just as critical as the material itself. For example, a small amount of gravel would have little effect on clay soil drainage if incorporated across the whole profile whereas as a French drain it can have a profound effect. The same is true of soil separators such as bark. Conversely other forms of organic matter may improve soil structure if incorporated across the entire site but may be value-less or harmful if used only in tree pits on the wrong soil type.

Above all it is important to remember that in habitat creation programmes it may be desirable to **make soil conditions worse rather than better**. In particular the 'problems' outlined above may be deliberately exploited to reduce fertility or increase water retention on poorly drained areas. It is vitally important that there is a detailed assessment of the conditions that are required to maximize the habitat value and rate of establishment. The way that soil factors influence diversity in particular will be looked at in more detail below.

Optimizing soil conditions for species rich communities

Soil type obviously needs to be matched to the type of habitat that is to be created, but where there are no particular targets regarding the exact nature of the vegetation to be produced, then there are certain principles which can be considered to maximize the likelihood of diversity in the vegetation system.

pH extremes

Moderately extreme pH is usually a significant advantage in soils intended for habitat creation. In particular high pH is almost always a great advan-tage. In the UK, limestone or chalk grassland habitats epitomize the condi-tions of moderate stress and disturbance that maximize species richness – 40 species of plants per square metre are often found.

A high pH, above 7.8, tends to encourage diversity in vegetation by limiting nutrient availability which in turn limits the invasion of competitive species. Low pH, below 5, may also reduce the vigour of aggressive species but for complex reasons there seems to be relatively few species in the UK flora which can tolerate acidic conditions and species richness does not usually result. Of course species richness is not the only measure that can be of importance. Habitats on acidic soils, or those prone to high stress may support only a few, highly tolerant, species but these species may still be valuable or attractive.

Some of the most fascinating 'industrial habitats' have arisen on poorly drained or moisture retentive, and highly alkaline wastes such as pulverized fuel ash. The flora on these spoils can include huge populations of relatively uncommon orchids for example. The flora of these industrial sites can be very attractive, unusual and worthy of conservation but again it is worth noting that they may not be particularly species-rich because they exist for too short a time to allow extensive colonization.

Low fertility

Nutrients and soil fertility are major factors which control plant community development. In particular the negative effects of over-fertility on conservation land are well understood. The management of nutrition will therefore be one of the greatest problems in successful habitat creation (Marrs and Gough, 1990). On the other hand the tools available to traditional conservation may not be adequate to combat this problem whereas in new habitats there is the potential to undertake a more fundamental alteration of the site soil such as large scale soil stripping or the importation of very infertile subsoils.

Carr and Lane (1993) document many failures in the attempt to establish new habitats and species rich plant communities in Bristol. Various methodologies and strategies, such as cropping to reduce fertility and turf introduction have been unsuccessful almost certainly because of excessive fertility encouraging the build-up of competitive plants.

Fertility reduction   Many habitat creation schemes are established on land which is inherently fertile such as set aside farmland (cf. the Countryside Stewardship initiative). Wells *et al.* (1981, 1986, 1989) have shown the practicality of creating wildflower meadows on ex-arable land at Royston, Hertfordshire, and at Great Chishill, Cambridgeshire. Nevertheless, in many situations the requirement for thorough site preparation, critical management during the establishment phase, and long-term management to prevent colonization by competitive species suggests the desirability of utilizing low-fertility sites if possible.

Supporting evidence also comes from the well-recorded losses of wildflower species during experimental additions of fertilizer to semi-natural grasslands. The decrease in species diversity characterizing high-fertility sites reflects dominance by highly competitive species and competitive exclusion of stress-tolerant species. The use of inorganic fertilizers, and especially nitrogen, rapidly leads to a grass-dominated sward.

Because of these problems attempts are often made to reduce the fertility of a new site by cropping off, i.e. growing a high-demanding crop as a means of extracting nutrients from the soil. The importance of removing clippings from mown grass to avoid nutrient enrichment is also often stressed.

However, a relatively simple quantitative analysis of nutrient cycles will soon reveal that such efforts may be misguided. Wells (1980) demonstrated by a combination of calculation and measurement that removal of clippings may make no practical difference to soil fertility. If this is of questionable importance to existing communities, its potential for reducing nutrient content on new over fertile habitats, must be extremely limited. Similarly it could take decades of crop removal to make any significant effect on site nutrient capital. In the research plots at Rothamstead, P levels have only declined by 40% after 70 years of continuous cropping (Johnston and Poulton, 1977). While cropping is likely to reduce nitrogen to a limiting level for commercial crop production, the absolute levels of nitrogen remain high for nature conservation purposes. Those crops with the highest nutrient demands, which would be expected to perform best as nutrient reducers, soon show a performance drop as available nutrient levels decrease.

Paradoxically the additions of nutrients limiting crop production may increase the effectiveness of cropping in reducing fertility. For example, removing a potassium deficiency may increase biomass and allow more phosphorus to be recovered in the crop. However, although high levels of apparent recovery, up to 150%, may characterize nitrogen additions to highly productive grazing systems apparent recovery in crops often falls below 100% (between 46% and 71% at Broadbalk, Rothamstead).

It is also important to recognize that although agricultural improvement is usually responsible for increasing site fertility, there are other sources including rainfall (in The Netherlands rainfall may contribute c.40 kg ha-1 yr -1 N (see Marrs and Gough, 1989) and in urban areas it may be difficult to remove nutrients at a rate that does more than compensate for new additions in rainfall. In areas where P levels are high, cutting may favour the growth of nitrogen fixing herbs such as clover (Bradshaw and Chadwick, 1980) which maintain the soil nitrogen levels.

Initial fertility levels are of course likely to make a difference, and in particular where naturally infertile soils such as sands have had their nutrient status artificially boosted by fertilizers significant reductions may be more feasible (Marrs, 1986; Marrs and Gough, 1989). Even so, there is obviously a need for more sophisticated studies of nutrient partitioning and flux in habitats. Cropping is more likely to have large effects on the pool of labile, readily available, nutrients but long-term fertility will not be substantially affected if there are large geological or organic nutrient stores that are slowly being made available.

Where habitat creation schemes are established on sites which have been recently disturbed there is a possibility that nutrient mineralization rates could be unusually high, leading to particular problems of high fertility and competition in the early years. Cropping may therefore be effective. However, where this is not the case cropping may temporarily and artificially lower the labile nutrient pool. This would give an underestimate of the true nutrient equilibrium. The community favoured in early years may become increasingly inappropriate and prone to competition as nutrient release continues and returns to its stable state.

Although the evidence for a **nutrient** effect is equivocal, there is frequently some indication that removal of cuttings significantly increases species richness. Removal of the cuttings reduces a build-up of thatch which would otherwise inhibit recruitment from seed. Parr and Way (1984) associate an increase in diversity with the disturbance and scarification accompanying hand-raking to remove cuttings and with alleviation of the smothering effect of cuttings on the stubble which allowed the preservation of 'regeneration niches' and incident light. In their trials, analysis of soil nutrients indicated that removing cuttings led to a decrease in extractable potassium, while other nutrients, including total and available nitrogen, were unaffected.

In certain circumstances grazing may also be utilized to reduce soil fertility, primarily by folding in sheep at night outside the management area (Marrs and Gough, 1989; Green, 1981). Burning also reduces soil fertility through losses of mineral nutrients in smoke, and removes the need to deal with clippings. Burning litter tends to remove nearly all of the nitrogen, and about a quarter of phosphorus and potassium. In addition, the remaining phosphorous is fixed and temporarily unavailable. In the short term, however, many available nutrient levels, especially of potassium, may increase.

Other options for nutrient reduction may be more effective. Habitat creation schemes differ from traditional conservation areas in that there may not be an existing vegetation cover that needs to be preserved. This allows scope for more dramatic interference with the nutrient capital.

When Dr John Handley's Groundwork team in St Helens in the UK undertook research into the establishment of wildflower grasslands in urban areas for English Nature (Ash *et al.*, 1992) the soils were too fertile to support floristically rich communities and the sites become dominated by aggressive, competitive perennial weeds. The research therefore has included studies of how these soils could be 'ameliorated' by the addition of large quantities of hostile material such as brick rubble, pulverized fuel ash or colliery spoil in order to make conditions less suitable for the competitors and more suitable for other flowering species. Topsoil stripping may be carried out first, with the resulting material available for fund raising or use in areas where fertile substrates are desirable, such as on a city farm.

Topsoil stripping from semi-natural vegetation was often undertaken to fertilize agricultural land and continues in some areas (e.g. Tenerife). On grasslands and heathlands topsoil stripping was also undertaken to provide fuel and fodder. In Holland, where nitrogen inputs from rainfall are resulting in a succession from heathland to grassland, sod stripping is undertaken for nature conservation purposes (Marrs and Gough, 1989).

Topsoil stripping is also used on amenity grasslands in Holland to control competitive species, including weeds, during establishment, and to reduce management costs by lowering productivity (Londo, 1977). Topsoil stripping may also be cost-effective in amenity landscapes where the use of low productivity grasslands in design allows the transfer of topsoil to decorative plantings elsewhere on site, or allows topsoil export and sale. Topsoil stripping is also useful to remove insoluble pollutants.

Following topsoil stripping the exposed subsoil still has to allow plant growth, and individual site characteristics will determine a satisfactory depth for stripping. Studies on recolonization of primary sites (see Grubb, 1986) and reclamation of derelict land after mining (see Bradshaw, 1986) indicate essential requirements for plant establishment. For example, a nitrogen capital of 700 kg ha-1 is required to establish a self-sustaining ecosystem of *Salix atrocinerea* on china clay wastes in Cornwall (Roberts *et al.*, 1981). Marrs (1986) suggests the removal of 20 cm of topsoil to assist in re-establishing heathland on former arable land at Roper's Heath in Suffolk.

Alternatives to topsoil stripping have been considered to reduce productivity on roadside verges such as adding a sufficient depth of infertile material to the surface. Another approach explored by the Groundwork Trust has been the use of bands of hostile material introduced into the soil by a sand slitter. The slits made are about 5 cm wide, 20 cm apart and down to 20 cm deep. The process adds 3 m^3 of waste for every 100 m^2 of soil surface and provides niches of different physical and nutrient characteristics. Simple low nutrient wastes are likely to be ineffective as competitive grasses could still thrive in the bands of normal soil. Groundwork used chemically active wastes such as limestone, PFA and sulphur as a source of ions or toxins that would influence the wider sward. However, they found that the soil disturbance is quite dramatic and leads to a flush of nutrient release and also growth of weeds like *Cirsium* that were semi-dormant in the turf.

Calcium makes phosphorous and many other nutrients less soluble and less readily available to plants. Because of these processes calcium rich soils usually run out of freely available nutrients faster than calcium-deficient soils once the application of fertilizer has been stopped. Calcium additions to soil may be worth trialing, but the calcium content of a soil is also important particularly because it influences the breakdown of organic materials. On calcium rich-soils this breakdown, which releases nutrients, proceeds much faster than on acid soils. Liming a humus-rich soil can therefore temporarily boost the fertility.

Other researchers have used low-nutrient organic amendments in order to dilute soils. Where the carbon:nitrogen and carbon:phosphorus ratios of the organic material are high the organic wastes may also reduce fertility by leading to uptake of available nutrient ions. However, the effect of such an amendment by what is essentially an ephemeral additive needs to be considered relative to the desirable life of the scheme.

The strategy of adding materials which introduce other stresses, but which do not directly influence nutrient levels, has been attempted on other occasions, most notably through trials on the use of iron sulphate additions as a grass growth retardant.

Machines have also been developed which invert the soil profile, placing infertile subsoil on the surface, or mixing the subsoil with the topsoil. The extent to which these are successful will be influenced by rooting patterns – for example, whether grass roots can reach the fertile layers deeper down. We also know little about the behaviour of plant systems where 'pockets' of fertile material may be distributed within a largely infertile matrix. Soil disturbance and mixing of this kind may also lead to unplanned effects, for example there may be a flush of nutrients if an organic-rich topsoil is aerated and mixed with a calcium-rich subsoil.

When discussing fertility it is necessary to take account of the habitat type to be created and the timescale that the project is planned for. Londo (1977) points out that the slower a spoil or subsoil is to revegetate, the more likely it will be to develop an interesting flora. Green (1986) discusses how successful exposed chalk subsoils can be at developing a species rich community after a few decades, where they are surrounded by existing chalk grassland. In some cases these 'new' communities are richer than the undisturbed grass which is becoming too fertile.

In very long term habitat creation schemes successional processes may also come into play. Ecology theory holds that as succession progresses, leading to woodland dominated by large forest tree species, there is an accumulation of living and dead biomass in the ecosystem. Increasingly nutrients are taken from the soil and become locked up in this biomass. A succession that begins on a soil that is too fertile for species-rich grass may still end up as a woodland with a diverse species complement, although the process may take decades or centuries. On the other hand, succession which starts from a more infertile soil supporting rich grass may finish with a very stressed, and hence species poor, woodland.

However, in the majority of habitat creation work it is difficult to take long term views. Instant results are often required politically and local people may want to see rapid greening rather than a bare subsoil.

Fertility building   An alternative scenario is where we are working predominantly on subsoils or skeletal soils, either deliberately imported or left as a legacy of some industrial process. Many of these sites are incapable of supporting vegetation, perhaps for decades, because of chronic nutrient shortage, so traditional restoration methodology has been geared towards increasing soil fertility.

For agricultural after-uses, high productivity is obviously desirable, but to meet conservation goals when reclaiming land presupposes an understanding of the minimum nutrient capitals required by different ecosystems. The objective is to restore the site to the point where plant communities can begin to function and to green the site enough to meet social or engineering goals. Early vegetation establishment requirements may mean that some initial nutrient inputs are necessary, even where the target vegetation, such as *Calluna* heathland, may be very tolerant of infertility as an established community (EAU, 1988). The use of small amounts of nitrogen fertilizer may aid establishment on very deficient soils, otherwise the seedlings remain vulnerable to additional stresses such as drought. Where the subsoil shows physical problems as well a thin covering of top soil can provide a favourable germination media and sufficient nutrients for seedling establishment.

Short-term fertilization may also allow rapid greening in order to reduce erosion, which would otherwise be a constraint on vegetation development. However, the desirable necessary size and likely fate of such inputs must be determined, given that it is often easier to raise fertility than it is to lower it.

New techniques therefore need to be determined to meet conservation rather than agricultural targets, but this presupposes an understanding of the minimum nutrient capitals required by different ecosystems. The use of nitrogen fixing plants in order to give early cover and to raise soil fertility is another common reclamation technique and again the manager needs to know how long these should be encouraged to remain as dominant parts of the community. To help provide guidance in such matters a high priority in research for habitat creation and restoration should be the development of guidelines indicating the minimum and maximum nutrient capitals that seem to be associated with different semi-natural plant communities. An attempt to undertake such an analysis for woodland creation was attempted by Kendle and Bradshaw (1992).

The major determinant of plant productivity in the long term is usually the phosphorus level of the soil (Marrs and Gough, 1989). This nutrient is highly immobile so that once the productivity of a system is raised it can be centuries before the effect starts to wear off; in some cases the effect may be permanent. Phosphorus also tends to encourage the growth of nitrogen fixing herbs, so it can indirectly lead to a build up of this nutrient as well. On the other hand, adding soluble nitrogen without phosphorus can lead to a short-term improvement in productivity but the N, because it is highly mobile, may soon be lost from the system. This prevents long term dominance by nutrient demanding species.

Addition of nutrients in manures or similar organic forms has been shown to be less damaging to existing plant biodiversity than soluble fertilizers, but it needs to be recognized that such organic sources are more likely to contribute more to the nutrient stores on the site, and if fertility is raised excessively then the effect will be long-lasting.

An area of research interest at Reading University relates to ways of getting rapid results from wildflower swards without compromising the long-term development of the habitat. There is the possibility of using very localized phosphorus additions in conjunction with the introduction of mature plants. Plug-grown wildflowers can have some phosphate fertilizer already in the soil plug. If these are planted at a low density into a sward which has been sown onto an infertile soil their visual effect may be quite considerable, particularly as these individuals will have limited competition. However, the net input of P into the site will still be very low and the chances of developing a species-rich sward in the long term will still be good.

Soil tilth

The aims of site preparation for sowing species are to create an environment favourable for seed germination and seedling establishment, and to reduce competitive interference from other species. Assuming the use of viable and ecologically appropriate seed, failures in establishing wildflower meadows from seed are often attributable to inadequate site preparation (Wells, 1987; Brown, 1989).

Traditional agricultural soil management has concentrated on ways of developing a good 'tilth' for sowing seed. A tilth is a uniform surface which ensures good contact between the soil and seed and encourages rapid and uniform germination. Even when we sow a wildflower seed mix, the percentage establishment will be higher where a high-quality tilth has been created, as long as weeds have been controlled. In practice the tilth will benefit from small irregularities which will increase the seed diversity and number, but large irregularities lead to poor initial establishment. However, in the long term such environmental uniformity will work to minimize diversity and it may actually be better to have a soil which produces erratic germination.

Variations in the surface texture of the soil are known to interact very closely with the particular form of seed (or other propagule) in order to encourage certain vegetation types. Ecologists refer to this effect as the 'regeneration niche' (Grubb, 1977). In a classic ecological experiment Harper *et al.* (1969) showed that very minor alterations in soil surface texture was enough to control the germination of different plant species. This understanding could also be used as a positive technique for landscape creation – diversity could be built into a design by treating the surface of patches of otherwise uniform soil in a variety of ways, perhaps by using different cultivation implements.

Soil disturbance

The colonization of urban waste spoils by uncommon plants is well documented and is attributed to the low nutrient status and lack of competition. Gemmell (1982) points out that in the Greater Manchester area there are more orchid sites on derelict industrial land than in more traditional habitats. Although the hostility of the soil helps to explain why competitors do so badly on such sites, it does not fully explain why orchids do so well. It has been well established that terrestrial orchids have effective dispersal mechanisms because of their very fine seed. However, this seed is so small that it lacks resources and can only produce a seedling with the support of a mycorrhizal fungus.

It must follow that the pattern of orchid distribution in the wild is largely a measure of the distribution of the symbiotic fungi. It is also well known that soil disturbance and sterilization can lead to dramatic changes in the abundance of the soil micro-flora and fauna. This may mean that the peculiar conditions of newly disturbed subsoils and wastes may in some way favour symbiotic fungi such as *Rhizoctonia sp.*, in competition with other soil fauna.

After a period of time many such 'disturbance' habitats gradually become less hostile and are invaded by scrub which in turn leads to a loss of the orchids. They are therefore essentially ephemeral communities. Management options for spoil tip habitats include re-creating the disturbance of the land using heavy earth-moving equipment to destroy the scrub and to exploit the hostility of the soil to control succession.

Landform and soil preparation for woodland creation

The minimum area necessary for the creation of a woodland or scrub area is larger than for low herbaceous vegetation while small differences in relief and in the soil of a woodland are less clearly expressed in the herbaceous layer than in a grassland. Relatively thin layers of different soils may not influence the woody species at all because they root so deeply.

Trees and shrubs are often tolerant of poor conditions and soil preparation can often be limited as long as critical steps are recognized. The most likely edaphic cause of immediate failure of woody transplants is poor aeration arising from impeded drainage. Woody root systems are much less able to adapt to such conditions compared to herbaceous plants. Over the medium term water shortages can often lead to failure, but most deaths are seen where herbaceous plants are allowed to compete and monopolize the resources that are available.

Moffatt (1986) outlines the approach on heavy clay soils at Warrington. Amelioration of topsoil compaction, and of exposed sub-soil by ripping to 450 mm depth at 500 mm centres, and improvement of structure by incorporating a 150 mm layer of local peat in a single operation in August or September is recommended. The site preparation is cost-effective, at around one-third of the cost of importing and spreading 300 mm of topsoil, and without the problems illustrated by Roberts and Roberts (1986) for imported topsoil.

Many trees and shrubs can maintain reasonable growth rates even when the soil is moderately infertile. In many cases it is not practical to make any large-scale changes to the planting site, but on derelict industrial sites in particular operators go to great expense in order to minimize diversity and produce uniform, fertile conditions in the name of good reclamation practice. It is essential as a first step to recognize that such variability, unless extreme, is not a problem, but should be seen as an asset that can be built upon rather than overcome. These conditions may encourage richness in the associated ground flora.

Although trees and shrubs do not need highly fertile soil, high fertility does not effect the opportunities for development of a species-rich system in the same ways as the grassland. A complex species mix and landscape structure can be introduced by design and management and this in turn will lead to diversity in associated species. Woodlands may therefore be a sensible choice of land use on fertile sites.

2. Species introduction

(A) HERBACEOUS

The main options available for introducing herbaceous plants are as follows.

- **Seed** – using either a commercial formulation or a mix taken direct from an existing plant community, such as a 'haymeadow' mix. The latter may be dominated by whichever species successfully set seed that season, and the proportions and content of the mix may bear little obvious resemblance to the plant community it came from. It may contain many components which are not currently commercially available, although this could be seen as both an advantage and a disadvantage. There are also particular advantages to this technique where it is important to obtain local genetic types.

Seeding should be onto bare soil. As well as reduced plant competition, bare ground avoids problems of thatch or organic litter preventing good seed contact with the soil, and some pest and disease problems, particularly that of slugs, will be reduced. Success rates of sowing into established grass are minimal, even if heavy harrowing or scarifying precedes sowing. However, there some other options, particularly through the use of a slot seeder as discussed below.

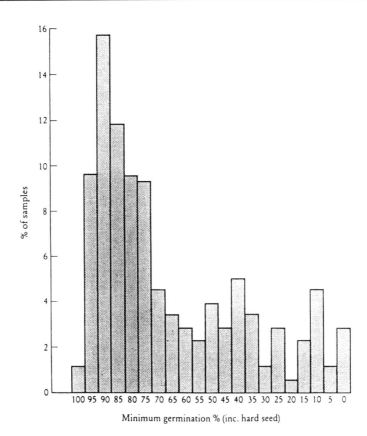

Figure 6.3 The variation in wildflower seed germination from different seed lots (Brown, 1989).

- **Transplants** – plugs or even pot-grown plants. This is expensive and best for those species that establish poorly because of slow or delayed germination. Again transplanting is often carried out into existing swards, although it is possible to plant into bare ground and to sow a low-rate grassland mix over the top.
- **Plant litter** – e.g. hay crop remains used as a substitute for a commercial seed mix.
- **Turves** – taken from a damaged site for 'inoculum', dotted into a new site, or as a complete cover.
- **Soil** – possibly the primary value of spreading topsoil salvaged from a damaged or destroyed habitat will be its role as a carrier of organisms.

Direct sowing (or 'direct seeding') of commercial wildflower seed mixes into prepared seed beds is the most common method of wildflower grassland establishment. Despite the publication of techniques established by Wells, Bell and Frost (1981) and the reiteration of these techniques in seed-house catalogues and technical leaflets, establishment of sown wildflower mixtures is often unsatisfactory in the field. Wells (1987) and Brown (1989) discuss the reasons for unsatisfactory establishment which includes poor seed quality (Figure 6.3).

Wells (1987) also reports on the success of 29 commercially available seed mixtures including a total of 119 dicotyledon species during the period 1982–84. 108 species failed to establish on some sites during the study. In addition to inadequate seed bed preparation and management, Wells attributes failures to:

- use of incorrectly stored or otherwise unviable seed;
- use of ecologically inappropriate species such as marsh species including *Lychnis flos-cuculi* and *Pulicaria dysenterical*;
- species with slow seedling growth (low seedling relative growth rates), such as *Campanula rotundifolia* and *Linum catharticum*;
- Species requiring vernalization sown in Spring, such as *Pimpinella saxifraga* and *Primula veris*.

Seed mixes are made available for a range of conditions. It is possible to buy 'general purpose' mixtures, anticipating that some species will not germinate. Effective commercial mixes for acidic soil conditions are not as widely available as those for neutral or alkaline soils. Bespoke mixes can also be ordered.

Clearly wasted seed is to be regretted but in complex habitats, with a lot of variation in soil conditions losses may have to be accepted. Since it is often impossible to assess in advance the likely subtleties of stress and disturbance that may operate in any given location it is often advisable that mixtures of species are introduced, knowing that only some will succeed as part of the long-term community. Much of the seed sown will remain dormant, and in some cases this can give second flushes and aid recruitment later. It will also be inevitable on many sites that species from the seed bank or blowing in from adjacent habitats will germinate in the newly cultivated soil (Figure 6.4).

Recommended sowing rates are low and frequently anything up to a tenth of the rate used for normal amenity grass establishment, although direct comparisons are complicated by the variation in seed size compared to simple grass monocultures.

Sowing is often done in autumn to mirror the natural time of most seed set. If other times are used there is likely to be some change in the species which emerge, but the overall effect is still usually satisfactory. However, if germination is particularly slow the seedlings will remain vulnerable and losses may follow. The optimum time of sowing may depend on whether winter adversity (frost etc.) is more severe than summer drought or vice versa.

The use of **hay or litter spreading** as an alternative to selected or commercially produced seed has been discussed in detail by Jones, Trueman and Millet (1995) and by EAU (1988). Important factors to consider to ensure success are:

- identification of a suitable donor site;
- careful timing of hay cut or harvest;
- control of the delay between cutting and strewing to avoid overheating

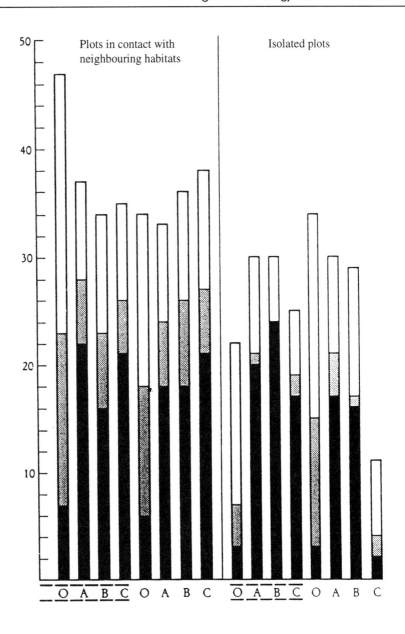

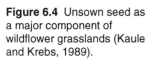

Figure 6.4 Unsown seed as a major component of wildflower grasslands (Kaule and Krebs, 1989).

18 A modified slot seeder developed to introduce wildflower seed into existing grass swards. The resulting establishment rates can be high. The seeding patterns can look artificial but can be modified by making several passes with the seeder.

19 Rattle plants are annuals that are hemi-parasitic on grasses and, if present in high enough densities, can reduce their vigour and allow other wildflowers to thrive.

20 Wildflower plants grown as plugs for introduction into existing grasslands. This technique is especially valuable for species with slow or complex germination.

and seed loss (freshly cut grass is superior in terms of quantity and species composition);

- spreading rates – if applied at high density, hay may need to be removed from the receptor site or it will smother the seedlings, but often seed content is high enough that adequate establishment can be obtained from light rates of hay strewing.

Inevitably, however, the use of hay or litter will provide less control over the composition of the seed mix. Certainly there may be a limited relationship between the nature of the donor site flora and the seed content of the material spread. Many dominant plants may be under-represented, while other species which are present in low numbers may produce large amounts of seed. Some of these problems may be overcome by phased cutting or collection. These sources do have the advantage of producing plants of known provenance, and may also contain seed of rarities that are not present in commercial mixes (although it is not always regarded as desirable to encourage the artificial spread of uncommon species).

21 Wildflowers grown as a crop to produce seed for habitat creation and restoration schemes. However, there are increasing concerns over restriction of the provenance of such seed.

Generally the presence of existing vegetation inhibits seed germination, unless it is present at such low densities that it acts as a nurse. However, there may be political reasons why existing vegetation may need to be maintained rather than destroyed, or it may be desirable to enrich but not replace an existing community. **Slot-seeding** retains existing visual amenity, reduces seed costs and removes costs associated with seed bed preparation. Diversification of existing swards through slot seeding may therefore be the most cost-effective method of establishing a wildflower grassland from existing amenity grasslands, although the difficulty of hiring suitable equipment, and capital costs involved in purchase and modification of standard equipment may prevent the application of slot-seeding to small sites.

Wells, Cox and Frost (1989a, b) discuss technical and ecological considerations in the use of slot seeding to introduce species to existing swards. A slot-seeder is used to apply herbicide (usually paraquat) in a band 10 cm wide and to drill a seed mixture into a slit 5 mm wide and 5–15 mm deep cut in the ground within the sprayed band. By exposing mineral soil and relieving competition during establishment, outstanding establishment of the sown species is possible. The sward surrounding the sprayed bands may also assist establishment by acting initially as a non-competitive 'cover' crop. Sprayed bands remain visible for up to six months following autumn herbicide application, whereas bands remain visible for only two months after spring application. Although the growth windows following autumn and spring application are similar, autumn sowing allows germination of species requiring vernalization and assists rapid establishment of autumn germinating species in the spring. Regional climatic differences are important in determining the best month for spraying.

Diversification of existing swards with seed-raised **wildflower transplants** presents a reliable option to slot-seeding. Transplants reduce `environmental sieving' during establishment and allow control of planting arrangements. In addition, seed-raised transplants may flower during the first season, whereas field sown seed may often only flower during the third (or even later) season. Purchasing (or raising) transplants and hand-planting increase costs compared with seed, although the reliability and flexibility of transplants may increase cost-effectiveness, especially on smaller sites. Transplants are also attractive as no specialized equipment is required and the existing sward is largely retained. Normally the grass immediately surrounding the transplant is controlled either by physical removal or herbicide application before the plant is introduced (Bisgrove, 1988).

Despite the advantages of using transplants, studies of long-term survival and reproduction of individual transplants are desirable. The early results of Wells *et al.* (1989a) indicate that ecological tolerances of individual species, and of seasonal factors may lead to losses even following good initial establishment.

Wathern and Gilbert (1978) report successful transplanting of **species-rich turf** using transplants 5–10 cm deep and interseeding with *Festuca* spp. The same approach was adopted on an opportunistic basis at Warrington New Town (Moffatt, 1986; Tregay and Gustavsson, 1983).

Park (1989) discusses a project relocating 5.5 ha of a Site of Special Scientific Interest of magnesian limestone grassland near Durham. Despite losses of 2–7% in area during donor-site preparation and transplanting, survival of the plants in the turves was satisfactory. Control of invasive weed species establishing in interstices between turves using glyphosate, and of woody species, were the only significant maintenance inputs. The flat terrain and shallow rendzina soils simplify the operation, as consideration of slope and aspect is unnecessary, and the entire topsoil is transportable. The use of earth-moving equipment from the quarrying operation threatening the grassland ensures the cost-effectiveness of the operation.

Where existing mature plants can not be salvaged or transplanted in a cost-effective way the use of **topsoil spreading** is a method of introducing seeds, rhizomes or other propagules. The importance of both soil or turf introduction is that they may bring fungi, mycorrhizae and invertebrates on to the site that may be invaluable in establishing a diverse and functioning habitat. Like the use of hay or litter they may also help to preserve plants that are impossible to buy through the trade and preserve local genetic variation. However, the proportions and composition of the mix are unpredictable

The transfer and storage of seed-rich topsoil presents as many problems as transplanting turf. As with hay, spreading of seed rich soil is likely to lead to dominance by whichever components of the buried seed bank have most rapid germination and respond best to disturbance. The soil seed bank may also be rich in legumes which can cause fertility problems. The unreliability of survival of some components of the seed bank as a result of storage compounds these problems. In the case of organic-rich topsoils poor storage may even lead to the initiation of a composting process that can lead to heat-death of the seed. The build-up of large seed populations of weeds characteristic of disturbed soils, such as *Rumex*, may also degrade the quality of the soil seed bank. Nevertheless in certain situations storage of topsoil may be necessary during site works, and satisfactory regeneration after re-spreading can result. For example, re-spreading of topsoil stored for two years during site works at the University of Bath resulted in good re-establishment of limestone grassland species on some areas. Londo (1977) has utilized seed rich topsoils collected from various regions in Holland with natural colonization for habitat construction on a small scale.

Sometimes seed can come from soil already present on site. Rotovation of sites which were likely once to have been diverse meadows may release associated species from dormancy in the seed bank (London Ecology Unit, 1985).

The extent to which plant introduction is a necessary or desirable component of habitat creation is a matter of some debate. With a few exceptions, transplanting is regarded unfavourably in traditional conservation as it decreases the naturalness of the resulting habitat, it may compromise local genetic stock and it also removes the opportunity to study the natural processes of plant dispersal which could improve our understanding of ecological processes (Rackham, 1986). **Natural colonization** is often overlooked as an option but there are those who see great advantage in waiting to see what comes up in areas which have not been sown (cf. Londo, 1977; Hermy, 1995). The particular advantage of this approach is that it:

- focuses attention on the importance of environment and management;
- indicates that there is at least some degree of fit between the species that arrive and the local environmental conditions, such that successful germination of future generations may be more likely;
- involves 'natural' processes which make the end result more 'valid' and acceptable to many traditional conservationists;
- is more likely to promote genetic continuity with the local ecotypes and regional varieties of wildlife;
- is likely to lead to more localized variation in species composition reflecting differences in the site edaphic status.

It is also important to recognize that the process of natural invasion is itself of value. We need to cherish the fact that things have happened despite man – the spontaneity and unpredictability of wildlife is in itself part of the importance of the natural world to many people. Scientifically the ecological processes at work in the urban countryside are educational and important for study. If natural colonization is allowed to take place, it is also an initial test that environmental conditions support the juvenile as well as adult stages.

Finally if rare species do arrive, which they sometimes do, their presence is legitimate and not clouded by ethical issues of planned manipulation of species boundaries.

The counter argument is of course that dispersal and establishment in the vulnerable seedling or propagule stage are major constraints in plant community creation. Loss of habitat increases fragmentation and dispersal distances, making it less likely that the same processes of species invasion that created existing semi-natural communities would be able to progress on new sites. It is therefore frequently stated that the contemporary distances from suitable seed sources will prove to be a limitation to wildflower establishment (Johnsons Seeds, 1991).

Because the process of colonization takes time, there is often a decrease in species richness associated with a change from one biome to another. This occurs in natural systems, for example during the move from grass to scrub woodland that follows a decline in grazing, but will also be characteristic of a planned and man-induced change in habitat. Transplanting may overcome these limitations and allow some plants to get a foothold where they would not have naturally arrived. For example, the products of natural colonization are likely to be heavily dominated by wind dispersed plants, some of which are of low competitive ability and low persistence. The sites may eventually be characterized by a closed community of low diversity dominated by common grasses and scrub that may even reduce opportunities for new colonizers (Ferris-Kaan, 1995).

However, transplanting in some forms, particularly the use of mature plants, can also overcome constraints to the establishment of seedlings or vegetative propagules that would normally never have been able to become components of an ecosystem. By artificially providing broad germination niches for the wildflowers we obviously raise the possibility that subsequent establishment of future generations will be largely unsuccessful, and the 'lifetime' of the community will be limited by the ability of the introduced species to regenerate vegetatively.

The accumulated experience of horticulturists, foresters and agronomists can already demonstrate certain principles. Nursery catalogues list several thousand taxa available for garden use with only pH requirement and hardiness regarded as worthy of mention in most cases. Domestic and botanic gardens testify to the fact that plant species can be taken from a variety of habitats around the world, placed in a wide range of combinations of species and vegetation structure and yet, once established, will thrive and grow for as long, or sometimes longer, than they do in the wild. They are therefore surprisingly tolerant of variation in edaphic and climatic factors. This contrasts sharply with the ecologists' perception of the highly subtle variations that can naturally control plant distribution when competition is allowed to happen.

Competition is most serious at certain vulnerable stages in the life cycle. Weins' (1977) theory of the 'ecological crunch' suggests that many natural communities are constrained by competition operating at certain vulnerable stages in the development of different species. This suggests that plant distribution is controlled by occasional very severe periods of environmental hostility rather than by prolonged low-level adversity. The landscape manager's role is often to nurture desired plants through such critical stages. The most likely time for a 'crunch' to prove dangerous is when a plant is young.

It is both a strength and a weakness of the transplanting process that it bypasses many of these natural constraints on dispersal. The danger is that establishment may create communities which appear to be successful but that have no long-term viability or ability to reproduce. This does not mean that the plants will not be able to establish and maintain a presence for decades or even centuries (cf. Oliver Gilbert's studies on the persistence of alien 'casuals' in urban flora as a result of past land use or industry). For many other plants, dynamic interactions are more critical in the short term and these may only survive in a community if they are able to compete successfully and re-establish.

Some of these issues are clearly complex, indeed they cut right to the heart of our understanding of natural community build-up and succession. In nearly all new habitats the initial species complement should be regarded as temporary and liable to change until the processes of natural invasion reach a balance and leave a species complement that suits the environmental framework and management. Whether this is really important for any given site does of course depend on whether the proposal is intended to mitigate for habitat loss or whether the intention is to make an artificial community for human enjoyment.

(B) WOODY PLANTS

Woody plants differ from herbaceous in several regards:

- they often have larger seed and therefore slower seed dispersal;
- they sometimes show much more complex dormancy and seed germination characteristics;
- establishment from transplants can be more difficult on some soil types due to a less flexible and adaptable root framework;
- adjustments in root:shoot ratio are less easily made, so some transplants can be initially very vulnerable to competition from grasses and to stresses such as drought;
- once established they can normally dominate the community and survive for very long periods without having to reproduce or to re-establish their position in the community.

Despite the greater challenges involved, one of the most important choices is still whether to allow woodland establishment to progress by natural colonization or to plant. If planting is chosen, plant material can be introduced at stages ranging from seed through small transplants up to large planting stock chosen for instant impact.

Colonization of woody plants is strongly coloured by the relationship between seed dispersal processes and competitive potential. In a survey of

22 Some industrial wastes have developed mature woodland that is of great benefit to local people.

47 urban and post-industrial sites in the UK that had been abandoned between 10 and 40 years three species *Fraxinus excelsior, Betula pendula* and *Crataegus monogyna* comprised 85% of the colonizing species (Hodge and Harmer, 1995). The proportions of seed arising from each source is influenced by the make-up of the urban area and the local tree species and distribution patterns. In some surveys species with small windblown seed made up 91% of the colonization found, in others this fell to 1% (Hodge, 1995).

Betula is wind dispersed and seed production rates are high. However, the seed is small and uncompetitive and it is unlikely to establish in sites with significant shade or ground cover. *Fraxinus* is also wind dispersed but has larger seed and can colonize some existing swards. *Crataegus* is dispersed

Table 6.2 *Forestry Authority monitoring of direct seeding*

	Site 1		Site 2	
Species	Seed sowing density (No ha⁻¹)	Percentage seedlings present after year 1	Seed sowing density (No ha⁻¹)	Percentage seedlings present after year 2
Sycamore	25 000	7.6	30 000	14.6
Norway maple	15 600	–	20 000	–
Field maple	5500	0.2	–	22.5
Ash	35 100	27	40 000	–
Oak	10 000	4.1	–	–
Wild cherry	9800	1.5	–	–
Hazel	2300	–	–	3.7
Beech	–	–	10 000	–

Source: from Harmer and Kerr (1995).

by birds and has a seed large enough to allow invasion into existing swards that are not too vigorous.

By allowing natural invasion there **may** be greater potential for encouraging local genotypes and thus helping to maintain a wider genetic range within a native plant species population. However, in UK towns and cities where there are parent trees nearby to act as a source for natural colonization it is also likely that *Acer pseudoplatanus* will play a major part of the mix. This can be unpopular with local wildlife groups, but unless there is existing vegetation that will be threatened there is a lot of wisdom in accepting the move towards a sycamore wood, since the species will undoubtedly seed in anyway and dominate any planting.

Once a relatively closed canopy has established new recruitment may fall off, so recent secondary woodlands can sometimes be poor in tree species compared to planted woodlands (Hodge, 1995).

Hodge and Harmer (1995) also found that the colonization ranged from extremely dense (30 650 trees ha⁻¹) to very sparse, with only 19% of the land having 'adequate density', and with the results often being slow and unpredictable. (However, there is clearly some value judgements incorporated in this statement, and the diversity of woodland structure described could be expected to be of value to some species.) They also confirm that natural colonization is most successful on land which is infertile enough to prevent the establishment of a rank competitive ground layer, but not so hostile that even trees could not grow. The sites studied had an average of three tree species. This low diversity may in turn limit the diversity of associated species such as birds (Fuller *et al.*, 1995). Some techniques could be used to increase the likelihood of establishment (such as ground preparation) and also to alter the proportions of specific tree groups (such as the use of bird perches to favour colonization by fleshy fruited seed species).

Where more control over species content and patterning are desirable, tree seeding can be undertaken. The limitations to deliberate tree seeding are quoted by Hodge and Harmer (1995) as being:

Table 6.3 *Operations which may be needed to ensure rapid woodland establishment within 15 years*

	Natural colonization	Direct seeding	Planting
Years 1–5			
Deer/rabbit fencing	++	++	++
Individual tree protection	+	–	++
Plants	–	–	++
Ground preparation	++	++	+
Vegetation management	++	++	++
Years 5–10			
Individual protection	+	+	–
Plants	+	+	–
Ground preparation	+	–	–
Vegetation management	+	+	–
Thinning	+	+	–
Maintenance	+	+	+
Years 10–15			
Individual protection	+	+	–
Plants	+	+	–
Ground preparation	+	–	–
Vegetation management	+	+	–
Thinning	+	+	–
Maintenance	+	+	+

Source: Harmer and Kerr (1995).

- losses due to predation, desiccation and shading;
- unpredictability of germination;
- difficulties of weed control;
- slow early growth relative to competing vegetation;
- browsing of seedlings.

Losses can therefore be intolerably high (Table 6.2). In some locations however the method has been practised with success and can give savings in cost as well as produce an effect which shows many of the advantages of natural colonization. The utilization of such techniques therefore seems to be dependent on a degree of flexibility and lack of pressure of time on the managing body.

Natural colonization or seed introduction has the advantage over transplants in that spacing and growth form will inevitably be more variable and appear more natural than any transplanting process. There may also be delayed germination in some species, giving a variable age structure. However, there is also a risk that some species may be suppressed by the early germinating species. To overcome this risk seed treated to break dormancy may be used, but these are often more fragile than dormant batches because of the emerging shoots and roots and so may need to be distributed by different means.

In addition it is often suggested that seed grown plants will be self-selecting, with species aggregating in those areas where environmental conditions best suit their germination. This again gives the woodland more potential diversity.

Both establishment by seed or natural regeneration need appropriate management. Indeed they can be slower than deliberate planting and hence spread the need for management inputs over a longer period, which can have budget implications (see Table 6.3).

The majority of woodlands, even in urban areas, will be established by the use of small transplants or whips (1+1, 2+1 etc.). With some species, such as *Salix* or *Populus*, establishment can be achieved by the use of hardwood cuttings.

It is well known that the size of tree stock planted can have an effect on the instant impact (as well as cost, chances of establishment success and vigour) of a plantation. What is sometimes overlooked is that the form of tree when planted can have a permanent effect on the shape of the mature tree. The country is littered with 'naturalistic' woodlands which have been planted with standard trees and as a result will **never** look natural. Standard tree shapes are appropriate for streets; they have nothing in common with woodland-grown specimens.

If large trees must be used they should be feathered or multistem specimens, and of course these should be carefully sited where instant impact really is necessary. Where money is not limiting standard trees can be scattered through larger areas of the mix within a matrix of smaller transplants. Within a relatively short time the smaller stock will catch up with the standards. The latter can then be left to become gradually more suppressed by competition, or coppiced to give them greater vigour and a more natural form (although some species may not regenerate well from large stock).

NURSE PLANTS

Wells (e.g. Wells *et al.*, 1981, Wells *et al.*, 1989b) suggests the use of nurse plants (or 'cover' crops), such as Westerwold's rye-grass (*Lolium multiflorum* cv.), sown (at 30–45 kg ha^{-1}) with a wildflower seed mixture to prevent soil erosion and provide acceptable 'greening' during the establishment phase on amenity sites, and to protect wildflower species during germination and establishment. With appropriate management to prevent seeding, these plants should disappear within two years. Alternative nurse crops could include species which are reliably annual, particularly cereals. Species which die young but maintain a persistent standing dead biomass may be particularly advantageous.

Annual wildflower species can also be included in sowing mixes with perennials. If this is done there can be a conflict with the need to cut the newly establishing perennial sward. It may be best to sow the annuals in the autumn so that flowering is completed early in the season and there is less public objection.

Nurse plants can of course also compete with the species to be established. It is essential that these are not too dense or growing too vigorously at the same time as the desired long-term species. Experimental evidence indicates a substantial part of the suppression suffered by a plant in the presence of another occurs during the first three weeks following germination (Harper, 1977). However, the medium-term ecological effects may be hard to predict since inevitably in very mixed seedling populations there are many possible interactions. One effect of the nurse may be to most significantly retard those components of the mix which are rapid to germinate and grow and this in turn may favour later germinating seed (Johnsons Seeds, 1991).

There also seems to be a strong interaction with fertility of the site; under fertile conditions nurse species may be expected to grow more quickly and more aggressively which could cause problems. In practice some authorities report that nurse additions are most harmful on low fertility soils where the competitive effect is presumably maximized (Johnsons Seeds, 1991).

Nurse crops work as long as the competitive interference is less important than the effect of the 'cover' crop in ameliorating the environment surrounding the seed. Some amelioration of the immediate environment of the seed due to changes in micro-climate at the soil surface may assist in germination and early establishment of wildflower species. In particular, protection from winds is likely to be important. Protection from soil erosion, predation, and extreme, and potentially lethal, soil surface temperatures are also possible as is an improvement in soil chemical and physical properties. They may also assist in suppressing and preventing flowering by more aggressive ruderal weeds.

Some studies on the use of such nurse plants are equivocal. Wilson (1989) investigated the use of exotic species to stabilize and nitrify severely eroded sites in order to assist prairie restoration in Manitoba, Canada. In fact, observations over eight years indicate that the introduction of exotic species restricts natural recolonization by native prairie species, relative to control sites.

The use of herbaceous 'nurse' species for tree crops is sometimes accepted. La Dell (1983, 1988) recommends the use of cereals (sown at a mean of 60 kg ha-1 depending on soils and environmental conditions) as a cover crop in direct seeding of trees. He considers that cereals provide a satisfactory balance between suppressing herbaceous weeds and ameliorating conditions to allow successful tree establishment.

With regard to woodland plantings it is also frequently suggested that trees associated with climax woodland, such as *Fagus*, need to be inter-planted with pioneer species to aid establishment. In practice Moffatt (1986) has found that frequently these nurse species overpower and suppress the trees that they were intended to support. At best they need thinning or removal and distract management resources into ephemeral tasks that are not really necessary. It seems extraordinary that people who would not think twice about planting a beech hedge, which is always exposed to the elements on two sides, seem to feel that the plant is incapable of growing as a free-standing specimen, or that beech transplants are not perfectly capable of sheltering each other as they grow.

Some of these misconceptions may arise from the forestry practice of using 'nurse' trees to draw up climax species and encourage the early formation of a clean stem. When grown in the open, trees such as oak often develop a scrubby habit for many years. In these cases the nurse tree is often a quick-growing species chosen in order that there could be a quick return from first thinnings. In habitat creation projects there will frequently be disadvantages, both visually and from the point of view of wildlife support, from encouraging the trees to develop uniform straight stems.

A more plausible need for shelter may occur when large stock is used on exposed sites causing the trees to bend or rock and making the root system unstable. This limits the rate of root re-establishment which can aggravate drought problems. However, even here nurse species are unlikely to grow fast enough to make a difference and the use of other forms of shelter, such as windbreak fencing, may be required.

(D) RECURRENT PLANT INTRODUCTION

The reinforcement of populations of desirable species may sometimes be necessary, requiring reseeding or further planting. Habitat creation schemes are usually based on a single sowing or planting, but research has shown that random or unquantifiable factors can influence colonization, and that several attempts may be necessary before any given species 'takes' (Simberloff, 1990). This does not mean that the plant species in question were not viable components of the community; rather it reflects the fact that plant establishment and maintenance are often influenced by recruitment from surrounding populations, and that establishment is frequently stochastic.

Interestingly, many traditional grasslands in the UK were oversown with hay sweepings and this may have played a role in maintaining species-richness at a level above that which would have characterized the community in isolation (Rodwell, 1993).

(E) PLANTING PATTERN

An important aspect of plant community ecology concerns the spatial distribution of species and of individuals relative to each other. This aspect receives limited attention in many habitat creation projects but it can be argued that the spatial relationship between plants will be a major factor determining whether or not they can function in the way desired. For example, spacing of trees will affect the growth form and long-term stability of the individuals and the shade cast which in turn will have a major influence on the development of the ground flora and on the suitability of the habitat architecture for the different animal species that may colonize. Spacing may also affect more subtle processes, for example Francis (1995) has shown that the spacing of some species of woodland herbs introduced into existing woodland has an influence on their long-term survival, presumably because the patterning affects the ability of pollinators to move between individual plants.

Frequently plant spacing in many projects is influenced primarily by the aesthetics, or the wish to make the construction or management phases easier rather than by a detailed analysis of the appropriate patterning of individuals for the target habitat type. For example, trees and shrubs are frequently planted in straight lines at regular spacings to simplify access for grass cutting or herbicide treatments. Although such considerations may be important in mass plantations which have a timber production component, they may undermine the long-term success of a woodland habitat creation scheme unless adequate allowance has been made for creative thinning. Another problem may be that the options for spacings are constrained by the requirements of forestry grants, and such benefits may need to be foregone for an effective restoration programme.

Much of the conservation importance in woodlands resides in structural diversity that comes from glades, varying tree density, varying tree form etc. There is a widely recognized relationship between the structural complexity of the landscape and the value to birds (Goode, 1995).

(F) Origin of seed

Significant professional use of wildflower seeds in the UK certainly dates back as early as the 1960s, and much earlier in many other European countries. For almost as long there has been a sense of disquiet among biological recorders and other botanists who found that the traditional patterns of geographical distribution of species were becoming blurred, and that many unusual species or ecotypes were appearing outside of their natural range. These plants showed unusual growth habit, unusual life form and doubtless also many exhibited atypical physiology and biochemistry which could be of great significance to feeding insects. More recently similar concerns have been voiced concerning the origins of trees and shrubs used in environmental improvement schemes.

The reason was of course that many wildflower seed mixes, even sometimes those claimed to be of native origin, contained seed harvested from other countries. Sometimes this was done out of ignorance by the seed supplier, sometimes as a result of sheer bad practice which was reinforced by customers looking for the cheapest possible supplies or even in some cases by EC seed legislation, but most often it was the consequence of gaps between demand and the supply from a fledgling wildflower seed industry.

The criteria for species selection determined by Wells *et al.* (1981) has profoundly influenced the development of the wildflower seed industry, and the seed-house catalogues usually adopt these objectives in principle. However, the seed mixtures have inevitably been modified by seed suppliers to reflect economic considerations of supply and marketing. Substitution with agricultural strains of native species in the absence of adequate local production increases supply and reduces costs. Rarely successful, but especially attractive native species, such as *Campanula* spp., *Linum* spp. and *Helianthemum nummularium* are often included in seed mixtures to assist marketing despite the consequent reduction in the cost-effectiveness of such mixtures.

The problems that arise from the use of seed from species or ecotypes outside their current range were documented by John Akeroyd for *Plantlife* in the report 'Seeds of Destruction' (1994). They can be summarized as:

1. Degradation of the biogeographical boundaries of plant distribution and general confusion of landscape character. In Holland for example existing patterns of plant distribution have been severely compromised by the long-established tradition of construction of nature parks.
2. Degradation of genetic patterns in native ecotypes, with possibly consequential losses of co-evolved invertebrates. Alien genotypes could also lead to greater susceptibility to disease. Agricultural legume cultivars may raise soil fertility more than unimproved forms and hence decrease diversity or increase the rate of succession (Ash *et al.*, 1992).
3. Project failure which may arise from using forms not closely adapted to prevailing conditions (although it is important not to fall into the trap of claiming that native plants 'grow better' than alien species, a contention frequently disproved by foresters and agronomists the world over). It is also possible that professional liability problems may arise if a consultant contracts to establish native plants and actually introduces alien types.

A related issue concerns the possibility that the process of commercial production of native seed (even of a local ecotype) may narrow the genetic base by favouring forms which have high germination rate (and possibly therefore reduced dormancy safeguards) or ease of harvest or by selecting just those forms which set seed around the modal peak of the community, thereby selecting against any forms which flower and set seed early and late within the species' range. The consequences may be less severe but could still be worrying if a small population is dwarfed by large numbers of re-introduced selected types.

Of course the ideal solution would be a supply of certified native seed of appropriate local provenance to the region in which they are to be used, but the practical realities are complex. Several issues confuse the picture.

Firstly, insisting on locally available seed may have an enormous impact on seed price (for example native birds-foot trefoil can cost 15 times as much as imported strains).

Secondly, it seems almost impossible, for many species, to define accurately what the extent of local provenance variation really is. Is seed sourced from the same county, or the same Natural Area, acceptable or do we need material from the adjacent field? We know next to nothing about the genetic patterning of wildflowers or whether stock from say Cornwall and Somerset are more similar than material from, say Cornwall and France. Hitchmough (1994c) argues that proximity alone is often a poor indication of genetic parity, especially for outbreeding or wind pollinated species. In some cases it may be possible that what appear to be widely separated populations are in fact the remnants of what was once one contiguous population. Mixing these genetic variants may therefore be an important aid to maintaining vigour in the isolated groups.

Research exists to show that in some species local variation is important, but we will be unlikely ever to see the day when we know the boundaries of such variation for all significant UK plants. This leaves us with the problem, not uncommon for nature conservation professionals, of trying to make our best judgements of how to proceed without complete supporting data.

Finally there is always the worry that for many species and ecotypes the greatest part of any likely damage has probably already happened. Historically huge quantities of forage variants of some native legumes were imported as seed, while it was quite common practice for seed from meadow harvests and barn threshings to be sold around the country by travelling merchants. Seed was of course also distributed as contaminants in grain. The proportions of seed used in environmental programmes may be a fraction of that used in agricultural or forestry operations.

Other threats to the genetic base of native species may arise from other directions. Garden forms of many native plants are also scattered far and wide, for example outbreeding is already very commonly seen among culti-vated *Primula* species. In the USA there is concern that plant breeders are rapidly blurring the line between wildflowers and cultivated perennials (Wilson, 1992). Wild species are being improved far beyond the discovery of unusual colour breaks, and there is now a new generation of pseudo wildflowers with larger, or even double flowers. Introduction of clearly 'exotic' and non-native species into wildflower meadows for example (cf. Hansen's work described in Chapter 3) may have the advantage that these plants are less likely to lead to genetic corruption of local ecotypes than when we plant selected, but locally incorrect, native forbs.

Similarly among trees and shrubs it is likely that importing stock or seed dates back for centuries. In the UK seed importation was probably common in order to grow the stock needed for creating the agricultural enclosures. It is likely that 'alien' gene combinations are widespread and attempts to rectify the situation now must be unlikely to succeed and should therefore take a lower priority than other investments. Given the economic importance of forest trees and the relatively limited number in the UK it is likely that we will see comprehensive genetic studies that allow us to map ecotypes with some precision (Ferris *et al.*, 1995). However, the problem is that when collecting seed these ecotypes may still not be 'pure', especially for wind-pollinated species.

Other issues of policing a regulation system may not be as simple as they first seem. For example, seed producers have traditionally grown many of their crops overseas for greater reliability of harvest, or even to **guarantee** that there will not be cross-breeding and confusion of genotypes. It therefore does not necessarily follow that a seed lot must be produced in the UK to be genetically native. Conversely selected provenances of some species may be offered that legitimately represent a subset of the local population's genetic range but may still be undesirable. For example, oak seed could be obtained from seed orchards produced by foresters to give an upright growth form, which may be undesirable from a conservation perspective. However, the issue then does not become one of genetic origin, but rather of diversity within the seed lots offered for sale. Similarly for wildflower seed, it may be that the seed harvesting process selects out a limited range of the natural variation which could have an impact on local invertebrates even though the seed is genuinely native.

Alternatives to the use of commercial wildflower seed do of course exist, for example natural colonization or the use of hay or litter. The disadvantages and advantages of such approaches have been discussed above from the perspective of the quality of the newly created habitat. In the case of small, sensitive remnant plant populations there are also concerns about the impact that seed harvesting may have on the health of those communities, both through physical damage during harvesting and also through impacts on seed inputs.

In many schemes a sensible way forward would be to use simpler wildflower mixes, relying on relatively common and freely reproducing species, and to plant at lower densities. This of course is actually close to the recommendations first set by Wells and co-researchers (Wells *et al.*, 1981).

Ultimately it is necessary to consider the deeper philosophical issues that have been discussed in Chapter 4 that relate to the need to find a balance between interventionist or protectionist nature conservation strategies. Professionals working regularly on habitat creation, restoration and mitigation schemes, for example, need to question whether they can stand by the premise that existing patterns of plant biogeography should be sacrosanct. We also need to find a way to strike a balance between the wish to conserve local sub-specific variation, much of which is, and will remain, unquantifiable, against the equally strong arguments for large scale and urgent habitat restoration to boost declining populations.

Clearly some practices are unacceptable and must be resisted; just as clearly 'ideal solutions' are unrealistic or unaffordable. The challenge will be to try and draw boundaries between these two extremes that can be accepted by professionals.

(G) OTHER ASPECTS OF PLANT INTRODUCTION

There are many other aspects of 'transplant ecology' that are of interest or practical import in habitat creation schemes. For example, some communities may only be viable if certain components are introduced after others (Gilpin, 1987). Trees may do best without ground flora, woodland herbs may need a developed canopy to control competitors (Buckley and Knight, 1990).

Many plants have a narrower physiological or ecological range as a transplant compared to an established mature specimen (Table 6.4).

The quality of transplanted stock may influence the performance of the plants in many ways (Kendle *et al.*, 1988), which in turn may influence the behaviour of the community.

Size is a major factor for consideration when establishing woody plants. A 15 cm tall tree seedling may be killed by grass competition, a 1.5 m tall individual may not be. On the other hand the larger the given tree or shrub, the more likely it is that it will suffer from the effects of poor aeration in a waterlogged or compacted soil. Woody plants grown to any significant size on a nursery will inevitably develop a root framework which reflects the balance of aeration and moisture on that soil. When such a root framework is transferred to a waterlogged soil, the majority of the roots will be plunged into an anaerobic zone and are likely to die off.

Table 6.4 *Habitat preferences of a range of aquatic plants*

Species	Oligotrophic	Water type Mesotrophic	Eutrophic	Guide to planting depth (mm)	Approx. max .depth (m)
Emergent					
Acorus calamus (sweet flag)	–	*	*	75–150	0.5
Alisima plantago-aquatica (water plantain)	*	*	*	0–150	1.5
Butomus umbellatus (flowering rush)	–	*	*	75–150	2.0
Glyceria maxima (reed grass)	–	*	*	50–150	0.7
Iris pseudacorus (yellow flag)	–	–	*	50–125	0.5
Mentha aquatica (water mint)	–	*	*	0–75	0.5
Phragmites communis (reed)	*	*	*	75–200	1.0
Rumex hydrolapanthum (great water dock)	–	–	*	0–75	0.4
Sagittaria sagittifolia (arrowhead)	–	*	*	75–150	1.5
Sparganium erectum (bur-reed)	–	*	*	75–150	0.5
Typha latifolia (great reedmace)	*	*	*	75–150	0.6
Floating leaved					
Callitache stagnalis (water starwort)	–	*	*	50–100	0.5
Lemna sp. (duckweed)	–	–	*	N/A	
Nuphar lutea (yellow waterlily)	–	*	*	up to 900	1.5
Nymphaea alba (white waterlily)	*	*	*	up to 900	1.6
Polygonum amphibium (water bistort)	*	*	–	0–300	1.0
Potamogeton natans (broadleaved pondweed)	*	*	*	150–300	2.0
Submerged					
Callitriche intermedia (water starwort)	–	–	*	–	1.0
Chara spp. (stonewort)	–	*	*	–	2.5
Elodea canadensis (Canadian pondweed)	–	*	*	–	3.0
Hippuris vulgaris (marestail)	–	*	*	–	4.0
Myriophyllum spp. (water milfoils)	–	*	*	–	1.5
Pontamegaton crispens (curled pondweed)	–	*	*	–	6.0
Zannichellia palustris (horned pondweed)	–	–	*	–	2.0

Note: The optimal depth for establishment is usually less than the maximum depth to which species will spread vegetatively. Submerged plants are usually just thrown in. The depth guides are very approximate since this depends almost entirely on the clarity of the water.
Source: Thornley (1979).

Small trees and shrubs will find it easier to develop and adapt the root system to the conditions operating on site. This will usually mean producing a shallow surface-running root system. The major threat to such plants may be the occurrence of severe droughts to which they will remain vulnerable.

Small plants are also generally more vigorous than very large stock, and this initial vigour can be the key to plant survival. The vigour may have multiple causes, for example the size of the root system will be closer to that of an undisturbed plant. The larger a plant is at the moment of transplanting, the smaller the percentage of root that can be preserved. Large trees may also have higher demands on carbohydrate reserves and on water translocation systems within the stems than small plants.

It can often be seen that survival relies upon growing a new root system in-situ. Site investigations have shown that there can be a strong interaction with climate, topography and stock handling. Often plants are at the margin of survival and if the year is excessively wet or dry, if the stock has been poorly treated (bare rooted plants allowed to dry out, or container-grown plants allowed to become root-bound), or if the topography is such that patterns of drainage and water infiltration aggravate the effects of compaction then establishment failures are more likely. In some instances even slight variation in the planting depth of the plants may mean the difference between success and failure.

(H) INTRODUCTION OF SPECIES GROUPS OTHER THAN PLANTS

The focus of almost all direct species introductions to the landscape is usually limited to higher plants, although as we have seen, some techniques such as the spreading of soil or species-rich turves also has the potential advantage of spreading invertebrates, fungi and other species groups.

In flagship habitat restoration programmes, particularly those associated with near-natural ecosystems, such as are found on recently degraded island sites in Australasia, the re-introduction of **animals** forms a major component of the procedure. Even in the UK there are sometimes discussions concerning the re-introduction of higher animals as a key component of habitat function. For example, the success of efforts to restore large tracts of Caledonian forest in Scotland has been linked to wolf introduction. This has had a particular focus on the need to control the unbalanced populations of deer that are causing excessive damage through over-grazing and thus preventing regeneration of woodland plants. However, these ideas are still contentious and difficult to accept even in the remote highlands. Very few opportunities can exist for deliberate animal introduction into urban areas.

A subject that has received some research attention with regard to tree establishment is that of **fungal** inoculation. Research evidence has been forwarded by Allen (1991) and others to show that growth responses among trees planted on disturbed sites or areas with poor soil status often improve as a result of artificial fungal introduction (although the form and history of the tree will be likely to be an important consideration, since many nursery grown transplants will already be carrying adequate inoculum). Similar research has been underway to address the value of inoculation of rhizobia bacteria on nitrogen fixing tree species. However, little is known of the effects of fungal inoculum on other plant groups, or of the degree to which fungal presence influences general patterns of plant community development.

Nevertheless the logical relationship is particularly clear for groups such as orchids which often have an obligate symbiotic dependence on fungi for seedling germination and establishment. We have already seen that large colonies of orchids are sometimes characteristic of ex-industrial sites and that random factors may influence symbiotic fungal development in these situations. The deliberate introduction of inoculum may be a technique that can encourage the earlier or more widespread establishment of such communities.

(i) KEYSTONE SPECIES

Traditionally ecologists tend to classify dominant species, particularly plants, as those which have the greatest population size or the greatest cover and biomass. However, there can be other species which, although present in small numbers, can control the processes operating in the habitat to a great extent – these may be termed process dominants or keystone species. Even where there are arguments against introducing species into new habitats, there may be value in artificially hastening the rate of colonization, or boosting the population of, keystone species.

Keystone species can be hard to identify without some detailed assessment of the processes in any one ecosystem but examples could be:

- a species which limits a potentially dominant competitor, e.g. a selective grazer, a species which inhibits seed germination or establishment, a species which attacks a predator or herbivore which would otherwise become too damaging;
- a species which plays a key role in dispersal or reproduction of some components of the system;
- a species which has a dramatic effect on the nutrient cycling or other processes e.g. a plant with litter very resistant to decay. The possibility of utilizing hemi-parasitic species, including *Rhinanthus minor*, to suppress grass and legume species in species rich swards is also under consideration (Grime *et al.*, 1988). *R. minor* is itself dependent on adequate regeneration conditions, as the species is an annual and forms no persistent seed. Harrowing the soil may help to ensure good contact between the seed and the soil. This plant may also be best sown after the sward has established for a year, since it seems to require existing grass cover.

3. Habitat design by management

In the majority of habitat creation, programmes management, while accepted as important, has been seen as a largely routine and one-dimensional operation by which a target plant community is preserved once created. However, it is also possible to consider management as a primary tool for habitat creation.

23 Urban vegetation fires may be a common factor influencing ecosystem development on rough ground.

Duffey *et al.* (1974) state that 'management is often the major factor affecting the floristic composition of a lowland grassland'. The semi-natural rural habitats that are treasured in Europe were created not by planting but by introducing repeated management onto an environmental framework. Management is often therefore the sole factor which has dictated whether different biotypes such as grassland or woodland cover have developed over most of the countryside.

Management can also indirectly encourage diversity by influencing whether refuges exist, the degree of disturbance, nutrient cycling and gap formation. Zonation in management can also reinforce patch dynamics and control structural diversity in the vegetation as well as the most fundamental characteristics of the habitat.

Of course, newly created habitats are, by definition, unstable and likely to undergo rapid changes. Management is an unusually critical component, and this may need to be much more flexible than with long-established sites. Often the key management activities take place many years after the first plant establishment, e.g. thinning of a woodland plantation.

It can be argued that in many grasslands the key process is the development of a rational management regime: the wildflower mix can be looked upon simply as an 'up-front' excuse and temporary justification for this more flexible management while in the long term quite a different flora could develop. Some studies have looked at the way different cutting regimes can lead to profound changes in grassland vegetation (Parr and

Way, 1984). Altering mowing height or frequency may only lead to a dominance by common flowering species that normally persist under intensive mowing, but nevertheless these can be surprisingly attractive. Such maintenance processes need more research so that they can be used in a less ad hoc way and so that the habitats that we create are reinforced over time rather than possibly degraded.

NICHE MAINTENANCE

In good examples of habitat creation, where the environment is well designed, the plants are well chosen for the site, and the management is well planned, the introduced species may sustain and regenerate themselves. Even then, it is likely that the initial species complement will only be a small subset of what would naturally be found in similar, long-established, ecosystems. Ideally the habitats should gradually improve over time as additional plants and animals colonize. It is therefore important that the habitat should be kept 'open' so that new species have the opportunity to invade. This can be done through disturbance introduced as part of the management, although it will of course also be dependent on other factors such as the soil type present.

Grubb (1977) stresses the role of the 'regeneration niche' in the recruitment of new individuals from seed. Recruitment and survivorship data for a number of herbaceous perennials analysed suggest that the contribution of seed to maintenance (rather than establishment) of populations may be negligible. Although annual germination may recruit a high percentage of individuals to a population, survivorship may be low and the contribution of seedlings to maintaining species populations may remain insignificant except perhaps following severe disturbance. (Of course seed recruitment may be more important in the first couple of years in the life of a new meadow with an open sward.)

Individuals of perennial species may be long-lived. For example, Kerster (1968) observes individuals of *Liatris aspera* surviving for at least 34 years, and even without any recruitment following initial establishment, decline from a plant community is extremely slow. The observation is especially interesting as *L. aspera* is a colonizing species of wind-blown sand, although as individuals persist during later successional stages, the relationships with the sub-climax plant communities are misleading. In this situation interpretation of the ecological niche may be extremely difficult, and descriptive ecology may be misleading in establishing a methodology for the re-creation of plant communities.

Harper (1977) uses a depletion curve to establish a half-life for a number of species from published data. For example, the half-life for *Ranunculus acris* in three separate studies conducted in North Wales, continental Russia and Finland is between two and three years, *Sanicula europea* has a half-life of around 50 years and *Filipendula vulgaris*, a half-life of 18.4 years, although the survival of individual species may vary considerably between sites. Tamm (1972) presents long-term data on the populations of perennials in Swedish meadows and forests. The depletion curve for populations of

Primula veris in a grove of *Fraxinus excelsior* has a half-life of 2.7 years, while a population in dry meadow has a half-life of nearly 50 years.

The variation in recruitment, survivorship and life-span of individual species clearly presents difficulties in predicting the fate of populations in the absence of detailed studies and the development of models taking account of apparently random catastrophes.

Long-term observations on wildflower meadows established from seed and observations on the survival of species transplanted into permanent grassland confirm the importance of seasonal factors and 'environmental sieving' on established plants (Wells *et al.*, 1989a). If established plants flower and set seed losses from seasonal factors may be compensated for by future recruitment of new cohorts from the seed bank. In these circumstances recruitment may require positive management of the meadow, for example, by scarifying with harrows in late autumn and early spring to create a 'regeneration niche'. Other species unsuited to the site may be permanently lost. Conventional mowing regimes set grass-cutter height at a level which ensures tillering and dense growth. For niche regeneration it may be advisable to produce a lower cut that 'scalps' the grass, or a medium height that prevents too much biomass build-up and yet encourages upright growth and gaps at the base of the grass rather than encourages tillering.

Jefferson and Usher (1987) suggest rotational scraping of areas within disused chalk quarries in the Yorkshire Wolds to provide a regeneration niche for the development of open field species otherwise surviving only in the seed bank. Wells (1987) suggests harrowing to promote recruitment in gaps and assist the establishment of less competitive species in sown wildflower meadows. Gibson *et al.* (1987) utilized sheep grazing to provide a regeneration niche to assist in recolonization of abandoned arable land near Oxford by semi-natural limestone grassland species. The project resulted in the re-establishment of 43 of the 75 calcicolous grassland species within 2 km of the site within two years.

REMOVAL OF DIVERSITY SUPPRESSING SPECIES

Sometimes it may be that the habitat in question is not limiting, but many of the existing sites are constrained by a factor that harms the desirable species. In the UK long grass is not a scarce habitat, but undisturbed long grass which is not patrolled by gamekeepers has become scarce. The creation of motorway networks with unmanaged verges has directly promoted populations of birds such as kestrels.

Often the constraining factor is one particular species or group of species that could be targeted for removal. In many island ecosystems, removing rats is a standard technique for ensuring diversity protection or restoration. The same may be true of aggressive, invasive plant species, e.g. *Rhododendron ponticum* in UK woodlands.

In a traditional nature conservation area there is a likelihood that the management programme will be oriented towards maintaining a plagioclimax. The major problem weeds often arise from later successional stages, e.g. scrub invading grassland. In new habitats the manager may be trying to encourage the movement towards a plagioclimax which has not yet been reached. There may therefore be a need to deal with species which belong to earlier successional stages or which are relicts from a previous land use.

The community dynamics and resilience of a man-made community will also differ from an established semi-natural community. The large storage organs and extensive root mat found in old grasslands withstands disturbances such as poaching and is likely to be more resistant to weed invasion (Hopkins, 1989). Depending on the previous land use the soil in a new habitat may contain a large reservoir of buried seed or propagules of persistent and vegetatively spreading weeds, such as *Urtica spp or Rumex spp.* Another characteristic of man-made sites is that there is likely to have been a substantial degree of soil disturbance during preparation work. This will influence water relations in summer and winter as well as patterns of nutrient mineralization and temperature fluctuations which in turn can encourage a ruderal flora.

To solve these weed problems may necessitate cleaning the site beforehand, the use of selective applications of translocated herbicide or hand weeding at a scale unheard of in normal conservation work. A reluctance to use chemicals may lead to a complete failure of wildflower establishment in some circumstances (Johnsons Seeds, 1991).

Sometimes management practices, such as mowing, will eventually eradicate weeds. However, some problem species such as *Cirsium arvense* may not be controlled without cutting at a frequency that also discourages desirable plants. Other management tools include grazing or burning, but in the early stages these may also have unexpectedly severe effects on a young mixed species sward. When introducing groundflora into existing amenity woodland, weed control may be achieved through the use of mulches or shade (Buckley and Knight, 1990).

Herbicides that select between germinated or germinating seedlings and mature plants may have interesting ecological effects by controlling gap colonization. Because of the wide range of species that may be present, possibly including desirable and undesirable plants that are closely related, the use of herbicides which work on the basis of physiological selectivity may seem ill advised. There is limited information available on the effect of chemicals on non-target species. In agriculture one crop needs to be protected against a large number of weeds while in conservation a large number of desirable species may need to be protected against only one or two weeds.

There has been some fascinating work done on the use of grass selective herbicides and growth regulators as a means of reducing vigour in competitive species (Marshall, 1988; Bisgrove, 1988). However, in practice, the use of chemicals alone to create species rich swards is not usually considered as an option. There is often ethical resistance to pesticide spraying in conservation areas which may be aggravated by increasing restrictions on amenity use of herbicides. Traditionally the effects of chemicals on food quality has received most attention from legislators, however in amenity areas public access is often much more uncontrolled than in farms, while the unusual and highly variable soil types, topography and varied range of planting which may be encountered make it harder to ensure even coverage or to be sure of the behaviour of applied chemicals. This is discussed in more detail in Chapter 8.

In woodlands weed control may be less important, since once established the woodland species are likely to survive and to influence their environment. However, in the short term, tree transplants are very vulnerable to weed competition. Moffatt (1986) presents details of the herbicide program in use at Warrington over a three-year period up to 1986 and reports a reduction in initial plant losses from 15–20% to 3–5% and a fourfold increase in growth rates compared with sites without maintenance.

Pest and disease attack may also be an issue that needs to be addressed. Early successional communities are prone to stress, and it has long been known that there are links between pathology and stress. Both stress and pest and disease attacks are important factors in natural systems. In many cases they maintain the integrity and characteristics of plant and animal communities by eradicating certain species, and it would be undesirable to intervene in those processes normally. However excess stress, beyond or different to what the component species are adapted to, can be expected where later successional communities are imposed on disturbed soils. For example, *Phytopthera* root disease is common on many urban sites which have been prone to soil damage, with consequent poor drainage. This fungal pathogen can have a major effect on the survival of some components of the plant community.

Unusual patterns of stress attack may also become evident where local populations of pests and their natural control agents have become unsynchronized. For example, the use of broad spectrum agrochemicals can sometimes be followed by a pest 'boom' as population levels rise faster than those of their predators. Similar processes may be seen on denuded land which is re-vegetated.

Another good example may be terrestrial mollusc attack, which is a major controlling factor in many UK plant communities. Many people never appreciate the scale of micro-grazing effects on plant population distributions. Successful plant species are often those which have some form of defence, or which exploit seed regeneration strategies that somehow avoid the worst attack.

Intensive soil disturbance or cultivation can dramatically reduce the mollusc population in a soil. In artificial plant communities it is sometimes possible to observe plants which have been established following disturbance, growing successfully for several years, becoming increasingly large and well established and then becoming almost completely grazed out by slugs as these populations have been re-established.

When establishing wildflower plants into existing swards slug attack can be a significant factor influencing success. Maintaining the frequency of cutting during the establishment phase can help keep the sward open and reduce the chances of slug attack, whereas the presence of a dense thatch will encourage them. It has, however, been found that clearing gaps can have complex effects, since this creates an area where the wildflower becomes an isolated target for the herbivore (Bisgrove, 1988).

The challenge to the manager is to distinguish between situations where natural slug levels are likely to prove always to be a limitation to that plant and those situations where initial problems may not persist. For example, slug populations may be temporarily and artificially high due to delayed colonization by predators. In the latter case the plants may survive if re-introduced later in the restoration programme.

The value of process and of the restoration of human/nature links

A critical analysis of the role of ecological restoration within nature conservation strategies would soon come to the conclusion that it is an activity that is disproportionately expensive, only partly successful, almost impossible to evaluate, produces a product which has an uncertain future and is least likely to succeed for the most important species. What, then, is its value? There is value in the process, but it needs to be carefully formulated.

The value of trying and failing

Bradshaw (1987) argues that habitat creation is 'an acid test of our understanding of ecology'. Most of the habitat creation work carried out is strongly product-oriented; however, one of the most important aspects may be the creation process itself. This may be of value in several ways. One is that it greatly improves our understanding of the way that ecosystems function. For example, in the USA early attempts to restore prairie habitats played a key part in identifying the role of fire as a controlling factor in these communities.

However, for these benefits to be realized requires that restoration is linked more closely to scientific programmes of research and evaluation (which is not the same as simple monitoring). It also requires that people will be prepared and almost eager to admit that they have some failures, something which is difficult to do in today's professional climate.

It is a paradox of habitat restoration that in many cases there will have to be a presumption of failure; despite our best efforts some habitats will never be restored to their former quality. A product-oriented vision of restoration always implies failure, but a process-oriented vision recognizes the value that comes from the effort.

Restoring some ghosts

We have seen that if we **were** technically able to restore, in perfect detail, a habitat such as an ancient chalk downland, there is still an argument that something is lost – a sense of authenticity and naturalness inevitably, and perhaps a spiritual quality that comes from centuries of human interaction and association with the land. If we really are to mitigate the damage that development does to the landscape we also need to consider what these more abstract qualities are, and whether these can also be restored in some way – whether the ghosts of the landscape can be put back by building stronger connections between people and the new landscape.

Once they started to focus on the importance of the habitat creation process rather than the product, the thinking of some American researchers moved rapidly to look at the value of the process as a means of environmental education. They see habitat creation as highly symbolic of a new, positive, healing relationship between man and nature. By being involved in the creation and subsequent aftercare of the landscape, the people also develop an emotional attachment with the land which goes some way towards restoring the spiritual dimension to the land which is otherwise lost. They have begun to explore the role of activities such as celebrations and rituals, the use of environmental art or many other approaches.

These are issues which cut to the heart of the future of the conservation movement globally. People need to be encouraged to care, to develop a stronger awareness of their dependence on the natural world. Even if all of the scientific and ecological debates outlined in the chapter were resolved, anyone who has ever really looked at the rate of global environmental degradation will recognize that we can only repair a fraction of the damage that the human race is currently doing to the natural world.

The real value of restoration is therefore its contribution to the human spirit and human education. Above all the subject can be a powerfully emotive symbol of the scope for a new, more positive, more caring relationship between people and nature. To maximize these benefits it is vital that ecologists involve as many members of the community as possible. Volunteer involvement in restoration projects can be the most positive thing that people have ever done for the natural world. As such it can capture their imagination in a powerful way, to encourage them to think, learn and redefine their position in the global ecosystem, to discover the possibilities of stewardship. The process of 'assembling' a new ecosystem provides a mechanism for capacity building in the population which can have knock-on benefits in the improved voluntary management of existing semi-natural habitat, improved social advocacy and so on.

The only real hope for global biodiversity is that people develop the will to change the way they live and the way that they consume resources. The value of restoration is that it teaches us to do this. Restoration or habitat creation projects, even if scientifically flawed or consisting of only the most common species, can do this as long as we put considerations of local involvement at the highest point in the agenda. It also pushes to the forefront the urban countryside as the key place for these activities and ideas to be explored. A new paradigm of the positive relation of man and nature needs to be forged where most people can participate.

Criteria for the assessment of habitat creation schemes

We have seen therefore that the issue of habitat creation is complicated by widely different goals. Landscape managers and conservation planners need to be continually conscious of the distinction between activities where the results need to be genuinely of conservation importance or where they are for popular impact. The distinction also needs to be maintained between sites where the goal is to use techniques that maximize potential biodiversity and those which aim to recreate previously existing states.

No matter how much environmentalists may deplore it, there is no doubt that habitat creation schemes will continue to be incorporated in development plans in the hope of disarming possible environmental objections. Planners will increasingly be asked to evaluate the worth of one habitat type against another, making a direct trade-off between different ecosystems in a way never seen in traditional conservation.

It is possible to produce some basic principles that can be adopted in the course of such evaluation. Obviously this can not be a hard science. Choices between rare and common, diverse and monotonous, small or large habitats are hard enough in traditional conservation but are made more complex by additional philosophical problems associated with the artificiality of man-made habitats.

One premise that must be understood from the start is that it is not enough for a habitat to be said to be 'good for wildlife'. Nature exploits almost any condition that man creates – whatever changes occur in a habitat are likely to be of benefit to some species, and at the same time will act to the disadvantage of others. This principle has often been exploited to justify a variety of activities. Conservation does not just mean encouraging wildlife, it means encouraging those species which are currently in decline or under threat. Conversely a habitat creation scheme that claims to have achieved benefits to nature conservation must also be evaluated in that light. Where only 'wildlife' is favoured, the project must involve high levels of community interaction or other human benefits.

Of course the criteria by which schemes are judged must also vary according to the goals which were set initially – for example where 'social' objectives rate higher than particular species then the criteria could relate to concepts such as local need, compatibility with local landscape or intrinsic appeal. In other situations it would be more appropriate to perhaps consider habitat size, environmental diversity and soil type as these factors can influence whether diverse communities can develop.

It does not therefore follow that a restoration programme that fails to match the pre-disturbance conditions will necessarily lack any nature conservation value, indeed it may at times be possible to make significant gains for local wildlife by a fundamental change in landscape and land use. On the other hand, we have also seen that it may be possible to match exactly the conditions and communities previously found on a site rich in wildlife, and yet there could still be a decline in the importance of the habitat in the eyes of conservation planners because of the loss of 'naturalness'.

Existing criteria for the assessment of sites of conservation value are inadequate to cope with skeletal ecosystems. Because the development of conservation interest must involve the passage of time, it is essential that criteria are developed for assessing the validity and **potential** of restoration proposals as well as evaluating the results on the ground. Although we have criteria for assessing sites of existing conservation value, identifying the qualities a landscape needs to have in order to provide the potential for supporting diverse plant and animal communities that may not yet have arrived is inevitably abstract.

In the USA standards have been defined based on certain target species which need to be present on the site at certain levels of abundance. The flaw is that, as discussed above, it is perfectly possible to simulate plant communities temporarily without being able to ensure that these can survive in the long term. Conversely it seems equally true that there could be cases where the potential for plant community development may still be high, even if particular species are still missing at the moment of assessment.

Criteria for evaluating quality may therefore be harder to identify for new habitats than for old, but it is still possible to highlight certain broad issues that need to be reviewed:

DIVERSITY

As with natural habitats, variety is better than uniformity. Sites with a range of habitats are preferred.

SIZE

As with natural habitats, large areas will be more valuable. With any mitigation scheme on development land the area of new habitat should usually be comparable in size to any premium habitats that have been lost.

RECORDED HISTORY

It is important to maintain quality records of the development of new habitats for several reasons. It may be important to know whether the techniques have failed both to aid technical understanding as well as helping to inform conservation planners of the reliability of such approaches. It may also be important in the future that 'man-made' sites or direct influences on species distribution can be distinguished from the results of natural processes.

WELL-DEFINED GOALS

It is apparent that there should be a clear vision of the nature of the target plant community, and the distinction between areas intended to develop significant biodiversity compared to areas that have primarily an amenity function. It is also important that the consequent implications for methodology are realized.

FEASIBILITY OF SUCCESS

It is debatable whether it is better to attempt to create the simple communities which are likely to work, or attempt to produce the familiar communities which are more valued by traditional conservation. The problem with the latter is that we do not really know in detail what makes most habitats tick – to claim to be able to create one anew is obviously over-ambitious if not exactly fraudulent.

As discussed above, some habitats are more 'recreatable' than others. The least feasible to emulate are those ecosystems which are most natural and least influenced by man, such as ancient woodland. On the other hand, simple scrub woodland of some description is relatively easy to produce.

FAVOURABLE POSITION IN AN ECOLOGICAL OR GEOGRAPHICAL UNIT

One of the possible functions of new habitats is to improve buffering of existing ecosystems. On the other hand new habitats are likely to accrue more conservation interest if adjacent to existing wild areas of a similar type.

HABITAT RARITY

Although there is sometimes a presumption against the use of rare species in habitat creation, it must be the case that a scheme will be valued more if the type of habitat is itself one which is under threat.

INTRINSIC APPEAL

Much of the value of man-made habitats is social. It is obviously particularly appropriate that they should be well designed and attractive.

LANDSCAPE APPROPRIATENESS

Obviously it is not always desirable to have limestone grass appearing in an acid soil area or vice versa, even though it would increase diversity in those regions.

COMPATIBILITY WITH EXISTING WILDLIFE

Some types of habitat creation could increase management problems with regard to existing sites. Tree planting adjacent to heath is a clear example as this is likely to increase the rate of scrub invasion.

MANAGEMENT PROVISION

The most important point to make about the management of new habitats is that there has to be some, but this is often easier said than achieved. It is clearly pointless to create new habitats unless the necessary management is allowed for. 'If you can't mow it, don't sow it' (Ash *et al.*, 1992). A natural habitat cannot be rated as any less valuable, whether or not there is a management plan for it; a planned habitat could very easily be judged on just such pragmatic criteria. Any scheme that puts into place the components of the original community but provides no solution for long-term management processes is a sham. It is better to have no plants and management than no management and plants.

The development must provide funding for the management. Far too often schemes seem to rely on some naive hope that community or volunteer groups will take on the maintenance. However, these organizations are often over-stretched looking after their existing responsibilities. It is asking too much to expect them to take on possibly valueless areas in the faith that they may develop into something useful?

It is important to identify critical inputs which are flexible enough to allow for contributions from a range of management organizations. Restoration goals which are highly dependent on regular management need to be recognized from the outset. The provision of greatly reduced but critical inputs by organizations such as naturalist trusts may encourage plant and animal communities to develop in more desirable ways.

New habitats must have a management plan associated with them. However, this plan will need to differ from those prepared for traditional habitats as it needs to take account of the evolution of the habitat from initial unstable conditions. The establishment phase may need very different management than the final condition. For example, management of newly sown wildflower grassland is often based on a frequency of cutting much greater than will be followed in subsequent years. Hay meadow grasslands are maintained below 150 mm, cutting down to 50–75 mm in each cut (Johnsons Seeds, 1991).

This need to anticipate habitat change also adds a new level of complexity to monitoring, particularly given that predictions of the way that a site could develop may at best be imprecise and at worst completely inaccurate.

Off-site management provision

Of course, where management has been successfully resolved it raises the paradox that some restored sites of questionable long-term value may have greater management security than existing high-quality semi-natural habitats perhaps just a mile or two away! Many precious communities in the UK were created by managing the land for other goals. The changes in farming practice which lead to agriculturists becoming destroyers rather than creators of habitats has produced a problem that conservationists still have not resolved. Lack of appropriate and adequate management is arguably a greater threat to protected habitats than any overt development disturbance.

There are circumstances therefore where the best conservation solution may not be to consider direct habitat creation or restoration, but to direct efforts towards the areas of surviving conservation importance.

For example, where there is an important and undisturbed semi-natural habitat suffering from lack of management in proximity to site it may be more suitable for a developer to consider paying for appropriate maintenance. Another scenario would be where part of a site gets separated and loses much of the justification or economic suitability of maintaining traditional land use. Mitigation in such circumstances may be to introduce a parallel management regime to the surrounding land to ensure that large enough area is treated in the same way so as to make the traditional management viable once more.

Provision for access and awareness

We have seen that perhaps the greatest justification for many habitat creation schemes, given that there are often complex questions about their long-term biological validity, is to act as a resource for people to gain greater contact with nature. Indeed they may serve a particularly important role if they reduce pressure on more pristine locations.

Success of many schemes could therefore be evaluated by consideration of the effectiveness of provision for access and interpretation. This does not necessarily mean that the site needs to be littered with distracting signs. The critical element in the educational and interpretation process is to make sure that people are aware of the site and of their right to have access to it. If choice of site location is possible, then issues such as the distance to schools or willingness of the local community to participate should be considered. In some cases the provision of visitor facilities may be justified.

In many cases optimum value will be obtained from public participation in the habitat creation and management process.

Other criteria obviously need to be considered. The site should be safe and not present an environmental hazard in the absence of more fundamental treatment. Ideally it should be in close proximity to the source of appropriate colonizing species, although there is also social value from encouraging conservation after-use in areas deficient in natural habitats.

7 Restoration and creation of the main biome types

Many of the techniques available for biome creation or restoration have been addressed in the review of the previous chapter. However, there are some more detailed issues which are specific to individual habitat types and these are considered below.

Grassland

The restoration of species-rich grassland is one of the best researched and established aspects of habitat creation, and several references have been provided that cover this aspect. Many of the comments made above refer directly to the difficulties and options available for grassland creation and this section will not recreate these, but rather will focus on a few issues that have not been adequately covered.

Wild grassland is often modelled on the diverse and colourful plant communities that have developed on agricultural land as a result of traditional agricultural practices. However, new opportunities are presented when grasslands can be designed and maintained deliberately to maximize conservation or amenity value. There will be scope to relax or alter cutting times and frequencies, as well as other management inputs, in order to encourage the desired effect. Frequently the time of peak hay cut is delayed in amenity situations compared to farming; the main objectives are that the maximum duration of flower can be exploited. Mowing timing may also be influenced by the presence of ground-nesting birds. On the other hand grassland management in urban situations also has certain limitations that arise from the methods of management available, i.e. mowing rather than grazing or burning.

One of the possible variants is a flowering lawn which is essentially not much taller than frequently mown grass. Ideally the sward will still have large populations of common species such as *Taraxacum vulgaris*, *Trifolium repens* or *Bellis perennis* that brighten up otherwise dull swards. The flower content of the lawn can be increased further by planting *Veronica filiformis* which prefers relatively fertile, moist soils and also grows well in semi-

Table 7.1 *The wildlife value of structurally simple lawns as against structurally complex meadows*

Meadow	Lawn
Flower layer: butterflies, bees, bumble-bees, hoverflies, bugs, beetles, seed-eating birds	Absent
Leaf and stalk layer: grasshoppers, bugs, beetles, web-spinning spiders, butterflies, caterpillars, insect eating birds	Regular mowing prevents inhabitation of any duration; nourishment for birds scanty
Litter layer: ground beetles, wood lice, daddy longlegs, ants, snails	Mosquito larvae, slugs, moth larvae
Soil layer: numerous soil organisms in the deeply-rooted soil layers	Soil organisms in shallowly rooted soil layer

Source: Muller and Wolf (1985).

shade. It is thought not to set seed in this country, although colour variants are sometimes seen, but the stems root easily. The plant gets dispersed as small cuttings whenever the grass is cut.

There may be other species more common in taller grass which can flower at a reduced height under this regime, such as *Scabious*. The comparison made by Muller and Wolf (1985) of the wildlife value of different structural layers of meadows and lawns is worth noting, however (see Table 7.1).

There are some quite long-established examples of 'habitat creation' which are not linked to agricultural activity. In particular, the descriptions of the formation of medieval flowery meads given in Bisgrove (1990) are fascinating. Turf was treated with boiling water in order to sterilize it and kill off the propagules of undesirable species. Turves were then cut and inverted and the soil beaten down. This process encouraged invasion by fine grasses and wildflowers.

The sward was not often cut, but they may have been re-turfed as often as every two or three years. The high rate of turnover means that these areas must have contained a higher than usual proportion of annuals, biennials and short-lived perennials. As the maintenance process continued, the seed bank of these species would have built up and gradually filled the soil with an inoculum of attractive plants. These meads would seem to have fulfilled a function halfway between beds of annuals and perennial grassland. They may have had much in common with the early years of colonization of an abandoned, not too hostile, waste site. At their best they would have been admirably effective at creating floral interest and diversity over quite a long season.

Beating down the soil would have increased the levels of stress in a relatively controlled way, in order to restrict the real competitors but at the same time not make conditions too harsh for annuals. Sterilizing the sward would have removed many of those problem perennials which thrive on compaction, such as dock or plantain, and these would have been slower to recolonize than more attractive plants such as *Bellis*.

The relation between maintenance and plant community development

In new habitats in amenity areas a species mixture should be chosen to give a season of effect that suits the programme of mowing. For example, spring flowering species can be planted into grass which is to be cut in midsummer. Naturalized bulbs will also do well in such a situation. Summer flowering species can be established in grass that is cut in spring and again in autumn.

The decision of when to cut is not just related to aesthetics. It is frequently reported that the cutting of meadows generally should be delayed until after seed has set, and that it is important to leave cut hay to ripen in the field, so that seeds can fall (e.g. Londo). Although it is clearly sensible to exploit opportunities for new seed recruitment when they occur, the evidence that seed regeneration is actually important in grasslands is rather limited, and many species may be maintained purely by vegetative spread.

Cutting changes the competitive relationships in grassland vegetation by reducing the dominance of highly competitive species (by altering plant growth habits and root:shoot ratios and by increasing the incidence of light at ground level). An increase in cutting frequency leads to a gradual change in species composition, with tall species declining and low-growing or prostrate species increasing. At intermediate levels of intensity cutting therefore usually leads to an increase in plant species diversity, whereas at high levels diversity may again decrease if the effect is to select out only those species highly tolerant of such disturbance.

Investigations into the management of roadside vegetation on Oxford clay at Keyston, West Cambridgeshire and on chalk at Ickleton, south-east Cambridgeshire, made comparisons of the effects of changes in cutting frequency (0, 1, 2 or 5 times per annum), cutting date for single cut (June or July), cutting machine (haymower, flail mower or rotary mower) and of leaving or removing cuttings by hand-raking over 18 years (from 1965 to 1982). Species richness was highest in plots cut twice per annum (in May and August) and lowest in uncut plots. The increase in cutting frequency led to a significant decrease in the frequency of ten coarse species and an increase in the frequency of eleven fine species (Parr and Way, 1984). The dates of cutting for these observations (June and July) had no affect on species richness, although Wells (1971) has observed significant differences between cutting at markedly different seasons (spring, summer and autumn) on chalk grassland. Species composition was unaffected by the type of machine used for cutting.

Logistical considerations are also important. If fertile meadows are not cut by July, the vegetation will probably be flattened by rain and wind. Conversely relatively infertile grasslands will be unlikely to lodge. If the cut is in June or early July some species may flower after that cut, particularly *Scabious*. There is some suggestion that a threshold of mowing frequency may be seen on many moderately fertile sites, where unless mowing is carried out twice per year and the cuttings removed there will be a decline in species richness (van Schaik, 1995). Fairly unproductive grassland that is only cut once a year should preferably be mown in the autumn when there is still a good chance of drying the hay so that it can be more easily transported. (The experience of being able to see, smell and even play in drying hay is also an aesthetic dimension that should be offered to users.)

Mowing different parts of the field at different times will give a varied and longer display of flowers. Rotational mowing may also be practised in order to ensure survival of associated species such as invertebrates.

Climatic or soil factors may also need to be taken into account. Wet grasslands are often mown during a specific midsummer window when the ground water table is low.

Some meadow areas may be left until the spring, since in some communities the standing vegetation can be beautiful and give character to the landscape in winter as well as being of potential value to over-wintering insects (although of course there are some communities where the standing vegetation is often very unattractive). However, Londo argues that removing the standing crop in spring tends to allow fertility to build up in potentially nutrient rich areas, since much biomass breaks down over winter. Leaving standing dead material may often be more successful in continental climates, with cold, dry and frosty weather often reliable, compared to the more mild but wet and windy weather experienced in the UK.

Figure 7.1 illustrates the typical mowing patterns. Probably the most important factor is that the mowing regime must stay the same every year.

Urban grazing is not usually considered as an option for deliberate management because of the difficulties associated with stock control, dog worrying etc., although this may be excessively pessimistic in areas where there can be close control over public access and very high levels of stock supervision. Some extensive and long established urban parks do contain grazing animals, such as Arthur's Seat in Edinburgh.

Harper (1977) stresses the distinction between cutting and grazing. Cutting is non-selective, whereas grazing is selective, favouring unpalatable herbs, patchy and accompanied by secondary consequences including trampling and the deposition of dung and urine which can be heavily localized. Further, distinctions between species of grazers in the mode of grazing are important. For example, cattle tear at leaves, uprooting weakly rooted grass tillers and are imprecise in species selection, whereas sheep crop closely and may even discriminate between individual leaves.

The distinctions between cutting and grazing on any particular site also vary depending on the frequency, timing and intensity of cutting, and on the duration, timing and intensity of grazing. Wells (1971) compares the effects of grazing and cutting on chalk grassland over a six-year period. Cutting in spring, summer and autumn and sheep grazing resulted in a similar species richness and diversity. Few long-term studies are available. Baker (1937) compared the flora of two grasslands in Oxfordshire – Port Meadow grazed by cattle, horses and geese for 900 years, and an adjacent meadow cut for hay. The grazed pasture contained 56 species, of which 26 occurred only in the grazed land, and the hay meadow contained 69 species, of which 39 occurred only in the meadow. Perennial grasses and laterally spreading clonal dicotyledons dominated the grazed pasture, and perennial and annual grasses and tall dicotyledons dominated the hay meadow. Analysis of life-forms and regenerative strategies suggests a similar picture.

When considering the degree to which mowing can substitute for grazing it is important not to underestimate the dramatic scale of disturbance to

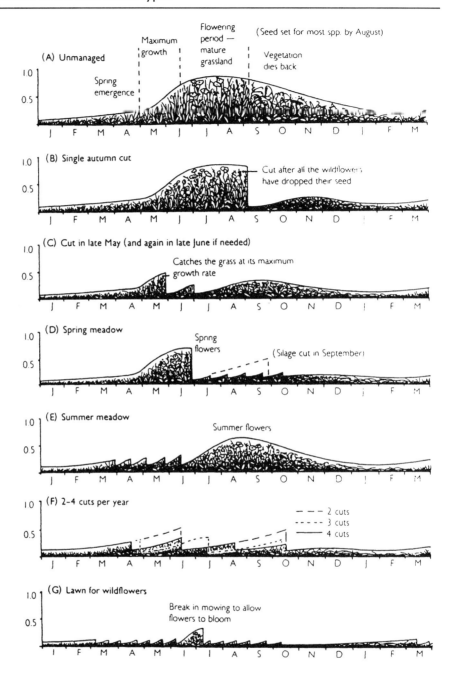

Figure 7.1 The typical mowing patterns for wildflower grasslands (Emery, 1986).

vegetation that grazing animals can cause by tearing, dunging and walking on the sward. Certain short-lived perennials may be encouraged by following mowing with a scarifier or similar soil disturbance machine.

In some ways mowers are as variable in their effect as different grazing animals. Flail mowers disperse the cuttings more than cutterbars, which may not actually be desirable when the wastes are to be collected. Flails may also cause more damage to invertebrates, but are more likely to encourage seed shedding.

Studies to develop finer resolution in vegetation management by grazing are desirable. For example, Willman and Simpson (1988) consider *Trifolium repens* growth in sown hill swards. Management recommendations to encourage *T. repens* in the presence of sheep grazing are quite precise, and require avoiding both overgrazing in spring, and undergrazing to reduce competition from *Agrostis tenuis* in summer.

Rabbits can graze many urban areas but their usefulness is limited by their unreliability, the problems arising from wildly fluctuating numbers and the difficulties in restricting their access where they are not wanted. Rabbits are also very selective feeders and very poor at reclaiming rough swards – they tend to prefer short turf and will persist in grazing this, perhaps too heavily, while other areas grow too rank.

Grazing by large flocks of geese is also increasingly seen in many urban areas, but here the problem is preventing the birds taking the grass, and all associated species, down to almost nothing.

In the urban fringe the most likely grazing animals to be encountered are horses and ponies. These are usually poorly regarded by conservationists since they are selective grazers that tend to avoid rather than control the coarse and less palatable perennial weeds. They also may encourage the spread of competitive plants through localized dunging.

Burning is usually avoided in urban areas, because of concerns about safety and disturbance to the public, although it may be practised in some country parks within the urban fringe and it may be essential in countries such as Australia where species are adapted to need fire for germination. However, even in Europe railway track-sides were often managed by regular burning and as a result many have become important conservation sites. We have already seen that unplanned and uncontrolled burns are typical in many urban nature areas as a result of vandalism or just accidents. It is therefore worth considering the likely ecological effects. In rural situations where burning is employed there is a widely recognized need to control the timing and extent of the burn in order to maintain species richness (e.g. Green, 1981). The impact of unplanned burns, such as fires set in long grass by children, also needs to be considered. Interestingly these may have more in common with the accidental fires typical of natural ecosystems than the planned winter burns usually undertaken by land managers.

Burning is often targeted at a time when the speed and intensity of spread of the fire is most easily controlled (often when the soil is wet). Because there are concerns that burning may be more destructive to animals than other management options it is also usual that a rotational treatment is employed, dividing the site into a series of parcels which are usually burnt in different years. Uncontrolled burning is likely to happen at the wrong time of year and with no control over the extent of the damage, with the net result that there may be a decrease in species richness.

A great challenge that landscape managers sometimes face is to investigate ways in which species richness can be encouraged and preserved in

Table 7.2 *Species suitable for enriching rough grassland*

Natives			
Yarrow	*Achillea millefolium*	Goats-beard	*Tragopogon pratensis*
Wild angelica	*Angelica sylvestris* **D**	Tufted vetch	*Vicia cracca*
Wormwood	*Artemesia absinthium*	Bush vetch	*Vicia sepium*
Mugwort	*Artemesia vulgaris*		
Knapweed	*Centaurea nigra*	**Naturalized species**	
Tease	*Dipsacus fullonem*	Michaelmas Daisy	*Aster novi-belgii*
Hemp-agrimony	*Eupatorium cannabinum* **D**	Canadian fleabane	*Conyza canadensis*
Perforate St John's-wort	*Hypericum perforatum*	Elecampane	*Inula helenium*
Field scabious	*Knautia arvensis*	Broad leaved everlasting pea	*Lathyrus latifolius*
Ox-eye daisy	*Leucanthemum vulgare*	Garden lupin	*Lupinus polyphyllus*
Common toadflax	*Linaria vulgaris*	Yellow loosestrife	*Lysimachia punctata*
Ragged-robin	*Lychnis flos-cuculi* **D**	Peppermint	*Mentha piperita*
Musk mallow	*Malva moschata*	Spear mint	*Mentha spicata*
Common sorrel	*Rumex acetosa*	Sweet cicely	*Myrrhis oderata*
White campion	*Silene alba*	Sainfoin	*Onobrychis viciifolia*
Marsh woundwort	*Stachys palustris* **D**	Soapwort	*Saponaria officinalis*
Hedge woundwort	*Stachys sylvatica*	Canadian goldenrod	*Solidago canadensis*
		Tansy	*Tanacetum vulgare*

D = best on damp sites
NB: The distinction between native and long established naturalized species is not always clear.
Source: Ash *et al.* (1992).

24 (top left) Plant communities which are low in species and also have a low floral impact can still be atmospheric and evocative of natural beauty.

25 (left) If management of grassland cannot be provided, the resulting sward will rapidly lose botanical interest. However, it may still be of value for small mammals and some invertebrates.

locations where management inputs are not feasible, such as the side of road verges. In areas where fertility is very low or the soil is very shallow it may be possible that the sward will continue to be quite short and open even when no cutting or grazing takes place. However, in many such cases, scrub invasion can still take place. Bushes can find regeneration niches in even quite stony ground. In the long term therefore the grassland would gradually turn to scrub.

Conversely, a sward on fertile ground will be relatively closed providing limited opportunity for scrub invasion. Therefore if a flower-rich grassland can be created (albeit not technically 'species rich') it may be more effectively self-maintaining than any more open unmanaged grassland on infertile land. Observations that some tall perennials such as golden rod and lupins can survive in these swards has led to experiments of deliberately planting and seeding these together with such species as purple and yellow loosestrife, mullein, evening primrose and tansy (Table 7.2). John Handley describes it as a type of 'zany prairie grassland'. Although composed of mostly alien plants many are valuable for wildlife, especially butterflies, and are attractive in late summer when many native flowers are over.

Although the complexity of grassland management arises from the need to control a complex and dynamic mix of thousands of individuals made up of tens of species, some situations require the manager to favour particular species. The following examples illustrate how an understanding of the ecology of different plants may help to develop a management strategy.

When studying the ecology of herb species it is important to distinguish between those that can spread vegetatively and invade gaps, and those that must, predominantly, spread by seed. The two groups are likely to show quite different characteristics and behaviour. Seedlings are likely to be vulnerable to changes in habitat that may be much less significant to mature or vegetatively reproduced individuals. A lack of new seedling recruitment is one of the earliest indicators of a loss in grassland richness, but this may be obscured for many years by survival of adults.

Preserving full diversity in a grassland means managing the grassland to encompass the periodic recruitment of these seed dependent types. Obviously recruitment does not need to happen every year, but the frequency must be related to the lifespan and ecology of the species concerned. This is well illustrated by contrasting the characteristics of some popular wildflowers.

Orchids are a classic example of a plant type which is usually associated in traditional conservation with old, undisturbed and stable grassland. In reality however, many species show ruderal characteristics and are found in great numbers on some types of disturbed land such as dunes and certain industrial wastes. Identifying the characteristics which encourage or limit orchid growth on disturbed land requires a more detailed review of their biology. However one point is certain, they can take many years to grow from seed and remain vulnerable to adverse conditions for many years. Establishment must rely in part on niches remaining open for a long time.

It is a truism that introduction of a plant or animal may be an ultimately pointless exercise if the habitat to which they are placed in is inappropriate or has been too severely damaged to function. Successful orchid recovery presupposes that the receptor habitat still exists, which in turn raises questions about why the plants disappeared in the first place.

Some of the reasons why orchids may become locally extinct even in an area which is suitable for them include:

- over-collection (which is believed to be the case for just a few species in the UK);
- random fluctuation in numbers which can have severe effects on small populations;
- temporary habitat hostility, for example shade or competition which may reach intolerable levels as a result of fluctuating management such as a reduction in grazing or cutting;
- a temporary fluctuation in the relative abundance of essential symbiots, e.g. pollinators or mycorrhizae.

Trying to determine whether any habitat still exists when some of the component species are no longer there raises some of the most imponderable abstractions and philosophical issues of plant ecology. To what extent do the species in a habitat create the habitat? However, when you are dealing with a species which is an obligate symbiot with a fungal mycorrhiza, the complexities begin to multiply.

There is still an unresolved debate concerning whether symbiosis is an advantage or a disadvantage to the species involved (Allen, 1991). Whichever, it is clear that the distribution of an obligate symbiot must depend on the relative abundance and the niche requirements of both partners. Orchid seed dispersal is known to be highly effective. Even individual plants can produce thousands upon thousands of seed, so rarity of many species must be caused by other factors such as the absence of a suitable host, or the absence of a suitable habitat. This in turn begs some difficult questions about which factors make a once acceptable habitat unsuitable.

Plant introduction can overcome the limitations that seedlings may experience. However, this does not mean that the 'habitat' is in place and able to support the next generation. (If pollinators are not present there will not even be a second generation.) By the same token there may be many orchid, or other plant, communities in existence that are really just relics; the 'habitat' has gone even if the individuals have not.

Again symbiots can be more complex than other plants. It must follow that this pattern of orchid distribution is also a measure of the distribution of the symbiotic fungi. Soil disturbance and sterilization are known to lead to dramatic changes in the abundance of the soil micro-flora and fauna. It may follow that the peculiar conditions of newly disturbed subsoils and wastes will also in some way favour symbiotic fungi such as *Rhizoctonia* sp., in competition with other soil fauna.

For many orchid species the planting programme inoculates the site with the fungus at the same time as the plant. It is possible that the absence of such a fungal inoculum was the key limiting factor to natural regeneration on that site. The boundaries between habitats, niches and the species that occupy them begin to look increasingly blurred!

Some UK orchids are able to spread vegetatively. The most notable are *Goodyera* which seems to be highly dependent on this form of growth habit in order to survive in woodland litter. *Dactylorhiza* are interesting in that in the ideal cultivation conditions seen in many private gardens they bulk up into clumps very easily, yet in wild communities this habit is rarely seen and the plants behave as single individuals. Doubtless the effect is opportunistic and limited in nature by competition or nutrient shortage. Many orchid types are not really capable of vegetative spread in or out of cultivation.

Primula vulgaris is an interesting species because individuals have the capability to survive surprisingly close mowing or grazing. Specific clumps may survive for decades; they may slowly get bigger but they can hardly be called invasive. The seed of *Primula* is heavy and not very mobile so distribution is not particularly fast. The seed also has a pronounced dormancy. To reach mineral soil, germinate and grow may need gaps to be maintained for two years or more.

Once established *Primula vulgaris* seem to be pretty competitive, they can tolerate some quite fertile grassland and are often seen in communities with limited overall diversity. They doubtless gain advantage from their phenology which gives them a strongly vernal growth peak. By midsummer they have almost died away.

Primula veris is equally capable of competing in swards which may be too aggressive for many other species. It is even possible to establish this species by scattering seed direct into turf, although the take is inevitably low.

Ox-eye daisy *(Leucanthemum vulgare)* is a short-lived perennial species that are often sown in wildflower mixes. It germinates extremely freely in bare ground. Visually it dominates swards in early years, but it usually completely fades out of the community as regeneration niches close.

Keeping *Leucanthemum* in the sward would involve maintaining quite a large proportion of open ground. Many of these 'disturbance perennials' are associated with banks and slopes, such as the roadside verges in Cornwall and Devon, where erosion maintains a regular supply of regeneration niches.

One aspect that needs further investigation relates to the conditions under which disturbance leads to a dominance by aggressive and generally undesirable 'weed ruderals' such as docks and thistles, and when it leads to a growth of desirable perennials. Obviously this in part depends on the relative availability of propagules, but there is also likely to be some interaction with soil fertility and perhaps pH. Ruderal perennials like *Primula* and *Dactylorhiza* may need niches to be maintained for some years, and this is unlikely to happen on fertile soils.

Companion **grasses** for wildflower mixtures are usually chosen by the seed suppliers from types which are non-aggressive and tussock forming rather than spreading rhizomatous types. Frequently the grass cultivars used are taken from sports or general landscape where dwarfer cultivars are common. The best grass cover can often be given by those cultivars assessed by sports turf organizations as patchy and unable to make a good turf.

The rapid and even germination of cultivated grasses is sometimes seen as an advantage in ensuring good soil stabilization and the rapid establishment of nurse conditions.

In Europe seed quality legislation has sometimes complicated the inclusion of grasses of true wild stock since minimum germination standards are difficult to achieve. In practice the government agencies do not always attempt to enforce the legislation in these cases. However, increasingly seed suppliers are able to include some component of those native grasses that are normally of no value for agriculture or amenity use.

Heaths

Heathland creation on a small scale, is a popular feature of many urban nature parks especially in continental Europe. A heather community will only develop naturally on nutrient poor and calcium deficient soils – sands, silts or peat but where these conditions are found heaths are relatively simple habitats to create – the vegetation diversity need not be particularly great and, being predominantly sub-shrubs, the degree to which individual components of the community interact is comparatively limited.

Heathlands in Europe are generally secondary, farming habitats. They were created by woodland clearance and land cultivation on poor soils, followed by a shift to low intensity grazing as the soil fertility and pH dropped and a low shrub community began to dominate the land. Some areas of upland heathlands may be primary habitats arising from a combination of climate and soil type, but inevitably it is the lowland types which are predominantly associated with urbanization.

Patches of original lowland heathlands dating from such farming use are not unusual in urban areas since they have often been retained as common land encompassed by urban development (indeed such land may be a prime target for building, since it is frequently topographically simple, with good drainage and of low farming value, which has tended to make it cheap and politically easy to obtain). Frequently however, changes in management and poor control over successional processes lead to an alteration of the flora in urban heaths which shift to a mosaic of scrub and secondary woodland together with bracken and grass.

Sheep grazing and burning of heather, mimicking the farming patterns that would have been used to manage the productivity and palatability of the heather, is practised in nature reserves but is often seen as not applicable to urban areas because of fire risks, complaints about smoke or the risks of dog attacks on sheep. Grazing with cattle may be an acceptable alternative. Ornamental heather gardens also show how, with precise cutting, heather can be kept young, vigorous and with an adequately closed cover for many years. These techniques have been under-researched since it was often the case with such encompassed urban heathlands that there was no original appreciation by the managers of why heath communities may be desirable. They certainly lack some of the utility of grassland open spaces, being difficult to walk over or sit on. They can also be prone to accidental summer fires which are both destructive to the habitat and also potentially more dangerous to people and property since they occur without adequate controls.

Interest in the management and re-establishment of genuine heath communities in urban areas is a relatively new phenomenon therefore, but it has become an important objective, particularly following the appreciation that lowland heaths are some of the most threatened and most rapidly declining habitat types in Europe. Frequently today professionals are exhibiting an interest in heathland re-creation, either within the boundaries of land that once contained such a habitat type, or on new sites such as road verges as part of an attempt to extend the habitat area and to provide links, stepping stones and corridor sites for supporting declining species.

In the UK *Calluna vulgaris* is the most common species of concern, with *Erica cinerea* becoming more important on dry soils, *Erica tetralix* on wet and a few other types having only localized presence. Heather seed is available commercially but many projects use locally collected sources. *Calluna* seed ripens about the middle of November so this is the best time to harvest it directly from the plant but different timings may be important where other species are important and in some cases several harvests may be required. To minimize the logistical complications of seed collection, heather cuttings, mown in the appropriate period, can be spread over the soil. It is also common practice to use the upper layers of the topsoil or litter layer from the soil surface beneath established stands, as a seed source, although it may be sensible to check the viable seed content. Heathlands are normally poor in burrowing invertebrates and the seed therefore does not get rapidly dispersed.

The germination patterns of the seed is erratic. Many plants may not germinate for one, or even several, years but seed collected in litter will often have a high proportion of individuals which have had dormancy broken. Low-temperature fire can also enhance germination. The soils of long-established heathlands are frequently very characteristic, having developed as acid-nutrient-poor soils with sometimes high degrees of podsolization and often a very clear undecomposed organic layer on the surface. However, it is interesting that the seed itself does not appear to have very precise requirements for soil type. In denuded heathland habitats heather often germinates in bare mineral soil as well as in areas where a peat cover still exists. It is, however, important that the seed is not buried too deep and that drought or waterlogging stresses are not severe.

Available nitrogen levels are often low in heathlands, as mineralization of organic stores is slow. Nevertheless on very impoverished areas the seed may benefit from some initial nitrogen fertilizer, and there is some evidence that nurse crops to stabilize the soil or raise humidity may be advantageous, although of course these must not be so dense that they become competitive (EAU, 1988). A variety of other methods for heather establishment have been tried, such as using transplants, cuttings and even moving heather turves from sites which are to be destroyed. These methods are far more expensive than using seed.

Heathland is at least superficially a rather uniform type of habitat. Despite this impression, it is important not to overlook the sources of the variation and diversity which do exist – the rock outcrops, the areas of blown-out sand, the patches of moister soil or more fertile zones.

Most research has concentrated on the performance of the Ericaceous shrubs. What is less well studied in heathland restoration is the performance or introduction of other, less dominant, but still important parts of the community such as gorses, rushes or plants such as cotton-grass (*Eriophorum angustifolium*). Heathland communities are not usually species rich, which is all the more reason for ensuring that other components are not unnecessarily omitted. What may perhaps turn out to be the most important operation is the introduction of pot-grown specimens of subordinate species.

It may also be important to recognize the value of bare ground. Heathlands are particularly important as very warm and dry refuges for certain animals, for example in the UK they contain a high proportion of the reptile fauna, many of which appreciate basking spaces. Invertebrates too may have a requirement for bare land, for example the Silver Studded Blue butterfly (*Plebejus argus*) has a symbiotic relationship with ants associated with extremely open heath vegetation.

On nutrient-rich or alkaline soil, problems will arise from the continual invasion of weeds and it may be necessary to use a soil-impoverishing technique, as discussed above. Acidification of soils using high rates of sulphur has been attempted on many sites with some success. This is clearly only sensible where the site itself has a natural tendency to be acidic, but where perhaps there is a short-term need to counteract lime additions e.g. where arable land is to be converted back to heath.

Perhaps more than any other type of habitat, however, the management implications of heathland restoration need to be considered with care to see how sustainable the project is likely to be. Heaths can not accommodate as many different recreation uses as grasslands, nor are they as capable as woodlands are of tolerating periods of neglect. Secondary succession can happen rapidly, with the establishment of pioneer trees and taller shrubs that soon threaten the integrity of the heath and raise management costs when work is attempted. Adding to the list of small isolated sites that receive poor management will be of little real use. On the other hand some management costs and problems are likely to go down when larger more coherent units are created. For example, it can become easier to introduce a rotational grazing regime or have a viable herd of animals, and the improved balance between edge and core habitat that is found on large rather than small sites can substantially reduce the rate of tree seed invasion.

Annuals

Creating an annual weed community is one of the simplest positive conservation options available to local authorities. It always seems remarkable how few seem to want to take up the challenge of doing this in rundown parks or pointless city greenspace areas. Not only are they a cheap way of putting back some of the colour that has been lost from parks, their maintenance is simple and can be easily administered through contract. They are suitable communities for establishment on land which is too fertile for most other wildflowers. They can make a genuine contribution to conservation; they include some plant species which are very endangered but which do not have very specific habitat requirements, while the whole community supports many insects which in turn support animals such as birds and bats. Annuals are also likely to be a relatively popular form of wildlife landscape; they are colourful and many older people will reminisce about seeing the familiar flowers of their childhood. They will therefore be relatively easy species to interpret, and they can act as the focus of a first step in a programme of environmental education and urban conservation.

Annuals include many of our most showy and attractive plants. This is because these species rely on the production of huge amounts of seed to ensure reproduction. They come from environments which experience regular disturbance, but which are fertile enough to allow rapid growth of the annuals in order to produce enough seed to survive the next disturbance. Nutrient reduction is therefore of less importance than for perennial wildflower establishment. However, there may be scope for some topsoil removal which can have the advantage of reducing weed problems.

Annuals need open ground to germinate. They cannot survive as members of a grassland community but can be encouraged by annual rotovating or through some other soil disturbance such as harrowing. Newly disturbed ground is also very attractive to some birds such as robins.

Some people feel that a cereal crop should always be sown with the annuals to act as a support and to prevent the annuals from lodging which is particularly likely in wet weather. Londo (1977) recommends wheat or rye as a cereal, since barley creates too dense a canopy. The cereal may also suppress the growth of grass weeds. Most of the time simple weed communities seem to work without cereal – the advantage being that the intensity of colour is greater and the herbage can be much easier to clean off in the winter. The appearance of a cereal crop in towns can look a bit peculiar unless well interpreted and may best be associated with city farms or the like.

The routine of soil disturbance and harvest is as important as the time of harvesting for many species. Some arable annuals are adapted to flower in the period after the crop has been harvested. It is therefore ideal if the soil is not redisturbed for a while after the herbage has been cleared off. Some of these species are rather dwarf in habit, such as Scarlet pimpernel, and will not do well if the old vegetation is left in place.

It has long been known that weeds can have very complex seed dormancy and germination mechanisms that prevent them from all coming up at once, and ensure that temporary setbacks, false springs, and other periods of adversity do not prove too damaging. Reliable prediction of germination patterns is therefore not possible and the following is a generalization only.

If community is started with a mixed annual seed population it will not be necessary to resow as long as the management is correct. From year to year there will be differences in which species are most successful – germination success will vary slightly in response to climatic variation to favour different plants in different years. However, if the management is stable there will gradually be an accumulation of seed that favours those types best adapted to the region, the soil and the management and the flora will tend to become dominated by a few main types. This should not be seen as a problem – it will add a welcome dimension of local distinctiveness and character to the plant communities.

If a cereal is used in the mixture, it will have to be re-sown every year. The same applies to those flowering weed species which do not normally form a persistent seed bank, such as *Agrostemma*.

Some species germinate in the autumn and do best from an autumn cultivation. Others germinate best in spring – they may come up following an autumn cultivation but they will experience more competition at this time and so will not play such a major part in the mix. The situation is further complicated in those situations where a new seed mix is being established for the first time. Some spring germinating plants will only come up if they have had a winter chilling, and so will not germinate unless they have been present in the ground since the autumn, regardless of the time of cultivation.

26 Cornfield annual weeds' are adapted to frequent disturbance, and usually need fertile soil conditions to complete their life-cycle. Here such annuals are being grown along the central verge of an urban road providing colour and wildlife interest to passers by.

As a general rule, autumn cultivation creates populations which are more diverse, but in specific cases where one or two autumn germinating types are too dominant this may not be true. It is always preferable to have a combination of both cultivation systems.

It may be beneficial to alter the timing of cultivation from year to year in areas where there appear to be undesirable levels of aggressive or problem weed species developing. Some perennial weeds are perfectly able to tolerate one or two deep cultivations in a year. In some cases it may be necessary to break the annual cycle in order to spray out the perennials. Most annuals with persistent seed banks will not suffer at all from this process, although some with short-lived seed may need to be reintroduced. An alternative to herbicide is to have a year of fallow where the soil is repeatedly cultivated to weaken the perennials gradually. This is likely to have a much more damaging effect on the annual seed bank than herbicide use, because each cultivation will encourage a new group of seedlings to come up.

The flowering season of both the autumn and spring sown fields can be extended if the surface of some of the field is topped with a mower before flowering. The cut plants will often regenerate and flower later in the year.

Wetlands

The technology of wetland creation is also well advanced, much of this due to the work of the Game Conservancy and Sand and Gravel Association sponsored projects (Andrews and Kinsman, 1990; Giles 1992) . The characteristics of wetland communities are so strongly dominated by the water

27 Wetland plants are adapted to changing conditions and can be very mobile, such as here where they are invading a poorly structured and waterlogged clay spoil.

relations that creation of diversity is almost easy, and is open to what is largely an engineering solution of landform grading and water-level control. Large water bodies are normally created for other purposes, and habitat creation opportunities are determined as a secondary treatment. However, ponds and smaller bodies are frequently created for no other purpose than to promote wildlife diversity in urban areas.

Wetland species often have good dispersal mechanisms, and can be easily introduced by adding mud and root fragments from nearby wetlands of similar characteristics. The water pH is an important variable that controls the community composition, but this is often beyond the scope for direct control. Excessively high nutrient levels can cause severe problems of eutrophication, and may require modification of the type of community aimed for.

The role of water as a design element and as wildlife habitat in urban areas is restricted by safety and management considerations. Siting, size and depth influence water quality. Moffatt (1986) recommends a depth of over 1 m to protect water quality, and of over 1.2 m to restrict the growth of aggressive emergent species such as *Typha* spp. and *Phragmites australis* (syn. *P. communis*). Shelving of banks allows establishment or colonization of aquatic plants, and assists in developing a zonation of species.

The most valuable wet areas for wildlife are inherently diverse with varying depths of water. This allows a range of plants to colonize. Patches of boggy soil are as important as open water and can be created by burying a butyl liner about 200 mm below the soil surface. Diversity in shore line (and above all a long and complex shoreline made by creating bays and inlets) is desirable. Different substrates at the shoreline may also be desirable to favour different species (e.g. shingle and mud).

Table 7.3 *The habitat requirements of some wetland birds*

Species	Status	Habitat characteristics	Food	Nest site
Great crested grebe	Widespread, mainly in lowland areas. Present throughout the year	Open lake-like sections of 1 ha 0.5–5 m deep, per pair during breeding season. Well-developed fringing emergent vegetation especially reeds	Fish, aquatic invertebrates	Nests of vegetation within emergent vegetation or trailing branches
Little grebe	Widespread and sometimes numerous especially in south. Presen throughout the year on lowland rivers	Shallow waters often <1m deep and < than 1 ha extent. Luxuriant aquatic, emergent and marginal vegetation, overhanging branches, bushes and scrub	Insects; molluscs; tadpoles; small fish	Floating nest platforms attached to emergent vegetation or trailing branches
Mallard	Very common and widespread on both lowland and upland rivers	Waters with emergent vegetation, bankside scrub; rank vegetation and submerged aquatics. Very adaptable	Omnivorous and opportunistic small young dependent on invertebrates	Generally on ground in thick cover but also in holes in trees. Where habitat in riverbank is not ideal will freely nest at distance from water in ditches, hedges or scrub. Young then brought to water

Source: from Ward *et al.* (1995).

The RSPB have developed sophisticated criteria for bank and water margin patterning, depth, substrate and other characteristics to the point where it is almost possible that wetland designers can guarantee that a certain water body will suit given species of water birds, or can make strong predictions concerning the likely species that will benefit from different features provided in association with wetlands (see Tables 7.3 and 7.4).

The presumption is nearly always to favour bank design that allows for a gradual transition from water to land, to aid easy movement of species such as amphibians. However, some species such as newts may favour the opportunity to pass quickly from aquatic to sheltered dry land conditions without being too vulnerable during the transition. Localized steeper edges are also beneficial for plants such as *Iris pseudacorus* and *Acorus calamus*. Of course rapid transitions to deep water increase the risk of drowning accidents.

Island design can also be approached with sophistication (see Figure 7.2).

Changes in ground water levels have a critical impact on marsh and bog vegetation. Where fluctuations between summer and winter are wide, i.e. on average more than 0.5–0.75 m, a less diverse vegetation will develop

Table 7.4 *The wetland bird species favoured by different habitat design and management options*

Feature or vegetation type	Species likely to benefit	Management recommendation	Benefit
Bankside scrub	Red-breasted merganser, mallard, tufted duck, sedge warbler and other species not restricted to rivers and wetlands	Should be managed in association with other bankside vegetation, if possible should be cut on a 10-year rotation to maintain thick cover down to ground level and various stages of growth	Can provide nest sites for mallard tufted duck, sedge warbler and a range of other species
Bankside trees	Goosander, moorhen, coot, kingfisher	Planting of native species particularly those associated with rivers or wetlands such as willows or alder should be encouraged in small areas along the bankside. Where present, older trees should be retained. Branches overhanging the water should also be retained where possible	Native trees contribute seed, fruit and invertebrates of value to birds, older trees with cavities are used for nesting by barn owls and goosander, overhanging branches are used as perches by kingfishers and trailing branches as nest anchorages by moorhens and coots
Earth cliffs	Kingfisher, sand martin	Natural erosion should be permitted wherever possible otherwise new sheer faces at least 2m high can be cut over water and recut at intervals	Earth cliffs provide opportunities for burrow-nesting birds such as kingfisher and sand martins to excavate nest holes

Source: from Ward *et al.* (1995).

compared to a more stable site. However, a completely stable water level may restrict opportunities for some species. For amphibian animals such as newts and other ruderal species periods when the pond dries completely may be an advantage in controlling populations of competitive or predatory fish.

Many urban ponds are small, and incapable of maintaining themselves. Small size can be an advantage since they will warm rapidly, have good light penetration and collect a high organic detritus. They hence become very rich in plant species and may also support many species that could not survive in deeper or larger water bodies (Andrews and Kinsman, 1990). Yet without management inputs they would relatively rapidly silt up and become completely covered by marginal species such as *Typha*. With careful planning of water depth it is possible to construct a pond in such a way that the management inputs can be reduced, although this is seldom done in the eagerness to make sure that it establishes quickly and with a full wildlife complement. To maximize bank variation it is almost inevitable that some shallows are created that will always need maintenance. The ability to compartmentalize and independently drain and flood different areas of the wetland is of enormous value.

Urban water is often a repository of a wide range of pollutants ranging

Figure 7.2. The design of topographical structure and boundaries of islands can greatly influence their value to birds (Andrews and Kinsman, 1990).

Island design

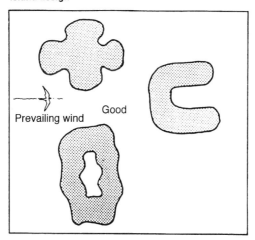

Good island forms to provide abundant 'edge' for feeding waders and dabbling ducks.

(a) Poor island design

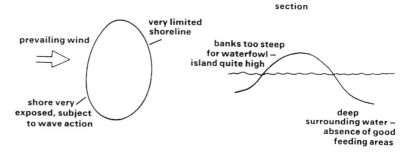

(b) Good island design

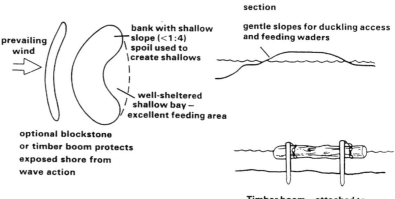

from excessive nutrients to shopping trolleys (although the latter may actually be functionally valuable even if unsightly, since they may help to develop structural diversity in the system). Problems can arise from inert sediments, pesticide runoff and build-up of organic matter but these pollutants can occur frequently in rural areas as well as urban. Where ponds are close to areas of hard surfacing frequented by traffic pollution by oil can be particularly harmful since it can interfere with oxygen uptake and gas exchange. It may be possible (and highly advantageous) to develop a local drainage system that keeps road and sewage water separate from storm water which can be safely diverted into the site water bodies (Moereels, 1995).

Biotic pollution may also occur, either accidentally through the spread of aggressive pond weeds or intentionally with people releasing fish that they no longer have room for. Human pressure may also become acute when the pond is large enough for angling. Frequently this will just have to be tolerated but good design may allow certain areas to be developed which are difficult to get access to.

Habitat mosaic in wetlands

The temptation to compartmentalize landscape features and to consider them in isolation from their surroundings seems particularly strong with regard to aquatic features such as ponds. With the exception of discussions about problems of overhanging trees, most pond creation guides make no reference to the surrounding landscape. Yet much of the life of ponds is determined by the patterns of the land around and this too also needs to be considered. In particular water birds and amphibians have certain extensive habitat requirements, such as the presence of grassland or rocky areas to act as refuges. Some amphibians spend the majority of their life-cycle on land, and they have clear terrestrial habitat requirements.

Trees

The longevity and size of trees make them special, unique, features in the landscape and gives them importance both collectively and individually. For example, all of the trees in a neighbourhood may help to modify the climate of the town beneficially through transpiration cooling and shade, shelter from winds. They may help to trap dusts and clean pollution from the air and hence improve conditions for a range of other species.

Urban development may increase the tree cover where this occurs in areas of relatively tree-less agricultural land. There seems to be a greater tendency for tree populations to increase in areas prone to planning control, or where landscape professionals are involved, but at the same time there may be less cover in privately owned gardens (Land Use Consultants, 1993). The net result of these trends needs is of course weighted by the extent of these different land categories, and as such there appears to be a small trend for

Table 7.5 *Tree numbers – results of a comparison between 302 sites assessed by aerial photography*

Land category	Current	Late 1960s	% change
Street	740	700	+6%
Parks/open space	1690	1090	+55%
Private, open	6550	5950	+10%
Private, enclosed	6500	7100	–9%
Woodlands (ha)	31	24	+29%
Overall	15480	14840	+4%

Source: Land Use Consultants (1993).

increased urban tree numbers from the 1960s to the present day (Table 7.5).

Recent research has also investigated the current patterning of the tree cover and the species distribution in more detail (Figures 7.3 and 7.4).

Failure rates of new tree planting can be high, however. Professionals questioned as to the primary causes of such failures ranked the following problems in decreasing order (Bradshaw *et al.*, 1995):

- vandalism;
- drought (which can be aggravated by weed competition);
- planting technique;
- soil compaction;
- stock quality;
- waterlogging;
- mower/strimmer damage;
- tie/stake/guard damage;
- soil fertility problems;
- disease;
- road salt;
- other.

However, in their own research studies Bradshaw *et al.* (1995) found that frequently damage attributed to vandalism was the result of poor management practices and inadequate after care which in some way physically weakens the tree such that die-back occurs or breakage of the stems or branches becomes easier (Figure 7.5).

Ecologically the special qualities of trees mean that they are not just things that live in a natural habitat, they actually are a habitat. They can be a home to many species, and there will be dependent animals or plants living on or in the roots, trunk, branches or leaves. From this perspective it is even possible to look on individual trees as isolated landscape fragments with patterns of migration and colonization between them.

Young trees are of course much less able to support a wide variety of life – the best trees for conservation are the hoary giant old specimens. These

Figure 7.3 Average cover of individual and woodland trees by urban land use type (Land Use Consultants, 1993).

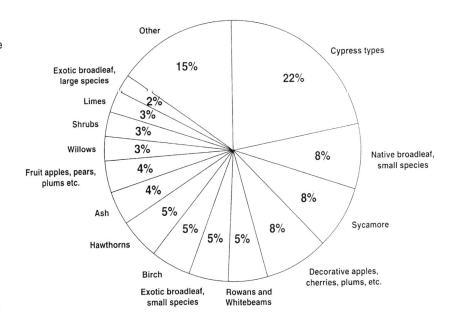

Figure 7.4 The contribution of different species groups to urban trees (Land Use Consultants, 1993).

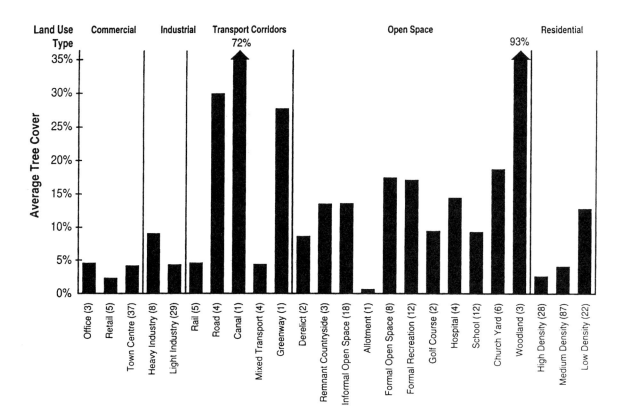

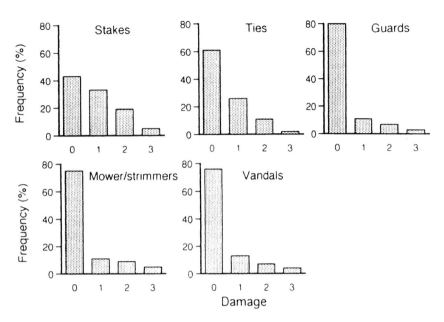

Figure 7.5 Surveyed causes of physical damage to trees 3–5 years after planting. Vandalism is much less significant than the combined problems from poor maintenance. Damage is assessed by degree of stem circumference affected. Column 0 – no damage, column 1 1–25%, column 2 25–50%, column 3 >50%. (Bradshaw *et al.*, 1995).

old trees are rare things in towns and even over much of the countryside, although it is rare that anyone ever tries to assess how many there are. No amount of young tree planting will fully make up for an absence of large established trees.

Trees are also almost certainly the most powerful symbol for use in environmental awareness projects. Historically trees have been fundamentally important in mythology and in religion and have been associated with powerful emotional, psychological and spiritual responses. In some cultures individual trees were identified which survived for thousands of years, tens of generations of people.

These responses obviously persist today to some degree. Trees often evoke powerful subconscious feelings and many people become very attached to particular trees in their area.

However, the rate of loss of mature trees in urban areas is again usually much higher than in rural settings. Stresses such as poor soils, pollution or vehicle damage may lead to a high mortality. These losses may be aggravated by peak events, such as local urban re-design or extensive earthworks, such as the recent expansion in cable laying. The acceptable lifespan of urban trees will often be curtailed by the managing authorities in the name of safety. There are therefore few opportunities for very large structurally complex specimens to develop. People obviously become concerned when trees start to develop dead branches or holes, or if they start to sprout mushrooms. Of course safety must be paramount whenever trees are growing in close proximity to housing and property but it is important to find ways to accommodate these specimens somewhere in the urban framework, or we lose a tremendous source of richness in the natural environment.

Arboricultural assessors are often in difficult positions, having to be overly cautious in their judgement of when a tree must come down in order to meet public liability concerns. The failing lies in research which has failed to clearly identify acceptable limits for decay, and species which can safely carry dead tissue.

Substantial advances have occurred in recent years through the research of scientists such as Shigo (1986) who have shown that trees can compartmentalize infected zones, i.e. they can develop internal protective barriers which stop the wound from spreading. After a time these infected areas can turn into extremely valuable habitats without in any way threatening the health of the tree or the people around. It is also important to identify those tree species that retain dead wood effectively without causing a significant hazard. Hollow trees may also be re-assessed, since not all are dangerous.

As part of habitat creation it is worth considering how new trees of character can be developed for both their visual and conservation value. 'Character trees' can be powerful local landmarks that are a focus of many activities. The simplest technique to begin with is to encourage nurseries and planters not to be too keen to grade trees by limited quality requirements. We may also want to explore how to make trees more gnarled and misshapen, perhaps by weaving them together or pegging them down.

Epicormic shoots are generally seen as a nuisance for street tree managers, and research has been underway to find ways of controlling these stem growths, however, in other settings epicormic shoots help to produce trees that look just like the hairy characters from children's books and this tendency can be enhanced by carving.

Pollarding has also been out of favour with many tree managers who see it as a mutilation of tree shape and form. Yet pollarding may also be a valuable technique for conservation that should be re-introduced into many towns since it can be used to keep old tree trunks alive in a safe form. Of course, for many tree species pollarding needs to be begun while the tree is still moderately young – old specimens may not respond when cut for the first time.

The habitat value of trees may also be favoured by establishing tree living plants. Lower plants, ferns, bryophytes and lichens, are often associated with moist habitats in many people's minds but they are frequently very drought-tolerant and only need moisture during certain phases of their life-cycle. They can therefore be established on trees as long as critical moisture input is given at the early stages.

Of course, many are very prone to air pollution since they absorb all of their moisture and nutrient needs from air and from bark surface, but many urban areas experience improved air quality and may be capable of supporting higher populations of these plants than they have done for most of this century. Some may also not be able to survive on young trees which still have rapidly expanding bark.

Hemi-parasites may be easier to establish as they get many resources from the tree sap. Mistletoe establishment is often a very worthwhile exercise, although it can require several attempts.

Climbing plants such as ivy should also be deliberately introduced sometimes. Large old hoary ivy-covered trees are some of the most distinctive and striking images to be seen in the landscape. The conservation advantages are that it flowers very late in the season and provides an invaluable source of nectar for bees. Its fruits also ripen in the spring and provide a useful food source at that time of year. Some birds like ivy-covered trees to roost and nest, especially during the winter period.

Many people think that ivy is a pest or parasite and wish to kill it off, but there is no direct exploitation of the tree. Any healthy deciduous tree should be able to grow faster than ivy, but it may be able to overtake and smother a tree which is not very vigorous or any old and declining specimen. However, the weight and leaf canopy in winter can make some trees more prone to windthrow.

Ivy is also an evergreen and it can cast a great deal of extra shade which in extensive populations may inhibit ground flora development and will suppress other bark living species such as lichens, mosses and liverworts.

Woodland

Techniques of creation of new, deliberately species-rich, woodlands are arguably less well developed, and certainly less well tested than with grassland. This at least in part reflects the prolonged timescales required before they mature. Additional problems in modern projects include hostile substrates, especially those resulting from the deterioration of soil structure during site construction and development, and the problems of funding skilled management and labour during both the establishment phase, and in later management. These problems may also be exacerbated by a requirement for the instantaneous creation of an acceptable living environment.

The approach to woodland establishment varies from site to site, although an indication of the best techniques available are outlined in Emery (1986), Hodge (1995) and Ferris-Kaan (1995).

Community, urban and multipurpose forestry

Community forestry or urban forestry initiatives attempt to exploit the 'multiple' benefits of woodlands to society. Typically the list of such potential benefits may include recreation opportunities, nature conservation, landscape improvement and timber production. The particular leanings of the organizations involved in promoting these woodlands affects the order in which the benefits are presented. As well as the above factors which seem to be obligatory additional returns will depend on circumstances and may include pollution control (including carbon fixation), noise reduction, provision of educational resources, biofuels and even just a simple, low maintenance land-bank 'filler' providing general environmental benefits on otherwise useless sites. In the UK the government has called for 'a doubling of woodland in England over the next half century' which would require coverage of about a million hectares of land, increasing woodland cover to a level which has not been seen since the compilation of the Domesday Book (Forestry Commission/Countryside Commission 1996).

The distinction between community forests (normally situated on the urban fringe) and urban forests (normally situated within urban boundaries) is often more important administratively than in terms of their intended range of functions. In both situations the manager would frequently encourage the involvement of the community in terms of planting or maintenance; indeed this is more likely within urban areas than outside. There are some important real differences between the two situations: within the city book prices for land value may make long-term woodland economic returns implausible, while the chances of high-quality timber being produced are considerably reduced.

The principle danger with 'multiple objective forestry' is that the term may start to become synonymous with 'muddled objective forestry'. The methodology by which these various goals can be reconciled, and what the product needs to look like on the ground in the early stages, is still unclear. Unfortunately there is a tendency for an implicit assumption to be made that forestry objectives are in many ways compatible with the other goals, and that there only needs to be a slight tweaking, particularly in terms of the species chosen, in order to make them adapt.

In reality, if different woodland systems are studied the inescapable conclusion must be that the objectives of multi-purpose forestry do not usually coincide with those of forestry as practised today. In particular in a crop production system the manager does everything possible to ensure uniformity – in good habitat and landscape design it is often far more important to introduce as much diversity as possible.

Take for example the paper by Moffat *et al.* (1991) discussing the problems of lack of uniformity in growth of woodland on once-derelict open-cast land in the Forest of Dean. This lack of uniformity of performance, arising from site variability, is a major limitation in the development of a productive forest. However, the very same variation would be a tremendous asset in conservation or amenity woodland and that would be reflected in the development of visual interest if a long enough perspective can be taken.

(Interestingly when Community Forests are discussed in the UK the Countryside Commission often refers to the ancient semi-natural New Forest in Hampshire as a model of what it would like to see. In reality the Forest of Dean makes a much better model, since it contains a large percentage of secondary woodland, much of it developed on derelict industrial land, in association with zones of productive forestry, recreation and also some interesting 'community' inputs such as the wonderful sculpture trail.)

The development and maintenance of conservation interest in woodlands is an area which is becoming moderately well researched. In general this work concentrates on the best way to maintain open space within woods. As is typical, the issue of amenity value of woodlands gets much less serious treatment. Assumptions are often made that imply that either this is not a very serious topic, or it is one where very simple answers exist and are immediately apparent to everyone. The idea that there may be a science and a methodology involved in growing amenity trees, a methodology that may differ from ordinary forestry practice, is rarely considered.

The community forestry plantings, for the most part, are based on standard forestry style plantings, using forestry-style planting stock, forestry tree shelters and above all forestry spacings on a uniform grid. The only movement towards the other goals is that if you look down into the rows of shelter tubes you will find inside, rather than one or two species, a mix of native trees. The risk is that these will turn into rows of straight, pole-like trees differing from a traditional productive forest only in that the yield will be drastically reduced and, if you take the trouble to peer upwards, at the top of each pole there is likely to be a range of different leaf shapes rather than just one or two. The only thing that will save these woodlands from developing into boring, dull, forestry plantations is some very careful management, and there is very little sign that this management is being planned or funded.

In fact there are many choices that face the designer and manager of an amenity woodland, each of which will influence the form and nature of the woodland that is produced.

Species mixtures

Woodlands differ from many other communities in that the influence of some plant species (the canopy trees) may be so dominant that they determine the nature of the plant community in a way which exceeds the influence of the environmental characters such as soil type.

The phenomenon of the mixed native woodland planting mix is not particularly new; landscape architects have been using this approach to develop diversity for many decades. However, increasingly planners seem to expect and demand a ubiquitous muesli of species collected together in random and characterless fashion. The landscape may also start to become populated with woodlands which have no regional flavour or sense of identity, that are essentially unmanageable, and that the concentration on species variety will divert attention away from other, perhaps more meaningful, considerations such as woodland structure.

Although diversity is often a good thing there is also a need for habitats of very strong character. A beechwood for example obtains its essential nature from the sheer dominance of beech. Plantings should therefore include many large blocks where a very limited number of species are used.

Where a particular woodland type or management system (such as coppice with standards) is aimed for it is naturally sensible to determine the species composition to suit the end point, yet it is amazing how rarely this principle is followed. Soutar and Peterken (1989) have presented some invaluable advice on species selection for conservation purposes in the UK. Rodwell and Patterson (1994) have also produced prescriptions for woodland creation in line with the UK National Vegetation Classification

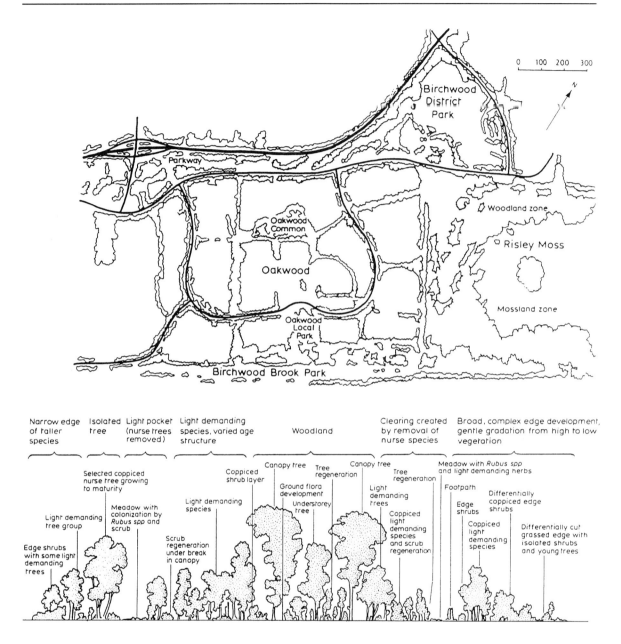

Figure 7.6 (top) The macro structure of woodland planting in Warrington New Town (Moffatt, 1986).

Figure 7.7 The micro structure of woodland planting in Warrington New Town (Moffatt, 1986).

categorization. It is obviously important to remain sensitive to and compatible with the local landscape when choosing a species mix, but also to remember that the objectives of multi-purpose forestry will not be met without some relaxation of adherence to any such preconceptions. Different objectives are likely to be best met by zoning the woodland, and by creating patches with very distinct species composition including, in some places, pure conifer stands. Native broadleaves should make up the bulk of the wooded landscape which has conservation or amenity objectives, but even

Figure 7.8 The individual planting patterns used to develop structural diversity in the woodlands at Warrington (Tregay and Gustavsson, 1983).

A. Situation in establishment phase

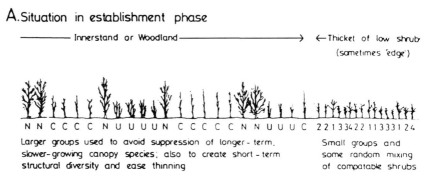

Innerstand or Woodland ⟶ ⟵ Thicket of low shrub (sometimes 'edge')

N N C C C C N U U U U N C C C C C N N U U U C   2 2 1 3 3 4 2 2 1 1 3 3 3 1 2 4

Larger groups used to avoid suppression of longer-term, slower-growing canopy species; also to create short-term structural diversity and ease thinning

Small groups and some random mixing of compatable shrubs

B. Situation in management phase

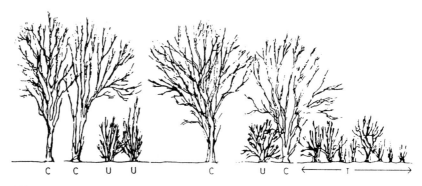

C   C   U   U   C   U   C ⟵ T ⟶

Wider spacing of canopy trees in innerstand relate to larger groups at planting stage and reflect management by thinning

Mixed species in thicket retained due to absence of a dominant, smaller stature of shrubs and management by differential coppicing

Notation :- N = nurse tree
C = ultimate canopy
U = understorey shrub
T = mixed thicket-forming shrub species
1 = species 1
2 = species 2
3 = species 3
4 = species 4

here the place of some exotic specimens should not be overlooked. These play a key role in the visual diversity of the countryside as well as urban areas, marking and denoting areas of 'civilization' or human activity. In small numbers exotics pose no threat to the conservation value of the wood, and in fact are likely to increase diversity.

The fundamental aim of breaking structural tree and shrub belts down into

Table 7.6 *Species category composition for structural tree and shrub belts*

Planting belt width	30 m	20 m	10 m	< 10 m
Species category				
Woodland	30%	10%	5%	–
Light demanding	30%	40%	20%	0%
Tall edge	20%	25%	50%	65%
Low edge	20%	25%	25%	25%

'Woodland' mix   1m centres, trees in groups of 10–50; shrubs in groups of 5–10. *Alnus* and *Corylus* planted randomly with occasional group.

25% *Corylus avellana*	20% *Fraxinus excelsior*	5% *Pinus sylvestris*
25% *Quercus robur*	5% *Ilex aquifolium*	2.5% *Sambucus nigra*
20% *Alnus glutinosa*	5% *Prunus avium*	2.5% *Ulmus glabra*

Scrub mix   0.75 or 0.5m centres; main species planted in groups of 5–30; additional shrubs and trees randomly planted; forms blocks detached from other planting mixes

75–100% *Crataegus monogyna*	75–100% *Ulex europaeus*	0–15% *Sambucus nigra*
75–100% *Prunus spinosa*	0–15% *Corylus avellana*	0–15% *Viburnum opulus*
75–100% *Rosa canina*	0–15% *Ilex aquifolium*	0–10% *Tree species*

Tall edge/hedgerow mix   1m or 0.75m centres; groups of 5–50; *Lonicera* planted randomly; frequently used as edge mixture; percentage of *Crataegus* increased when used as a hedge

42.5% *Crataegus monogyna*	10% *Alnus glutinosa*	5% *Lonicera periclymenum*
17.5% *Corylus avellana*	5% *Acer campestre*	2.5% *Salix caprea*
15% *Prunus spinosa*	5% *Sambucus nigra*	

Light demanding mix   1m centres; all species in groups of 5–100; may occasionally form edge to a planting; mostly group coppiced on a rotation

22.5% *Corylus avellana*	17.5% *Sorbus aucuparia*	5% *Ilex aquifolium*
17.5% *Alnus glutinosa*	10% *Acer campestre*	5% *Populus tremula*
17.5% *Betula pendula*	7.5% *Sambucus nigra*	2.5% *Pinus sylvestris*

Low edge mix   0.75m or 0.5m centres; all species in groups of 5–30; percentages and combinations used very flexibly, with great attention paid to small-scale variation

50% *Rosa arvensis*	30% *Prunus spinosa*	20% *Rosa pimpinellifolia*
50% *Rosa canina*	20% *Cornus sanguinea*	20% *Viburnum opulus*
30% *Corylus avellana*	20% *Ilex aquifolium*	
30% *Crataegus monogyna*	20% *Ulex europaeus*	

Source: after Moffatt (1986); Greenwood and Moffatt (1982); Emery (1986).

four basic mixes and by single-species group planting is to minimize maintenance and management, simulate natural regeneration and structurally diverse woodlands and overcome the problems encountered in the early structural planting schemes, particularly competition by aggressive species (Moffatt, 1986; Tregay and Gustavsson, 1983) (see Figures 7.6, 7.7 and 7.8 and Table 7.6). The recognition of the ecological relationships of narrow woodland plantations at Warrington has provided a significant contribution to British ecological landscapes.

The species choice may be influenced by other factors, such as the opportunities for craft use or other forms of revenue gathering, or even the rate of decay and rot formation. Long-lived trees with slowly decaying wood may be of greatest value for insects in the long term, but short-lived trees are probably important for the rapid development of invertebrate interest in new woodlands (Hodge, 1995).

Tree spacing and density

As discussed, many of the community woodland plantations that are being created have very simple structures with trees being planted on a grid system at standard forestry spacings. There is no clear consensus on whether such spacings really are essential.

Moderately high planting densities are advocated by Hodge (1995) for ensuring adequate stands despite failures and also for creating mutual shelter. They allow the rapid establishment of woodland conditions, both visually and ecologically. Fast-growing trees at 2 m spacing under intensive forestry techniques may close canopy after four years, whereas slower growing species at 3 m spacing may not close canopy for 15 years (Harmer and Kerr, 1995). High densities may reduce the need for weed control by the rapid establishment of shade, and also more rapidly create litter conditions that allow the establishment of more sensitive understory species (Ferris-Kaan, 1995), although it should be remembered that excessive shade can also be inhibitory to many desirable woodland herbs.

In the UK grant aid support from the Forestry Commission for woodland establishment imposes a lower limit on spacing of 3 x 3m. This has been argued to be too low for either rapid canopy closure or the production of quality timber (Harmer and Kerr, 1995). The same authors also argue that wider spacings may create conditions that favour deer.

Conversely the advantages of low spacing density include the reduced costs of stock (and protection). Where locally collected ecotypes are used only small tree numbers may be available (Soutar, 1991). Above all, wide spacing eventually allows the development of the broad tree canopies and extensive swathes of understory that are sometimes required in habitat creation (Ferris-Kaan, 1995).

There is also the question of whether spacing needs to be uniform or distributed in clumps or other more natural forms. One of the most common arguments given for uniformity is ease of management. However, it is a moot point why simplicity at planting is in any way preferable to simplicity of management. In fact it seems rather naive to rely on skilled management in many of these situations where capital funding is often scraped together on the back of a rag tag of grants and donations, but where reliable funds, or indeed a system, for maintenance seem almost non-existent. Emery (1986) suggests that trees should not be planted closer than 1.8 m centres, and that at this density they will require thinning within 15 years, whereas at twice this spacing there will be no need for thinning for perhaps 25 years.

In Warrington New Town trees were primarily established from whips between 450 and 600 mm high. Planting centres were usually at 1 metre, although planting distance varies from 70 cm centres (2 plants m^{-2}) to 2 m centres (0.25 plants m^{-2}). These planting distances vary depending on species, site and function. Apart from on heavy clays susceptible to water-logging, mulches are used to reduce weed competition and retain moisture. However, with this approach unless creative thinning begins within the very first few years of establishment the options for developing a full range of mature tree forms will be extremely limited.

Where early canopy closure is desired, but the long-term aim is to let the trees develop the form and branch structure and final spacing that is associated with woodlands of high conservation value, then a suitable technique is to include moderately vigorous but low growing shrubs in the planting mix. These may need to dominate the mixture at a ratio of 15:1 to the trees (Thoday, personal communication).

The size and shape of the planted area

The Forestry Commission have produced some excellent work on aspects of landscape design for forests (Bell, 1995) which discuss in detail the influence of boundaries and shape on perceived naturalness. However, in many urban woodlands, where plantable areas are dictated by land availability and where the concept of a harmonious natural landform is often meaningless, these design rules are of limited value.

Nevertheless size and shape is still an issue. Like many habitats, there are relationships between size and the composition of the wildlife species found within, but these can be more complex than is often realized. For example Fuller *et al.*, (1995) identify that:

- woodland area is a strong predictor of the number of bird species;
- the area of woodland is also related to the composition of the associated bird communities, with some species avoiding the smallest woods;
- woodland area is generally inversely related to the density of breeding birds as a consequence of edge effects;
- the stability of bird populations is lower in small woods and the turnover of individual birds is higher.

Where opportunities exist for extensive planting a careful analysis is therefore required of the optimum shape and size of the planted zones. Open spaces should be planned from the beginning so that non-woodland species can be retained. Even in quite small areas, the ratio of edge length to centre can be addressed by choosing complex or simple boundaries and edges. In large areas rides will be especially valuable if their orientation is east–west. Their width should be variable but in many places equal to at least the expected ultimate height of the surrounding trees. However, straight rides will lack shelter and are visually dull. Open glades on the southern edges of the woodland are also valuable. Both will need frequent maintenance. Open patches and glades may need to be maintained by cutting. It may also be worth allowing additional open areas which are intended to be allowed to close in through natural colonization or scrub development.

It is currently argued that within the woodland itself open space should make up something like 20% of the total (Ferris-Kaan, 1995). However, in many community forest programmes in the UK the woodland cover itself is targetted at perhaps only 30% of the total landscape (Forestry Commission/Countryside Commission, 1996). Bell (1995) also identifies that visually lowland woodland looks most natural if it covers between one-third to two-thirds of the landscape.

The amenity woodland plantings in Warrington New Town place great emphasis on the use of woodland edge species adjacent to open spaces or grassland. Light-demanding trees and shrubs added greatly to the diversity and richness of the wood. At Warrington woodland plantations are primarily restricted to large-scale open spaces and linking structural plantings. The desirability of private gardens, and a domestic scale for other curtilage and structural plantings, together with problems of scale for a woodland setting with tree belts less than 10 m in width, preclude the extension of woodland into low-density housing.

The difficulty of measuring success in the absence of social survey data is apparent. Attempts to include woodland within low-density housing are only partially successful. The difficulty of balancing lawn and woodland areas on a restricted scale has forced the Haarlem Parks Department to abandon woodland areas in low density housing (Dick Vonk, Haarlem Parks Dept, personal communication). Conversely they find that woodland plantings in high-density housing are successful, both aesthetically and ecologically, although residents opinions are still divided. The woodland plantings are successful both in softening the architecture, and in providing visual interest in the view from the flats.

When new woodlands are being established, inevitably there is a likelihood that existing habitat patches may be incorporated. If treated in the right way these can add greatly to the diversity of the overall feature, but careful attention needs to be given to their preservation through design and management. These issues have been addressed in detail for invertebrates by Key (1995) (Table 7.7).

Introduction or treatment of understory

Of course in conservation terms the 'value' of a woodland lies not in the trees but in the associated species; trees are viewed more as the 'habitat' than as members of the plant community. In fact under some management regimes, the trees must be seen as ephemeral and regularly cut – the woodland is sustained by the survival of the understory and associated species.

Woodlands or scrub are much more complex communities than grassland; they consist of more layers of vegetation, they have a wider range of rooting depths and they take a much longer time to stabilize.

In ancient woodland the understory species will exist in a complex mosaic

Table 7.7 *The benefits and problems to invertebrate conservation of incorporating blocks of other habitat in new woodland, together with potential management solutions*

Incorporated habitat	Benefits	Problems	Possible solution
Woodland	Source of colonization of new woodland.	Edge fauna may suffer	Maintain internal edges.
	Enhanced visibility of fauna of small woodland.		
Hedgerow and trees	Source of colonization of new woodland.	Overtopping or shading of shrubs or older trees.	Maintain as internal edges.
	More diverse tree age structure in new woodland.		
	Good nectar sources.		
Scrub	Source of colonization of wood and ride edges.	Overtopping or shading of shrubs	Maintain as internal edges.
	Good nectar sources.	Rarely appreciated and often neglected.	Education.
		Eventually becomes too mature and fills available space.	Manage on coppice style rotation.
Grassland and heathland	Source of colonization of rides and glades. Increased shelter and warmth.	Danger of shading small patches. Tree/shrub regeneration into habitat.	Coppice edges, especially south and east sides. Manage specifically as open space.
		More remote from graziers or difficult access for machines.	Design ride system to allow easy access.
'Waste' ground	Ruderal nectar plants.	Rarely appreciated.	Education.
	Sunny bare ground for basking and burrowing.	Danger of shading small patches.	Coppice edges, especially south and east sides.
	Cover and shelter.	Tree/shrub regeneration into habitat.	Manage specifically as open space.
Wetland	Increased shelter.	Danger of shading small patches.	Coppice edges, especially south and east sides.
	Less likelihood of pesticide or fertilizer input.	Increased evapotranspiration leading to drying out.	Is woodland planting appropriate here?
		Nutrient input from leaf fall.	As above.

Source: Key (1995).

that reflects environmental conditions and it is not recreatable. However, stands of many of these species can be established if the appropriate conditions of shade and humidity can be provided. Although some woodland herbs have a positive requirement for shade and humidity, many have a broad physiological tolerance but are not very competitive. The challenge therefore is primarily to produce conditions which suppress the establishment of competing and aggressive weed species (Cohn and Millett, 1995; Buckley and Knight, 1989).

There is a range of these environmental conditions where the woodland species survive but weeds do not, but achieving the right balance of conditions can be difficult in a young plantation and it may be necessary to introduce the understory once canopy closure has been achieved. Young woodlands are often planted at very high densities to give instant impact, and these have to go through complex thinning stages before a final and stable plant density can be achieved.

Planting shrubs and smaller trees around the edges of small woodlands may help to make the shade and humidity conditions closer to that which is desired. Shade in particular, while it may not be directly necessary to establish the woodland herbs, is essential to prevent competition and dominance by potentially more competitive grasses.

Francis (1995) has found that woodland herbs can be categorized as those which regenerate easily from seed and are mobile, often associated with gaps and woodland edges which can be variable habitats, and those which are not very successful from seed and are associated with more stable conditions. These may need to be introduced as transplants.

Some of the rarest and more demanding species have complex soil requirements with high levels of woodland humus, and we are a long way from being able to establish these with certainty.

The most important woodland species are perhaps the lower plants and invertebrates which are not usually mobile. These may be introduced on sites where soil and litter transfer takes place, but are normally unlikely to colonize a secondary woodland for perhaps centuries, if ever.

Londo (1977) identifies a link between ground flora, soil type and leaf litter. On fertile soils species with nutrient-rich rapidly decomposing leaves, such as poplar and alder, will favour a rank course undergrowth. Species with slowly decomposing leaves such as oak and beech will encourage a richer understory.

Woodland management

Woodlands are much more robust and able to withstand neglect compared to plagioclimax habitats such as grassland. Producing woodlands designed to remain unmanaged may be a viable option to meet some objectives. However, in most cases, new woodlands are modelled on types which do require some management input, or require some form of intervention to maximize the environmental benefits. Provision of long-term management is therefore critical and yet there is a stark contrast between the management operations that can be identified by trained foresters and the complete lack of input that is actually typical for most new urban woodland schemes.

For example, many of the most critical management inputs in a new coppice woodland will come after 15 years and recurrently after that. Simple

28 Some woodlands have their structural characteristics determined by long-term but infrequent management. Where the aim is to create new woodlands that match these patterns the necessary management inputs must be planned for.

management programmes which do not meet the need for such long-term provision can not be seen as effective.

The essential complement to the planned initial spacing of the trees and the patterning of species is:

- manipulating species composition by additional planting or removal of dense stands or aggressive species;
- the decision of how the trees should be thinned, how quickly this process should commence and at what frequency it must be repeated thereafter and the choice of which species and proportions need to be favoured.

Brashing and pruning can also influence the final form of the trees in a woodland. In traditional forestry these operations were used in order to ensure that a clean stem free from knots is developed. Occasionally it is possible to come across situations where over-enthusiastic maintenance gangs have brashed specimens where the lower branching habit is essential to their function.

A key decision is also whether to manage the woodland as coppice or high forest, and if the latter whether to favour clear felling in coupes or selection felling. Ideally this decision will have been made at the earliest design stages, and the woodland mixtures and densities chosen accordingly. However, there must also be an adequate mechanism for ensuring follow-through management when the right time arrives.

The frequency of the harvest interval (and hence the age of the trees before cutting) is also an important consideration. These choices will obviously partly be dependent on financial and management issues and whether timber production is a high priority among the multiple objectives. The choices will of course affect ground disturbance, patterns of light and shade and many other factors that ultimately influence species composition. Above all it is essential that the entire process of design and establishment of the woodland is driven by a clear understanding of the likely long-term management system, so that the choice of species, spacing etc. supports rather than conflicts with the final objectives.

Hodge (1995) suggests that some habitat models that are favoured by conservationists (such as coppice with standards) are difficult to establish on new sites and very vulnerable to poor planning or neglect. Slightly modified approaches may be more successful, such as the creation of mosaics of high woodland cover alternating with pure coppice.

Even when these problems have been resolved, woodland management is sometimes hard to sell to the public because people can not 'see' what the implications of the options are; many subtleties are too complex to visualize. It is sometimes particularly hard to promote the idea that tree cutting is necessary because it sustains the woodland and because the trees are less important than the overall system. A key component of urban woodland management is therefore education and participation opportunities. These will be considered in the next chapter.

8 Strategic management issues in the urban countryside

A.D. KENDLE, R. CANDY and S. FORBES

This chapter addresses many of the strategic issues facing the manager who has to implement an urban conservation policy. Many of these relate to technical problems concerning vegetation maintenance and budgeting. However, arguably the greatest challenge and responsibility is that of ensuring that the needs of the human users are addressed. An important dimension of this is the need to allow for local people to participate in management of the sites.

Choosing the appropriate management method and pattern

Once the presence of areas of possible urban conservation significance has been identified it is important to assess what the best level of intervention should be to safeguard the site quality. We have seen above that there are many options for management of grasslands, for example.

Management plans have been seen as the cornerstone of conservation management programmes in order to ensure the necessary continuity of objectives and techniques over the long timescales involved. They have their roots in forestry work where it is inevitable that processes begun by a manager will often not reach fruition within her/his working life. The key elements of a management plan require that the necessary information about the site, the objectives, the resources available and the proposed methods of working are specified. The precise composition of the report can be as flexible as required, but in the UK strong guidelines regarding the desirable layout have been produced by the Countryside Commission and the Nature Conservancy Council. Many conservation groups have become so familiar with these styles that something of a *de facto* standard has emerged and there is often a pressure to conform.

However, landscape management is not just about efficient deployment of resources, it must be value-driven. Often the area that is most neglected is a thorough review of the opportunities and desirable directions of the work programme. In connection with this, it seems easy to put too much emphasis on the format of management plan presentation; in reality the demands of the style can be readily picked up by any professional – the hard part is learning the skills that underlie the content, making the correct decisions about management tasks and resource allocations.

There are a lot of complex questions still to be resolved in conservation and it is important not to be tempted into generalizations. Ecology is a science which attempts to deduce underlying trends and principles from a mass of sometimes conflicting data. Sometimes it is necessary for ecologists to overlook the minutiae in order to arrive at such theories; however, when the manager is trying to do the reverse, and apply ecological principles to a specific site, it is important to remember to consider the needs of the exceptions and minority plant and animal groups as well. This is why generalizing about 'good' conservation practice can be such a dangerous thing.

Urban nature conservation throws some of these problems into sharp perspective. So many things are malleable; so many judgements have to be made about the appropriate level of intervention or the potential value of certain habitats. The need for a strategic overview is arguably even more important than with many traditional rural conservation areas which can be evaluated in a rather more empirical way that takes regard primarily of what is there, and with questions related to the origins of that diversity being inevitably of only secondary importance.

An urban conservation management plan may need to differ from those prepared for established rural habitats as it needs to take account of what may be there in the future rather than attempting to preserve what is. Unless the objective is to model the system on a particularly closely defined semi-natural plant community, the manager has the task of setting the appropriate management inputs in the knowledge that this decision will directly affect the type of plant community that develops. This adds a new level of complexity to the monitoring and evaluation of 'success', particularly given that predictions of the way that a site could develop may at best be imprecise and at worst inaccurate.

Determining the levels of safe intervention depends upon the ability to recognize the key processes and environmental factors that are maintaining the overall diversity in the systems. Managers of many established sites of conservation interest usually have the particular advantage that the baseline management input, both in terms of overall strategy as well as technique, is relatively easy to determine. Since conservation value has often developed over centuries of traditional land management, which has favoured a species group adapted to such circumstances, then the obvious treatment to be followed in the absence of any other criteria is to maintain the traditional inputs. In **relict countryside** in urban areas this may still be a sensible approach, but very often there are few very sensitive species surviving and it may be that attempts to revive traditional management patterns or methods, such as grazing, may be far more of a headache than can be justified.

For example, road verges were often adopted from existing agricultural grassland. They were previously managed by grazing, cutting for hay or burning. These techniques helped to maintain a diversity of species and to create a distinctive sward character. Roadside management in more recent years has probably lead to a reduction in species diversity. Many grass verges are no longer cut at all, except where necessary for sight lines and access. Some areas were regularly treated with herbicide to control broadleaved species. It is likely that many locations could again support a more diverse flora. However, this can only be achieved under appropriate management and in some cases it may require the re-introduction of plants.

An alternative scenario is where there has been substantial management input, but where this has changed to a form and frequency which is more typical of the patterns of work and abilities of urban local government. For example, regular gang mowing may have changed the appearance and composition of a grassland but there may still be many interesting species surviving vegetatively, especially on any areas of very poor soil or wet patches. If left uncut for periods to allow flowers to become visible this richness will become more evident. Of course, if the management programme has included the use of herbicides or broad spectrum pesticides (fortunately usually a rare occurrence) then it is likely that a far more serious loss of biodiversity will have occurred.

The objectives of urban conservation may therefore best be served by determining a programme of maintenance and inputs which are above all realistic and viable and which favour maximum diversity within the framework of that particular biotype rather than attempt to support any specific groups of species.

Non-intervention is often an important strategy for true **early successional urban communities** with value arising from seeing what develops in the way of robust, cost effective and locally appropriate vegetation. However, as we have seen in earlier chapters there is also a value in trying to maintain some unique plant and animal assemblages that arise from the early stages of a primary succession, where it is clear that the later stages of such a succession are likely to have less interest or importance.

An experimental approach to management is often necessary as of course rural landscape managers are building, even unconsciously, on centuries of human experience of how plants and animals respond to different inputs. Inevitably parallel work on new urban communities will initially be crude and poorly focused and will need to be supported by informed guesswork, based on an understanding of the autecology of the different species encountered.

Often the unique communities found in urban areas may reflect patterns of activity which simply can not be duplicated in their original form (such as artificial heating of waterways by factory wastes mentioned above) but in many cases experiments to find the correct management to support or encourage particular aspects of the biota are still worthwhile.

It is also necessary for the management trials to be widely replicated. Any complex urban plant community is often the result of an accumulation of colonization episodes occurring over a very long period of time. Some of those colonization events may have occurred as a result of stochastic processes that may have only occurred once in very many years. Short-term or one-off experimental work is likely to miss many key processes. Therefore a certain management regime may create exactly the right gaps for colonization to occur but this may happen in a year where, because of the climate or lack of pollinating agents or dispersal agents, no seed arrives or in a year where a certain seed pathogen is particularly successful so that no seed germinates.

Given their origins, it is possible to predict that regular disturbance of some kind will be important in maintaining some of the unusual plant communities found in towns and cities. However, we know relatively little about the subtleties of management (such as timing of disturbance) that could be used to encourage specific components or maintain particular phases of the succession. The plant communities we see are largely the product of acute environmental disruption that is far more severe in intensity than will be encountered normally in rural areas. On the other hand they are often characterized by a reduced frequency of chronic disturbance compared to rural sites which may have been maintained by long-term farming inputs.

Mistimed or over-enthusiastic disturbance in closed rural grassland communities often has the result that it encourages invasion of undesirable or exotic plants. Caution is often appropriate therefore. Conversely in many urban settings, where exotics may not only be tolerated but may be desired and where a rich and colourful flora may be the result of unusual patterns of disturbance in previous times, the opportunity exists for a more adventurous approach to management to cast more light on urban plant population dynamics.

The timing and the nature of disturbance will have a major effect on the species which can colonize. Exposure of bare ground consisting of subsoils and spoils which lack a seed bank favours species with small wind distributed seeds. These can travel very effectively in urban areas because of the effects of car slipstreams and building turbulence. Conversely soil movement and dumping often favours aggressive 'weed' species with a good seed bank, or those which survive and spread vegetatively such as through underground rhizomes. These processes are common in most urban areas and as such the species concerned are widespread. Species which have more complex dispersal and establishment mechanisms form the more unique components of the plant communities that often give regional distinctiveness to different areas.

(Unplanned management may also be a useful controlling factor. Regular fires on unmown grass in St Helens have been suggested as being of value for the development of diversity in the landscape (Handley, personal communication).

Far more damaging than over-management is usually any process which leads to the accumulation of excessive fertility which encourages dominance by competitive species and the loss of diversity. This may have occurred through deliberate fertilization, or through the dumping of garden wastes and organic rubbish which may also contain the propagules of persistent and competitive weed species.

Such degraded sites may never be capable of returning to the vegetation patterns that they previously supported, and high species richness may not be easy to achieve. Nevertheless fertile land may be capable of supporting woodland and scrub communities of interest or of developing tall herb grassland communities composed of competitive species which may be visually striking even if not particularly diverse.

The economics of urban vegetation management

One of the most common assumptions about a transition from formal to naturalistic landscape style is that the managing authority should be able to sit back and reap the rewards of greatly decreased management costs. There are of course inevitably many cases where this must be true, for example Crowe (1956) estimated the cost of maintaining Wimbledon Common at 3% that of Kensington Gardens. However, the actual scale of savings will be dependent on the style and content of the previous landscape pattern. Savings are most likely to be seen where the previous landscape contains costly and labour-intensive features, but these sort of showcase sites are arguably the least likely to be converted to a completely different style.

The Groundwork Trust has accumulated figures that show substantial cost saving opportunities linked to the choice of different styles of landscape (Table 8.1).

Of course the term 'native' here is not strictly accurate, since it relates less to the origin of the plant material than to the design decision to work with whatever arises through natural colonization. What is also striking is that the 'naturalistic' styles, which frequently would be dominated by native plants chosen by the designer, can be costly.

Where the 'formal' amenity landscape is a fairly ordinary mix of trees,

Table 8.1 *The costs of establishing and maintaining three types of open space (£ ha^{-1})*

Type of scheme	Capital cost		Estab. cost (0–5 yrs)		Maintenance cost (5–10 years)	
	Mean	Range	Mean	Range	Mean	Range
Native	4482	609–9854	1767	519–3870	640	303–2160
Naturalistic	36166	6734–57091	10600	2560–15718	3578	1738–5950
Amenity	20679	4952–56000	7488	1450–20942	5513	1450–17592

Key
Native – derelict areas that have colonized adequately to allow minimal reclamation thus retaining the colonized vegetation.
Naturalistic – derelict areas that have been treated so that they simulate natural habitats.
Amenity – derelict areas that have had traditional reclamation to grassland with or without trees and shrubs.

Source: from Groundwork Trust (1986).

shrubs and mown grass cost savings will be much harder to realize. It may be that a naturalistic style may give better value for money invested, but the case that needs to be presented to the managing authority will of course need to be very different.

The experience in botanic gardens is sometimes pessimistic. As Apel (1977) notes,

> the ecological principle leads to a plant sociological conception in which the environmental conditions of the site are so largely simulated that it is attempted to show plant communities as may be encountered in the landscape. In theory such a solution appears attractive and simple; one might come to the conclusion that maintenance costs can be saved. In practice, however, such a solution is costly, difficult and risky and possibilities are limited.

There is a vital need to be realistic about costs and the financial backing required for adequate habitat care. Administrators will be keen to take on board the idea that natural is cheap because it means little or no management, but little or no management is **not** usually what conservation is all about. If cost savings are promised which cannot be delivered the net result will be a general discrediting of the approach.

When determining comparative costs it is not possible to make direct comparisons with rural habitat management. In urban areas the need to provide for new machinery and to accommodate poor economies of scale with scattered sites that are slow to travel between can increase associated costs. Urban areas also have a higher profile than rural areas. Public acceptance of short-term abandonment will be low, and there is often a need to undertake high-frequency management at the site fringes to maintain an impression of tidiness.

It sometimes seems that there is a widespread assumption that ecological management, particularly of grasslands, must be cheaper simply because operations are carried out less often. For example, standard amenity grasslands may be mown on a 16 cuts/year basis, whereas meadow grasslands may be cut perhaps just twice. Surely the latter will cost less to maintain? Unfortunately this is not necessarily so. Actual costs will depend on a variety of factors, most particularly on the size and slope of the grassland, which affect the speed and efficiency of the grass-cutting machinery used.

Among the most cost-effective management systems available for land is to use tractor driven gang mowers on large levels sites. Despite the fact that regular cuts are needed, each cut is so quick per unit area that the annual costs are low. For many years the machinery available for cutting long grass was by comparison slow and unwieldy, and the additional costs required for collection of meadow cuttings more than outweighed any potential saving that could be gained. The situation has changed more recently because of the introduction of new machines such as amenity forage harvesters which are capable of cost-effective collection of cut grass. However, even with these machines available, research by the Groundwork Trust (Table 8.2) showed

Table 8.2 *Estimated costs for managing amenity and wildflower grasslands*

	Number of cuts/yr	Machinery	Estimated costs £/cut	£/ha/yr
Small areas				
(<0.2 ha)				
Amenity med quality	16	Ped. Rotary	187.5	3000
Amenity low quality	8	Ped. Flail	350.0	2800
Wild flower grassland	3	Ped. Flail + hand rake	666.7	2000
Medium areas (0.2—0.8 ha)				
Amenity med quality	16	Triple	39.4	630
Amenity low quality	8	Compact flail	100.0	800
Wild flower grassland	3	Compact flail + sweeper	400.0	1200
Wild flower grassland	3	Amenity forage harvester	200.0	600
Large areas (>0.8 ha)				
Amenity med quality	16	5 unit gang	21.9	350
Amenity low quality	8	Compact flail	55.0	440
Wild flower grassland	3	Compact flail + sweeper	116.7	350
Wild flower grassland	3	Amenity forage harvester	100.0	300

Source: Ash *et al.* (1992).

Table 8.3 *Approximate maintenance costs of various landscape vegetation types*

Vegetation type	Typical annual maintenance in hours/100m^2		Cost of maintenance relative to lowest cost vegetation type	
	Small units	Large units	Small units	Large units
Gang mown general recreational turf (5 unit gang mower 24 cuts per annum)	0.24	0.14	2	1
Recreational turf and widely spaced trees (as above)	1.5	0.9	10.7	6.4
Rough grass (flail mown 4 times/year)	0.20	0.17	1.4	1.2
Intermediate mown turf on steep banks (rotary cut, 500 mm, 12 times/year)	8.0	5.0	57.1	35.7
Ground cover and shrub massing (mulched and hand weeded)	8.0	5.0	57.1	35.7
Annual bedding (2 plantings per year and weed control)	80	80	571.4	571.4

Notes: Figures reflect labour only and do not take into account the cost of equipment. Ground cover costs can of course vary depending on species and stage of establishment. Some established cover may require almost no annual maintenance. Information on how mowing costs change relative to slope is hard to come by for flail mown vegetation. The costs of flail mown vegetation may of course be greatly influenced by the costs of disposal of cuttings, if these are not to be allowed to lie.
Source: Hitchmough (1994b), adapted from Wright and Parker (1979).

that comparative costs are still of the same order of magnitude with traditional grass-mowing machinery. For some grasslands requiring mowing by smaller machinery, costs are still cheaper where regular cutting is carried out.

Similar cost relationships were suggested by Wright and Parker/Hitchmough (Table 8.3).

Of course these are general estimates, actual costs depend on a myriad of factors such as how far the machines need to travel between sites, the amount of work and the degree to which they are effectively employed through the year and so on. The most efficient harvesting machinery would be expensive to buy, or hire into inner city areas, if the area to be cut was comparatively limited.

The disposal costs of grass cuttings may be one of the most important factors for consideration in a costing exercise. Oland (1986) calculates that the costs of removal of grass clippings can exceed the actual cost of cutting several times, especially in isolated sites in urban areas where access to a suitable waste recycling site may be difficult. Long grass places greater strain on machinery, also leading to higher repair and replacement costs. Rain also increases the difficulty of grass cutting, and this effect is often much worse on long grass which can be prone to lodging and tangling; the effort involved in removing cut grass is also greatly magnified when the season has been wet, meaning that cost variations from year to year may be more significant in naturalistic areas.

Even where there are very clear reductions in direct costs from a shift to ecological management styles there may also need to be a shift in the type of labour force required. Instead of predictable schedules that detail the nature and frequency of inputs, complex plant communities more often need sensitive intervention that reflects the season and shifts in the species balances.

There is also the problem that budgets and staffing levels are often compartmentalized in a way which means that savings in one sphere may not be desirable if they mean cost increases in another area. Many superficially 'low-maintenance' landscapes in fact require higher inputs of new kinds, such as greater, if irregular, attention from more highly skilled staff in order to determine the best treatment to maintain complex plant communities. Management patterns may change, perhaps reducing underemployment of labour at some times of the year, but placing less value on routine and simple, predictable tasks and requiring more professional attention. Intermittent tasks may be less supported by mechanization and hence lead to the need to rely more heavily on manual labour when a task is required.

(Direct parallels exist with volunteer management. Volunteers often do not save money. They need supervision and support, often by more senior professional staff. They may be valuable if the budgets for manual labour are deficient and there is sufficient professional time, but otherwise they can prove costly. In Camley Street Nature Park in London, annual labour costs are arguably £0, since all work is carried out by volunteers. However, there is a recurrent cost of over £60 000 to fund permanent staff whose job it is to supervise the volunteers and to develop and maintain the level of public interest that provides the labour force in the first place. Of course in terms of 'value' this may be money well spent, with the community gaining much in terms of environmental awareness and stewardship capabilities, but this makes it all the more important that realistic and adequate funding levels are identified from the outset.)

As an example of the pitfalls, some German towns have learnt that Hansen-style ecological plantings are virtually impossible to maintain in public open spaces without fencing, regular supervision and specialist maintenance (Weigel, 1992). By their nature, such complex perennial plantings are reliant on qualitative management. Karl Foerster perhaps summed up the management style required when he entitled his book *Gardens for Intelligent Lazy People* in 1928 (van Groeningen, 1994). Actual costs available for the style seem to vary enormously depending on circumstance. In Berlin's Sudpark, herbaceous woodland areas proved to require almost no maintenance, while the open ground habitats became a very expensive feature (Meyer, 1992). Records at the trial gardens in Hermanshoff show that established species rich plantings require only 4 minutes per square metre per year (Walser, 1994).

Munich Parks Department has its own grounds maintenance team which looks after all their sites. Those employees with a higher level of knowledge and experience are left to make their own decisions, particularly as far as weeding and intervention go. At the other end of the scale, less skilled employees are given very simple tasks, such as removing all of a single species of weed.

The generalization probably cannot be sustained that landscapes can be maintained more cheaply if they are managed in an ecological way. However, it is still plausible that quality landscapes, landscapes which are not completely sterile or devoid of interest, can be managed cheaper.

As a parallel concept it has sometimes been argued that management costs and intensity can be related to the successional stage of the landscape, with the general trend that the closer a landscape is to its climax state the less effort that is required to maintain it (e.g. Figure 8.1). This too is a potentially misleading generalization which needs careful qualification. In particular issues of the timescale and timing of vegetation change need to be clarified.

For example, although the costs of woodland management may be generally low over its life compared to some other landscape features, a neglected over-mature woodland which approaches a stage where extensive felling or regenerative work is required can require extremely high levels of investment. Conversely on some early successional sites the rate of vegetation change can be rather slow and require very little in the way of maintenance for several years if not decades. Where the soil is infertile it may even be possible for grasslands to be maintained without cutting.

The timescale of the management assessment, and the nature of the plant community will of course have a great bearing. Short-term costs and labour requirements may be considerably higher, and will include expenditure on training and new machinery. Cost-effectiveness also reflects the degree to which the system created will be expected to survive in the envisaged form, rather than requiring regeneration. Initial planning and design to limit

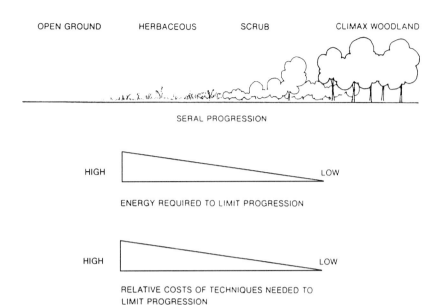

Figure 8.1 The assumed relationship between ecosystem successional stage and management inputs (Corder, 1986).

management and maintenance must therefore consider the relationship between capital costs in site preparation and establishment and recurrent costs for management and maintenance in analysing cost-effectiveness. A high initial cost may be recouped (or discounted) by low maintenance costs, and a minimum capital cost recovery time ('break-even' point) may be established.

Establishment costs for naturalistic landscapes may, but again need not be, cheaper than formal and ornamental designs. Emery (1986) argues that formal landscape approaches are likely to lead to higher costs in terms of site preparation, drainage, topography adjustment etc., compared to an ecological style that can utilize existing site diversity. However, where the site is inherently monotonous requiring high inputs for diversification, or where specific habitat types such as ponds are to be created, ecological designs can also have high capital costs (Tregay and Gustavsson, 1983).

The capital costs of the William Curtis Ecological Park when it was created in 1977 were £2000 for 0.8 ha, but this design built very much on the existing site structure. Where earthmoving and other major activities are required the costs can be much higher. Gillespie Park in London cost £350 000 for 1.6 ha in 1981/82 and Camley Street cost £150 K for 0.9 ha, also in the early 1980s (setting aside costs of site purchase and clearance) (Johnston, 1990). The latter figures reflect a highly complex design involving much landforming and also the disproportionate fencing costs associated with small, almost linear, areas of land.

There is one aspect of ecological landscape construction which **is** widely reported as leading to substantial cost savings, which is the scope to avoid topsoil purchase and spreading (Emery, 1986; Ruff, 1979; Tregay and

Gustavsson, 1983). Ruff (1979) emphasizes that the ratio between input and return may be favourable for ecologically managed landscapes. He also confirms that the treatment may still be high-cost, and that costs are likely to be influenced by the degree to which the prevailing situation can be exploited or needs to be modified. He argues that costs can be saved by:

- not levelling the surface area;
- not filling in ponds and ditches;
- not lowering the ground water level by drainage;
- not importing fertile topsoil;
- using little or no fertilizer;
- mowing less frequently;
- using less expensive planting material, with native as opposed to exotic species.

However, costs can be high where:

- the site has to be modified because currently it is inappropriate for the development of the type of system or level of diversity required;
- hand or mechanical weeding is required;
- small-scale operations are carried out by hand or machinery, such as woodland thinning.

Redistribution of work load may lead to some cost savings, for example by putting grass cutting out of the spring/early summer peak flushes. The labour demand of Camley Street Natural Park in London is higher in the winter than the summer.

Traditionally one of the greatest impediments to a change in landscape style by local authorities was the need to consider the limitations of the machinery fleet and also the skills profile of the workforce. New grassland management styles could only be introduced gradually, and with careful consideration of the impact on work patterns and training needs.

Arguably the changes brought about by Compulsory Competitive Tendering legislation have made it easier for local authorities to implement such management changes. The tenders for the revised contracts should only be attractive to those contractors able to supply the machinery and to ensure sufficient and suitably skilled supply of labour to meet the demands of the site. However, in practice it seems that CCT has acted as a constraint that has slowed landscape development (Swann, 1994).

Over the last few decades it has not been uncommon that a conflict has arisen between ecologists and horticultural maintenance staff, where the latter are accused of insensitive or incorrect management of wild areas. However, even where such criticism is justified the problems usually reflect a larger problem of the poor financial rewards and low standards of training for many casual workers in horticulture.

Horticulture is an industry that absorbs people from all walks of life. However, because of its relationship with gardening there are many people working who feel that they know what to do simply because they have had a garden and who make spontaneous decisions that are based at best on the eccentric priorities of gardening magazines rather than on sound management principles.

There has been a gradual deskilling of the workforce in amenity horticulture, yet the system is still geared up to the days when the workforce had skills and were trusted to make line management decisions. These decisions were expected to further the implicit goals of the organizations, but rarely were these goals ever stated. Traditionally almost no public urban landscapes in the UK had management plans or a stated objective for the workforce to aim at, and there were no clear management sanctions that could be applied. Local authorities did not really have clear ideas of what they planned to achieve with regard to open space; yet at the same time they were totally confident of their ability to achieve it. It was not surprising therefore that problems arose as land management objectives became more complex.

Contract management has had a profound impact on some of these issues. It represents a key procedure by which sanctions can be imposed and by which clear objectives and acceptable methods of work can be spelt out. Land managing authorities have been obliged to assess their land holding and to specify in detail what exactly their plans for the area are. Undirected, unconsidered or random maintenance should become a much less common problem.

On the other hand there is also evidence that CCT is contributing to a further decline in skills within the industry as training is cut back in an attempt to remain competitive (Swann, 1994).

For the advantages of the CCT system to be realized there is a very real challenge of translating ecological concepts and habitat management requirements into the prescriptive schedules normally required for contract management.

Cole (1986) observes that:

> cheap maintenance often equates with unskilled, easily programmed repetitive mechanised tasks, such as grass cutting, and not with infrequent but intensive tasks, such as hand scything or woodland thinning. In addition, aesthetic requirements, especially on small urban sites, may require constant intervention and management to maintain species diversity and the general attractiveness of the site.

Contract management can of course be approached in several different ways, and some methods provide for more flexibility than others. Probably the optimum solution is based on a schedule of rates, which can provide some leeway to modify the planned maintenance in the light of changing needs, or a performance based specification which sets targets for the goals to be achieved.

To maximize these opportunities ecologists need to consider the problems of defining complex management principles in ways that can be implemented under a contract management system. On a broader level other deficiencies in current contract arrangements may be highlighted, such as the difficulty in using contract staff as a focus for encouraging community participation, and also the problems of maintaining a sense of safety in parks which no longer have a permanent staff presence. These issues are addressed in more detail below.

Revenue opportunities from urban landscapes

To offset the costs of management inputs attention often turns to the scope for obtaining revenue from the urban landscape. Even where this is insufficient to cover the costs, revenue can still provide a useful addition to the budget, although there are far too often instances where any income generated is absorbed into coffers which are not accessible by the landscape manager.

There are several direct opportunities for income generation as a by-product of landscape maintenance but the main by-products of activity are usually grass, timber, prunings and other green wastes.

Hay from cutting long grass can sometimes be sold to local farmers, or it may even be of great financial advantage if a farmer can just be persuaded to collect the material at cost. However, this is not always possible, particularly where small quantities are involved and transport distances are great. Perhaps of greater concern is the possibility that urban grasslands may be so contaminated with airborne dusts, other pollutants and even physical contaminants that they are unsuitable for feed.

The pressure on local authorities to find a positive use for green wastes has increased dramatically since the government introduced targets for recycling. It is now common practice for prunings to be chipped and used as mulch even around long-established trees and shrubs. The ecological impacts of this activity are not entirely clear but are probably likely to be of benefit to woodland organisms, many of which appreciate a litter layer. However, there may be in some cases a risk of spread of woodland pathogens.

Composted green wastes and materials such as leaf litter can be disposed of to allotment holders or amateur gardeners as soil conditioning materials. In many countries where landfill taxes are high, composting can lead to substantial cost savings for the local authority even where no attempt is made to generate direct revenue by charging for the product. However, again problems can arise from contaminants which are sometimes found in the product. Small waste wood and chippings can also be used as a fuel, sold as firewood or sometimes used in specially adapted boilers.

Timber obtained from management of urban woodlands and street trees can also be a potentially attractive revenue source. The best example documented in the UK is certainly the Leeds City Council who have invested in machinery for timber processing (Oland, 1986). There are of course sometimes quality problems with urban timber, such as the presence of nails in the wood or more often poorly shaped and knotty timber that arises when trees are grown or managed for amenity or conservation rather than optimal timber production.

Although these initiatives are clearly desirable it is essential to recognize that these 'incomes' are of course just a means of reducing the financial scale of the management investment. They do not really help to justify the presence of greenspace in urban areas, as in most cases it would be cheaper not to have any vegetation at all.

Of far more importance are the many indirect financial benefits that can come from urban vegetation. For example, the degree to which tree screening and shelter can improve the energy balance in buildings leading to heating cost reductions deserves increasing attention. Similarly tree cover may help to reduce airborne pollution, leading to potential savings in health-care or building maintenance. There is also some evidence that there may be more subtle but no less significant health benefits arising from contact with nature in cities (Ulrich, 1984).

But by far the greatest financial return from urban landscapes probably arises from the influence on the desirability of living and working in the area. Clear relationships between environmental quality and property prices have often been demonstrated (Harris, 1992). Undoubtedly the greatest of such financial rewards can arise when large companies are attracted to invest in a region. Although it is difficult to quantify the contribution that a green landscape plays in such decisions, it is clear that many companies consider the need to offer employees somewhere pleasant to live when they are planning expansion or relocation. Indirect benefits can outweigh the direct returns by several orders of magnitude, and ultimately these form the real justification for investment in greenspace management by local authorities. The problem of course is that the financial returns are almost never recognized formally, making it possible for short-term political goals to lead to cutbacks in the landscape maintenance programme.

One of the greatest problems facing the manager therefore is how to balance the temptation to gain direct returns against the risk that these will decrease the indirect benefits. The production of timber from urban trees is a good example. Optimum revenue would be obtained by managing trees in a way which encourages a long, straight trunk with few branches whereas the best trees for landscape and conservation value may be of a very different form. Similarly timber production can be maximized by harvesting the timber when the trees are at their marketable prime, which can be many years before they reach their biological or aesthetic prime. Indeed there can be an almost direct relationship between increasing conservation interest, as trees begin to develop rots, hollows and burrs, and the decline of timber value.

Critical inputs and risk assessment

The view of agricultural, horticultural and silvicultural management as a series of critical inputs determining a crop yield is relevant to urban country-side management, although the diversity of amenity plantings, the problems in characterizing environmental constraints, and the difficulty of deter-mining aesthetic or social values precludes the accuracy of models associated with crop production. Although an ecological approach may aim to eliminate husbandry, critical inputs are usually required to achieve and retain design objectives but intelligent design and management can aim to minimize these.

Risk assessment requires accurate assessment of losses in amenity plantings. Losses are commonly absorbed into development and renovation budgets and are difficult to assess; nevertheless losses in supposedly low risk strategies may be high. Gilbertson (1987) reports that 9.7% of urban trees studied during a survey in the north of England were dead, and considers this a considerable underestimate as contractors are required to replace losses during the first year. The selection of trees for urban plantings generally reflects past successes (and failures) and results in a *de facto* selection for species with wide environmental tolerances. Nevertheless tree survival and growth on hostile sites depends on some basic husbandry during establishment, and losses reflect poor nursery stock and inadequate or inexpert maintenance during establishment. Most losses are attributable to stress, with 50% of stress a result of competition from grasses. Gilbertson (1987) distinguishes water deficit as the principal environmental stress, although nutrient deficiency may act secondarily by preventing the development of an adequate root system. Inadequate site preparation, resulting in planting in compacted soils, is responsible for around 5% of losses, and the remainder of losses are attributed to physical damage from vandalism or poor husbandry, such as the incorrect use of ties or guards.

Traditionally low-risk strategies are adopted for amenity plantings, through a reliance on species which are generally 'known to be reliable'. Low-risk plantings generally utilize competitors and stress-tolerant competitors for woody plantings and herbaceous plantings, and C-S-R strategists and competitive ruderals in herbaceous plantings (*sensu* Grime *et al.*, 1988) introduced as transplants, extensive site modification and a maintenance program to reduce stress and competition during establishment. Such a system can be refined by an improved understanding of the relationship between genotype, environment and husbandry. The use of competitors on productive sites and of stress tolerators on hostile sites, suggest straightforward refinements to planting. The potential for competitors to reduce costs as a result of rapid establishment, mechanization of maintenance and possible sale of produce requires consideration.

Comparison of the establishment of wildflower meadows from seed with the establishment of a fine grass sward from seed and subsequent diversification with transplants provides an opportunity to contrast a high-risk and low-risk approach. The reliance on wildflower seed is a high-risk, low-input system, whereas use of grass seed and wildflower transplants is a low-risk, high-input system. In the absence of critical management, establishment of wildflower meadows from seed may be erratic establishment. Although establishment from seed is cost-effective the requirement for critical inputs in site preparation and management is less flexible.

Another example is in the preference of local authorities for containerized nursery stock. The preference reflects the difficulty of efficiently handling other stock. Despite some evidence that with correct handling open-grown and bare-rooted plants are likely to be more successful in amenity sites the preference reflects the flexibility allowable in the handling of containerized plants. The preference may also be interpreted as an inability to deliver the critical inputs required for the use of open-grown and bare-rooted plants.

High-risk strategies are apparent where stress-tolerators or stress-tolerant competitors are introduced as seed. On productive sites risks from weed competition (or inter-specific competition) increase, while on unproductive sites risks from environmental stresses depressing recruitment and reducing ground cover are increased. Other high-risk strategies, such as the use of species with a poor establishment rate or marginal environmental fitness, are usually avoided in landscape design (although they are sometimes a source of delight in garden design).

Social objections to high-risk strategies involving establishment from seed may also be significant. The requirement for an instant landscape effect may interfere with establishment of amenity plantings from seed, although the use of a cover crop and initial fencing may be successful, as in direct tree seeding (e.g. La Dell, 1988).

If the use of competitive tendering is able to enforce critical inputs, it provides a possible route for increasing cost effectiveness by the adoption of high-risk strategies. Cost-effectiveness in amenity plantings, however, reflects a compromise between minimum or critical inputs and the desirability of a low-risk strategy. A low-risk strategy increases flexibility of management inputs and the reliability and predictability of the result. Definition of the risks involved in minimum-input–high-risk systems and in high-input-low-risk systems provides a possible route for an ecological approach to increase success in amenity plantings.

Hopkins (1989) presents another perception of risk assessment in differentiating a 'skill requirement' for different grassland creation strategies. The predictability, reliability and flexibility of a high-input system may enhance apparent cost effectiveness. Although establishment, management and maintenance techniques are available for high-risk strategies, the requirement for critical inputs during the establishment phase reduces flexibility in programming management and maintenance operations and may reduce apparent cost-effectiveness. The possibility of utilizing high-risk experimental plantings with local community involvement, as in the social landscapes in Holland (see Chapter 3), is attractive, although clearly difficult to program. The challenges, and also the advantages of community involvement are discussed in more detail late in this chapter.

Safety in the urban countryside

One way in which the latter part of the twentieth century is going to be characterized is by a phenomenal growth in urban fear and anxiety associated with the perceived risk of crime in urban areas. In many cases this anxiety is almost completely unfounded, residing most strongly in those sections of society that are least at risk, and focused on the wrong potential threats. We have lost the ability to judge accurately the degree of personal risk and to some extent the fear is self-fuelling. Women and older people are increasingly frightened of using some open spaces, which increases the sense of isolation and worry of those that do venture out. Parents are increasingly preventing children from playing outside, such that the health risks of increased inaction among the young is beginning to cause serious medical concern. Landscape managers are increasingly going to have to address this sense of fear when within their strategic planning.

One possible solution is to consider the degree to which safety perception can be influenced by design. Sangster (1995) discussed in detail the problem in relation to community woodlands. He suggests the following design approaches to reduce or alleviate the anxieties:

- **Sightlines** – ensure that paths have good longitudinal visibility, avoiding sharp bends.
- **Margins** – paths should have open space to either side. Where the vegetation comes up to a path it should be opened up to allow visibility through it. Open verges also are recommended for nature conservation.
- **Path widths** – they should be wide enough or have passing places so that people can pass comfortably.
- **Lighting** – in some circumstances this will be appropriate.
- **Thinning** – differentially thin woodland to provide low stem densities and good visibility into the crop close to paths and roads.
- **Undergrowth** – bushes and tall herbaceous vegetation are viewed with great suspicion by many townspeople. Mown verges and low vegetation are preferred.

However, in taking such an approach it is recognized that the result will be a taming of the experience which may not be welcomed by all users, and as such a choice of visiting more natural areas should also be provided (Sangster, 1995).

In trying to find solutions to this problem a valuable parallel can be drawn with work that has looked at the impact of environmental design on crime rates and risks in housing estates. The vast majority of modern estates incorporate the principles devised by Oscar Newman with regard to defensible space and clear and precise zoning of activity (Bird, 1996). In particular *cul de sac* designs are intended to prevent opportunities for strangers to enter within the local communities territory without being obvious. Surveillance opportunities are maximized, and urban layout is phased so that casual visiting of those spaces is not encouraged.

This approach has then often been built upon by police forces working on principles of target hardening, i.e. making it harder for the crime to happen. Sightlines are maximized. Bushes and places of concealment are removed or replaced with spiny or prickly species such as *Berberis*; barriers and locks are reinforced.

However more recently some limitations to this approach have been recognized. In many cases surveillance is not as effective as was originally anticipated, partly because the outside environment becomes too boring and devoid of action to bother looking at. Target hardening may increase security (the physical risk of a crime happening) but can raise perceptions of a lack of safety (try walking down a street at night where all windows and doors are shuttered and padlocked). By zoning, some estates become dominated by single age and social groups, such that in some areas there is almost no one around at certain periods of the day. Above all, by making the streets devoid of passing activity there is a whole spectrum of supporting surveillance and potential help that disappears, whereas genuine criminals are not so easily put off.

Drawing upon the ideas of another planner, Jane Jacobs, a new generation of principles are emerging based on the idea that active streets are safe streets. Strangers should not be regarded as a threat, but rather as a positive potential source of social support. The proponents of this approach argue for a return to traditional styles of urban design where complex, high-density towns are created that integrate various mixed activities. In part it is the richness of the environmental quality, the sense of vibrancy that comes from lots of activity, that is the key to this strategy (Bird, 1996).

The possible lessons for urban green areas are that design changes that maximize surveillance and minimize risk by removing opportunities may give a short-term improvement in perceived safety, but in the long term are likely to undermine use and lead to a worse situation than before. The most secure landscape may be a featureless, flat green desert, yet it is exactly such styles that are seen around some of the most difficult urban estates. Designers and managers need to hold to the conviction that what is needed is a rich and stimulating environment that encourages many people in, and by stimulating activity increases the sense of safety.

Another possible component to the solution may be to develop a team of ecological wardens with responsibilities for ensuring safety, monitoring and clarification of maintenance methodology and the development of education and interpretative programmes to encourage public use. There is clearly a cost, but the alternative will be that many urban spaces become abandoned, social malaise continues to mount, and environmental quality becomes increasingly threatened by safety lobbies.

One of the challenges with regard to urban nature areas is to find ways to accommodate many people without undermining the opportunity for privacy and sense of 'getting away' that many users want. However, with careful design and structuring of the environment it is possible to assimilate many people. Division of space into small, screened pockets may allow people to remain within shouting distance without them being constantly visible.

It has been found that habitat patterning is important (see also Chapter 5). Dense woodlands provide fewer benefits and a greater sense of unease. A ratio of one-third wooded area to two-thirds open has been suggested by Bussey and Coles (1995), but they argue also that it is probably important that the environment is structurally rich with variation in appearance and feel.

Habitat size is also of significance. Bussey and Coles also found that woodland sites of less than 2 ha, although perhaps superficially easier to escape from, were less likely to receive regular use. They argue that size is important since it influences the extent to which people feel that they have 'got away' from the urban experience.

The design solutions are therefore not all obvious, and still need refinement, but the key first step is to recognize that the solutions do not lie in sterilizing surroundings or removing all complexity.

Poisonous plants

Another aspect of safety in the landscape that is receiving increasing attention is that of contact with poisonous plants. It seems often the case that the perception many people have is that there are a few rogue species, such as *Laburnum*, that can be easily identified and eradicated from the landscape, allowing us to live safely evermore. The truth is of course very different. All plants contain complex cocktails of biochemicals that frequently include materials which are potentially harmful. Sometimes there seems no particular reason why a given chemical is harmful, it may just be unfortunate coincidence, but of course many species have had to evolve defence strategies that rely on the manufacture of toxins that discourage grazing for example.

Even those species which may have highly edible and desirable parts, such as fruit bearing shrubs and trees, may wish to exploit animal feeding as a seed dispersal agent and also wish to discourage uncontrolled browsing on other organs. Otherwise very benign plants may have some part of their structure which is potentially harmful. It is also necessary to take into account the seasonal production of chemicals or of harmful plant parts, such as potentially harmful pollen in bracken.

There are inevitably also complexities that arise when considering the criteria for the definition of poisonous. The degree of risk may have to be tempered against the volume of plant material that has to be ingested before there is any danger (Thoday, 1995). (The risk will of course also vary according to the body weight, age, health and physiology of the individual.)

Of course the problem is that almost any material, including many foodstuffs, will prove to be toxic if eaten in large enough quantities. The risk of death must be tempered by some assessment of the likelihood of the required quantity of the dangerous parts of any plants to be ingested. Unfortunately the fact to be borne in mind is that people sometimes do the most extraordinary things, for example a search through the literature may reveal that some people have died from ingesting kilograms of bluebell bulbs for example (Thoday, personal communication). Does this merit their inclusion on a list of hazardous species? Is the risk of people chewing through large quantities of leathery leaves enough to require that a plant is regarded as poisonous?

Beyond the question of lethal poisoning is the often less serious but probably even more complex problem of allergic reactions. People may develop allergies to contact with chemicals at extremely low doses, such that a very very low percentage presence of a plant in a landscape may be enough to cause problems.

There seems little possibility therefore that hazard can be removed from the landscape, particularly from complex plant communities containing many species that arrive by natural colonization, without extraordinary environmental degradation and impossibly high management costs. Scares have arisen and are likely to arise again, with naturalistic or wild plant communities being regarded as possibly dangerous repositories of risk and danger. The landscape manager needs to be aware of a balanced assessment of the true levels of risk under such circumstances.

The use of agrochemicals

The issue of the use of chemicals in urban landscapes is another aspect of management which invariably raises strong feelings. There are various positions on a spectrum of opinion, ranging from the argument that no chemicals should be used at all, through to the grudging acceptance of some chemicals and even, although this is becoming less common, outspoken support for all forms of chemical management. At all times the debate needs to recognize that urban and amenity use of pesticides has been almost totally discontinued in some European countries. There is clearly a possibility that such constraints may become embodied in European legislation.

Can 'safe' pesticides be identified?

Agrochemical availability for landscape management is controlled by the much larger and more lucrative forestry and agriculture markets. The development of alternative systems and techniques often also come from the agricultural industry, so in exploring the scope for more 'organic' forms of landscape management it seems reasonable to look at the approaches, both practical and philosophical, that characterize organic farming.

Many people's attitudes towards chemicals are often characterized by ambiguities, unproven assertions and even sometimes contradictions that many scientifically trained land managers find difficult to accept. For example, it is often the case that organic farmers will use some pesticides or other chemicals as long as these are of natural origin. Yet there are of course very many naturally occurring chemicals which are extremely toxic and which have a wide spectrum of activity, affecting many organisms as well as the target pest.

In contrast it is argued by supporters of artificial agrochemicals that huge research and development programmes are targeted towards the production of ever safer products which have highly specific action and rapid breakdown. Of course many chemicals have been withdrawn from the market as concerns have developed about their safety, but the manufacturers will still argue that this does not necessarily undermine their case that there is a gradual shift towards materials which are far more environmentally friendly, and indeed may have less harmful impacts than other forms of land management. While it is inevitably true that pesticides harm some wildlife – that is their very function in life, after all – alternative forms of maintenance, such as digging, will also harm some species. All forms of vegetation management are in essence based on decisions that some species will be favoured, and others will be destroyed or, to use the more common euphemism, 'discouraged'.

The organic philosophy is however based on a precautionary principle that argues that it is ultimately impossible to prove that any agrochemical is safe, and that confidence can only be placed in materials of natural origin which are therefore unlikely to prove to be excessively persistent or harmful in the biosphere. Organic attitudes are therefore based on an ideology which has its own logic, but the very essence of the precautionary principle is that it avoids any suggestion that the risk needs to be 'proven'. As with many environmental issues it can be argued that it is undesirable to wait for the time when evidence of widespread damage becomes apparent.

Since amenity landscape management is a subject which is concerned very often with people's preferences and attitudes to the natural world perhaps it is only right and proper that the manager carries out work in accordance with those attitudes. However, the landscape manager is also often in the position where low-density weed content, which would be of little or no significance to the growth rates of the desired species, are aesthetically disruptive and unacceptable to the public. A difficult challenge can therefore result which requires the evaluation of the weight of different opinions from different social groups.

Perhaps most important of all is the issue of how much pest control can be achieved with and without chemicals. With the possible exception of high-profile sports areas and some prestigious horticultural landscapes, fungicides and insecticides tend to be used on a reactive basis and are rarely fundamental to the maintenance of amenity landscapes. Herbicides however are used on a more routine basis because they have the potential to lead to direct cost savings.

Moffatt (1986) argues that herbicides are an essential management tool for conservation. For example, when establishing new woodlands herbicide use could keep ground clean for a fraction of costs of using manual techniques and even for a fraction of the costs of mulch where the latter has to be bought in from off-site. Obviously this means that a much greater area of new woodland can be created within the constraints of a budget. In the UK there is a clear contrast between many professional conservation agencies that have adopted herbicide use and the attitudes of public membership environmental groups that deplore the idea of these chemicals. Frequently the professionals avoid conflict simply by not publicizing the extent to which the chemicals are used.

There are many other situations internationally where herbicides are recognized as an irreplaceable tool for conservation management, such as when trying to control alien weed invasion in Australian bushlands (Hitchmough, 1994b). Hitchmough identifies certain potential roles for herbicide use in habitat management that merit more research: the use of weed-wiping technology with systemic herbicides to selectively remove dominant and invading species from grassland; the use of contact herbicides to mimic fire effects; the use of herbicides in woodlands to create regeneration gaps for seedling trees; the use of low rates of herbicides to stress and reduce selectively the vigour of some ecosystem components.

The current compromise that is being reached in many local authorities is to try to target pesticide use in a way which minimizes the risk of environmental harm. We have therefore seen the rise of 'green chemicals' of which the best example must be glyphosate, being a material which is believed to have a low mammalian toxicity and very rapid breakdown. It does, however, have a broad spectrum of activity on plants and may be harmful to some animal groups. The least acceptable herbicides for many people are those which have high persistence and broad spectrum activity, such as those which may be used to treat hard surfaces and land around established trees and shrubs to slow seedling development.

When deciding upon safe materials there is a need to take account of difficulties of using chemicals in an urban landscape. Ensuring even application can be difficult in a situation where the topography is complex, the plant spacing variable and the species and varieties diverse in both their growth habitats and tolerance of different chemicals. Despite great improvements in training for pesticide application there are still cases where the operator inevitably does not have as much concern for the plants as a farmer would have for his crop. Finally, there are often soil aspects which limit the degree to which the pesticide activity can be predicted. For example shallow soils, coarse soils with low organic matter and location exchange capacity, or poorly drained soils where rooting is superficial, may influence herbicide retention in the soil, or may lead to increased or decreased plant susceptibility.

Strategies for safe and effective herbicide use increasingly involve limiting their application to situations where they are used to solve a particular, localized and hopefully temporary problem, such as to aid the establishment of new transplants. Establishment stages of course often require management inputs of a type and frequency which are very different from the later stages of maintenance of the site. In these situations safe technology should be favoured such as low-volume, pre-formulated 'no-mix' sprayers.

New techniques and machinery for non-chemical approaches to weed control should of course be favoured wherever these are not excessively costly or inefficient. There should also be a focus on re-education of the public to tolerate landscapes with higher levels of weed presence. At times there may also be an argument for re-educating the professionals who may impose their own value judgements to classify some plants as weeds when the public may have no such concerns (cf. exotic species among a native plant community).

However, there is certainly nothing to be gained by failing to recognize those situations where mechanical or alternative weed control methods are likely to be ineffective. The clearest examples are those persistent perennial weed species which regenerate easily from underground roots or other storage organs. Not only is it often impossible to eradicate these by sporadic cultivation or cutting, but cultivation may actually increase their population numbers dramatically. Of course frequent and persistent manual control methods will eventually eradicate even these plants from the landscape, but practice almost invariably shows that these extraordinarily high levels of inputs can not be sustained in public landscapes.

Translocated herbicides such as glyphosate, if applied at the right time and with sufficient coverage of foliage, have allowed almost complete control of some previously highly troublesome weed species. In the case of perennial grasses such as *Agropyron*, grass-selective herbicides are able to achieve excellent control among dense communities of other plants that would inevitably be harmed by any other control measure.

Prioritizing weed problems

It may be impossible to avoid chemical-based weed control in some circumstances, for example when it is important to maintain biodiversity in rural sites threatened by invasive species. However, in many urban situations, and especially in man-made communities, there may be a strong argument for modifying the site objectives or content, such as establishing plant communities which are more tolerant of weed content, or to find ways to tolerate the weed presence such as public re-education.

This may just require the simple acceptance of changes which in more sensitive situations would have been regarded as undesirable, such as the colonization of existing woodland by sycamore, *Acer pseudoplatanus*. In such circumstances the manager is faced with two alternatives. Young seedlings can be controlled by cutting or pulling, but once past about three years old they will be too extensively rooted for easily pulling and will begin to develop the capacity to regenerate strongly from the cut base. Eradication may then require cutting back linked to herbicide treatment of

29 Avoiding the use of topsoil can help to reduce weed problems. Frequently soil storage methods lead to an explosion in the population numbers of 'disturbance' weeds.

the re-growth. The alternative option is to live with the change in the community and regard a mixed sycamore community as the likely climax of many urban woodland sites.

Careful design, and in particular attention to environmental factors, may also help to control weed invasion. The likelihood of weed invasion is probably reduced on sites where soil conditions are extreme, which will create conditions outside of the ecological niche of the competitive species. Weed invasion may also be more likely when certain habitat types are adjacent. For example, Londo (1977) recommends that arable land systems should not be established directly adjacent to grassland.

However, there are inevitably cases where weeds have become established. This problem may be particularly severe in urban areas even in habitat types which are normally trouble-free, reflecting the level of disturbance and the high inoculation pressure from invasive species. In such cases it may still be worth distinguishing the reasons why a particular species is classified as a weed in the first place and distinguishing between:

- weeds which are clearly biologically damaging to desirable plants or animals through competition;
- weeds which are potentially harmful to humans, especially through toxins;
- weeds which are unacceptable on aesthetic grounds;
- weeds which are unacceptable on ideological grounds (such as non-natives).

As an aid to developing a management strategy for the site, the weed flora of an area may need to be classified into categories related to its functional behaviour. The most important sub-divisions relate to colonizing behaviour, and to population build up:

COLONIZING BEHAVIOUR

- Weeds favoured by disturbance or characteristic of establishment phases which may be competitive with desirable plants in the short term.
- Weeds favoured by disturbance or characteristic of establishment phases which, once established, may persist and become a long term member of the plant community.
- Weeds capable of colonizing mature or undisturbed sites.

POPULATION BUILD-UP

- Weeds which persist as a member of a community but are rarely totally dominant.
- Weeds which are typically capable of developing dominance within the plant community.
- Weeds which may persist as a subordinate member of a community unless favoured by certain environmental circumstances (such as a cessation of mowing or grazing).

Depending on which of the above is the motivating concern, very different populations of the weed in question may be tolerated, and where control is not possible very different outcomes may be expected. In the first case an adjustment in ideological or aesthetic criteria may resolve the problem. In the last case the system can be expected to undergo fundamental changes in composition which may or may not be acceptable.

Community participation in urban land management

The picture has already been clearly painted of the way in which urban nature conservation is more about process than it is about product – the actual concrete manifestation of species and habitats usually means less than the opportunity and need to work with ecological processes. In terms of the role of urban nature conservation strategies within wider biodiversity programmes, the obvious priority is to find ways in which people can experience richer lives and also develop greater environmental concern through contact with nature. The importance to nature of improved levels of public participation and concern have been discussed in Chapter 4. The potential value and importance to people of greater contact with nature in cities will be discussed in more detail in Chapter 9. This section addresses the strategic challenges to the professional landscape manager who needs to determine how to incorporate and balance community participation programmes within the work schedule.

While the use of volunteers and systems of encouraging participation are well established in rural conservation areas, and indeed the management inputs by volunteers is critical to fill a labour gap, the tradition and the need is less well established in urban green space (Bradley, 1986). The use of community workers may therefore be viewed with suspicion rather than in a spirit of partnership, and people who wish to play an active role have sometimes had to campaign for the opportunity.

Johnston (1990) reviews the potential advantages to managing organizations of encouraging community participation in the development of nature areas in cities (Table 8.4).

Table 8.4 *Benefits to providers from community involvement*

- Achievement of appropriate design – by consulting people there is a much greater chance of arriving at a design solution which is suited to local circumstances.

- Improved long-term maintenance – people who have volunteered to help establish a nature reserve are usually very keen to see that it succeeds.

- Early warning of problems and conflict – if consulted, people will usually say what they like and don't like.

- Reduced cost in the long term – if local people are keen to help with maintenance, educational materials, wardening and so on this can reduce costs.

- Kudos – a nature area that is well designed and maintained, and in constant use for a variety of activities, will reflect well on the organization responsible for providing it.

- Reduced vandalism – the community tends to protect places which they feel belong to them.

However, these issues are focused on the benefits to the professionals; arguably of far greater significance is the value to the community itself. Encouraging participation can help to ensure that far greater richness and value is obtained from the green space which does exist. At the same time it can lead to spin-off benefits in both social function and environmental awareness that is increasingly high on the political agenda following the development of local Agenda 21 programmes.

The particular educational focus of participative approaches in urban land management are:

- to produce an urban community that is better informed of how habitats work and has a deeper understanding of environmental issues;
- to develop a more positive attitude towards nature and support for the work of conservation agencies;
- to demonstrate to individuals the opportunity for positive change, and to develop an awareness of how effective action can be taken at a local level.

It is vital to appreciate that from the viewpoint of the local authority or other government agencies, community action is to be encouraged because of the long-term benefits it brings, not because it is a cheap or more 'vandal-proof' approach to landscaping.

Following the Rio Conference in 1992 the development of Local Agenda 21 programmes has formalized the commitment that local authorities have for encouraging community work. However, in many cases, they have not completely anticipated the resulting resource implications. Where communities have been encouraged to take action for environmental improvement they often, and not unreasonably, turn to these encouragers for help. If such help can not be produced then the resulting disappointment can undermine the whole relationship.

There are two main means by which people should be able to benefit from participation in the creation and management of their environment.

1. CREATE AN ENVIRONMENT THAT FULFILS THE NEED OF THE USER

As Wates and Knevitt (1987) state:

> The key is to get the process of development right; to ensure that the right decisions are made at the right time . . . And the main lesson to emerge from the pioneering projects is that the environment works better if the people who live, work and play in it are actively involved in its creation and management.

To create and manage the built environment successfully demands an intricate knowledge and understanding both of how its physical components relate together and of how the end result will relate to the specific people who inhabit them. Every part of the environment is essentially unique and specific to location (Wates and Knevitt, 1987). The landscape professional can gain a valuable insight of how a place functions by conducting surveys and simply observing. But based on this alone, perception is bound to be limited. It takes years to understand the qualities of a particular environment and what makes it tick:

> Behind unassuming front doors lie years of intimate experience of what makes a neighbourhood work and what doesn't, and where the council might just be going wrong (Nicholas Hinton, Director of the National Council for Voluntary Organisations).

Further, the community knows most about the site's history and how it fits in with other spaces in the area, and how it is likely to be used in the future (Millward, 1987). In short, the participation of 'users' is essential to gain the necessary knowledge to ensure that any environmental improvements carried out will address their needs, and will attain the intended objectives in the most efficient way (Wates and Knevitt, 1987).

2. CREATE A STRONG, PARTICIPATING COMMUNITY

The second reason for participation is the positive effect it has on the participants themselves and on the strength and vitality of society. Creating one's own environment makes one more confident and self-fulfilled. Community projects draw people together in participation, which improves people's ability to work together and strengthens the community. Involvement leads to understanding, which in turn leads to the ability to act, both individually and collectively.

The most obvious effect is that people take a pride in their surroundings. Environments are cared for and looked after, and respond to people's needs and aspirations. Less obvious is the faster diffusion of landscape-making skills into our largely incompetent population, and a faster spread of awareness of what the landscape profession has to offer to society (Spray, 1994). 'The underlying premise is that visible signs of change lift the spirits of an otherwise depressed people, raise their horizons, and begin the process of instilling the confidence from which self-help and community development can flow' (Young, 1990).

In parallel with increasing specialization and bureaucracy, we have witnessed the deskilling of consumers in environmental matters. Lack of involvement has led to a lack of knowledge and understanding. With the public perceiving environmental issues more and more as the role of the professional, more barriers have been presented to the 'layman'. In addition to this, the environmental movement has traditionally been dominated by the rural and wildlife conservationists, not by people who believe the environment starts at home. This has led to a lack of grassroots input in urban areas which serves to exclude those living in these environments.

The result is a vicious circle of environmental paralysis:

> People are not in a position to solve their own problems because they lack the knowledge and skills and because the whole system is geared to intervention only by experts. Experts cannot solve the problems

because they have been divorced from the people they are meant to serve (Wates and Knevitt, 1987).

However, recent trends in planning suggest the emergence of a new spirit of urbanism which seems to reinstate civic life and an urban realm in cities (Cregan 1990), and to discard the anti-urban tradition. The 'city green' movement, from which community landscape owes much of its pedigree, is in essence pro-city. It starts from the place and the people **that exist**.

There is no definite blueprint. The greening movement is perceived as an instrument for economic regeneration, to encourage people to come back. Local greening initiatives are perceived as vehicles to 'reactivate communities that economic and environmental pressures have shattered into the fragmented, individual alienations and insecurities that make people most vulnerable to poverty' (Higgins, 1986).

The principles of community involvement

The problems in the built environment and the means used to achieve socially desirable and environmentally effective results by the local community are extremely varied. However, three principles have emerged which when applied together, help make human environments more successful.

- People willingly take responsibility for their environment and participate both individually and collectively in its creation and management.
- A creative working partnership is established with specialists from one or more disciplines.
- All aspects of people's environmental needs are considered simultaneously and on a continuing evolutionary basis (Wates and Knevitt, 1987).

The urban environment is extremely complicated. In some instances spaces may be almost identical, yet individuals use spaces differently and this use changes according to their needs and lifestyle. Needs differ according to a multitude of variables including age, social class, cultural background, past experience motives, and the daily routine of the individual. Despite these complications, it is possible to suggest certain broad categories of inner needs defined on the basis of observed behaviour, empirical evidence and social analysis (Laurie, 1986).

MOTIVATIONAL FORCES AND PSYCHOLOGICAL NEEDS

Social needs

These include the need of the individual for social interaction, for group affiliation, for companionship, and for love. The family group and the peer group are obvious manifestations of these needs.

The creation of green space can engender communality, i.e. this is created when 'representatives' of a community meet for the purpose of pursuing new interests and goals, establishing unfamiliar patterns of exchange and sharing.

Table 8.5 *What makes community landscape different*

	Conventional landscape architecture	*Community landscape architecture*
Status of user	Users are passive recipients of an environment conceived, executed, managed and evaluated by others: corporate public or private sector landowners and developers with professional 'experts'	Users are – or are treated as – the clients. They are offered (or take) control of commissioning, designing, developing, managing and evaluating their environment, and are often physically involved in construction
User/expert relationship	Remote, arm's length. Little if any direct contact. Experts – commissioned by landowners and developers – occasionally make superficial attempts to define and consult end-users, but their attitudes are mostly paternalistic and patronizing	Creative alliance and working partnership. Experts are commissioned by, and are accountable to, users, or behave as if they are
Expert's role	Provider, neutral bureaucrat, elitist, 'one of them', manipulator of people to fit the system, a professional in the institutional sense. Remote and inaccessible	Enabler, facilitator and 'social entrepreneur', educator, 'one of us', manipulator of the system to fit the people and challenger of the status quo; a professional as a competent and efficient adviser. Locally based and accessible
Scale of project	Generally large and often cumbersome. Determined by pattern of land ownership and the need for efficient mass production and simple management	Generally small, responsive and determined by the nature of the project and the participants. Large sites generally broken down into manageable packages
Location of project	Fashionable and wealthy existing residential, commercial and industrial areas preferred. Otherwise a green-field site with infrastructure	Anywhere, but most likely to be urban, or periphery of urban areas; area of single or multiple depravation; derelict or decaying environment
Use of project	Likely to be a single function	Likely to be multi-functional
Design style	Self-conscious about style	Un-selfconscious about style. Any 'style' may be adopted as appropriate. Most likely to be 'contextual', 'regional' (place-specific) with concern for identity. Loose and sometimes exuberant; often highly decorative, using local artists
Technology/ resources	Mass production, capital intensive	Tendency towards: small-scale production, on-site construction, individuality, local supply of materials, re-use of materials, labour and time intensive
End product	Static, slowly deteriorates, hard to manage and maintain, high-energy consumption	Flexible, slowly improving, easy to manage and maintain
Primary motivation	Private sector: return on investment and narrow self-interest. Public sector: social welfare. Experts: esteem from professional peers. Response to general social needs and opportunities	Improvement of quality of life for individuals and communities. Better use of local resources. Social investment. Response to specific localized needs and opportunities
Method of operation	Top-down, emphasis on product rather than process, bureaucratic, compartmentalized, impersonal, paper management, secretive	Bottom-up, emphasis on process rather than product, flexible, localized, holistic and multi-disciplinary, evolutionary, continuous, personal, people management, open
Ideology	Big is beautiful, competition, survival of the fittest	Pragmatic, humanitarian, responsive and flexible, small is beautiful, collaboration, mutual aid

Source: from Wates and Knevitt (1987).

Any system of living should also respect the individual's need for privacy and freedom. We cannot design for community/privacy as such, but we can assist by creating contexts in which the needs for these feelings are satisfied.

Stabilizing needs

We have a need to be free from fear, anxiety and danger. We have a need for clear orientation, a need to develop and to hold a clear philosophy of life, a need to organize the environment, to have a say in its form and content.

The concept of advocacy planning (self-help and self-determination) is to an extent related to this desire for stability through participation in decisions concerning one's own local environment. Self-help projects give rise to a form of design that satisfies this human need for stability.

Individual needs

The need for privacy in the residential environment has been mentioned above. Further, there is a strong need for a certain amount of self-determination, for an identity and sense of personal uniqueness in the environment, and related to this is a need to be able to choose or make individual decisions about one's life.

Self-expression

Needs which constitute self-expression include the need for self-assertion and exhibition, for dominance and power (Laurie, 1986). Most people also have the need for accomplishment and achievement, to be held in esteem by others. This is the need for status, which manifests itself in the environment as the concept of territory (Ardrey, 1967).

Enrichment

People have thirst for knowledge. Related to this is a need for self-realization and personal creativity, plus a need for beauty.

User participation in the environment

> Environmental experts, just like doctors in the health service, have a vital role, but cannot exercise it effectively unless the patient willingly takes responsibility and participates (Wates and Knevitt, 1987).

Community participation works at various levels, likened by the American sociologist, Sherry Arnstein, to a ladder with eight rungs (Figure 8.2). It is only at the top two or three rungs of the ladder, where some form of commitment exists, that the real benefits come about. When residents are given the major decisions and are free to make their own contribution to the design of the residential environment, both the process and the environment produced stimulate individual and social well being.

The higher up the ladder one gets, the more power is given to the user and the more fruitful the outcome is likely to be. Furthermore, the process of emotional engagement to one's environment leads to the impetus for the care of that environment.

Figure 8.2 The ladder of community participation.

Citizen control
Delegated power
Partnership
Placation
Consultation
Informing
Therapy
Manipulation

Enabling – the new professional services

While community groups have been gearing themselves up to take on the role of developers, environmental professionals have been exploring ways of helping them. One element common to all successful schemes is the presence of an 'enabler', an individual who not only has the perception and enthusiasm to see the potential of the project, but is someone who is able to communicate a vision which gives meaning to the work of others, a 'leader' being thought of as inseparable from the group – as the linking-pin in the middle of a wheel.

Community participation takes time, and is not necessarily a cheap option. The work is time-consuming and it is tempting for the professional to do the task in half the time, but the group will only gain confidence by realizing they can do it themselves. Scale fees, under pressure from competitive tendering, do not recognize the amount of time required in establishing a project.

In discussion with various professionals involved in community participation, the following roles have been identified: executive, planner, 'expert', arbitrator, exemplar, representative of the group, scapegoat, counsellor, friend and teacher.

The landscape professional may have to carry out several roles in the same situation. The expectations of each role may be quite clear and the expectations compatible for each role, but the roles themselves may be in conflict. Many local authorities now see the benefits of working through voluntary sector agencies, for the statutory functions of a local authority and its role in collecting local taxes can get in the way of securing voluntary participation in council schemes.

Most people can handle some form of role conflict, i.e. a collection of roles that do not precisely fit. There comes a time, however, when the number of roles that one person has to handle becomes just too much. He or she then experiences role overload. Several interviewees expressed a relief to get back to the relative quietness of the office. Role ambiguity, conflict and overload can all lead to stress.

The local authority as facilitator

Instead of the local authority acting as 'gate-keeper' or supplier, professionals can become 'facilitators' who help things happen rather than
stopping them by:

- 'cutting red-tape';
- adopting a policy of encouraging the voluntary provision of suitable
  temporary uses;
- adopting a procedure for land in their ownership; whereby licences are
  granted speedily for the interim use of sites, so that each proposal doesn't
  have to be dealt with as a 'one-off' case;
- completing surveys of dormant land; they could suggest suitable sites to
  tackle;
- providing skips, equipment and technical advice;
- naming an officer for dealing with requests from voluntary groups;
- giving small grants for practical schemes;
- establishing partnerships involving the public sector, with developers and
  private institutions, working closely with the voluntary sector (Cantell,
  1977).

An enabler has to provide professional expertise to the community group
as well as acting as a link and interpreter between them and other professionals. However, there is also often a role for inspiration, requiring that
opportunities and new visions can be conveyed to the public who may previously have had a limited idea of the full range of possibilities.

This role transcends the traditional role of providing meticulous drawings,
thick reports and schedules that result in schemes being supplied for the
local community. Instead, it involves 'facilitating' residents groups;
organizing meetings and contacts for people unused to doing so, and using
back-of-envelope sketches and language free of jargon to help people think
through and develop their own ideas for their own places (Spray, 1994).

The incorporation of environmental education objectives into the brief of
projects is invaluable. Agenda 21 recognizes that environmental education is
critical for the promotion of sustainable development and urban greening
projects at the local level provides a means for this. But, the greatest benefit
urban greening projects offer, is the faster diffusion of environmental
stewardship skills into the population (Spray, 1994) and hopefully greater
environmental awareness that manifests as political and personal support for
global biodiversity protection initiatives.

Ensuring effective participation

A denial of participation to an individual can carry its costs. However, this
does not imply that the opposite is always true, i.e. that 'participation is
good'. The general criteria for the use of participation methods, extracted
from various case studies and literature (Croft and Beresford, 1988; Hodge,
1995; Johnston, 1990) are as follows.

- There must be understanding of people's need for a feeling of relatedness to others and to the life of the community.
- It is necessary to be proactive in order to build positive links with local people. A long-term outlook should be linked with patience, persistence and commitment.
- It is necessary to avoid a preoccupation with esoteric or obscure issues of significance to professionals.
- The invitation to participate must be genuine. Any feeling by the community that participation is but a token gesture for democracy when the decision has already been taken will produce a 'compliance' response. In other words the individual is doing what he is doing because he has to do it. The onus for seeing that the community does what it is supposed to do remains with the initiator of the scheme.
- There should be small, but attainable goals for change.
- Provide well-focused, relevant and low level initiatives rather than formal and high-profile initiatives which attract unbalanced responses. Foster a down to earth local image with which local people can identify.
- The 'problem' must be worth the time and effort in the eyes of all concerned. Participation takes time and energies. If the task is trivial, or foreclosed, and everyone realizes it, participative methods will boomerang. Issues that do not affect the individuals concerned will not, on the whole, engage their interest.
- There must be attractive benefits to the community from the project and particularly to individual members of the community.
- The 'contract' must be clear. If the group is asked for a decision then that decision must be accepted. If advice is required then this should be stated. There should be no decisions made 'behind closed doors'.
- Conditions of responsibility in return for the benefits should be worked out by the community themselves wherever possible.
- Ideally, the individuals concerned must have the skills and the information to enable them to participate effectively. It may be necessary to develop these skills further. However, one must be careful not to erect an 'educational barrier' to involvement, i.e. people must not hold back, because they feel they must be 'educated' to make a worthy contribution.
- The 'manager', whether national government, local authority or landlord, must want participation and not indulge in it because of a sense of obligation. The manager must be prepared to give up some responsibility and give advice and guidance without dominating.
- People should be involved from the earliest possible stages in the project.
- Involvement should progress to ownership of the project by the community.
- The manager should listen carefully to people's own concerns, wants and needs.
- The resource implications of increased community involvement must be recognized and addressed with commitment.
- Opportunities for involvement should be easy to identify and without unnecessary barriers or bias.
- Opportunities for social benefits should be maximized, for example having fun.

Finding a suitable 'entry point' to participation

Not all groups want to participate in each and every stage. It should also be remembered that volunteers generally prefer to implement than to maintain. It can be argued that after a working day, certain members of the community are not willing to do yet more hard work, unless there is an element of fun involved. However, the professional mustn't simply do a job which the community was unwilling or seemingly unable to do. If the dialogue isn't to lapse into a one-way consultation process, the landscape professional needs to elicit an input from the group.

The professional should recognize what the local community can achieve, and advise the group accordingly. At whatever stage the community is involved, people need to learn how land-use decisions are made, what potential a site has in terms of design, and what skills they already possess that would be of use to the project.

Community involvement in landscape management does require supervision, otherwise enthusiasm dwindles. People need to be instructed and directed, particularly when performing tasks they are unaccustomed to, for then they know how to 'do the job properly'. This also saves time and effort for everyone concerned; it is vital not to appear as to be wasting their time.

The threshold of participation

Obtaining a truly representative view of the demands and wishes of a group is difficult, since people have various thresholds of participation, i.e. some are more able to speak up than others, and the larger the group, the larger the problem.

Indifference often prevails until a threat to a site occurs which identifies a 'common enemy'; i.e. the task of saving the site from development becomes sufficiently salient and clear to all members of the community, that people sink any potential differences and come together for the collective purpose. However, it is a pity that we have to rely on outside events to produce this change in peoples' perception of the collective purpose. This is often seen at the level of aftercare. It is not hard to initiate interest in environmental improvement, but the difficulty lies in sustaining that interest. Various strategies have been employed, namely: the rules-and-rewards strategy; the controlled access strategy; and the key-person strategy (Bradley, 1986). The latter approach recognizes that an important aspect of group dynamics is the identification of a 'key person' who will be prepared to invest exceptional amounts of time and energy to ensuring that things happen and that people are motivated. Employees of environmental groups and local-authority 'enablers' are often unable to proportion equal effort into one of many sites that they have a brief for, but sometimes the right person can be identified and given the specific task of being the motivator and organizer for community projects (Bradley, 1986).

Involvement is also very much a function of the level of funding: 'once funding dries up, then enthusiasm for community involvement dries up as well' (Cooper, personal communication). This can present the local authority with financial difficulties after being expected to take projects on to mainstream funding. The more active an authority has been, the more difficult are these 'time-expiry' difficulties which they now face. Many organizations have found that community projects that they have inspired remain as a long term commitment requiring resources and time (Bradley, 1986).

Working in groups

Groups fit well with democratic culture, with representative systems of government. Participation and involvement go well with assumptions of man as an independent individual. Groups there must be. But, individuals need to be co-ordinated and their skills and abilities meshed and merged.

The problem is this: if groups or committees are constructed for an inappropriate task, or with impossible constraints; if they are badly led or have ineffective procedures; if they have the 'wrong' people, too many people, too little power or meet too infrequently; frustration will set in and dissonance will be created.

Conclusions

One important concept is that we shouldn't expect too much from community groups.

> If a project fails because the group wasn't strong enough, or if a once successful community landscape falls into neglect for a period, that should not necessarily be seen as a bad thing. The process perhaps matters more than the end product, and it has to be that way, if we want to promote active caring by local people of their local places (Millward, 1987).

Some view community involvement in a greening project as a means of preventing vandalism completely. This is an over-simplified view of the situation. Participants respect the site more, but that doesn't stop others from nearby areas from doing damage. Often the best strategy to employ is to immediately undo the damage done to restore the public image of the site, for if it is left, people's respect for the site starts to decline, further perpetuating the problem.

Not all stages in the creation and management cycle of the landscape may be suitable for participation or community work. The professional teams must be prepared to provide support through critical inputs, some of which have to be very flexible and ready to come into operation whenever necessary. If this after-care is not provided it reflects badly upon the organizations involved.

Just as we hope that the act of planting a tree or a bulb may be a momentous one for those involved (especially children) equally momentous may be the disillusionment later should the tree fail due to weed competition, the wildflower meadow be overtaken by nettles and docks, or the neat lawn become rank and overgrown (Bradley, 1986).

The challenge is to ensure these inputs, without undermining the communities' ownership and commitment to the project.

Lessons learnt from many projects are summarized below, and together they present a manifesto for the further development of community landscape.

VOLUNTARY SECTOR

- Voluntary organizations should willingly accept more responsibility for the creation and management of the environment.
- Community organizations should have access to sufficient funds to employ the varied expertise they need to implement environmental projects.

GOVERNMENT

- Central and local government should learn to trust community organizations and should actively assist them in their formation and development.
- Government should help fund the services offered by community technical aid centres, and link funding with a long-term commitment to urban greening. Why not offer a simplified grant scheme for urban greening, as part of the Agenda 21 initiative?
- Accountability procedures for the receipt of public funds should be defined to encourage community initiatives and provide voluntary organizations with consistent, long-term funding, to facilitate forward planning.
- Urban greening projects should form part of a package of environmental improvements on a broader scale.
- Land ownership should be public information. Further, land in public ownership should be sold or leased to those wishing to develop it for the most sociably desirable ends.

ENVIRONMENTAL PROFESSIONS

- All landscape projects should have simple maintenance manuals.
- The construction process should be demystified, wherever possible using methods and materials which are easily understood and usable by lay members of the community, and construction methods which are labour- rather than capital-intensive and flexible for future adaptation.
- Recommended professional fee scales should be adjusted to take account of the extra time needed to involve users.
- The education of landscape professionals should include the first hand experience of the landscape and the people who use it.

- Information systems should be established to make data about successful examples of community landscape widely available.
- Programmes should be established to encourage more exchange of experience between the various groups involved in the process – public, private, professional and voluntary.
- Environmental education programmes for the public should be expanded so that people learn how the urban environment works and how they can take part in improving it.
- Methods should be devised for exchanging information internationally so that relevant lessons may be learned and action implemented in the shortest possible space of time.

9 Nature for people

C.L.E. ROHDE and A.D. KENDLE

Psychological value of nature for people in urban areas

In the UK challenges to landscape managers' budgets are becoming difficult to defend as it is a time when many open spaces seem to have lost their purpose and are under-utilized. Landscape managers increasingly need to have sound information on the benefits of urban landscapes and nature for society, and on the preference for different landscape styles that people show.

Public parks were created in the nineteenth century in British cities by visionaries who were not interested so much in the aesthetic sensibilities of the urban poor, but rather had a strong belief in the possible health advantages (both physical and social health) which would result from open space. Parks were hoped to reduce disease, crime and social unrest, providing 'green lungs' for the city and areas for recreation. Certainly they were appreciated by the people and the first examples were so rapidly threatened by overuse that barriers and restrictive by-laws were soon introduced (Nicholson-Lord, 1987).

It is interesting that these values were held as important by a society whose collective problems of poor housing and other more direct causes of ill health were far greater than ours are today. Yet approaching the next millennium many parks seem increasingly tired and out of place. They are over-mature, poorly policed and poorly used. Decades of funding cutbacks have led to a gradual erosion of features that required intensive inputs. The overgrown and patchy remnants of the original design style seem of little relevance to the needs and interests of inner-city populations. Attitudes towards parks and green spaces are confused and ambivalent. They are often perceived as locations for crime and moral degeneracy rather than positive experiences.

The parks have not entirely lost their connection with health, but the focus is on active sport, meeting the demands of a lobby that represents no more than a small percentage of society and yet has been successful in re-directing resources to football pitches and expensive leisure centres (Elliott, 1988). The wider values of landscape and the scope for contribution to a sustainable

Table 9.1 *Personal benefits of participation of an urban wildlife area*

Emotional
- relief of escaping from the city
- opportunities to identify with nature
- sense of freedom
- a peaceful retreat to repair emotions
- sense of pride and achievement

Intellectual
- seeing nature at work
- learning about the variety of flora and fauna
- learning about local history
- new skills

Social
- getting to know people better
- pleasure from team and community spirit
- becoming more responsible citizens

Physical
- appeals to the senses
- feeling fit
- a safe place to exercise or play

Source: from Mostyn (1979).

society have been largely forgotten, but it seems clear that urban green has potential value for humans on many levels. Urban nature areas in particular may embody some of these values particularly strongly (Table 9.1).

These returns may of course differ for people in different circumstances of life, and in particular may be influenced by personal qualities but also by the extent to which they have opportunities for control over the contact with nature in their lives. Many groups in society lack such opportunities and one of the main benefits of urban nature is therefore to provide an element that is missing from their environments.

The following benefits of contact with nature have been identified for ethnic groups (Wong, 1997):

- increased sense of identity and ownership of the country they live in;
- a sense of integration rather than isolation;
- a reunion with nature (many first-generation immigrants come from very rural backgrounds and move to completely urban inner-city experiences);
- the re-awakening of a sense of possibility, of widening horizons;
- restoration and a relief from daily struggle;
- empowerment, skills development and the enabling of the opportunity to participate in environmental care.

These benefits may be most strongly expressed when people can visit the rural countryside, but for many this is not easy or even possible. Urban countryside can meet many of these ends as long as it is well designed and interpreted in a visionary way. However, this may require a new recognition that the UK landscape, and that of much of the urbanized world, is in fact a multicultural landscape, and that care for this landscape carries powerful messages that can inspire a holistic view of the world and of global bio-diversity conservation as well (Wong, 1997). The challenge of finding ways to implement such a holistic approach is discussed later in this chapter.

The development of urban nature sites also has benefits that may express in more formal ways through education. For example, urban schools can undertake fieldwork that is flexible with regard to travel arrangements and timing and can respond to weather changes and reduce travel costs. Long-term and repeated visits are possible.

Psychological well-being and landscapes

Psychological well-being is not easily defined and has received relatively little study, most psychologists having been concerned with mental illness rather than health. Nevertheless the current focus of much research on the relationship between people and nature focuses on how contact with the living world may help to maintain well-being, which may in turn be preventative of illness, or may raise us to a higher level of fulfilment in our lives. This latter issue, quality of life, is of no less importance than health. Modern medicine has made extraordinary advances in prolonging life in developed countries yet society is not so clear about how to make these extra years worth living.

The research evidence for the impact of urban nature on psychological well-being can be classed under five main headings (Rohde and Kendle, 1994):

- emotional (e.g. through reduction in stress and increase in happiness);
- cognitive (e.g. through reduction in mental fatigue);
- developmental (e.g. through encouraging higher levels of mental activity, especially among children);
- behavioural (e.g. through encouraging explorative and adventurous behaviour, which in turn can support or build self-esteem);
- social (e.g. natural settings can facilitate contact, encourage conversation across social boundaries and even, in some cases, engender a broader social concern).

It has also been suggested that there can be links between these improved psychological states and greater physical health. One of the most widely quoted pieces of research in this field concerns patient's greater recovery from surgery when they had views of a tree from the hospital window (Ulrich, 1984). The mechanisms for this relationship are speculative, but are linked perhaps to the relationship between stress and the immune system (Antonovsky, 1979).

The particular reasons why nature is believed to have these de-stressing and thus health-promoting qualities are not clear but the process is often linked to psycho-evolutionary theories of human development. Unfortunately these areas are under-researched and remain speculative. Many of the psychological studies have methodological problems, and they certainly may not work for all people at all times (there is evidence that some people are focused entirely on their social life and see their physical environments as 'a grey backdrop against which people move'). We know almost nothing about cultural, social, age or personality differences in response, but know that they do exist.

Creating ecological landscapes that are valued

The theme of this book reflects the current fashion among landscape professionals in northern Europe towards the production of more natural landscapes where ecological criteria are taken into account and attempts are made to encourage wildlife within the urban fabric. However, it is essential that these fashions are not just dictated by the interests of the professionals concerned and that they genuinely reflect the needs of the user. Certainly the professional interest in ecological landscapes has been very strong across Europe for the last few decades. With constant pre-occupation and contact with green spaces professionals often learn to enjoy the richness of the small intimate pictures that nature creates compared to the simpler structures and lines of man-made designs. We appreciate the surprises that come from letting nature have more control. We also find open spaces familiar and easy to relate to. However, constantly, there are small pieces of evidence that show that other groups in society can differ; that they prefer bright flowers, tidiness and order and see wilder forms of nature as unkempt, valueless or even frightening (Burgess, 1993; Burgess et al., 1991).

It is not just a matter of academic interest if we can clarify the mechanisms by which urban people relate to nature – the potential ramifications are far ranging. Nature conservationists are recognizing that battles to save biodiversity can not be won if they are only fought in habitats such as the rain forest. The urban population are the key group to be motivated. Attitude change has to come in the areas of greatest political importance and highest resource consumption, and it is well recognized that such changes need to begin close to hand. If urban communities do not care for the nature on their doorstep it is almost impossible to make them care for distant and abstract problems. It is perhaps not surprising therefore that English Nature, the government agency concerned with nature conservation, has a deep concern for promoting the importance of, and chances for contact with, urban wildlife. In 1994 the organization commissioned a research review of the possible mental health value of contact with nature in cities (Rohde and Kendle, 1994).

As part of this review it was necessary to explore the question of what 'urban nature' or 'natural urban landscapes' mean when for many people the very terms seem counter-intuitive. People **are** selective and judgmental about what they see as natural. In a strictly objective sense all living things are a part of nature – this applies as much to a highly bred hybrid rose as to a wildflower, yet many people would see the rose as somehow unnatural, as if the human influence of breeding and selection had erased or corrupted its origin.

If an analysis is made of what is meant by the ecological style of landscaping many different approaches and forms of planting can be identified (see Chapter 3). It is often seen as a style that involves using only regionally indigenous plants. However, this is a particularly sterile and meaningless distinction in an urban context where naturalized exotic species add so much to the ecological interest and local character. A more meaningful concept would focus on those styles which allow plants and animals to be dynamic, to interact, to determine to an extent their own patterns and population size.

Perhaps the greatest distinction between the 'natural' and the 'unnatural' hinges therefore on the degree of perceived control and human influence that is associated with the landscape. An area will lose its 'naturalness' if it is too closely maintained, modified or controlled by people. This distinction between the controlled and the uncontrolled is, after all, embodied in the very term '**wildlife**'. If this definition is accepted, are there any unique benefits that urban wildlife may offer that differs from nature in a more ornamental or formal setting? Does it matter whether Ulrich's 'view' is of wild vegetation or manicured topiary? It seems that it may do.

Unexpected or subversive nature

A very great part of the pleasure that comes from urban wildlife comes from its vitality, subversiveness and unpredictability, from a feeling that it is surviving somewhere where it shouldn't. A badger in the heart of a city symbolizes nature's ability to reinvade and reassert itself in the most unpromising environments. It embodies natural renewal more strongly than can be achieved by a formal landscape.

Linked with this is a suspicion that some benefits that arise from contact with nature may have their roots in experiences which are so uncommon and hence exhilarating that they force a greater intensity of perception and emotion. Many of us will know, for example, of a jogger who can tell of his unexpected encounter with a fox in the local park with excitement still shining in his eyes many years after the event. In some cases such `peak moments' have had such a profound effect that people have completely changed their work or life interests.

Mysterious and complex nature

Often parks and green spaces are the setting for physical actions, such as jogging or walking the dog, but these are activities which could have taken place in the most concrete urban streets if necessary. More important, perhaps, are situations where nature is an inducement or motivator for an activity which would not have happened otherwise.

Some natural settings can inspire exploratory and adventurous behaviour because they offer a combination of a sense of mystery and yet are also comparatively easily deciphered and understood (Kaplan and Kaplan, 1989). This can be of great developmental and health importance, especially in children. In medical circles inaction in children is currently attracting concern as it is seen as storing up health problems for the future. Exploration can also build up self-esteem. However, the wish to explore is easily destroyed. Millward and Mostyn (1989) cite an example of where a fence designed to keep out dogs also effectively excluded people from a pond despite a clear and accessible gate.

The natural environment has many characteristics which may make it ideally suited to foster perceptual integration and perhaps other areas of development. 'The stimuli of the natural environment simultaneously assault the senses at an uncontrolled strength' (Sebba, 1991), which means that an adaptational effort is required which engages awareness. In the natural environment stimuli occur over a relatively large range and their changes are continual over time or space, which gives rise to a refinement of the perceptual analysis and may foster behavioural control. In contrast the stimuli of man-made environments tend to be simple, clearly defined, repetitive and static or only change through discreet progression.

Compared to the built environment, the natural environment is therefore characterized by variety and surprise. This triggers not only alertness and attention and captures the senses but also encourages thought and imagination. Natural shapes are usually soft and rounded, and mostly ambiguous and infinitely varied, which allows for endless projection and interpretation. Finally, life springs from the natural environment and it causes objects to move. This gives a person a feeling that s/he is in contact with living elements which have force and meaning and to which s/he cannot be indifferent.

Unrestrained nature

Many direct psychological benefits may come from uncontrolled settings, where people are able to feel relief from the complex constraints of modern society. Freedom of thought and feeling may be particularly likely to occur in settings which appear 'natural'. In nature there is also little external pressure to conform, and therefore a person can perhaps confront 'the world' and her/himself more immediately and directly than in any other setting. It is through such circumstances that people who are mentally fatigued can be restored by means of a relaxed state which has some parallels with meditation and has been called 'soft fascination' (Kaplan and Kaplan, 1989).

These aspects may only emerge if the environment is perceived as non-judgmental and unrestrained. Too many 'rules' must surely undermine any feelings of mental freedom and lack of restriction. (In German city parks it is now common to see signs instructing people to keep off wildflower meadows, while 'horticultural' grass is free to be walked on!)

People who do not value wildness and people who only value wildness

One of the most important things to understand about amenity landscape management is that the most fundamental objective is to produce the sort of living environment that people like and respond to. The subject is arguably about people more than plants or animals; it is a strange science that needs to make decisions based on whim, interest, aesthetics, fashion and many other qualities as well as on a sound understanding of technical aspects such as plant ecology.

Despite the potential benefits from wildness there are some people that need more control and order in landscape. Inevitably we probably all have complex attitudes towards different components of the natural world. Even so, there may be evidence for a fundamental and basic dichotomy of reaction in that some people see nature ultimately as spiritually good, a thing to be cherished, others as symbolic of 'anti-civilization' and a thing to be feared. Developing a sense of 'mystery' in the landscape may be the key to cognitive benefits in some people, but must at the same time increase the scope for feelings of anxiety to develop in others. Clearly psychological benefits will not be experienced by people where the natural settings are perceived as threatening rather than inviting, or where they simply do not inspire the people that visit them.

For people familiar with traditional park and garden landscapes, it can be difficult to learn to appreciate the interest and beauty in natural landscapes. Many of these, even when not degraded, have relatively limited amounts of colour. Carr and Lane (1993) document the difficulties that the Avon Wildlife Trust have had in getting visitors to appreciate the nature areas created in Branden Park, and the even great difficulties they have had in developing a community participation programme.

In Australia attempts were made to classify the typical response of different social groups to naturalistic landscapes (see Table 9.2).

For people familiar with formal or more showy landscapes often a complete change in the scale of perception is needed in order to see the beauty that nature areas hold, to spot and enjoy small, relatively shy, flowers or even the patterns hidden deep within them, the sunlight on leaves and the flickering shadows beneath trees, the combination of subtly different greens in a landscape. On the other hand, once you have tuned in to such pleasures the patterns and bright colours of traditional gardens can seem brash, obvious, overblown. (Incidentally it is worth noting that landscape evaluation research studies often work with photographs as an attempt to standardize scenery and to make comparisons more objective. However in so doing, they prevent our ability to change the scale of perception and focus of what we see, our ability to choose to see the wood or the trees depending on what pleases us most.)

What is particularly interesting is that many people with traditional tastes can not see beauty in wild landscapes even when they too are dominated by colour splashes of some quite exotic flowers, for example people will often

Table 9.2 *Recreational preferences of potential park users in Melbourne in relation to value segments*

Value segment and description	Most important facilities; features in large parks in metropolitan Melbourne	
	Natural bush/ wildlife areas (%)	Picnic and barbecue areas (%)
Basic needs: traditional views on life, older, lower income	28.6	42.9
A fairer deal: dissatisfied with life, often lower income, less than 35 years old	15.2	21.2
Conventional family life: average income, seek security, generally satisfied, 25–49 years old, with children	24.2	46.8
Traditional family life: older group, traditional family values, grandparents, often retired	39.6	29.7
Look at me: younger, seeking exciting, prosperous life, no tertiary education	39.4	21.8
Something better: well educated, good job, more progressive family types	35.3	31.8
Real conservatism: cautious of new ideas/things, over 35, not educated to tertiary level	33.0	44.0
Young optimism: student population, interest in style, new technology, career, tertiary educated	45.5	20.5
Visible achievement: visible success plus traditional values, high incomes	40.4	30.2
Socially aware: community-minded, socially responsible, high incomes, well educated	52.2	14.2

Source: Ernst and Young (1991), adapted by Hitchmough (1994).

walk past a large stand of rosebay willowherb, and not see it as anything but a weedy mess.

Much of the research work on evaluating landscape preferences flounders on the belief that 'scenery' can be objectively measured, without recognizing the full implications of the fact that 'beauty is in the eye of the beholder'. Scenery is not anywhere as important as the meaning that we invest the scenery with when we view it. Experience shows that people do not really see what is there; they see what their mind interprets from a mass of information. Every scene, every landscape, is loaded with imagery, groaning under the weight of layers of meaning. None of us can avoid pre-judging, or focusing on what we choose to focus on.

More than anything we interpret what we see in terms of what we know about the scene and have learnt to value: a naturalist may be excited about a puddle if she believes it may contain a fairy shrimp; gardeners get exited about displays of spicily scented roses and may completely overlook the faint smudge of a blue butterfly travelling past; both groups probably care nothing for daisies in a lawn – the beauty of this plant is neglected because it is a common colonist, which means to one group it may be a weed, to another it may be simply uninteresting.

30 Maintaining a tidy, high-maintenance edge to wild landscapes can make them more publicly acceptable.

If you want to test this, take a naturalist and a member of the Royal Horticultural Society and let them both loose in a rose garden and in an area of scrub woodland and study their comparative reactions – in many cases their assessment of beauty would be so profoundly different that it is difficult to believe that they come from the same human ecotype.

There is a tendency for naturalists in particular to underestimate the degree to which they place value judgements on the natural world, yet no one could really deny that they get a buzz from some plants or insects simply because they are rare; or that the way that sycamore gets despised is often based simply on completely spurious grounds that neglects the wildlife that it does support. It is similarly not uncommon to hear urban ecologists exhorting local homeowners to remove ornamentals such as flowering cherries for replacement with native trees. For many ecologists the very term 'gardening' implies a rather meaningless and obsessive activity. By taking such a position, and ignoring the value that ornamental plants have for many people, the conservation groups risk defeating their own cause by imposing limits on the legitimate relationships between people and plants.

To a large extent the different reactions of people to urban wildlife may reflect their feelings towards the loss of control that its presence represents. People who value formal ornamental landscapes most strongly will often see wild areas as 'untidy', 'unmaintained' or in some other way degraded. For others the degradation is associated with too much human influence, when an area becomes 'manicured', 'over-formal' or loses its 'naturalness'. Intolerance is found on both sides.

'Horticultural' designs also have an important place in new landscapes and by arguing too strongly for natural treatments to land there is a risk of alienating others from their surroundings. At worst this may lead to a negative reaction, a lack of public support or even opposition when it really matters. In one study local residents showed a lack of desire, or even active hostility, for the conservation of a site of wildlife interest that was threatened by development. Among the reasons expressed was the resentment they felt against conservationists who, in their view, had illegitimately claimed control over their neighbourhood site. They felt 'spatially disenfranchised' by the conservation movement. They saw in development a means of regaining access to and control over land which they felt ought to belong to them and give them pleasure (Burgess, 1993).

The simple reality is that, regardless of growing trends for wildlife gardens, the majority of people still choose to live with gardens that have a semi-formal design with ornamental plants. Arguably, such people are more important to the environmental movement than those that already have a deeper appreciation of wildlife. Instead of fighting against their wishes we need to recognize the positive value of ornamental designs.

The values of formal landscape

There are many positive benefits that may arise from more traditional and formal types of landscape and gardens where the human influence on nature's forms and patterns is more obvious. Grahn (1993) has shown that familiar plants can act as a mental stimulus for elderly people delaying the onset of dementia. Research has also shown that a shared interest in showy flowers can act as an incentive for conversation and social contact, and they are something that the growers can be proud of (Lewis, 1992). However, perhaps the most important aspect of formal gardens in domestic situations is that they are not passive but clearly require people in order to survive. Man-made landscapes differ from 'wildscapes' because the public understand more clearly the role of management of these plant communities. (Although many semi-natural habitats need careful human intervention to survive, it is typical that an awareness of this is not widespread; for example, few people will understand that wildflowers survive in a meadow because they **are** cut every year rather than despite the cutting.)

Perhaps most important of all is that the traditional concept of a garden embraces the idea of nurturing, i.e. deliberate human activity is carried out in order to foster the life of another species.

A gardener handles nature with respect but without self abnegation, manipulating nature intelligently and creatively, benefiting and nurturing other species while at the same time exercising a wide range of human aptitudes and leaving a distinctively human mark on the landscape (Jordan, 1994).

Gardening and habitat restoration and management are therefore parts of the same spectrum (Manning, 1979) and differ in the degree to which there is creativity expressed in the landscape formation, as opposed to the conservative approach that focuses on natural patterns and processes.

In appropriate circumstances this process can lead to many positive outcomes such as psychological benefits, increase in local pride, better social interactions among local communities and physical health benefits (Kaplan and Kaplan, 1989). In fact it could be argued that the concept of 'wilderness' protection as the most important goal of conservation is potentially dangerous since it involves an unrealistic abdication of choice about what happens on the land. Natural freedom needs to be balanced by areas where people are encouraged to participate, to develop a nurturing spirit and to learn to make informed choices about what a healthy landscape consists of.

A garden is made from the dance of humans and nature in partnership and in tension. It is the one piece of land where most urban dwellers have the right and power to model the landscape into a form that pleases them and meets their needs. It is where they most clearly express the shape of their relation to nature and where they may learn the importance of positive human inputs into landscape most clearly. Of course this puts gardening in a favourable light, which does not accord always with the motivations or emphasis. For some people, and certainly for some periods in history, gardening was often an expression of dominance over nature rather than nurturing (see Chapter 3). Equally there are many people who garden simply because they have inherited a patch of land that is open to scrutiny by neighbours and which needs to be kept 'tidy'. Nevertheless for many gardeners the goal of 'nurture of nature' is strong, even if not allied to an ecological vision or understanding of traditional regional conservation paradigms. Successful environmental education and the development of a greener society relies upon the support and the development of effective partnerships between all such groups.

We have already seen that sustainable environmental and conservation strategies need to be based on a change in attitude and relationship towards nature among urban people. Above all there is a need to foster a sense of stewardship for the environment. Formal landscapes may involve some members of society who would otherwise not be interested. The challenge will be to progress some of these people from a situation of looking for control over nature to one of more sympathy for natural processes.

It is inevitable that highly anthropogenic landscapes will still have their place in the sustainable city of the future. But rather than being just a sterile provision for people who happen to like loud flowers, they can be used as a potential seed bed for new ideas. However, for the development of maximum returns from a horticultural style it is important to build on the issue of 'necessary care'. This means exploring the value of process rather than product. Local communities should be provided with opportunities to participate in landscape creation and maintenance rather than showpieces to stand and admire.

One obvious issue is that access to natural environments, or to the benefits of nature and land is not equitable. Gardens or leafy settings are the privilege of the wealthy. Easier access to the countryside with greater car ownership is often also cited as a major cause for the decline in the need for parks, yet these opportunities are usually out of reach of the urban poor. Much of the urban population is removed from the opportunity to own land, the opportunity to have an input into the use of urban land or even, arguably, their ability to understand or have a concern for land conservation. This is what Aldo Leopold, a prophet of sustainable development if ever there was one, called a 'land ethic'. There needs to be opportunities for observing wildlife created in the city, but there also needs to be opportunities for participation in gardening the land.

Conflicts between the objectives of amenity and conservation

Inevitably there may be conflicts arising between the wish to develop a site for conservation value, and the need to integrate and allow for the pressures imposed by people. In rural conservation sites there is often a clear guiding principle, sometimes known as the Sandford Principle, that states that if recreation pressure ever threatens landscape quality, it is the recreation that should be curtailed.

The priorities may, however, be different in an urban site which contains habitats created almost solely for the purpose of allowing for human enjoyment. For example, it may be that human presence will lead to disturbance of nesting birds, or require the removal of ageing trees just as they are becoming most valuable as habitats, but these problems may have to be accepted.

However there may be some activities which are unacceptable to the managing authority, such as fly tipping, excessive trampling or vandalism. The importance of zoning and the provision of tidy managed edges and components within a naturalistic landscape has been emphasized by Corder (1986). Patterns of space, enclosure, access, and interfaces with and transitions to other sites can all influence the appearance and perceptions of a site. Also important are high standards of litter collection and interpretative or information systems.

Nevertheless there are still problems of conflict between many people's aesthetic preferences and naturalistic landscapes. Wildflower areas for example, while stunningly beautiful in season, can look untidy, unmanaged or even vermin infested to many people for much of the year. In particular the need to incorporate dead vegetation and to promote a cycle of decay can appear equivalent to neglect. Studies on the spontaneous flora of 'urban commons' by Oliver Gilbert (1989) have shown that the flowering season can be very long, but also that the aesthetic effect is weakened by the tendency of many of these species to maintain standing dead vegetation for long periods of time (see Figure 9.1).

In many ways the exotic species component of urban ecosystems may improve matters relative to more natural landscapes which can have relatively limited amounts of colour. But still people often do not see these

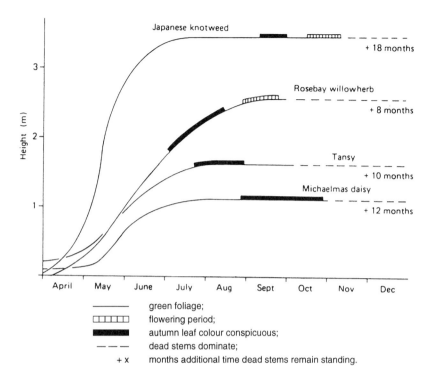

Figure 9.1 Phenological data collected from individual plants of a range of common urban species in Sheffield, 1980.

things as beautiful until somehow they have been shown how to do so – it is often striking how quite beautiful plants are only seen as 'weeds' by people who have been used to applying that label.

These problems will tend to become less common as people become more familiar with the idea and appearance of wildlife sites, but in the interim there may be a need to employ a range of tactics to promote positive associations. For example, there may be value in promoting the links found in nature, such as the way that popular birds may be dependent on less popular weeds. Wildflower areas may first be introduced to the public by planting spring bulbs into the sward; the need to allow bulb foliage to die down provides a useful justification for not cutting the grass. When the bulbs have finished flowering the flowering grassland herbs will have grown quite tall and be giving a good display that hides the dying foliage. When the *Leucanthemum* etc. has finished flowering the bulb's leaves will have yellowed enough to allow mowing. From then onwards the grass can be maintained as a normal lawn until the bulbs begin to re-appear, perhaps August or September with *Colchicum* spp.

It is also important to recognize the priorities outlined above and to ensure that people are encouraged to make maximum use of the landscape. By encouraging a sense of the personal value and rewarding experiences associated with wild plants people will learn to appreciate them more.

A particularly clear example is shown by the development of wildflower trails and celebration days in the town of Knowsley by the urban environmental charity Landlife. Wildflower fields, established partly to provide a

commercial seed crop for habitat creation, are opened to the local community, and people are positively encouraged to come and pick the flowers
(Drury, 1992). This can seem surprising and disturbing at first to anyone
who has the idea that conservation is about leaving nature alone, but the
point is of course that none of the wildflowers used are rare and the real
value to conservation is to encourage people to develop a connection with,
and hence care more about, the natural world.

Gobster (1994) also discusses the ways of overcoming or minimizing the
visual conflict and perceptual conflicts associated with natural areas. One key
is to consider 'design cues' that equate the activities with human care and
stewardship. This requires careful framing of views and use of sharp and
defined barriers. Another important activity is interpretation, through signs,
leaflets or word of mouth. Public participation is one of the most effective
ways of encouraging an appreciation of the site and the overall aims.

Gobster also argues that the manager should explore means to move
towards promoting a more holistic appreciation of the links between the
structure and function of the landscape. These concepts take the emphasis
away from superficial modifications or compromises that reflect current
public aesthetic attitudes, and instead raise the idea that habitat creation and
restoration can be a means to improved environmental education, if the
issues raised are seen as an opportunity rather than just a problem.

Education for urban conservation

Managing people's perceptions through education is as important as
managing the actual landscape. This is an area that landscape managers have
only just started to come to grips with. The relatively new profession of
environmental psychology may help, but to date most of the people interested in this field seem to get highjacked by geographers and sent off to do
yet more studies of tourist preferences in National Parks. We need to drag
the psychologists down from the hills and set them loose in the inner city.

One particular area that will prove challenging is the need to encourage a
wider understanding that there is a distinction between two approaches to
environmental ethics:

- that which aims to preserve diversity and species (but which often recognizes the need to sacrifice individuals as a consequence);
- that which manifests as animal welfare or protection of individual trees
  where the goal of protecting individuals is given highest priority, but
  where issues relating to the good of the wider population of that, or other,
  species may be poorly considered.

If saving the environment is equated by the local community as saving
every tree, then quickly the professional is going to find herself in conflict
with the public. However, the impetus to save the trees contains the essence
of a wider global consciousness that needs to be nurtured. 'Think global, act
local' is not an easy concept to implement in practice.

It is clear that interpretation and environmental education will have to be given greater attention and higher status in all aspects of professional life. However, interpretation and education need not be as dull, staid or as 'worthy' as is often considered necessary. Somehow it needs to speak to the emotional levels of our response to nature.

Environmental education theory recognizes that there may be three distinct themes to an educational approach:

1. education **about** the environment (often using traditional teaching methods to provide information);
2. education **through** the environment (for example using the outdoors as a teaching resource that can be adapted to several ends);
3. education **for** the environment (developing awareness and concern for environmental issues.

There does seem to be a conceptual muddle involved in this paradigm, since it confuses objectives (1 and 3) with methods (2). However, even if the division were accepted it is important to note that in practice education programmes frequently have multiple aims and overlay different methods in quite subtle ways. Teaching about the environment may also be teaching for the environment, if the information provided is selective and of course **all** information we are provided with is selective and chosen to meet a particular bias.

On the other hand, it has often been shown that providing information alone is a particularly ineffective method of environmental education. People seem to be able to adjust the facts to suit their deeper convictions. More effective education, leading to attitude change, will only come about if we find a way to really captivate and inspire people. Above all, participation and the opportunities for direct action that leads to positive change seem to be among the most powerful motivating factors that exist.

The debates about the finer minutiae of environmental education practice and policy are of course important, but the key first step is that people care enough to see nature, and that they see enough nature to care. The motivation, the connection, the inspiration for people are at the heart of urban nature conservation. The ultimate focus of such policies must therefore be to find ways in which everyone, regardless of cultural background, sex, age, disabilities and even personal preference has opportunities to find a way to better relate to the natural world.

There are several potential benefits that can come from ecological parks rather than from field studies in rural habitats including safety, freedom to explore, high habitat density within a small area and the opportunity to become involved practically. Urban nature areas can therefore present an invaluable opportunity for participatory environmental education that integrates the three strands identified above.

Of course education strategies should address all ages of the population. One example of an organization that has followed a fascinating approach to adult environmental education is Common Ground. Rather than

31 The opportunity to see wild species in the heart of the city is a key component of many strategies for environmental education.

campaigning to save particular habitats or fighting particular local issues they have a commitment to promote the value of green space to people, and by value they don't mean the potential drugs or chemicals that may exist somewhere in the rain forest, but rather all of the romance, poetry, mystique and richness that the natural world can evoke.

Among the initiatives they have carried out in recent years have been campaigns to promote 'local distinctiveness' in the landscape. They work with environmental artists such as Andy Goldsworthy to encourage people to see more clearly the beauty of commonplace nature. They have published *In a Nutshell*, a book on tree planting that puts as much emphasis on the mythology and folklore of trees, and the contribution trees can make to society as on the techniques of tree establishment. They have an over-riding concern for the links between art and landscape and have also published an anthology of poetry about trees. They have active campaigns for preserving old orchards and old apple varieties which culminates in the annual apple day, already a popular institution that attracts a great deal of media coverage. Most recently the work completed by Richard Mabey on the *Flora Brittanica* (1996), a compendium of the meaning that native and introduced species have for people, is one of the most exciting developments of the 1990s.

There are many lessons here that can be put to good use by landscape managers. When working with people it is important to capture their imagination by evoking the romance and the excitement of the natural world, to

32 The wildflower fields of Kirby, developed by the environmental group Landlife, have become the focus of an outstanding community initiative.

exploit the sense of adventure and the richness that contact with the wild can provide. This may be done by linking art, parties and picnics with nature conservation; we need to be happy to work with exotic plants and common habitats as well as with natives and rarities as long as they have a story to tell. We also need to remember to be aware of the beauty of the natural world, without putting unnecessary value judgements on that beauty. Above all however, we need to find ways to help people learn to value things even if they are useless, pointless, ugly and without a colourful history – that is the final step in developing a sense of nurture and stewardship, and it is only then that the full range of purpose of nature conservation can be realized (see Chapter 4).

For real benefits from nature to be realized in urban areas the dichotomy of town and countryside must be broken down. Nature needs to become recognized as an integral part of the fabric of urban life but just as importantly human life needs to become reconciled as a part of nature. The conservation movement must not be slow to learn these lessons. The natural world is our origins. It must already be calling to our subconscious in a voice that has taken us centuries to learn to ignore. To teach people to listen again, we need to learn how to blend all of the skills of the artist or the entertainer with those of the ecologist. Above all, we need to keep a clear vision of the relationship between people and wildlife – they need each other and urban nature conservation is the art that expresses that truth.

Bibliography

Akeroyd, J. (1994) *Seeds of destruction, Plantlife*, London.

Allen , M.F. (1991) *The Ecology of Mycorrhizae*, Cambridge University Press.

Andrews, J. and Kinsman, D. (1990) *Gravel Pit Restoration for Wildlife*, Royal Society for the Protection of Birds, Sandy.

Andrews, J. and Rebane, M. (1994) *Farming and Wildlife*, Royal Society for the Protection of Birds, Bedfordshire.

Andrews, M. (1989) *The Search for the Picturesque: Landscape Aesthetics and Tourism in Britain, 1760–1800*, Scholar Press, Gower Publ. Co. Ltd, Aldershot.

Anon (1991a) *Plant more British Trees says Society.* Horticulture Week, vol 209, 24, p. 6.

Anon (1991b) *The Greater Bristol Nature Conservation Strategy*, Nature Conservancy Council, Taunton.

Antonovsky, A. (1979) *Health, Stress and Coping*, Jossey-Bass Publishers, San Francisco.

Apel, J. (ed.) (1977) *The Social Significance of a Botanical Garden*, Gartnerisch-Botanische Briefe, nos 54/55.

Ardrey R. (1967) *Territorial Imperative.*

Ash, H.J. (1991) Soils and vegetation in urban areas. In P. Bullock and P.J. Gregory (eds), *Soils in the Urban Environment*, Blackwell, Oxford.

Ash, H.J., Bennett, R. and Scott, R. (1992) *Flowers in the Grass*, English Nature, Peterborough.

Avon Wildlife Consultants (undated) *Hospital Wildlife Gardens*, UK2000/RSNC, Nettleham, Lincs.

Baines, C. (1985) *How to Make a Wildlife Garden*, Elm Tree Books, London.

Baines, C. (1986a) Design considerations at establishment. In A.D. Bradshaw, D.A. Goode and E. Thorp (eds), *Ecology and Design in Landscape. The 24th Symposium of the British Ecological Society*, Blackwell, Oxford, 73–82.

Baines, C. (1986b) Wildlife and the community. In R. Brooker and M. Corder (eds), *Environmental Economy*, E&FN Spon, London, 138–54.

Baines, C. (1986c) *The Wild Side of Town*, Elm Tree Books, London.

Baines, C. (1989) Choices in habitat re-creation. In G.P. Buckley (ed.), *Biological Habitat Reconstruction*, Belhaven, London, 5–8.

Baines, C. and Smart, J. (1984) *A Guide to Habitat Creation*, London Ecology Unit, London.

Baker, H. (1937) Alluvial meadows: a comparative study of grazed and mown meadows, *J. Ecol.*, **25**, 408–20.

Barker, G. (1984) Urban nature conservation abroad, *The Planner*, **70**(6), 21.

Barker, G. (1986) *An Introduction to Nature Conservation in Urban Areas*, unpublished report. Nature Conservancy Council, Peterborough.

Bastin, L. and Thomas, C.D. (1995) Plant metapopulations and conservation in urban habitat fragments, *Land Contamination and Reclamation*, **3**(2), 70–2.

Bath City Council (1990) *Nature in the City*, a report of the Bath Wildlife Survey, Bath City Council.

Beckett, P. and Parker, D. (1990) The use and management of plant species native to Britain. In B. Clouston (ed.), *Landscape Design with Plants*, Heinemann Newnes, 103–29.

Beebee, T. (1992) Trying to save the natterjack toad, *British Wildlife*, **3**(3), 137–45.

Bell, S. (1995) New woodlands in the landscape. In R. Ferris-Kaan (ed.), *The Ecology Of Woodland Creation*. John Wiley, Chichester, 27–48.

Bernatzky, A. (1978) *Tree Ecology and Preservation*, Elsevier Scientific Publishing Co., Amsterdam.

Bird, A. (1996) Unpublished MSc thesis, University of Reading.

Bisgrove, R.J. (1988) Flower rich grasslands: using wild flower plants and growth retardants. In G. Taylor and J. Shildrick (eds), *Wildflowers '87. Workshop Report*, No.14. (University of Reading, 29 September, 1987), National Turfgrass Council, Bingley.

Bisgrove, R. (1990) *The National Trust Book of the English Garden*, Viking, London.

Bisgrove, R. (1992) *The Gardens of Gertrude Jekyll*, Frances Lincoln, London.

Bland, R.L. and Taylor, S.M. (1991) The birdlife of Bristol. In A.E. Frey (ed.), *Bristol's Urban Ecology. Proceedings of the Bristol Naturalist's Society*, **48**, 63–83.

Boothby, J. and Hull, A.P (1995) Restoring and rehabilitating pond landscapes: thinking strategically. In G.H. Griffiths (ed.), *Landscape Ecology, Theory and Application*. IALE (UK), Aberdeen, 186–99.

Box, J. (1993) Conservation or greening? the challenge of post-industrial landscapes, *British Wildlife*, **4**(5), 273–9.

Box, J. and Harrison, C. (1993) Natural spaces in urban places, *Urban Nature*, **2**, 18–19.

Bradley, C. (1982) An ecological approach: a brief review. In R. Tregay and A.R. Ruff (eds), *An Ecological Approach to*

Urban Landscape Design, Paper 8, Dept of Town and Country Planning, University of Manchester, 31–8.

Bradley, C. (1986) *Community Involvement in Greening Projects*, Groundwork Foundation, Bolton.

Bradshaw, A.D. (1979) Derelict land – is the tidying up going too far?, *Planner* (May), **3**, 85–8.

Bradshaw, A.D. (1983a) Ecological principles in the landscape. In A.D. Bradshaw, D. Goode and E. Thorpe (eds), *Ecology and Design in the Landscape*, Blackwell Scientific Publications, 15–36.

Bradshaw, A.D. (1983b) The reconstruction of ecosystems, *J. Appl. Ecol.*, **20**, 1–17.

Bradshaw, A.D. (1986) Ecological principles in landscapes. In A.D. Bradshaw, D.A. Goode and E. Thorp (eds), *Ecology and Design in Landscape. The 24th Symposium of the British Ecological Society*, Blackwell, Oxford, 15–36.

Bradshaw, A.D. (1987a) The reclamation of derelict land and the ecology of ecosystems. In W.R. Jordan, M.E. Gilpin and J.D. Aber (eds), *Restoration Ecology*, Cambridge University Press, Cambridge.

Bradshaw, A.D. (1987b) Restoration: an acid test for ecology. In W.R. Jordan, M.E. Gilpin and J.D. Aber (eds), *Restoration Ecology*, Cambridge University Press, Cambridge, 23–30.

Bradshaw, A.D. and Chadwick, M.J. (1980) The restoration of land. In *Studies in Ecology*, Vol 6,. Blackwell Scientific Publications, London.

Bradshaw, A.D., Hunt, B. and Walmsley, T. (1995) *Trees in the Urban Landscape*, E & FN Spon, London.

Bristol Naturalists Society (1991) *Bristols Urban Ecology*, Bristol Naturalists Society, Bristol.

Brooker, R. and Corder, M. (1986) *Environmental Economy*, E & FN Spon Ltd, USA.

Brown, J.H. (1981) Two decades of homage to Santa Rosalia: toward a general theory of diversity, *Am. Zool.*, **21**, 877–88.

Brown, R.J. (1989) Wild flower seed mixtures supply and demand in the horticultural industry. In G.P. Buckley (ed.), *Biological Habitat Reconstruction*, Belhaven, London, 201–20.

Buckley, G.P. (ed.) (1990) *Biological Habitat Reconstruction*. Belhaven Press, London, 363 .

Buckley, G.P. and Knight, D.G. (1990) The feasibility of woodland reconstruction. In G.P. Buckley (ed.), *Biological Habitat Reconstruction*, Belhaven, London, 171–88.

Burgess, J. (1993) Representing nature: conservation and the mass media. In F.B. Goldsmith and A. Warren (eds), *Conservation in Progress*, John Wiley, Chichester, 51–64.

Burgess, J., Harrison, C. and Maiteny, P. (1991) Contested meanings: the consumption of news about nature conservation, *Media, Culture and Society*, **13**, 499–519.

Burrows, A.G. and Boulger, G.S. (1983) Epping Forest – its present condition, with suggestions for future management, *Trans Essex Field Club*, **3**(7), Appendix 1, pt VI, xxxv–xiii.

Bussey, S. and Coles, R. (1995) Recreation patterns in an urban community forest, *Quarterly Journal of Forestry*, **83**(3).

Byfield, A. (1990) The Basingstoke Canal. Britain's richest waterway under threat, *British Nature*, **2**(1), 13–21.

Byng, I. and Johnson, P. (1995) Environmental management of wetlands formed following brick clay extraction at Peterborough Southern Township, UK, Land Contamination and Reclamation, **3**(2), 145–7.

Cantell,T. (1977) Urban wasteland, *Civic Trust*, October.

Caradine, E., Page, S. and Bullock, J. (1995) Spider and harvestman communities of urban wetlands, *Land Contamination and Reclamation*, **3**(2), 77–8.

Carr, S. and Lane, A. (1993) *Practical Conservation – Urban Habitats*, The Open University, Hodder & Stoughton, London.

Chatto, B. (1989) *The Green Tapestry*, Collins, London.

Christy, S. (1989) Jens Jensen. In Tishler W. (ed.), *American Landscape Architecture Designers and Places*, The Preservation Press, 78–83.

Clements, E.J. and Foster, M.C. (1996) *Alien Plants of the British Isles*, Botanical Society of the British Isles, London.

Cohn, E.V.J. and Millett, P. (1995) Problems of the implementation and management of urban woodland habitat creation schemes, *Land Contamination and Reclamation*, **3**(2), 89–92.

Cole, L. (1984) Urban nature conservation. In Warren and Goldsmith (eds), *Conservation in Perspective*, John Wiley & Sons, Chichester.

Cole, L. (1986) Urban opportunities for a more natural approach. In A.D. Bradshaw, D.A. Goode and E. Thorpe (eds), *Ecology and Design in Landscape. The 24th Symposium of the British Ecological Society*, Blackwell, Oxford, 37–54.

Collingwood, W.G. (1903) *Ruskin Relics*, Isbister & Co. Ltd, London.

Coppin, N.J. and Richards, I.G. (1990) *The Use of Vegetation in Civil Engineering*, Butterworths, London.

Corder, M. (1986) Naturalistic techniques and the urban local authority. In R. Brooker and M. Corder (eds), *Environmental Economy*, E & FN Spon, London, 113–37.

Cotton, J. (1982) The field teaching of ecology in Central London – The William Curtis Ecological Park, 1977–80. In R. Bornkamm, J.A. Lee and M.R.D. Seaward (eds), *Urban Ecology*, Blackwell, Oxford, 321–7.

Coventry, F. (1753) Extract from The World (15), reprinted in Hunt, J.D. and Willis, P. (1975) The Genius of The Place, Paul Elek, London. 274–6.

Cramer, M. (1993) Urban renewal: restoring the vision of Olmstead and Vaux in Central Park's woodlands, *Restoration and Management Notes*, **11**(2), 106–16.

Craul, P.J. (1992) *Urban Soils in Landscape Design*, John Wiley & Sons Inc., New York.

Crawley, M.J. (1986) The structure of plant communities. In M.J. Crawley (ed.), *Plant Ecology*, Blackwell, Oxford.

Cregan, M. (1990) Open spaces and quality of urban life, *Landscape Design*, June.

Croft and Beresford (1988) A third approach to city regeneration, *Town and Country Planning*, **57**(2), 82–4.

Crozier, J. (1992) Flower fields and Alpine meadows, *The Hardy Plant*, **14**(2), 89–93.

Davis, B.N.K. (1976) Wildlife, urbanisation and industry, *Biological Conservation*, **10**(4), 249–91.

Davison, J.G. (1983) Weed control in newly planted amenity trees. In P.R. Thoday (ed.), *Tree Establishment: Proceedings of the Symposium Held at the University of Bath*, Bath, 59–67.

Dawe, G.F.M. (1995) Species-density in relation to urban open space, *Land Contamination and Reclamation*, **3**(2), 114–16.

Dawson, D. (1994) Are habitat corridors conduits for animals and plants in a fragmented landscape?, *English Nature Research Report 94*, English Nature, Peterborough.

Dean, J. and Slewellyn, A. (1990) *Open Space Management for Nature Conservation*, Leicester City Council, Leicester.

Department of the Environment (1989) *Cost Effective Management of Reclaimed Derelict Sites*, HMSO, London.

Department of the Environment (1992) *The National Survey of Vacant Land in Urban Areas in England in 1990*, HMSO, London.

Diamond, J.M. (1975) The island dilemma: lessons of modern biogeographic studies for the design of natural reserves, *Biol. Conserv.*, **7**, 129–46.

Drury, S. (1992) Children of the sunflowers, *Horticulture Week*, 28 August, 40–2.

Druse, K. (1994) *The Natural Habitat Garden*, Clarkson Potter.

Duffey, E., Morris, M.G., Sheail, J. *et al.* (eds) (1974) *Grassland Ecology and Wildlife Management*, Chapman & Hall, London.

Dutton, R.A. and Bradshaw, A.D. (1982) *Land Reclamation in Cities*, HMSO, London.

Eaton, L.K. (1964) *Landscape Artist in America: The Life and Work of Jens Jensen*, University of Chicago Press, Chicago.

Ellenberg, H. (1988) *The Vegetation Ecology of Central Europe*, Cambridge University Press, Cambridge.

Elliott, B. (1988) From people's parks to green deserts, *Landscape Design*, **171**, 13–17.

Emery, M. (1986) *Promoting Nature in Cities and Towns*, Croom Helm, Beckenham.

Environmental Advisory Unit (1988) *Heathland Restoration - A Handbook of Techniques*, British Gas, Southampton.

Ernst and Young (1991) *Market Research Report: Yarra Valley Park Management Plan*, Melbourne, Victoria.

Evelyn, L. (1662) *Sylva, or a Discourse of Forest-Trees and the Propogation of Timber in His Majesties Dominions etc.*, J. Wlathoe, J. Knapton, D. Midwinter etc, London, reprint 1979. Stobart & Son Ltd, London.

Eyre, M.D. and Luff, M.L. (1995) Coleoptera on post-industrial land: a conservation problem?, *Land Contamination and Reclamation*, **3**(2), 132–4.

Fairbrother, N. (1970) *New Lives New Landscapes*, Architectural Press, London.

Falk, S. (1995) Insects in urban and post-industrial settings, *Land Contamination and Reclamation*, **3**(2), 75–6.

Ferris, C., Oliver, R.P., Davy, A.J. and Hewitt, G.M. (1995) Using chloroplast DNA to trace postglacial migration routes of oaks into Britain, *Molecular Ecology*, **4**, 731–8.

Ferris-Kaan, R. (1995) Ecological planning in new woodlands. In R. Ferris-Kaan (ed.), *The Ecology of Woodland Creation*, John Wiley & Sons, Chichester, 225–36.

Fiedler, P.L. and Jain, S.K. (1992) *Conservation Biology: The Theory and Practice of Nature Conservation – Preservation and Management*, Chapman & Hall, London.

Forbes, S. (1989) Nature and ecology in landscape design. Unpublished MPhil thesis, The University of Bristol.

Forestry Commission/Countryside Commission (1996) *Woodland Creation: Needs and Opportunities in the English Countryside*, CCP 507, Countryside Commission, Cheltenham.

Francis, J.L. (1995) The enhancement of young plantations and new woodlands, *Land Contamination and Reclamation*, **3**(2), 93–8.

Fuller, R.J. (1982) *Bird Habitats in Britain*, T & A.D. Poyser, Calton.

Fuller, R.J., Gough, S.J. and Marchant, J.H. (1995) Bird populations in new lowland woods. In R. Ferris-Kaan (ed.), *The Ecology of Woodland Creation*, John Wiley & Sons, Chichester, 163–82.

Gemmell, R.P. (1982) The origin and botanical importance of industrial habitats. In R. Bornkamm, J.A. Lee and M.R.D. Seaward (eds), *Urban Ecology*, Blackwell Scientific Publications, Oxford.

Gibbons, B. and Gibbons, L. (1990) *Creating a Wildlife Garden*, Hamlyn, London.

Gibson, C.W.D., Watt, T.A. and Brown, V.K. (1987) The use of sheep grazing to recreate species rich grassland from abandoned arable land, *Biol. Cons.*, **42**, 165–84.

Gilbert, O.L. (1989) *The Ecology of Urban Habitats*, Chapman & Hall, London.

Gilbert, O.L. (1992) The ecology of an urban river, *British Wildlife*, **3**(3), 129–36.

Gilbertson, P. (1987) *The Survival of Trees in Urban Areas*, unpublished PhD thesis, University of Liverpool.

Gilbertson, P., Kendle, A.D. and Bradshaw, A.D. (1987) Rootgrowth and the problems of growing trees in urban and industrial areas. In D. Patch (ed.), *Advances in Practical Arboriculture*, Bulletin 65, Forestry Commission, Edinburgh, 59–66.

Giles, N. (1992) *Wildlife after Gravel*, The Game Conservancy/ARC Fordingbridge.

Gill, D. and Bonnett, P. (1973) *Nature in the Urban Landscape: A Study of Urban Ecosystems*, York Press, Baltimore.

Gilpin, M.E. (1987) Experimental community assembly: competition, community structure and the order of species introductions. In W.R. Jordan, M.E. Gilpin and J.D. Aber (eds), *Restoration Ecology*. Cambridge University Press, 151–62.

Gobster, P.H. (1994) The urban savanna: reuniting ecological preference and function, *Restoration and Management Notes*, **12**(1), 64–71.

Goode, D. (1984) Conservation and value judgements. In R.D. Roberts and T.M. Roberts (eds), *Planning and Ecology*, Chapman & Hall, London, 188–205.

Goode, D. (1986) *Wild in London*, Michael Joseph, London.

Goode, D. (1995a) Designing for nature in urban parks. In J. De Waal (ed.), *Ecological Aspects of Green Areas in Urban Environments. Proceedings of the 1995 IFPRA World Conference*. Vereniging Voor Openbaar Groen, Bruge. 567–9.

Goode, D. (1995b) New values new ecological landscapes, *Land Contamination and Reclamation*, **3**(2), 59–60.

Goode, D.A. and Smart, P.J. (1983) Designing for wildlife. In A.D. Bradshaw, D. Goode and E. Thorpe (eds), *Ecology and Design in the Landscape*, Blackwell Scientific Publications, 219–36.

Grahn, P. (1993) Planera för Bättree Hälsa. In B. Kullinger and

U.B. Strömberg (eds), *Planera för en Bärkraftig Utveckling*. Byggforskningsrådet, Stockholm.

Green, B. (1981) *Country Side Conservation*, 2nd edn, Unwin Hyman Ltd, London.

Green, B.H. (1986) Controlling ecosystems for amenity. In A.D. Bradshaw, D.A. Goode and E. Thorp (eds), *Ecology and Design in Landscape. The 24th Symposium of the British Ecological Society*, Blackwell, Oxford, 195–210.

Griffith, G.H. (1995) *Landscape Ecology: Theory and Application*, IALE, UK.

Grime, J.P (1979) *Plant Strategies and Vegetation Processes*, John Wiley, Chichester.

Grime, J.P. (1983) Manipulation of plant species and communities. In A.D. Bradshaw, D. Goode and E. Thorpe (eds), *Ecology and Design in the Landscape*, Blackwell Scientific Publications, 175–94.

Grime, J.P., Hodgson, J.G. and Hunt, R. (1988) *Comparative Plant Ecology*, Unwin Hyman, London.

Griswold, M. and Woller, E. (1991) *The Golden Age of American Gardens*, Harry N. Abrams and the Garden Club of America.

Groundwork Trust (1986) *Report of the Working Party on the After-Care of Reclaimed Land in St Helens and Knowsley*, Groundwork Trust, St Helens.

Grubb, P.J. (1986) The ecology of establishment. In A.D. Bradshaw, D.A. Goode and E. Thorpe (eds), *Ecology and Design in Landscape. The 24th Symposium of the British Ecological Society*, Blackwell, Oxford, 83–98.

Grubb, P.J. (1977) The maintenance of species-richness in plant communities: the importance of the regeneration niche, *Biological Reviews*, **52**, 107–45.

Gryseels, M. (1995) Orientations for the promotion of the biological heritage in Brussels capital region. In J. De Waal (ed.), *Ecological Aspects of Green Areas in Urban Environments. Proceedings of the 1995 IFPRA World Conference*, Vereniging Voor Openbaar Groen, Bruge, 530–3.

Gustavsson, R. (1982) Nature-like parks and open spaces in housing areas in Sweden. In Tregay and Ruff (eds), *An Ecological Approach to Urban Landscape Design*, Paper 8, Dept of Town and Country Planning, University of Manchester, 119–34.

Gustavsson, R. (1983) Analysis of vegetation structure. In R. Tregay and R. Gustavsson (eds), *Oakwood's New Landscape*, Swedish University of Agricultural Sciences, Sweden 85–140.

Handley, J. (1984) Ecological requirements for decision-making regarding medium-scale developments in the urban context. In R.D. Roberts and T.M. Roberts (eds), *Planning and Ecology*, Chapman & Hall, London, 224–37.

Handley, J.F and Bulmer, P. (1987) The design and management of cost effective landscapes. In B. Rigby (ed.), *Proceedings of the 27th Askham Bryan Amenity Technical Course*, Askham Bryan, Yorks, 40–57.

Handley, J.F. (1996) *The Post Industrial Landscape*, Groundwork, London.

Hansen, R. (1986) Spontaneous or designed ground flora?, *Garten Und Landschaft*, 5/86, 31–5.

Hansen, R. (1987) More nature in public green spaces, *Garten Und Landschaft*, 5/87, 17–22.

Hansen, R. and Stahl, F. (1993) *Perennials and Their Garden Habitats*, Cambridge University Press, Cambridge.

Harding P.T and Rose, F. (1986) *Pasture Woodlands in Lowland Britain*, Institute of Terrestrial Ecology, Abbots Ripton.

Harmer, R. and Kerr, G. (1995) Creating woodlands: to plant trees or not? In R. Ferris-Kaan (ed.), *The Ecology of Woodland Creation*, John Wiley & Sons, Chichester, 113–28.

Harper, J.L. (1977) *Population Biology of Plants*, Academic Press, London.

Harper, J.L., Williams, J.T. and Sagar, G.R. (1969) The behaviour of seeds in soil. In A.S. Boughey (ed.), *Contemporary Readings in Ecology*, Dickenson, CA.

Harris, L.D. and Silva-Lopez, G. (1992) In P.L. Fiedler and S.K. Jain (eds), *Conservation Biology*, Chapman & Hall, London and New York.

Harris, R.W. (1992) *Arboriculture – The Care of Trees, Shrubs and Vines in the Landscape*, 2nd edn, Prentice Hall, New Jersey.

Harris, S. (1986) *Urban Foxes*, Whittet Books, London.

Harris, S. (1996) Foxy come home, *BBC Wildlife*, **14**(7), 28–32.

Harris, S. and Cresswell, W.J. (1991) Bristol's badgers. In A.E. Frey (ed.), *Bristol's Urban Ecology. The Proceedings of the Bristol Naturalists' Society*, **48**, 17–30.

Harris, S. and Woolard, T. (1991) Bristol's foxes. In A.E. Frey (ed.), *Bristol's Urban Ecology. The Proceedings of the Bristol Naturalists' Society*, **48**, 3–15.

Harrison, C., Burgess, J., Millwood, A. and Dawe, G. (1996) *Accessible Natural Greenspace in Towns and Cities: A Review of Appropriate Size and Distance Criteria*. English Nature, Peterborough.

Hayter, S. (1995) Painting the town green, *Horticulture Week*, **16** (6/1/95), 16–19.

Hennebo, D. (1955) *Staubfilterung Durch Gruenanlagen*, VEB Verlag Technil. Berlin, 79.

Henrey, B. (1975) *British Botanical and Horticultural Literature Before 1800*, Oxford University Press, Oxford, 3 vols.

Hermy, M. (1995) Ecological principles and development of urban green spaces. In J. De Waal (ed.), *Ecological Aspects of Green Areas in Urban Environments. Proceedings of the 1995 IFPRA World Conference*, Vereniging Voor Openbaar Groen, Bruge, 570–1.

Higgens, S. (1986) City Green, *Architects Journal*, February.

Hill, W.T. (1956) *Octavia Hill: Pioneer of the National Trust and Housing Reformer*, Hutchinson, London.

Hitchmough, J. (1994a) Natural neighbours, *Landscape Design* (4/94), 16–22.

Hitchmough, J. (1994b) *Urban Landscape Management*, Inkata Press, Australia.

Hitchmough, J. (1994c) The wild garden revisited, *Landscape Design* (5/94), 45–9.

Hobbs, R.L. and Sanders, D.A. (1993) *Reintegrating Fragmented Landscapes*, Springer-Verlag, New York.

Hodge, S.J. (1995) Creating and managing woodlands around towns, *Forestry Commission Handbook*, 11, HMSO, London.

Hodge, S.J. and Harmer, R. (1995) The creation of woodland habitats in urban and post-industrial environments, *Land Contamination and Reclamation*, **3**(2), 86–8.

Holden, R. (1988) Parks of the future, *Landscape Design*, **171**, 11–12.

Hopkins, J. (1989) Prospects for habitat creation, *Landscape Design*, **179**, 19–23.

Horbert, M. (1978) and Kirchgeorg, A. (1980) *Kilmatische Und Lufthygienische Aspekte Zur Planing Innerstädtischer Freiräume, Dargestellt Am Biospiel Des Grossen Tiergartens In Berlin West*, Stadtbauwelt, Berlin, 270–6.

Hottentrèger, G. (1992) New flowers new gardens, *Journal of Garden History*, **12**(3), 207–27.

Hough, M. and Barrett, S. (1987) *People and City Landscapes, a Study of People and Open Space in Metropolitan Areas of Toronto*, The Conservation Council Of Ontario, Toronto.

Hunt, J.D. and Willis, P. (1988) *The Genius of the Place: The English Landscape Garden 1620–1820*, MIT Press edn, Cambridge, Massachusetts from 1782, 2nd edn.

Insley, H. and Buckley, G.P. (1986) Causes and prevention of establishment failure in amenity trees. In A.D. Bradshaw, D.A. Goode and E. Thorpe (eds), *Ecology and Design in Landscape. The 24th Symposium of the British Ecological Society*, Blackwell, Oxford, 127–42.

IUCN/UNEP/WWF (1991) *Caring for the Earth*, IUCN, Gland, Switzerland.

Jacques, D. (1983) *Georgian Gardens: The Reign of Nature*, Batsford Press, London.

Jarvis, P.J. (1990) Urban cats as pests and pets, *Environmental Conservation*, 17(2), 169–71.

Jefferson, R.G. and Usher, M.B. (1987) The seed banks in soils of disused chalk quarries in the Yorkshire Wolds, England: implications for conservation management, *Biol. Cons.*, **42**, 287–302.

Jekyll, G.O. (1899) *Wood and Garden*, 2nd edn, Longman, Green & Co., London.

Johnson, J. (1989) Gardens. In Tishler W. (ed.), *American Landscape Architecture Designers and Places*, The Preservation Press, 136–41.

Johnsons Seeds (1991) *Wildflower Manual*, Johnsons Seeds, Boston.

Johnston, A.E. and Poulston, P.R. (1977) *Yields on the Exhaustion Land and Changes in the NPK Content of Soils due to Cropping and Manuring*, Report Rothamstead Experimental Station, 1976 (2), 53–86.

Johnston, J.D. (1990) Nature areas for city people, *Ecology Handbook*, 14, London Ecology Unit, London.

Jones, G.H., Trueman, I.C. and Millet, P. (1995) The use of hay strewing to create species-rich grasslands. (1) General principles and hay strewing versus seed mixes, *Land Contamination and Reclamation*, 3(2), 104–7.

Jordan, W.R. (1994) Sunflower Forest: ecological restoration as the basis for a new conservation paradigm. In A.D. Baldwin, J. De Luce and C. Pletsch (eds), *Beyond Preservation – Restoring and Inventing Landscapes*, University of Minnesota Press, Minneapolis.

Jordan, W.R., Gilpin, M.E. and Aber, J.D. (1987) *Restoration Ecology: A Synthetic Approach to Ecological Research*, Cambridge University Press.

Jordan, W.R. and Packard, S. (1989) Just a few oddball species: restoration practice and ecological theory, In G.P. Buckley (ed.), *Biological Habitat Reconstruction*, Belhaven Press, Pinter Publishers, London, 18–26.

Joyce, D. (1989) *Garden Styles*, Pyramid Books.

Kaplan, R. and Kaplan, S. (1989) *The Experience of Nature: A Psychological Perspective*, Cambridge University Press, New York.

Kaule, G. and Krebs, S. (1989) Creating new habitats in intensively used farmland. In G.P. Buckley (ed.), *Biological Habitat Reconstruction*, Belhaven, London, 161–70.

Kendle A.D. (1990) Soil ameliorants for landscape planting, I: Principles. *Plant User*, **3**, 3–5.

Kendle, A.D. (1992a) Adaptation of reclamation methodology to maximise conservation benefits – application of ecological principles. In *Proceedings of the International Symposium on Land Reclamation*, Nashville USA. American Society of Agricultural Engineers.

Kendle A.D. (1992b) The management of man-made habitats, *Aspects of Applied Biology 29: The Management of Vegetation in Forestry, Amenity and Conservation Areas*, Association of Applied Biologists, Wellesbourne, 25–32.

Kendle, A.D. and Bradshaw, A.D. (1992) The role of nitrogen in tree establishment and growth on derelict land, *Arboricultural Journal*.

Kendle, A.D., Gilbertson, P. and Bradshaw, A.D. (1988) The influence of stock source on transplant performance, *Arboricultural Journal*, **12**(3), 257–73.

Kennedy, C.E.J. and Southwood, T.R.E. (1984) The number of insects associated with British trees; a re-analysis, *J. Anim. Ecol.*, **53**, 455–78.

Kerster H.W. (1968) Population age structure in the prairie for *Liatris aspera*, *Bioscience* **18**, 430–2.

Key, R. (1995) Invertebrate conservation and new woodland in Britain. In R. Ferris-Kaan (ed.), *The Ecology of Woodland Creation*, John Wiley & Sons, Chichester, 149–62.

Kingsbury, N. (1994) *The Wildflower Garden*, Conran Octopus.

Kirby, K. (1995) Rebuilding the English countryside: habitat fragmentation and wildlife corridors as issues in practical conservation, *English Nature Science*, **10**, English Nature, Peterborough.

Kirby, P. (1992) *Habitat Management for Invertebrates*, Joint Nature Conservation Committee/RSPB, Sandy, United Kingdom.

Kitz, N. and Kitz, B. (1984) *Painshill Park: Hamilton and His Picturesque Landscape*, Norman Kitz, Painshill, Cobham, Surrey.

Koch, W. (1995) Nature in the city: wildflowers and perennials in urban open spaces in Stuttgart. In J. De Waal (ed.), *Ecological Aspects of Green Areas in Urban Environments. Proceedings of the 1995 IFPRA World Conference*, Vereniging Voor Openbaar Groen, Bruge, 595–6.

Koningen, H. and Leopold, R. (1992) Nature and garden art in Holland: some features, *Proceedings of the Symposium on Perennial Planting*, Alnarp, Holland.

Kunick, W. (1982) Comparison of the flora of some cities of the central European lowlands. In R. Bornkamm, J.A. Lee and M.R.D. Seaward (eds), *Urban Ecology*, Blackwell, Oxford, 13–22.

Kunick, W. (1992) The introduction of wild perennials, *Garten Und Landschaft*, 5/92, 27–31.

La Dell, T. (1983) Tree seeding on amenity sites, *Landscape Design*, **144**, 27–31.

La Dell, T. (1988) The establishment of amenity trees and shrubs by direct seeding: management and weed control, *Aspects of Applied Biology 16: The Practice of Weed Control and Vegetation Management in Forestry, Amenity and Conservation Areas*, Association of Applied Biologists, Wellesbourne, Warwickshire, 47–52.

Land Capability Consultants (1989) *Cost Effective Management of Reclaimed Derelict Sites*, DOE, HMSO, London.

Land Use Consultants (1993) *Trees in Towns*, DOE, HMSO, London.

Laurie, I. (ed.) (1979) *Nature in Cities*, John Wiley, Chichester.

Laurie, M. (1986) *Landscape Architecture*, Elsevier, Amsterdam and London.

Lewis C.A. (1992) Effects of plants and gardening in creating interpersonal and community well-being. In D. Relf (ed.), *The Role of Horticulture in Human Well-Being and Social Development*, Timber Press, Oregon.

Londo, G. (1977) *Natuurtuinen En Parken. Aaneg En Onderhoud*, Thieme, Zuphen.

Londo, G. and Den Hengst, J. (1993) *Tuin Vol Wilde Planten: Natuur In Tuin En Park*, Terra, Warnseld.

London Ecology Unit (1985) Nature conservation guidelines for London, *Ecology Handbook*, 3, London Ecology Unit, London.

Lord, A. (1996) *The RHS Plant Finder*, Moorland Publishing Company, London.

Lott, D. and Daws, J. (1995) The conservation value of urban demolition sites in leicester for beetles, *Land Contamination and Reclamation*, 3(2), 79–81.

Loudon, J.C. (1834) Arboretum Brittanicum, *Gardener's Magazine*, 10, 558–64.

Lunn, J. and Wild, M. (1995) The wildlife interests of abandoned collieries and spoil heaps in Yorkshire, *Land Contamination and Reclamation*, 3(2), 135–7.

Mabey, R. (1973) *The Unofficial Countryside*, Collins, London.

Mabey, R. (1980) *The Common Ground*, Hutchinson, London.

Mabey, R. (1996) *Flora Brittanica*, Sinclair-Stevenson, London.

McAndrews, S., Morris, P. and Rogers, S. (1986) Environmental education. In R. Brooker and M. Corder (eds), *Environmental Economy*, E & FN Spon, London, 155–75.

MacArthur, R.H. and Wilson, E.O. (1967) *The Theory of Island Biogeography*, Monographs in Population Biology, 1. Princetown University Press, Princetown.

MacGregor, H. (1995) Crested newts – ancient survivors, *British Wildlife*, 7(1), 1–8.

McPeck, E. (1989) Beatrix Jones Farrand. In W. Tishler (ed.), *American Landscape Architecture Designers and Places*, The Preservation Press, 94–9.

Main, A.R. (1993) Landscape reintegration – problem definition. In R.J. Hobbs and D.A. Saunders (eds), *Reintegrating Fragmented Landscapes*, Springer-Verlag, New York, 189–208.

Manning, O. (1979) Designing for nature in cities. In I. Laurie (ed.), *Nature in Cities*, Wiley & Sons, Chichester, 3–36.

Marder, J. (1995) Unpublished MSc thesis, University of Reading.

Marrs, R.H. (1986) Techniques for reducing soil fertility for nature conservation purposes, *Biological Conservation*, 34, 307–32.

Marrs, R.H. and Gough, M.W. (1989) Soil fertility - a problem for habitat restoration. In G.P. Buckley (ed.), *Biological Habitat Reconstruction*, Belhaven, London, 29–44.

Marshall, E.J.P. (1988) Some effects of annual applications of three growth-retarding compounds on the composition and growth of a pasture sward, *Journal of Applied Ecology*, 25, 619–30.

Meyer, C. (1992) Maintenance of perennials, *Garten Und Landschaft*, 5/92, 24–6.

Millward, A.M. (1986) *Community Involvement in Urban Greening*, Groundwork Foundation, London.

Millward A.M. (1987) *Community Involvement in Urban Nature Conservation*, unpublished PhD thesis, Aston University, Birmingham, UK.

Millward, A.M.. and Mostyn, B. (1989) People and nature in cities: the changing social aspects of planning and managing natural parks in urban areas, *Urban Wildlife Now*, **2**, Nature Conservancy Council, Peterborough.

Moereels, J. (1995) Ecological aspects of water drainage systems in Brasschaat. In J. De Waal (ed.), *Ecological Aspects of Green Areas in Urban Environments. Proceedings of the 1995 IFPRA World Conference*, Vereniging Voor Openbaar Groen, Bruge, 579–81.

Moffat, A.J., Bending, N.A.D. and Roberts, C.J. (1991) The use of sewage sludge as a fertiliser in the afforestation of opencast coal spoils in South Wales. In M.C.R. Davies (ed.), *Land Reclamation: An End To Dereliction?*, Elsevier Applied Science, London.

Moffatt, D. (1986) The natural approach to open space. In R. Brooker and M. Corder (eds), *Environmental Economy*, E&FN Spon, London, 79–112.

Moggridge, H.T. (1983) Blenheim Park – 1: The restoration plan, *Landscape Design*, **12**, 9–10.

Morrison, D. (1989) Restored natural landscape. W. Tishler (ed.), *American Landscape Architecture Designers and Places*, The Preservation Press, 190–4.

Mostyn, B.J. (1979) Personal benefits and satisfactions derived from participation. In *Urban Wildlife Project – A Qualitative Evaluation*, Nature Conservancy Council, London.

Muller, N. and Wolf, G. (1985) Blumenwiesen in Siedlungsräumen, *Garten & Landschaft*, **95**, 33–40. English translation in Sukopp and Werner (1987).

Naveh, Z. and Liebermann, A. (1994) *Landscape Ecology – Theory and Application*, 2nd Edition, Springer-Verlag, New York.

Newbold, C. (1989) Semi-natural habitats or habitat re-creation: conflict or partnership. In G.P. Buckley (ed.), *Biological Habitat Reconstruction*, Belhaven, London, 9–17.

Nicholson, M. (1970) *The New Environmental Age*, Billing & Sons Ltd, Worcester.

Nicholson. M. (1987) *The New Environmental Age*, Cambridge University Press, Cambridge.

Nicholson-Lord, D. (1987) *The Greening of the Cities*, Routledge & Kegan Paul, London.

Nicholson-Lord, D. (1994) Calling in the country: ecology

parks and urban life, Working Paper No. 4 from *The Future of Public Parks in the UK*, Comedia/Demos.

Oehme, W., Van Sweden, J. and Frey, R. (1991) *Bold Romantic Gardens*, Acropolis Books.

Oland, L. (1986) The management of amenity grasslands and woodlands. In R. Brooker and M. Corder (eds), *Environmental Economy*, E&FN Spon, London, 176–200.

Owen, J. (1991) *The Ecology of a Garden: The First Fifteen Years*, Cambridge University Press, Cambridge.

Owen, J. and Owen, D.F. (1975) Suburban gardens: England's most important nature reserve?, *Environmental Conservation*, **2**, 53–9.

Owen, M., Atkinson-Willes, G.L. and Salmon, D.G. (1986) *Wildfowl in Great Britain*, Cambridge University Press, Cambridge.

Paine, R.T. (1966) Food web complexity and species diversity, *Am. Naturalist*, **100**, 65–75.

Park, D.G. (1989) Relocating magnesian limestone grassland. In G.P. Buckley (ed.), *Biological Habitat Reconstruction*, Belhaven Press, London, 264–80.

Parr, T.W. and Way, J.M. (1984) The effect of management on the occurrence of agricultural weeds in roadside verges. In *Aspects of Applied Biology 5: Weed Control and Vegetation Management in Forests and Amenity Areas*, AAB, Wellesbourne, 9–18.

Peterken, G. (1981) *Woodland Conservation and Management*, Chapman & Hall, London.

Plummer, B. and Shewan, D. (1992) *City Gardens: An Open Space Survey in the City of London*, Belhaven Press, London.

Rackham, O. (1978) Archaeology and land-use history. In D. Corke (ed.), *Epping Forest - The Natural Aspects? Essex Naturalist* (2), Essex Field Club, London, 16–57.

Rackham, O. (1986) *The History of the Countryside*, J.M. Dent & Sons Ltd, London.

Ranson, C.E. (1978) Nature conservation in Epping Forest. In D. Corke (ed.), *Epping Forest - The Natural Aspects? Essex Naturalist* (2), Essex Field Club, London, 58–79.

Ratcliffe, D.A. (1977a) *A Nature Conservation Review* (2 vols), Cambridge University Press, Cambridge.

Ratcliffe, D.A. (1977b) *The Nature Conservation Review*, Cambridge University Press, Cambridge.

Repton, H. (1802) *Observations on the Theory and Practice of Landscape Gardening including Some Remarks on Grecian and Gothic Architecture*, J. Taylor, London.

Roberts, R.D. and Roberts, J.M. (1986) The selection and management of soils in landscape schemes. In A.D. Bradshaw, D.A. Goode and E. Thorp (eds), *Ecology and Design in Landscape. The 24th Symposium of the British Ecological Society*, Blackwell, Oxford, 99–126.

Roberts, R.D. and Roberts, T.M. (1984) *Planning and Ecology*, Chapman & Hall, London.

Roberts, R.D., Marrs, R.H., Skeffington, R.A. and Bradshaw, A.D. (1981) Ecosystem development on naturally colonised china clay wastes, I. Vegetation changes and overall accumulation of organic matter and nutrients, *J. Ecol.*, **69**, 153–61.

Robinson, W. (1894) *The Wild Garden*, 4th edn, John Murray.

Robinson, W. (1900) *The English Flower Garden*, 8th edn, Windus, London.

Rodwell, J.S. (1993) Grasslands and montane communities, *British Plant Communities*, Vol 3, Cambridge University Press.

Rodwell, J.S. and Patterson, G. (1994) Creating new native woodlands, *Forestry Commission Bulletin*, 112, HMSO, London.

Rohde, C.L.E. and Kendle, A.D. (1994) Human well-being and nature in urban areas, *English Nature Science*, No. 22, English Nature, Peterborough.

Ruff, A.R. (1979) *Holland and the Ecological Landscapes*, Deanwater Press, Stockport.

Ruff, A.R. (1985) Ecology and landscape design. In S. Harvey and S. Rettig (eds), *Fifty Years of Landscape Design 1934-1984*, The Landscape Press, London.

Ruff, A.R. (1986) Ecology and gardens. In G. Jellicoe and S. Jellicoe (consultant eds) and P. Goode and M. Lancaster (executive eds), *The Oxford Companion to Gardens*, Oxford University Press, Oxford, 152–4.

Ruff, A.R. (1987) Holland and the ecological landscapes, 1975–1987: an appraisal of recent developments in the layout and management of urban open space in The Low Countries, *Urban and Regional Studies*, Vol. 1, Delftse Universitaire Pers, Delft, Netherlands.

Ruff, A.R and Tregay, R. (1982) *An Ecological Approach to Urban Landscape Design*, Occasional Paper 8, Department of Planning and Landscape, University of Manchester, Manchester.

Sangster, M. (1995) Planning and designing new woodlands for people. In R. Ferris-Kaan (ed.), *The Ecology of Woodland Creation*, John Wiley & Sons, Chichester, 17–26.

Scmid, A. (1995) Green structures and green networks. In J. De Waal (ed.), *Ecological Aspects of Green Areas in Urban Environments. Proceedings of the 1995 IFPRA World Conference*, Vereniging Voor Openbaar Groen, Bruge, 518–21.

Sebba, R. (1991) The landscapes of childhood, *Environment and Behavior*, **23**, 395–422.

Selman, P. (1992) *Environmental Planning: The Conservation and Development of Biophysical Resources*, Chapman & Hall, London.

Shafer, C.L. (1990) *Nature Reserves: Island Theory and Conservation Practice*, Smithsonian Institution Press, USA.

Shepherd, P.A. (1995) A review of urban floras and plant communities, *Land Contamination and Reclamation*, **3**(2), 67–9.

Shigo, A.L. (1986) *A New Tree Biology*, Shigo & Trees Associates, Durham, New Hampshire.

Simberloff, D. (1990) Reconstructing the ambiguous. In D.R. Towns, C.H. Dougherty and I.A.E. Atkinson, *Ecological Restoration of New Zealand Islands*, Dept of Conservation, Wellington, New Zealand.

Sinden, N. (1989) *In a Nutshell*, Common Ground, London.

Smart, J. (1989) Common sense approaches to the construction of species-rich vegetation in urban areas. In G.P. Buckley (ed.), *Biological Habitat Reconstruction*, Belhaven, London, 115–28.

Smyth, B. (1987) *City Wildspace*, Hilary Shipman, London.

Snow, B. and Snow, D. (1988) *Birds and Berries: A Study of an Ecological Interaction*, T & A.D. Poyser.

Soutar, R.G. (1991) Native trees and shrubs for new woodlands in Scotland, *Scottish Forestry*, **45**, 186–94.

Soutar, R.G. and Peterken, G. (1989) Regional lists of native trees and shrubs for use in afforestation schemes, *Arboricultural Journal*, **13**, 33–43.

Spellerberg, I.F. (1995) Biogeography and woodland design. In R. Ferris-Kaan (ed.), *The Ecology of Woodland Creation*. John Wiley & Sons, Chichester, 49–62.

Spray, M. (1994) Educating the not quite professional, *Landscape Design Extra*, August.

Sterndale-Bennett, J. (1994) Cultivated weeds, *The Hardy Plant*, **16**(1), 51–5.

Sukopp, H., Blume, H.P and Kunick, W. (1979) The soil flora and vegetation of Berlin's wastelands. In I. Laurie (ed.), *Nature in Cities*, John Wiley, Chichester.

Sukopp, H., Trautmann, W. and Korneck, D. (1978) *Auswertung Der Roten Liste Gefährdeter Farn Und Blütenpflanzen In Der Bundesrepublik Deutschland Für Den Artenund Biotopschutz. Schriftenreihe Für Vegetationskunde*, Bonn-bad Godensburg, **12**, 1–131.

Sukopp, H. and Werner, P. (1987) Development of flora and fauna in urban areas, *Nature And Environment*, Series No. 366. Council Of Europe, Strasbourg.

Swann, W. (1994) Unpublished MSc thesis, University of Reading.

Tamm, C.O. (1972) Survival and flowering of perennial herbs, III: The Behaviour of *Primula veris* on permanent plot, *Oikos*, **23**, 159–66.

Teagle W.C. (1978) *The Endless Village*, Nature Conservancy Council, London.

Thacker, C. (1979) *The History of Gardens*, Croom Helm, London.

Theophrastus (C.300BC) *Enquiry into Plants*, trans., Introduction and Notes by A.F. Hort (1916) Loeb Classical Library, Wm Heinemann, Harvard Univ Press, Cambridge, Mass., 2 vols.

Thoday, P.R. (1983) Tree establishment in amenity areas. In *Tree Establishment Symposium Proceedings*, University Of Bath.

Thoday, P.R. (1995) *Poisonous Plants*.

Thomas, K. (1983) Man and the natural world, *Changing Attitudes in England 1500–1800*, Penguin Books, London.

Thomas, G.S. (1990) *Perennial Garden Plants*, J.M. Dent & Sons.

Thomas, J.A. (1989) The return of the large blue butterfly, *British Wildlife*, **1**(1), 2–13.

Thompson, J. (1992) *Prairies Forests and Wetlands in Iowa*, publisher unknown.

Thornley (1979) In A.E. Weddle (ed.), *Landscape Techniques: Incorporating Techniques of Landscape Architecture*, Heinemann, London.

Tishler, W.H. (1989) *American Landscape Architecture Designers and Places*, The Preservation Press.

Towns, D.R., Daugherty, C.H. and Atkinson, I.A.E. (eds), *Ecological Restoration of New Zealand Islands*, Conservation Sciences Publication 2. Department of Conservation, Wellington, New Zealand.

Tregay, R. (1986) Design and ecology in the management of naturelike plantations. In Bradshaw A.D., Goode D. and Thorpe E. (eds), *Ecology and Design in the Landscape*, Blackwell Scientific Publications, 275–84.

Tregay, R. (1988) *New Approaches to Landscapes Design and Management*, unpublished address to Institute of Horticulture Annual Conference, 1988, Royal Agricultural College, Cirencester.

Tregay, R. and Gustavsson, R. (1983) *Oakwood's New Landscape*, Swedish University Of Agricultural Sciences, Sweden.

Tuffs, L. (1994) Perennials go public, *Horticulture Week*, 14/7/94, 25–7.

Turner, T.H.D. (1982) Loudon's stylistic development, *J. Gard. Hist.*, **2**(2), 175–88.

Ulrich, R.S. (1984) View through a window may influence recovery from surgery, *Science*, **224**, 420–1.

Usher, M.B. (1986) *Wildlife Conservation Evaluation*, Chapman & Hall, London.

Vallance, A. (1897) *William Morris – His Art, His Writings and His Public Life*, George Bell & Sons, London (reprinted 1986, Studio Editions, London).

van Groeningen, I. (1994) Karl Foerster (1874–1970), Chapter 3 from unfinished Phd thesis, University of York, 133.

van Schaik, A.W.J. (1995) Management of road verges: a ten year experiment, *Land Contamination and Reclamation*, **3**(2), 119–20.

Von Schoenaich, B. (1994) The end of the border, *Landscape Design*, 4/94, 9–14.

Von Schoenaich, B. and Rees, T. (1994) Introduction to new trends in planting design, *International Symposium*, 29/6/95.

Walpole, H. (1780) *History of the Modern Taste in Gardening*, excerpts reprinted from 1782, 2nd edn in Hunt and Willis (*op. cit.*)

Walser, U. (1987) Perennial plant communities: a new park culture?, *Garten Und Landschaft*, 5/87, 2326.

Walser, U. (1994) From infancy to maturity designing and maintaining sustainable perennial schemes for landscapes public and private, *Designing with Perennials New Trends in Planting Design Symposium*, Schoenaich Rees, 17–22.

Ward, D., Holmes, N. and José, P. (1995) *The New Rivers and Wildlife Handbook*, RSPB, Sandy.

Ward, L.K. (1979) Scrub dynamics and management. In S.E. Wright and G.P. Buckley (eds), *Ecology and Design in Amenity Land Management. Conference Proceedings*, Wye College, Wye, Kent, 109–27.

Wates, N. and Knevitt, C. (1987) *Community Architecture. How People Are Creating Their Own Environment*, Penguin, London.

Wathern, P. and Gilbert, O.L. (1978) Artificial diversification of grassland with native herbs, *J. Environ. Manag*, **7**, 29–42.

Webb, N.R. and Haskins, L.E. (1980) An ecological survey of heathlands in the Poole Basin, Dorset, England, in 1978, *Biol. Conserv.*, **17**, 281–96.

Weigel B. (1992) Perennials in public parks, *Garten und Landschaft*, **5**, 30–1.

Weins, J.A. (1977) On competition and variable environments, *American Scientist*, **68**, 590–7.

Wells, T.C.E. (1971) A comparison of the effects of sheep grazing and mechanical cutting on the structure and botanical composition of chalk grassland, *Symposium of the British Ecological Society*, **11**, 497–515.

Wells, T.C.E. (1980) Management options for lowland grassland. In R. Hunt and I.H. Rorison (eds), *Amenity Grassland*. John Wiley & Sons, Chichester, 175–96.

Wells, T.C.E. (1983) The creation of species rich grassland. In A. Warren and F.B. Goldsmith (eds), *Conservation in Perspective*, J. Wiley & Sons, Chichester, 215–32.

Wells, T.C.E. (1987) The establishment of floral grasslands. In P. Thoday (ed.), *The Scientific Management of Vegetation in Urban Areas, Acta Hort.*, **195**, 59–69.

Wells, T.C.E., Bell, S.A and Frost, A. (1981) *Creating Attractive Grasslands Using Native Plant Species*, Nature Conservancy Council, Shrewsbury.

Wells, T.C.E., Cox, R. and Frost, A. (1989a) Diversifying grasslands by introducing seed and transplants into existing vegetation. In G.P. Buckley (ed.), *Biological Habitat Reconstruction*, Belhaven Press, Printer Publishers, London, 283–98.

Wells, T.C.E., Cox, R. and Frost, A. (1989b) The establishment and management of wildflower meadows, *NCC Focus On Nature Conservation*, 21, Nature Conservancy Council, Peterborough.

Wells, T.C.E., Frost, A. and Bell, S. (1986) Wild flower grasslands from crop-grown seed and hay-bales, *Focus on Nature Conservation*, 15, Nature Conservancy Council, Peterborough.

Western, D. and Pearl, M. (1989) *Conservation for the Twenty First Century*, Oxford University Press, New York.

Western, D. Pearl, M.C., Pimm, S.L. *et al.* (1989) An agenda for conservation action. In D. Western and M.C. Pearl (eds), *Conservation for the Twenty First Century*, Oxford University Press: New York, 304–23.

Whitcomb, C.E. (1983) Why large trees are difficult to transplant, *Journal of Arboriculture*, **9**(2), 57–8.

Wiener M.J. (1981) *English Culture and the Decline of the Industrial Spirit, 1850–1980*, Cambridge University Press, Cambridge.

Williams, C. (1995) Beacon Wood – a post industrial country park, Land Contamination and Reclamation, 3 (2), 143–4.

Willman, D. and Simpson, D. (1988) The growth of white clover (*Trifolium repens*) in five sown hill swards grazed by sheep, *J. Appl. Ecol.*, **25**, 631–43.

Wilcox (1980) Insular ecology and conservation. In M.E. Soulé and B.A. Wilcox (eds), *Conservation Biology: An Evolutionary-Ecological Perspective*, Sinauer Associates Inc., Sunderland, Mass., 95–117.

Wilson, E.O (1989) Conservation: the next hundred years. In D. Western and M. Pearl (eds), *Conservation for the Twenty First Century*, Oxford University Press, New York, 1–10.

Wilson, J. (1992) *Landscaping with Wildflowers: an Environmental Approach to Gardening*, Houghton Mifflin Company.

Wilson, S.D. (1989) The suppression of native prairie by alien species introduced for revegetation, *Landscape and Urban Planning*, **17**, 113–19.

Wiren, M. (1995) The relationship between fauna and horizontal vegetation structure in urban parks. In J. De Waal (ed.), *Ecological Aspects of Green Areas in Urban Environments. Proceedings of the 1995 IFPRA World Conference*, Vereniging Voor Openbaar Groen, Bruge, 525–9.

Wittke, K. (1994) Perennials and their garden habitats naturalistic planting schemes at Professor Hansen's trial garden at Weihenstephan, *Designing with Perennials New Trends in Planting Design*, Symposium Paper (29/6/94), 14.

Wittkugel, U. (1988) Urban park management in Berlin, *Landscape Design*, **171**, 23–5.

Wolschke-Bulmahn, J. and Groning, G. (1994) From open-mindedness to naturalism: garden design and ideology in Germany during the early 20th century. In J. Flagler and R.P. Poincelot (eds), People–Plant Relationships: Setting Research Priorities, Food Products Press, New York.

Wong, J.L. (1997) The cultural and social values of plants and landscapes. In J.A. Stoneham and A.D. Kendle (eds), *Plants and Human Well-Being*, The Federation To Promote Horticulture for Disabled People, Gillingham.

Wright, T.W.J. and Parker, J. (1979) Maintenance and conservation. In A.E. Weddle (ed.), *Landscape Techniques*, Heinemann, London, 204–36.

Yahner, R.H. (1983) Population dynamics of small mammals in farmstead shelterbelts, *J. Mammal*, **64**, 380–6.

Young, K. (1990) *Inner City Policy*, Institute of Local Government Studies, London.

Index